W9-BWP-418

Keto Meal Prep Cookbook For Beginners

By Kira Peterson

Contents

INTRODUCTION

A few years ago, I started gaining weight despite my healthy eating habits and regular physical activities. I was tired and bloated all the time; it was annoying, disrupting my everyday activities. I've even suffered from back pain and it got worse and worse as time went on. I was frustrated, feeling like a granny. Ironically, I was mostly eating organic and healthy foods. There are many reasons for putting on weight – hormone imbalance, aging, an underactive thyroid (hypothyroidism), genetic predisposition, food addiction, high insulin levels, stress, neurologic problems, and so on. For all the reasons above, it's important to weigh the risks so you should consult a physician before starting this or any other diet.

When attempting to lose weight, changing eating habits and reducing calorie intake are important parts when it comes to the effectiveness of your dietary regimen. Therefore, I started a restrictive diet and I lost some pounds successfully. Shortly after that, I gained them all back! In fact, I experienced so-called yo-yo effect! I realized that diets and restriction can disrupt hormones that control appetite (for instance, leptin is the hormone that helps to control hunger levels and regulate energy balance). Experts suggest that an inappropriate diet can result in a reduction in muscle mass instead of the body fat. Thus, the body automatically adapts to the new situation by slowing down your metabolism. It was the rude awakening for me! With the advice of a nutritionist, I decided to change some eating patterns completely and set realistic goals that fit my lifestyle and meet specific needs. I discovered a nutrition plan that focuses on plenty of fat and a good amount of protein; it also includes zero to low-carb foods. A weight loss without dieting? Come on! I was skeptical at first; notwithstanding, that intrigued me and I decided to learn more about the ketogenic lifestyle. I decided to give it a try and lost about five pounds in the first month.

At that time, I worked 12-plus hours a day and had no time to cook at home. I always put my own needs on the back burner. I needed to change my routine so meal prepping was a turning point! Cooking big batches of food sounds like a great idea to me. I can store my meals in the refrigerator or freezer for long-term storage! I usually spend Sunday morning cooking several meals for the upcoming week. In this way, I never fall into "there-is-nothing to eat" situation. With meal prepping, you can balance your diet and make better food choices on a daily basis!

We can watch our portions and exercise regularly, but if we do not eat real, health-promoting foods, we can't expect long-lasting results. In fact, the real food is unprocessed food so you should cook at home as much as possible. I also applied the other healthy eating principles (not skipping meals, planning meals in advance, eating smaller portions, choose a variety of food and so on). And voilà! I never gained weight again! The ketogenic diet changed my life so I wanted to share my experience and help you live a happier life. From fast and easy breakfast to decadent casseroles and desserts, you'll learn how to make the best keto recipes and store them for later use.

I know, weight loss is extremely challenging. This is going to be a long journey since our eating habits are difficult to change; but it is worth the effort. Once you notice all benefits of keto lifestyle, you will never slip back into your old and destructive habits. If you feel overwhelmed by the vast amount of information out there, there are a lot of tricks that will help you stay on track and achieve your goal. For example, try to set realistic expectations, carry healthy snacks with you and keep junk food out of your house. In essence, opt for local and seasonal foods that have grown in soil and haven't been artificially created. If you are looking for fail-proof keto recipes, check this book out. And remember whatever you are going through, you can succeed!

What is so Fascinating about Ketogenic Diet?

Human beings ate some versions of the ketogenic diet for thousands of years. This dietary regimen promotes whole foods and foods that are not heavily processed as high-quality sources of all beneficial nutrients. You can eat low-carb foods, a good amount of high-quality protein, and plenty of healthy fats.

What is ketosis? It is a natural metabolic process the body initiates to help us survive when we don't have enough calories or carbs to burn for energy. This usually happens over 3 to 4 days of eating fewer than 30 grams of carbohydrates per day. When you reach ketosis, your body simply uses ketones to generate energy. It means that your body creates ketones for energy instead of glucose.

What foods are included in the ketogenic diet? Here is a short list of keto foods that can help you properly organize your keto pantry.

- <u>Above ground vegetables</u> – asparagus, peppers, tomatoes, broccoli, celery, mushrooms, onions, bok choy, greens, arugula, cauliflower, cabbage, and Brussels sprouts; canned and pickled vegetables (preferably homemade, no sugar added);
- <u>Meat</u> – pork, beef, poultry;
- <u>Fish and Seafood</u> – white fish, fat fish, shrimp, lobster, mussels, sea scallops, clams, oysters, and crabmeat (fresh or canned);
- <u>Dairy Products</u> – full-fat milk, heavy cream, full-fat yogurt, cheese, sour cream, butter, and ghee;
- <u>Eggs</u>;
- <u>Nuts and seeds</u> – hazelnuts, pine nuts, pecans, coconut, macadamia nuts, walnuts, almonds and peanuts, chia seeds, sesame seeds, flax seeds, sunflower seeds, unsweetened nut, and seed butter.
- <u>Oils & Fats</u>;
- <u>Fruit</u> – avocado and berries;
- <u>Condiments and seasonings</u> – mustard, vinegar, unsweetened cocoa powder, and herb mix, and coconut aminos;

- Vegetarian keto foods – coconut yogurt, unsweetened dairy-free milk, tofu, tempeh, and seaweed;
- Beverages – coffee, tea, and sparkling water. Alcoholic beverages include brandy, rum, whiskey, vodka, and dry wine;
- Sweeteners – xylitol, erythritol, Swerve, Stevia, and monk fruit powder.

Foods to avoid on a ketogenic diet include:

Almost all types of fruits;
- Starchy vegetables – potatoes and yams;
- Common types of flours – all-purpose flour, cake flour, cornmeal, and arrowroot;
- Grains & pseudo-cereals – rice, oats, barley, millet, corn, quinoa, amaranth, and buckwheat;
- Legumes – lentils, beans, and dried peas;
- Sugars – all types of sugar including honey, molasses, agave nectar, maple syrup, sorghum syrup, corn syrup, and rice syrup.

In addition to these foods, you should avoid trans fats and hydrogenated oil. Keep in mind that packaged foods often contain hydrogenated oils. You should also limit premade baked foods, ready-to-use dough, coffee creamers, and packaged snacks.

Benefits of the Ketogenic Diet

1. Weight loss

   Did you know that the American Medical Association (AMA) defines obesity as a disease? It wasn't my intention to scare you, but an obese person has a higher risk of high blood pressure, hypertension, diabetes, heart disease, stroke, metabolic syndrome, degenerative arthritis, and cancer. If you've been searching for a solution, you may have stumbled upon some popular short-term weight loss plans and instant diets. Remember, healthy BMI is not just about how you look. It should become your ongoing lifestyle with new healthy habits. If you tend to look your best and feel your best, you should find the best lifelong diet for you.

   I maintain my healthy BMI by practicing a carb cycling (a planned alteration of carb intake). I usually rotate no carb, low carb, moderate carb, and high carb days throughout the week. Remember – everyday activities also count – your carb intake depends on the intensity and duration of the exercise. I consume moderate to high amounts of carbs on days with high activity, which helps my body to refuel muscle glycogen and improve performance.

2. Health benefits

   Eating fewer carbs has a direct result in lowering insulin levels and reducing the risk of heart disease. The ketogenic diet may benefit your health by significantly reducing the risk factors that contribute to certain cancers as well.

3. Neuroprotective benefits

   The keto diet may protect your mental health and prevent conditions such as Parkinson's, dementia, and Alzheimer's; it can also cure epilepsy in children. Studies have proven that a keto diet may protect your brain and help with chronic memory issues.

Tips for Success with the Ketogenic Diet

Calculate and track your macros. Macronutrients (macros) are carbohydrates, fats, and proteins. On the ketogenic diet, use these recommendations as a guideline: you should consume 65–75 percent of calories from fat, 20–30 percent of calories from protein and 5–10 percent of calories from carbs. After a certain amount of time, you will be able to determine your ideal macronutrient breakdown according to your individual nutritional needs. In fact, macronutrient ratios can vary depending on your goals and specific needs. An average person would need more fat and fewer carbs, while a professional athlete may need more protein and high carbohydrate consumption.

Track your calorie consumption. Skipping a meal here or there isn't harmful when it's occasional but restricting calories for longer periods can have negative effects on your health. Carb cycling also involves calorie cycling so you can switch from low-calorie to higher-calorie periods.

Keep an eye on the amount of cholesterol. If your cholesterol level is high, avoid saturated fats (found primarily in red meat) and opt for monounsaturated fats. Trans fats such as partially hydrogenated vegetable oils are out of the question; they can be found in margarine and other spreads, fried foods, packaged foods, and fast foods. On the other hand, you should increase soluble fiber, foods rich in omega-3 fatty acid (herring, salmon, mackerel, flaxseeds, and walnuts).

Replenish electrolytes. Just make sure that you are eating foods that contain electrolytes such as bouillon, leafy green, avocado, and Himalayan salt. Taking magnesium supplements may be beneficial on a keto diet.

A few more tips. Consume at least 8 glasses of water per day to stay hydrated on the ketogenic diet. Further, get regular exercise. It doesn't have to be anything special and time-consuming. Simply find an activity that fits into your schedule like walking, cycling, or stair climbing. Keep it simple since the ketogenic diet requires a little pre-planning. Stick to real and nutrient-dense foods and find good alternatives for your favorite carbs. I am sure you will find inspiration and motivation in these six hundred recipes. You will learn how to prepare keto pancakes, granola, desserts, waffles and snacks. It is all about variety and smart food choices, not rigid rules and restrictive diet plans. And remember – you are beautiful just the way you are, take a deep breath and love yourself.

Turn a Chore into a Lifelong Habit with Meal Prepping

Processed foods became popular in the 20th century. Ready-to-eat meals and savory snacks are convenient choices but they are harmful to our health. Generally, these foods are loaded with sodium, sugar, and trans-fats. To make matters worse, they contain a lot of chemicals and additives that are strongly associated with serious diseases including diabetes, cardiovascular disease, obesity, and mental disorders. In the hectic pace of modern life, we lose sight of the main point - good food choices are the best investments in our overall health.

As I said before, I was very busy and had no time to cook at home. My husband and I rarely had time for a good sit-down meal. Luckily, I discovered meal prepping! I realized – I can double or triple whatever I make and freeze leftovers. If you always have a stash of freezer meals, you can serve a great dinner almost every night, without spending an entire evening in the kitchen! My favorite freezer meals include stews, casseroles, and roasted chicken.

Meal planning might sound difficult at first glance, but planning ahead of time is not rocket science. It's easier than you think! This book will help you to find a lot of inspiration and great recipes that you can adapt to your own meal plan. I hope this collection will help you to simplify your cooking routine and tackle meal prepping once for all! This simple routine can transform your life in a way you couldn't even imagine. Meal prepping can save you tons of time and boost your productivity on a daily basis. It also means spending less money on takeout and restaurants. It reduces food waste because you can pack your leftovers in the freezer. And last but not least, meal prepping can help you have the best keto diet results. An average restaurant meal usually contains too much sugar and salt, while packaged meals can contain artificial colors and flavorings. Many studies suggest that families who eat together are less likely to be overweight.

Here are a few tips from chefs and food experts   that can help you master your meal prep:

- **Create a list of must-have items.** Stock your pantry with keto staples such as nuts, seeds, olive oil, coconut oil, and non-starchy veggies. And remember – always buy what you can use up. It doesn't mean you need to embrace meal monotony. On the contrary, you can cook your favorite foods and mix them up to create the best food combinations ever! Add different spices and combine vegetables in different colors; in this way, you will get a variety of vitamins and minerals throughout the week. Let's suppose you like chicken. Double your recipe for oven-roasted chicken and keep leftovers in your freezer. You can make salads, sandwiches, tacos, chowders, stews, and so on. You can pack your own lunch or invite your friends over for dinner.
- **Invest in goof kitchen gear.** You can throw your favorite meat, vegetables, and seasoning into your slow cooker or pressure cooker and let it simmer on Sunday morning. In addition, you can cook a good 6-8 portions at once and get on top of your game!
- **Simplicity is the key to a successful meal prepping.** If you are short on time, look for easy meals that can be thrown together in less than 1 hour. This recipe collection is chock-full of easy-to-follow, delicious recipes that require less than 30 minutes from start to finish. Simply accept not doing everything perfectly and keep going!

A Few Words about Our Recipe Collection

Nowadays, the ketogenic cooking and meal prepping are a form of art that is constantly revamping itself with new findings and techniques. Doubtlessly, cooking at home is one of the most important things you can do for your health. This recipe collection may help you to turn cooking at home into a habit. These 600 recipes contain the ingredients that are available everywhere as well as detailed step-by-step instructions. I have classified the dishes into categories according to food group, so you can easily search for a certain recipe.

From traditional grandma's favorites to classic dishes and contemporary innovations, these recipes will make their way to your kitchen with fascinating results. The secret ingredient is… shhh! A heaping spoonful of love!

3-Week Meal Plan

This is a sample menu for three weeks on a ketogenic diet that can help you kick-start your keto adventure.

DAY 1

Breakfast – Keto Belgian Waffles

Snack – Goat Cheese Deviled Eggs

Lunch – Crispy Chicken Drumsticks; 1 handful of iceberg lettuce

Dinner – Easy Halibut Steaks

DAY 2

Breakfast – Breakfast Eggs in a Mug

Lunch – Creamed Greek-Style Soup; 1 serving of cauliflower rice

Dinner – Easy Cod Fritters; 1 medium tomato

Dessert – Cashew and Pecan Fat Bombs

DAY 3

Breakfast – 1 slice of bacon; 1 hard-boiled egg; 1 shake with 1/2 cup of coconut milk and protein powder

Lunch – Easy and Spicy Sloppy Joes; 1 serving of coleslaw

Snack – Autumn Cheese and Pepper Dip

Dinner – Grilled Flank Steak; 1 keto dinner roll

DAY 4

Breakfast – Nutty Breakfast Porridge

Lunch – Old-Fashioned Beef Mélange; 1 serving of coleslaw

Dinner – Easy Keto Broccoli Pilaf; Tangy Cabbage Soup

Dessert – Mom's Coconut Tarts

DAY 5

Breakfast – Breakfast Beef Sausage Quiche

Snack – Italian-Style Tomato Crisps

Lunch – Pork Spare Ribs with Peppers; 1 handful of mixed green salad with a few drizzles of a freshly squeezed lemon juice

Dinner – Italian-Style Turkey Wings; 1 keto dinner roll

DAY 6

Breakfast – Spicy Breakfast Sausage

Lunch – Chicken with Avocado Sauce; 1 serving of cauliflower rice

Dinner – Super Easy Fish Cakes

Dessert – Hazelnut Cake Squares

DAY 7

Breakfast – Breakfast Mug Muffin

Snack – Nana's Pickled Eggs

Lunch – German Szegediner Gulasch (Beef with Sauerkraut); 1 large tomato

Dinner – Broccoli with Gruyère Cheese Sauce

DAY 8

Breakfast – Scrambled eggs; 1 tomato; 1/2 cup of Greek-style yogurt

Lunch – Ground Pork Skillet; 1 serving of cauliflower rice

Dinner – Breaded Chicken Fillets

Dessert – Classic Chocolate Fudge

DAY 9

Breakfast – Greek-Style Egg and Apple Muffins; 1/2 cup of unsweetened almond milk

Snack – Alfredo Cheese Dip

Lunch – Rustic Hamburger and Cabbage Soup; Mozzarella-Stuffed Meatballs

Dinner – Herbed Chicken Breasts; 1 keto dinner roll

DAY 10

Breakfast – Breakfast Muffins with Ground Pork

Snack – Classic Cheese and Artichoke Dip

Lunch – Autumn Ground Chuck Casserole; 1 scallion; 1/2 tomato

Dinner – Oven-Baked Avocado; a dollop of sour cream; 2 tablespoons tomato paste

DAY 11

Breakfast – 1 tablespoon of peanut butter; 1 slice of keto bread

Lunch – Old-Fashioned Turkey Chowder; 1 serving of cabbage salad

Dinner – Zingy Tuna Steaks with Spinach

Dessert – Easy Lemon Panna Cotta

DAY 12

Breakfast – Decadent Scrambled Eggs

Snack – Sesame Shrimp Bites

Lunch – Cream of Cauliflower Soup; Beef Tenderloin with Cabbage

Dinner – Artichoke Salad with Mozzarella Cheese

DAY 13

Breakfast – Cheese and Prosciutto Stuffed Avocado

Lunch – Chicken Fillet with Brussels Sprouts

Dinner – German Pork Rouladen

Dessert – Classic Chocolate Bars

DAY 14

Breakfast – Egg and Bacon Salad

Lunch – Spicy Ground Beef Bowl; 1 handful of baby spinach with 1 teaspoon of mustard and 1 teaspoon of olive oil

Dinner – Oven-Baked Sole Fillets; Coleslaw with a Twist

Dessert – Tangerine Chocolate Pudding

DAY 15

Breakfast – Scrambled Eggs with Crabmeat; 1/2 cup of Greek-style yogurt

Snack – Festive Zucchini Boats

Lunch – Chicken Breasts with Mustard Sauce; 1 serving of roasted keto veggies

Dinner – Cheesy Tuna Pâté

DAY 16

Breakfast – Genoa Salami and Egg Balls; 1/2 cup of Greek-style yogurt

Lunch – Mexican-Style Pork Chops

Dinner – Parmesan Chicken Salad

Dessert – Mixed Berry Scones

DAY 17

Breakfast – Banana Blueberry Smoothie

Snack – Glazed Oyster Mushrooms

Lunch – Saucy Flank Steak with Leeks; 1 fresh bell pepper

Dinner – Caciocavallo Cheese and Spinach Muffins; 1 cucumber

DAY 18

Breakfast – Greek-Style Spicy Tofu; 1/2 tomato

Snack – Hemp and Chia Pudding

Lunch – Rich Pork and Bacon Meatloaf; 1 serving of steamed broccoli

Dinner – Duck and Eggplant Casserole

DAY 19

Breakfast – Keto Pancakes with Blueberry Topping; 1 cucumber

Lunch – Beef and Tomato Casserole

Dinner – Roasted Chicken with Cashew Pesto

Dessert – The Best Chocolate Cake Ever

DAY 20

Breakfast – Autumn Nut and Seed Granola

Lunch – Easy Roasted Turkey Drumsticks; 1 dollop of sour cream

Snack – Pepper Boats with Herring

Dinner – Paprika Cauliflower Soup; Classic Cajun Shrimp Skewers

DAY 21

Breakfast – Easy Vegan Granola; 1 serving of blue cheese

Lunch – Porterhouse Steak with Sriracha Sauce

Snack – Pepperoni and Ricotta Balls

Dinner – Easy Chicken Tacos

PORK

1. Melt-in-Your-Mouth Ribs

(Ready in about 4 hours 30 minutes | Servings 4)

Per serving: 412 Calories; 14g Fat; 4.3g Carbs; 43.3g Protein; 0.7g Fiber

INGREDIENTS

1 ½ pounds spare ribs
1 tablespoon olive oil, at room temperature
2 cloves garlic, chopped

1 Italian pepper, chopped
Salt and black peppercorns, to taste
1/2 teaspoon ground cumin
2 bay leaves

A bunch of green onions, chopped
3/4 cup beef bone broth, preferably homemade
2 teaspoons erythritol

DIRECTIONS

Heat the olive oil in a saucepan over medium-high heat. Sear the ribs for 6 to 7 minutes on each side.
Whisk the broth, erythritol, garlic, Italian pepper, green onions, salt, pepper, and cumin until well combined.
Place the spare ribs in your crock pot; pour in the pepper/broth mixture. Add in the bay leaves. Cook for about 4 hours on Low setting.

STORING

Divide the pork ribs into four portions. Place each portion of ribs along with the cooking juices in an airtight container; store in your refrigerator for 3 to 5 days.
For freezing, place the ribs in airtight containers or heavy-duty freezer bags. Freeze up to 4 to 6 months. Defrost in the refrigerator. Reheat in your oven at 250 degrees F until heated through. Bon appétit!

2. Mom's Meatballs in Creamy Sauce

(Ready in about 30 minutes | Servings 6)

Per serving: 378 Calories; 29.9g Fat; 2.9g Carbs; 23.4g Protein; 0.3g Fiber

INGREDIENTS

For the Meatballs:
2 eggs
1 tablespoon steak seasoning
1 tablespoon green garlic, minced
1 tablespoon scallions, minced

1 pound ground pork
1/2 pound ground turkey
For the Sauce:
3 teaspoons ghee
1 cup double cream

1 cup cream of onion soup
Salt and pepper, to your liking
1/2 teaspoon dried rosemary

DIRECTIONS

Preheat your oven to 365 degrees F.
In a mixing bowl, combine all ingredients for the meatballs. Roll the mixture into 20 to 24 balls and place them on a parchment-lined baking sheet.
Roast for about 25 minutes or until your meatballs are golden-brown on the top.
While your meatballs are roasting, melt the ghee in a preheated sauté pan over a moderate flame. Gradually add in the remaining ingredients, whisking constantly, until the sauce has reduced slightly.

STORING

Place the meatballs along with the sauce in airtight containers or Ziploc bags; keep in your refrigerator for up to 3 to 4 days.
Freeze the meatballs in the sauce in airtight containers or heavy-duty freezer bags. Freeze up to 3 to 4 months. Reheat on the stove pot or in your oven. Bon appétit!

3. Old-Fashioned Stew with Pork Butt

(Ready in about 25 minutes | Servings 4)

Per serving: 295 Calories; 15.6g Fat; 6.3g Carbs; 17.3g Protein; 1.1g Fiber

INGREDIENTS

3/4 pound boneless pork butt, cubed
1 ½ cups vegetable stock
1 tablespoon lard, room temperature
1 teaspoon Serrano pepper, deveined and minced

2 garlic cloves, minced
1/2 teaspoon ground cloves
1 yellow onion, chopped
1 carrot, chopped
1 tablespoon fresh coriander, chopped

2 ounces cream cheese, full-fat
Himalayan salt and ground black pepper, to taste

DIRECTIONS

Melt the lard in a soup pot over medium-high heat.
Now, sauté the onion, carrot, and Serrano pepper for about 4 minutes or until tender and fragrant.
Add in the boneless pork butt and cook for a father 5 to 6 minutes, stirring continuously to ensure even cooking.
Add in the garlic, vegetable stock, ground cloves, salt, black pepper, and coriander; bring to a rapid boil. Now, reduce the temperature to medium-low.
Cook for 15 to 20 minutes or until everything is thoroughly cooked. Bon appétit!

STORING

Spoon the stew into four airtight containers and store in your refrigerator for up to 3 to 4 days.
For freezing, place the stew in airtight containers. Freeze up to 4 to 6 months. Defrost in the refrigerator. Serve in individual bowls, dolloped with cream cheese.
Bon appétit!

4. Mexican-Style Pork Chops

(Ready in about 30 minutes | Servings 6)

Per serving: 356 Calories; 20.3g Fat; 0.3g Carbs; 45.2g Protein; 0g Fiber

INGREDIENTS

2 Mexican chilies, chopped
1 teaspoon dried Mexican oregano
1/2 teaspoon red pepper flakes, crushed

Salt and ground black pepper, to taste
6 pork chops
1/2 cup chicken stock

2 garlic cloves, minced
2 tablespoons vegetable oil

DIRECTIONS

Heat 1 tablespoon of the olive oil in a frying pan over a moderately high heat. Brow the pork chops for 5 to 6 minutes per side.
Then, bring the Mexican chilies and chicken stock to a boil; remove from the heat and let it sit for about 20 minutes.
Puree the chilies along with the liquid and the remaining ingredients in your food processor. Add in the remaining tablespoon of the oil.

STORING

Divide the pork chops and sauce into six portions; place each portion in a separate airtight container or Ziploc bag; keep in your refrigerator for 3 to 4 days.
Freeze the pork chops in sauce in airtight containers or heavy-duty freezer bags. Freeze up to 4 months. Defrost in the refrigerator and reheat in a saucepan. Bon appétit!

5. Easy Pork Tenderloin Gumbo

(Ready in about 35 minutes | Servings 6)

Per serving: 427 Calories; 16.2g Fat; 3.6g Carbs; 33.2g Protein; 4.4g Fiber

INGREDIENTS

1 pound pork tenderloin, cubed
8 ounces New Orleans spicy sausage, sliced
1 tablespoon Cajun spice mix

1 medium-sized leek, chopped
2 tablespoons olive oil
5 cups bone broth
1/2 cup celery, chopped

1 teaspoon gumbo file
1/4 cup flaxseed meal
3/4 pound okra
2 bell peppers, deveined and thinly sliced

DIRECTIONS

In a heavy-bottomed pot, heat the oil until sizzling. Sear the pork tenderloin and New Orleans sausage for about 8 minutes or until browned on all sides; set aside.
In the same pot, cook the leek and peppers until they softened. Add in the gumbo file, Cajun spice and broth. Bring it to a rolling boil.
Turn the heat to medium-low and add in celery. Let it simmer for 18 to 20 minutes longer.
Stir in the flax seed meal and okra along with the reserved meat. Then, continue to simmer for 5 to 6 minutes or until heated through.

STORING

Spoon your gumbo into six airtight containers; keep in your refrigerator for up to 3 to 4 days.
For freezing, place the chilled gumbo in airtight containers or heavy-duty freezer bags. Freeze up to 5 months. Defrost in the refrigerator and reheat on the stove pot. Enjoy!

6. Pork and Carrot Mini Muffins

(Ready in about 35 minutes | Servings 6)

Per serving: 303 Calories; 17g Fat; 6.2g Carbs; 29.6g Protein; 1.7g Fiber

INGREDIENTS

1 egg, whisked
1 ounce envelope onion soup mix
Kosher salt and ground black pepper, to taste
2 cloves of garlic, minced

1 cup carrots, shredded
1 cup tomato puree
1 tablespoon coconut aminos
1 tablespoon stone-ground mustard
1 ½ teaspoons dry basil

1 cup Romano cheese, grated
1 pound pork, ground
1/2 pound turkey, ground

DIRECTIONS

In a mixing bowl, combine all ingredients until everything is well incorporated. Press the mixture into a lightly-oiled muffin tin.
Bake in the preheated oven at 355 degrees F for 30 to 33 minutes; let it cool slightly before unmolding and serving.

STORING

Wrap the meatloaf muffins tightly with heavy-duty aluminum foil or plastic wrap. Keep in your refrigerator for up to 3 to 4 days.
For freezing, wrap the meatloaf muffins tightly to prevent freezer burn. They will maintain the best quality for 3 to 4 months. Defrost in the refrigerator. Bon appétit!

7. Bacon Blue Cheese Fat Bombs

(Ready in about 5 minutes | Servings 4)

Per serving: 232 Calories; 17.6g Fat; 2.9g Carbs; 14.2g Protein; 0.6g Fiber

INGREDIENTS

1 ½ tablespoons mayonnaise
1/2 cup bacon, chopped
3 ounces blue cheese, crumbled

3 ounces cream cheese
2 tablespoons chives, chopped
2 teaspoons tomato puree

DIRECTIONS

Mix all ingredients until everything is well combined.
Shape the mixture into 8 equal fat bombs.

STORING

Place the fat bombs in airtight containers or Ziploc bags; keep in your refrigerator for 10 days.
To freeze, arrange the fat bombs on a baking tray in a single layer; freeze for about 2 hours. Transfer the frozen bombs to an airtight container. Freeze for up to 2 months. Serve well chilled!

8. Creole-Style Pork Shank

(Ready in about 30 minutes + marinating time | Servings 6)

Per serving: 335 Calories; 24.3g Fat; 0.8g Carbs; 26.4g Protein; 0.4g Fiber

INGREDIENTS

1 ½ pounds pork shank, cut into 6 serving portions
1 tablespoon Creole seasoning
A few drops of liquid smoke
Salt and cayenne pepper, to taste

3 teaspoons vegetable oil
2 clove garlic, minced
1 ½ tablespoons coconut aminos

DIRECTIONS

Blend the salt, cayenne pepper, vegetable oil, garlic, liquid smoke, Creole seasoning, and coconut aminos until you get a uniform and creamy mixture.
Massage the pork shanks on all sides with the prepared rub mixture. Let it marinate for about 2 hours in your refrigerator.
Grill for about 20 minutes until cooked through.

STORING

Put the pork shanks into six airtight containers or Ziploc bags; keep in your refrigerator for 3 to 4 days.
For freezing, wrap tightly with heavy-duty aluminum foil or freezer wrap. It will maintain the best quality for about 3 months. Defrost in the refrigerator and reheat in your oven. Enjoy!

9. German Pork Rouladen

(Ready in about 1 hour + marinating time | Servings 6)

Per serving: 220 Calories; 6g Fat; 2.8g Carbs; 33.3g Protein; 0.4g Fiber

INGREDIENTS

1 ½ pounds boneless pork loin, butterflied
2 garlic cloves, pressed
1 tablespoon ghee, room temperature
1 tablespoon Mediterranean herb mix
1 teaspoon mustard seeds

1/2 teaspoon cumin seeds
1 cup roasted vegetable broth
1 large-sized onion, thinly sliced
Salt and black peppercorns, to taste
1/2 cup Burgundy wine

DIRECTIONS

Boil the pork loin for about 5 minutes; pat it dry.
Now, combine the Mediterranean herb mix, mustard seeds, cumin seeds, garlic and ghee.
Unfold the pork loin and spread the rub all over the cut side. Roll the pork and secure with kitchen string. Allow it to sit at least 2 hours in your refrigerator.
Place the pork loin in a lightly greased baking pan. Add on wine, broth, onion, salt, and black peppercorns.
Roast in the preheated oven at 390 degrees F approximately 1 hour.

STORING

Divide the pork and sauce between six airtight containers or Ziploc bags; keep in your refrigerator for up to 3 to 5 days.
For freezing, place the pork and sauce in airtight containers or heavy-duty freezer bags. Freeze up to 4 months. Defrost in the refrigerator and reheat in your oven. Bon appétit!

10. Rich Pork and Bacon Meatloaf

(Ready in about 1 hour 10 minutes | Servings 6)

Per serving: 396 Calories; 24.1g Fat; 5.1g Carbs; 38.1g Protein; 0.5g Fiber

INGREDIENTS

1 ¼ pounds ground pork
1/2 pound pork sausage, broken up
6 strips bacon
2 garlic cloves, finely minced

1 teaspoon celery seeds
Salt and cayenne pepper, to taste
1 bunch coriander, roughly chopped
1 egg, beaten

2 ounces half-and-half
1 teaspoon lard
1 medium-sized leek, chopped

DIRECTIONS

Melt the lard in a frying pan over medium-high heat. Cook the leek and garlic until they have softened or about 3 minutes.
Add in the ground pork and sausage; cook until it is no longer pink, about 3 minutes. Add in the half-and-half, celery seeds, salt, cayenne pepper, coriander, and egg.
Press the mixture into a loaf pan.
Place the bacon strips on top of your meatloaf and bake at 390 degrees F about 55 minutes.

STORING

Wrap your meatloaf tightly with heavy-duty aluminum foil or plastic wrap. Store in your refrigerator for up to 3 to 4 days.
For freezing, wrap your meatloaf tightly to prevent freezer burn. Freeze up to 3 to 4 months. Defrost in the refrigerator and reheat in your oven. Bon appétit!

11. Pork and Vegetable Souvlaki

(Ready in about 20 minutes + marinating time | Servings 6)

Per serving: 267 Calories; 10.6g Fat; 5.3g Carbs; 34.9g Protein; 1.3g Fiber

INGREDIENTS

1 tablespoon Greek spice mix
2 cloves garlic, crushed
3 tablespoons coconut aminos
3 tablespoons olive oil
1 tablespoon stone-ground mustard

2 tablespoons fresh lemon juice
1 pound brown mushrooms
2 bell peppers, cut into thick slices
1 red bell pepper, cut into thick slices
1 zucchini, cubed

1 shallot, cut into wedges
2 pounds pork butt, cubed
Bamboo skewers, soaked in cold water
for 30 minutes

DIRECTIONS

Mix the Greek spice mix, garlic, coconut aminos, olive oil, mustard, and lemon juice in a ceramic dish; add in pork cubes and let it marinate for 2 hours.
Thread the pork cubes and vegetables onto the soaked skewers. Salt to taste.
Grill for about 15 minutes, basting with the reserved marinade.

STORING

Divide the pork and vegetables between six airtight containers or Ziploc bags; keep in your refrigerator for up to 3 to 5 days.
For freezing, place the pork and vegetables in airtight containers or heavy-duty freezer bags. Freeze up to 4 months. Defrost in the refrigerator. Bon appétit!

12. Pork Cutlets with Kale

(Ready in about 25 minutes + marinating time | Servings 6)

Per serving: 234 Calories; 11g Fat; 2g Carbs; 29.8g Protein; 0.9g Fiber

INGREDIENTS

Sea salt and ground black pepper, to
taste
2 teaspoons olive oil
1/4 cup port wine

2 garlic cloves, smashed
2 tablespoons oyster sauce
2 tablespoons fresh lime juice
1 medium leek, sliced

2 bell peppers, chopped
2 cups kale
1 ½ pounds pork cutlets

DIRECTIONS

Sprinkle the pork with salt and black pepper. Then, make the marinade by whisking 1 teaspoon of olive oil, wine, garlic, oyster sauce, and lime juice.
Let the pork marinate for about 2 hours in your refrigerator
Heat the remaining teaspoon of olive oil in a frying pan. Fry the leek and bell peppers for 4 to 5 minutes, stirring continuously, until they have softened slightly; set aside.
In the same pan, sear the pork along with the marinade until browned on all sides.
Stir the reserved vegetables into the frying pan along with the kale. Continue to cook for 5 to 6 minutes more.

STORING

Place the pork chops and veggies in airtight containers or Ziploc bags; keep in your refrigerator for 3 to 4 days.
Freeze the pork chops and veggies in airtight containers or heavy-duty freezer bags. Freeze up to 4 months. Defrost in the refrigerator. Bon appétit!

13. Pork and Broccoli Stew

(Ready in about 2 hours | Servings 6)

Per serving: 326 Calories; 13.9g Fat; 6g Carbs; 23.5g Protein; 1.2g Fiber

INGREDIENTS

2 tablespoons lard, at room temperature
1 ½ pounds pork shoulder, cubed
1 teaspoon smoked paprika
Sea salt and ground black pepper to taste

1 brown onion, chopped
1 stalk celery, chopped
1 teaspoon garlic, finely minced
1/4 cup dry red wine
3 cups water
2 bay leaves

1/2 teaspoon celery seeds
2 bell peppers, chopped
1 chili pepper, chopped
1 cup broccoli, broken into florets
1 tablespoon beef bouillon granules
1 tablespoon flax seed meal

DIRECTIONS

Melt the lard in a heavy-bottomed pot over a moderate flame. Now, cook the pork for 5 to 6 minutes or until browned on all sides. Season with paprika, salt, and black pepper; reserve.

In the same pot, sauté the onion, celery and garlic until they've softened. Add a splash of dry red wine to scrape up any browned bits from the bottom of your pot.

Add in the water, bay leaves, celery seeds, bell peppers, and chili pepper. Reduce the temperature to simmer and add in the reserved pork. Continue to simmer for 1 hour 20 minutes. Add in the broccoli and beef bouillon granules and cook an additional 15 minutes.

Add in the flax seed meal to thicken the cooking liquid. Taste and adjust the seasonings.

STORING

Spoon the stew into six airtight containers or Ziploc bags; keep in your refrigerator for up to 3 to 4 days.

For freezing, place the stew in airtight containers. Freeze up to 4 to 6 months. Defrost in the refrigerator and reheat on the stove pot. Bon appétit!

14. Bavarian-Style Ham and Cabbage

(Ready in about 45 minutes | Servings 4)

Per serving: 123 Calories; 4.4g Fat; 6.8g Carbs; 9.8g Protein; 2.8g Fiber

INGREDIENTS

6 ounces smoked ham, chopped
1 yellow onion, diced
2 cloves garlic, pressed

1 pound red cabbage, shredded
2 cups vegetable stock
Sea salt and ground black pepper, to taste

1/4 teaspoon paprika
1 bay leaf

DIRECTIONS

In a heavy-bottomed pot, cook the ham in over medium-high heat for 7 to 8 minutes.

Then, sauté the onion and garlic for about 6 minutes or until tender and aromatic. Add in the cabbage and continue cooking for 10 minutes more. Add in the other ingredients and reduce the heat to simmer. Cover and continue to simmer for 20 to 25 minutes or until cooked through.

STORING

Spoon your stew into four airtight containers or Ziploc bags; keep in your refrigerator for up to 3 to 4 days.

For freezing, place the stew in airtight containers. Freeze up to 4 months. Defrost in the refrigerator. Bon appétit!

15. Mediterranean Meatballs in Tomato Sauce

(Ready in about 50 minutes | Servings 6)

Per serving: 237 Calories; 12g Fat; 5.6g Carbs; 26.4g Protein; 1.6g Fiber

INGREDIENTS

For the Meatballs:
3/4 cup grated parmesan cheese
1 teaspoon garlic paste
1 pound beef, ground
1 egg, beaten
Salt and ground black pepper, to taste

1 white onion, finely chopped
1/2 tablespoon chili powder
1 teaspoon onion flakes
2 tablespoons fresh parsley, chopped
1/4 cup almond flour
2 ounces full-fat milk

For the Sauce:
2 tablespoons olive oil
1 cup marinara sauce
1 tablespoon Mediterranean herb mix
Salt and ground black pepper, to taste

DIRECTIONS

Mix all ingredients for the meatballs. Then, roll the mixture into bite-sized balls and arrange them in a single layer on a lightly greased baking sheet.

Mix all ingredients for the sauce. Pour the sauce over the meatballs.

Bake in the preheated oven at 365 degrees F for 40 to 45 minutes or until they are golden brown on the top.

STORING

Place the meatballs along with the sauce in airtight containers or Ziploc bags; keep in your refrigerator for up to 3 to 4 days.

Freeze the meatballs in the sauce in airtight containers or heavy-duty freezer bags. Freeze up to 3 to 4 months. Reheat on the stove pot or in your oven. Bon appétit!

16. Italian Pork Soup

(Ready in about 1 hour | Servings 4)

Per serving: 331 Calories; 17.6g Fat; 4.4g Carbs; 37.4g Protein; 0.9g Fiber

INGREDIENTS

1 shallot, chopped
4 cups beef bone broth
1 tomato, crushed
1 Pepperoncini, seeded and cut into
very thin strips with scissors

1 tablespoon Italian herb mix
1 teaspoon green garlic, minced
1/2 cup Marsala wine
1 carrot, thinly sliced
2 tablespoons olive oil

1 ½ pounds pork stew meat, cubed
1 Italian pepper, thinly sliced
Salt and black pepper, to taste

DIRECTIONS

In a soup pot, heat the oil over a moderately high flame. Brown the pork for about 6 minutes until no longer pink; set aside.
In the same pot, cook the shallot until tender and fragrant. Stir in the garlic and continue to sauté for 30 seconds more or until aromatic.
Add in wine to deglaze the bottom of the soup pot.
Add in the remaining ingredients along with the reserved pork; bring to a rapid boil. Reduce the heat to medium-low; continue to simmer, partially covered, for about 45 minutes.

STORING

Spoon the soup into four airtight containers or Ziploc bags; keep in your refrigerator for up to 3 to 4 days.
For freezing, place the soup in airtight containers. Freeze up to 4 to 6 months. Defrost in the refrigerator. Bon appétit!

17. Warm Pork Salad with Blue Cheese

(Ready in about 20 minutes | Servings 2)

Per serving: 431 Calories; 22.9g Fat; 5.2g Carbs; 42.2g Protein; 5.2g Fiber

INGREDIENTS

1/2 pound ground pork
1/2 cup Greek yogurt
1/2 cup blue cheese, crumbled
1 tablespoon lard
1/4 teaspoon thyme

1 bell pepper, deveined and chopped
1/4 cup beef bone broth
1/2 cup radicchio, trimmed and sliced
2 teaspoons fresh lemon juice

Kosher salt and black pepper, to your
liking
1 small head of Iceberg lettuce, leaves
separated

DIRECTIONS

In a frying pan, melt the lard over medium flame; cook the ground pork until browned, crumbling with a fork.
Add the peppers and cook until they have softened. Pour in the bone broth to deglaze the pan; season with salt, pepper, and thyme; cook
for a further 5 minutes and set aside.

STORING

Place the ground pork mixture in airtight containers or Ziploc bags; keep in your refrigerator for up to 3 to 4 days.
For freezing, place it in airtight containers or heavy-duty freezer bags. Freeze up to 2 to 3 months. Defrost in the refrigerator.
Garnish with Iceberg lettuce, radicchio, Greek yogurt and blue cheese. Drizzle fresh lemon juice over everything and serve.

18. Maiale al Latte (Milk-Braised Pork)

(Ready in about 1 hour 35 minutes | Servings 8)

Per serving: 293 Calories; 15.4g Fat; 5.4g Carbs; 31.4g Protein; 0.4g Fiber

INGREDIENTS

2 pounds pork sirloin roast
2 cup full-fat milk
Salt and pepper, to taste

1 teaspoon dried marjoram
1/2 cup onion, sliced
3 teaspoons butter, room temperature

2 bell peppers, deveined and thinly
sliced

DIRECTIONS

Melt the butter in a saucepan over medium-high flame. Sear the pork for about 7 minutes until just browned.
Lower the pork sirloin roast into a baking dish. Season with salt, pepper, and marjoram. Scatter the onion and peppers around the pork.
Pour in the milk and cover the dish with a piece of aluminum foil. Roast in the preheated oven at 330 degrees F for 1 hour 20 minutes,
turning the pork halfway through the cooking time.
Let it sit for 10 minutes before slicing.

STORING

Divide the pork loin and vegetables between airtight containers; keep in your refrigerator for 3 to 5 days.
For freezing, place the pork loin and vegetables in airtight containers or heavy-duty freezer bags. Freeze up to 4 to 6 months. Defrost in
the refrigerator. Bon appétit!

19. Barbecue Saucy Pork

(Ready in about 2 hours | Servings 8)

Per serving: 561 Calories; 34g Fat; 1.7g Carbs; 52.7g Protein; 0.4g Fiber

INGREDIENTS

2 tablespoons olive oil
1 teaspoon fresh garlic, halved
2 pounds pork butt

Sea salt and freshly ground black
pepper, to taste
1/3 teaspoon hot paprika
A few drops of liquid smoke

1/3 teaspoon ground cumin
1/2 cup marinara sauce
1 teaspoon hot sauce
1 teaspoon stone-ground mustard

DIRECTIONS

Rub the pork with the olive oil and garlic. Sprinkle with salt, pepper, and hot paprika.
Roast the pork at 410 degrees F for 20 minutes. Turn the heat to 340 degrees F and roast for about 1 hour.
In a mixing bowl, whisk the remaining ingredients. Spoon the sauce over the pork and continue to roast an additional 20 minutes. Enjoy!

STORING

Divide the pork between airtight containers or Ziploc bags; keep in your refrigerator for up to 3 to 5 days.
For freezing, place the pork in airtight containers or heavy-duty freezer bags. Freeze up to 4 months. Defrost in the refrigerator. Bon appétit!

20. Pork Stuffed Zucchini Boats

(Ready in about 50 minutes | Servings 8)

Per serving: 302 Calories; 21.2g Fat; 5.2g Carbs; 18.2g Protein; 1.1g Fiber

INGREDIENTS

1 pound ground pork
1 yellow onion, chopped
1 garlic clove, pressed

4 medium-sized zucchinis, cut into
halves
1/2 cup chicken broth
2 tablespoons olive oil

Salt and ground black pepper, to taste
1 cup tomato puree
1 cup cheddar cheese, freshly grated
1 cup Cremini mushrooms, chopped

DIRECTIONS

Start by preheating your oven to 365 degrees F. Use a spoon to carefully scoop the flesh out of the zucchinis to create indentations.
In a sauté pan, heat the oil in over medium-high flame. Cook the onion for about 3 minutes until tender and translucent.
Stir in the garlic, pork and mushrooms; continue to sauté for 4 to 5 minutes more. Add in the salt, pepper, tomato puree and chicken broth. Continue simmer for 10 to 12 minutes or until thoroughly cooked.
Spoon the filling into the zucchini boats and bake in the preheated oven approximately 20 minutes. Top with grated cheese and place under the preheated broiler for 5 minutes more until hot and bubbly.

STORING

Place the zucchini boats in airtight containers or Ziploc bags; keep in your refrigerator for up to 3 to 4 days.
For freezing, place the zucchini boats in airtight containers or heavy-duty freezer bags. Freeze up to 2 to 3 months. Defrost in the refrigerator. Bon appétit!

21. Polish Sausage and Sauerkraut

(Ready in about 35 minutes | Servings 6)

Per serving: 309 Calories; 20.6g Fat; 4.2g Carbs; 19.3g Protein; 3.8g Fiber

INGREDIENTS

4 slices Polish bacon, chopped
2 pork sausages, sliced
1 onion, chopped
1/3 cup dry white wine

1 Serano pepper, finely minced
1 teaspoon garlic, finely minced
1/2 teaspoon fennel seeds, ground
1/2 teaspoon mustard seeds

1 cup vegetable broth
1 ½ pounds prepared sauerkraut,
drained

DIRECTIONS

In a saucepan, fry the bacon over medium-high heat for 7 to 8 minutes; reserve.
In the same pan, cook the sausage until no longer pink for 4 to 5 minutes; reserve. Then, cook the onions until tender and translucent for 5 to 6 minutes.
Add a splash of wine to deglaze the pan.
Add in the remaining ingredients and bring to a boil; turn the heat to simmer and continue to cook for 15 to 18 minutes or until everything is cooked through.

STORING

Divide the sauerkraut between six airtight containers or Ziploc bags; keep in your refrigerator for up to 3 to 5 days.
For freezing, place the sauerkraut in airtight containers or heavy-duty freezer bags. Freeze up to 5 months. Defrost in the refrigerator and reheat on the stove pot. Bon appétit!

22. Easy Pork Sausage Frittata

(Ready in about 35 minutes | Servings 4)

Per serving: 423 Calories; 35.4g Fat; 4.1g Carbs; 22.6g Protein; 0.8g Fiber

INGREDIENTS

1/2 pound pork sausages, thinly sliced
8 eggs, whisked
1 teaspoon Serrano pepper, finely minced

2 garlic cloves, minced
1 teaspoon salt
1/2 teaspoon ground black pepper
1/4 teaspoon cayenne pepper

1 teaspoon dried thyme, crushed
3 tablespoons olive oil
1 cup onion, chopped

DIRECTIONS

Start by preheating your oven to 410 degrees F.
In a frying pan, heat the oil over a medium-high flame. Sauté the onions, Serrano pepper and garlic for about 5 minutes until they have softened.
Sprinkle with salt, black pepper, and cayenne pepper. Then, cook the sausage until no longer pink, crumbling with a fork.
Transfer the sautéed mixture to a lightly greased baking pan. Pour the whisked eggs over the top and sprinkle with dried thyme.
Bake in the preheated oven for 22 to 25 minutes.

STORING

Cut your frittata into four pieces. Place the pieces in airtight containers; place in your refrigerator for up 3 to 4 days.
To freeze, place in separate Ziploc bags and freeze up to 3 months. To defrost, place in your microwave for a few minutes.

23. Breakfast Mug Muffin

(Ready in about 10 minutes | Servings 2)

Per serving: 327 Calories; 16.6g Fat; 5.8g Carbs; 40g Protein; 1.2g Fiber

INGREDIENTS

1/2 cup marinara sauce
1/2 cup cheddar cheese, shredded
1/2 pound ground pork

1 teaspoon garlic paste
1/2 teaspoon shallot powder
Salt and ground black pepper, to taste

1/2 teaspoon paprika

DIRECTIONS

In a mixing bowl, combine all ingredients until everything is well incorporated.
Spoon the mixture into two microwave-safe mugs.
Microwave for 5 minutes until set but still moist.

STORING

Place your muffins in the airtight containers or Ziploc bags; keep in the refrigerator for a week.
For freezing, place your muffins in a Ziploc bag and freeze up to 3 months. Defrost in your microwave for a couple of minutes. Bon appétit!

24. Easy Pork Bistek

(Ready in about 30 minutes | Servings 4)

Per serving: 305 Calories; 20.6g Fat; 3.7g Carbs; 22.5g Protein; 0.6g Fiber

INGREDIENTS

1 red onion, peeled and chopped
1 garlic clove, minced
2 tablespoons olive oil
1 ½ pounds pork blade steak

1/4 cup dry red wine
1/2 teaspoon salt
1/2 teaspoon freshly ground black pepper

1/2 teaspoon cayenne pepper
1 teaspoon mustard seeds

DIRECTIONS

In a frying pan, heat 1 tablespoon of the olive oil over a moderate heat. Now, sear the pork steaks for 8 to 9 minutes per side.
Pour in a splash of wine to deglaze the pot. Sprinkle with spices and continue to cook for 10 minutes more, adding additional water if necessary; reserve.
In the same frying pan, heat the remaining tablespoon of olive oil and cook the onions and garlic until they have softened.

STORING

Place the pork blade steak in airtight containers; keep in your refrigerator for up to 3 to 4 days.
For freezing, place the pork blade steak in airtight containers or heavy-duty freezer bags. Freeze up to 2 to 3 months. Defrost in the refrigerator. Bon appétit!

25. Pork Spare Ribs with Peppers

(Ready in about 2 hours | Servings 4)

Per serving: 370 Calories; 21.3g Fat; 4.3g Carbs; 33.7g Protein; 1.6g Fiber

INGREDIENTS

1 tablespoon lard, melted
1 tablespoon crushed sage
1 red onion, chopped
1 garlic clove, minced
1 tablespoon tamarind paste

1 cup beef broth
1/2 cup dry sherry
Salt and pepper, to your liking
1 rosemary sprig
1 thyme sprig

1/2 cup coconut aminos
1 pound pork spare ribs
2 Italian peppers, deveined and chopped

DIRECTIONS

Melt the lard in an oven-proof skillet over medium-high heat. Cook the meat on all sides until just browned; sprinkle with seasonings.
Add in the remaining ingredients. Roast in the preheated oven at 330 degrees F for 1 hour 40 minutes.

STORING

Divide the ribs into four portions. Place each portion of ribs in an airtight container; keep in your refrigerator for 3 to 5 days.
For freezing, place the ribs in airtight containers or heavy-duty freezer bags. Freeze up to 4 to 6 months. Defrost in your refrigerator. Bon appétit!

26. Italian-Style Pork Casserole

(Ready in about 50 minutes | Servings 6)

Per serving: 478 Calories; 36g Fat; 4.9g Carbs; 33.5g Protein; 0.3g Fiber

INGREDIENTS

1 ¼ pounds ground pork
6 eggs, lightly beaten
2 tablespoons fresh Italian parsley

2 ½ cups almond meal
1 Italian peppers, thinly sliced
1 cup double cream

1/2 teaspoon celery seeds
1 stick butter, melted
Salt and pepper, to the taste

DIRECTIONS

Start by preheating your oven to 350 degrees F
Thoroughly combine the eggs, almond meal, and melted until well combined. Press the mixture into a lightly oiled baking dish.
In a nonstick skillet, cook the ground pork for about 4 minutes, breaking apart with a wide spatula; season with salt and pepper to taste.
Add in the remaining ingredients and stir to combine well.
Spread this mixture over the crust, using a wide spatula. Bake in the preheated oven at 350 degrees F for about 40 minutes. Let it stand for 10 minutes before slicing.

STORING

Cut the pork casserole into six pieces. Place each piece in a separate airtight container or Ziploc bag; keep for 3 to 4 days in the refrigerator.
To freeze, place each piece in a separate heavy-duty freezer bag. Freeze up to 2 to 3 months. Defrost in the microwave. Bon appétit!

27. Chinese-Style Pork Tenderloin

(Ready in about 20 minutes | Servings 6)

Per serving: 356 Calories; 19.5g Fat; 6.4g Carbs; 33.1g Protein; 1.8g Fiber

INGREDIENTS

1 ½ pounds pork tenderloin, boneless
1 (8-ounce) can bamboo shoots
1 ½ tablespoons olive oil
1 shallot, chopped

1 head cauliflower, broken into florets
Kosher salt and ground black pepper, to taste
1/4 teaspoon dried thyme

1/2 teaspoon dried rosemary
1/2 teaspoon granulated garlic
2 tablespoons fish sauce
1/4 cup vodka

DIRECTIONS

Place the pork, salt, black pepper, thyme, rosemary, granulated garlic, fish sauce, vodka and 1/2 tablespoon of olive oil in Ziploc bag; shake to coat on all sides.
Now, heat the remaining tablespoon of the olive oil in a frying pan over medium-high flame; sauté the onions until translucent.
Add the shallot and cauliflower for about 6 minutes or until they have softened; reserve.
In the same frying pan, brown the pork for 3 to 4 minutes per side. Add in the reserved marinade along with the shallot/cauliflower mixture and bamboo shoots.
Continue to cook for a further 5 minutes or until cooked through.

STORING

Divide the pork and veggies between six airtight containers or Ziploc bags; keep in your refrigerator for up to 3 to 4 days.
For freezing, place the pork and veggies in airtight containers or heavy-duty freezer bags. Freeze up to 3 months. Defrost in your refrigerator. Bon appétit!

28. Roasted Pork Rib Chops

(Ready in about 30 minutes + marinating time | Servings 4)

Per serving: 452 Calories; 34.8g Fat; 4.7g Carbs; 26.3g Protein; 0.6g Fiber

INGREDIENTS

4 (2- 1 1/2"-thick) pork bone-in pork rib chops
1 teaspoon mustard seeds
2 tablespoons fresh lime juice

1/2 teaspoon celery salt
1/2 teaspoon freshly ground black pepper
1 garlic clove

2 tablespoons butter, room temperature
1 cup leeks, sliced
2 carrots, sliced
1 celery stalk, diced

DIRECTIONS

Place the pork, mustard seeds, fresh lime juice, celery salt, salt, pepper, and garlic in a ceramic dish. Cover and let them marinate in your refrigerator for about 3 hours.

In an oven-safe skillet, melt the butter over medium-high heat. Sear the pork cutlets until bottom side is golden brown, about 2 minutes. Flip them over and cook on other side about 2 minutes.

Repeat the process, turning about every 1 to 2 minutes, until an instant-read thermometer inserted into the thickest part registers 150 degrees F.

Add in the leeks, carrots, and celery and continue to cook, partially covered, for 5 minutes more.

Transfer the skillet to the oven and roast the pork with the vegetables for about 10 minutes.

STORING

Place the pork chops and veggies in airtight containers or Ziploc bags; keep in your refrigerator for 3 to 4 days.

Freeze the pork chops and veggies in airtight containers or heavy-duty freezer bags. Freeze up to 4 months. Defrost in the refrigerator and reheat in your oven or microwave. Bon appétit!

29. Classic Pork Stew

(Ready in about 45 minutes | Servings 8)

Per serving: 390 Calories; 27.8g Fat; 4.7g Carbs; 28.3g Protein; 5g Fiber

INGREDIENTS

1 cup fresh brown mushrooms, sliced
1/2 cup fresh cilantro, chopped
1 habanero pepper, minced
3 cups beef bone broth, no sugar added
2 ripe tomatoes, chopped

1 teaspoon garlic, pressed
2 carrots, peeled and chopped
1 celery stalk, chopped
2 tablespoons dry red wine
1/2 teaspoon dried oregano
2 tablespoons lard, at room temperature

2 pounds Boston butt, cut into 3/4-inch cubes
1 teaspoon sea salt
1/2 teaspoon black pepper
1 medium leek, chopped
1 teaspoon dried marjoram

DIRECTIONS

In a heavy-bottomed pot, melt the lard until sizzling. Once hot, brown the pork for 4 to 5 minutes; season with salt and pepper and reserve. Then, cook the leeks, habanero pepper, garlic, carrots and celery until they have softened. Pour in the wine to deglaze the bottom of your pot. Add in the broth, tomatoes, oregano, marjoram, and mushrooms. Partially cover and continue to cook for 35 to 40 minutes.

STORING

Spoon the stew into airtight containers or Ziploc bags; keep in your refrigerator for up to 3 to 4 days.

For freezing, place the stew in airtight containers. Freeze up to 4 to 6 months. Defrost in the refrigerator and reheat on the stove pot. Serve with fresh cilantro. Bon appétit!

30. Hungarian-Style Pork Goulash

(Ready in about 25 minutes | Servings 6)

Per serving: 228 Calories; 11.7g Fat; 6g Carbs; 23.1g Protein; 1.7g Fiber

INGREDIENTS

1 tablespoon olive oil, room temperature
2 teaspoons paprika
2 bay laurels
1/2 cup loosely packed fresh parsley, roughly chopped

2 slices bacon, chopped
Salt and red pepper, to taste
1 cup tomato sauce, no sugar added
1 cup onions, chopped
2 garlic cloves, minced

1 ¼ pounds pork stew meat, cubed
2 cups beef bone broth
1/2 teaspoon celery seeds

DIRECTIONS

Heat the olive oil in a stockpot over a moderately high flame. Sauté the onions and garlic until they've softened.

Add in the pork and continue to cook for 7 to 8 minutes. Add in the bacon, salt, red pepper, and continue to cook for about 3 minutes.

Add in the tomato sauce, beef bone broth, celery seeds, paprika, bay laurels, and parsley. Turn the heat to simmer. Continue to simmer for about 12 minutes until cooked through.

STORING

Spoon the goulash into six airtight containers or Ziploc bags; keep in your refrigerator for up to 3 to 4 days.

For freezing, place the goulash in airtight containers. Freeze up to 4 to 6 months. Defrost in the refrigerator. Enjoy!

31. Mom's Signature Pork Meatloaf

(Ready in about 45 minutes | Servings 6)

Per serving: 251 Calories; 7.9g Fat; 4.5g Carbs; 34.6g Protein; 1.4g Fiber

INGREDIENTS

1 cup tomato puree, no sugar added
1 ½ tablespoons Swerve
1 tablespoon champagne vinegar
1/2 teaspoon dried rosemary
1 teaspoon fresh coriander

1/3 cup almond meal
1 large egg
Sea salt and ground black pepper
1 teaspoon celery seeds
1 ½ pounds ground pork

1/4 cup pork rinds, crushed
1 large onion, chopped
2 cloves garlic, finely minced

DIRECTIONS

In a mixing dish, thoroughly combine the almond meal, egg, salt, black pepper, celery seeds, ground pork, pork rinds, onion, and garlic. Press the meatloaf mixture into a lightly greased loaf pan.

In a saucepan, cook the remaining ingredients until the sauce has thickened and reduced slightly. Spread the sauce evenly over the top of your meatloaf.

Roast in the preheated oven at 365 degrees F for 35 minutes. Place under the preheated broiler for 5 to 6 minutes.

STORING

Wrap your meatloaf tightly with heavy-duty aluminum foil or plastic wrap. Then, keep in your refrigerator for up to 3 to 4 days.

For freezing, wrap your meatloaf tightly to prevent freezer burn. Freeze up to 3 to 4 months. Defrost in the refrigerator. Bon appétit!

32. Authentic Greek Souvlaki

(Ready in about 20 minutes + marinating time | Servings 6)

Per serving: 216 Calories; 4.1g Fat; 1.7g Carbs; 30g Protein; 0.2g Fiber

INGREDIENTS

2 ½ pounds pork tenderloin, trimmed of silver skin and excess fat, cut into 1-inch cubes
1 teaspoon Greek oregano
3 cloves garlic, smashed

Sea salt and ground black pepper, to taste
1/3 cup wine vinegar
2 tablespoons coriander, chopped
2 tablespoons fresh lime juice

DIRECTIONS

Thoroughly combine all ingredients in a ceramic dish. Cover tightly and let it marinate in your refrigerator for 2 to 3 hours. Thread the pork cubes onto the skewers.

Prepare the outdoor grill and brush the grates with a nonstick cooking spray.

Grill your skewers until well browned and internal temperature registers 160 degrees F on an instant read thermometer.

STORING

Divide the pork skewers into six portions; place each portion in a separate airtight container or Ziploc bag; keep in your refrigerator for 3 to 4 days.

Freeze the pork skewers in airtight containers or heavy-duty freezer bags. Freeze up to 4 months. Defrost in the refrigerator. Bon appétit!

33. Pork Rib Soup with Avocado

(Ready in about 20 minutes | Servings 6)

Per serving: 423 Calories; 31.8g Fat; 6g Carbs; 25.9g Protein; 3.2g Fiber

INGREDIENTS

1 ¼ pounds pork spare ribs, boneless and cut into chunks
2 tablespoons butter, room temperature
Sea salt and ground black pepper, to taste
A pinch of dried Mexican oregano
2 vine-ripened tomatoes, undrained
1 celery, chopped

1 onion, peeled and chopped
1 teaspoon garlic, crushed
1 teaspoon habanero pepper, seeded and minced
3 cups beef broth, less-sodium
1/4 cup fresh coriander, roughly chopped
1 medium-sized avocado, pitted and sliced

DIRECTIONS

Melt the butter in a heavy-bottomed pot over a moderate heat. Sauté the onion, garlic, pepper and celery approximately 3 minutes.

Then, sear the pork for 4 to 5 minutes, stirring continuously to ensure even cooking. Add in the broth, salt, black pepper, oregano, tomatoes, and coriander.

Continue to simmer, partially covered, for about 12 minutes.

STORING

Spoon the soup into six airtight containers or Ziploc bags; keep in your refrigerator for up to 3 to 4 days.

For freezing, place the soup in airtight containers. Freeze up to 4 to 6 months. Defrost in the refrigerator. Reheat on the stove pot and serve with avocado. Bon appétit!

34. Mediterranean-Style Pork Medallions

(Ready in about 30 minutes | Servings 4)

Per serving: 335 Calories; 26.3g Fat; 1.5g Carbs; 18.3g Protein; 0.2g Fiber

INGREDIENTS

4 pork medallions
2 tablespoons coconut aminos
1/4 cup dry white wine

2 tablespoons olive oil
1 red onion, thinly sliced
2 cloves garlic, minced

1 teaspoon dried marjoram
1/2 teaspoon fresh ginger root, grated

DIRECTIONS

In a saucepan, heat the olive oil over a moderate heat. Once hot, sauté the onions and garlic until browned.
Cook the pork for about 20 minutes. Add the dry white wine to scrape up any browned bits from the bottom of your pot; add in the coconut aminos, marjoram, and ginger root.
Continue to cook for 8 to 10 minutes or until cooked through.

STORING

Divide the pork medallions into four portions; place each portion in a separate airtight container or Ziploc bag; keep in your refrigerator for 3 to 4 days.
Freeze the pork medallions in airtight containers or heavy-duty freezer bags. Freeze up to 4 months.
Defrost in the refrigerator. Reheat the pork medallions in the same way you prepared them, if possible. Bon appétit!

35. Creamed Pork Soup

(Ready in about 25 minutes | Servings 4)

Per serving: 490 Calories; 44g Fat; 6.1g Carbs; 24.3g Protein; 2.2g Fiber

INGREDIENTS

3/4 pound pork chops, cubed
2 tomatoes, pureed
1 cup double cream
1/2 teaspoon Tabasco sauce
1 tablespoon chicken bouillon granules

4 cups water
2 tablespoons butter, melted
1 white onion, chopped
1 celery stalk, chopped
1 carrot, chopped

Seasoned salt and freshly cracked
black pepper, to taste
1/2 teaspoon red pepper flakes
1/2 cup avocado, pitted, peeled and
diced

DIRECTIONS

In a soup pot, melt the butter over medium-high heat. Cook the onion, celery, and carrot until tender and fragrant or about 6 minutes.
Heat the remaining tablespoon of butter and sear the pork for 4 to 5 minutes, stirring periodically to ensure even cooking.
Add in the water, pureed tomatoes, chicken bouillon granules, salt, black pepper, and red paper flakes, salt, and pepper. Partially cover and continue to simmer for 10 to 12 minutes.
Fold in the double cream and Tabasco sauce. Let it simmer for 5 minutes until cooked through.

STORING

Spoon the soup into four airtight containers or Ziploc bags; keep in your refrigerator for up to 3 to 4 days.
For freezing, place the soup in airtight containers. Freeze up to 4 to 6 months. Defrost in the refrigerator. Reheat on the stove pot and serve with avocado. Bon appétit!

36. Mississippi Pulled Pork

(Ready in about 6 hours + marinating time | Servings 4)

Per serving: 350 Calories; 11g Fat; 5g Carbs; 53.6g Protein; 2.2g Fiber

INGREDIENTS

1 ½ pounds pork shoulder
1 tablespoon liquid smoke sauce
1 teaspoon chipotle powder

Au Jus gravy seasoning packet
2 onions, cut into wedges

Kosher salt and freshly ground black
pepper, taste

DIRECTIONS

Mix the liquid smoke sauce, chipotle powder, Au Jus gravy seasoning packet, salt and pepper. Rub the spice mixture into the pork on all sides.
Wrap in plastic wrap and let it marinate in your refrigerator for 3 hours.
Prepare your grill for indirect heat. Place the pork butt roast on the grate over a drip pan and top with onions; cover the grill and cook for about 6 hours.
Transfer the pork to a cutting board. Now, shred the meat into bite-sized pieces using two forks.

STORING

Divide the pork between four airtight containers or Ziploc bags; keep in your refrigerator for up to 3 to 5 days.
For freezing, place the pork in airtight containers or heavy-duty freezer bags. Freeze up to 4 months. Defrost in the refrigerator. Bon appétit!

37. Saucy Boston Butt

(Ready in about 1 hour 20 minutes | Servings 8)

Per serving: 369 Calories; 20.2g Fat; 2.9g Carbs; 41.3g Protein; 0.7g Fiber

INGREDIENTS

1 tablespoon lard, room temperature
2 pounds Boston butt, cubed
Salt and freshly ground pepper
1/2 teaspoon mustard powder
A bunch of spring onions, chopped

2 garlic cloves, minced
1/2 tablespoon ground cardamom
2 tomatoes, pureed
1 bell pepper, deveined and chopped

1 jalapeno pepper, deveined and finely chopped
1/2 cup unsweetened coconut milk
2 cups chicken bone broth

DIRECTIONS

In a wok, melt the lard over moderate heat. Season the pork belly with salt, pepper and mustard powder.
Sear the pork for 8 to 10 minutes, stirring periodically to ensure even cooking; set aside, keeping it warm.
In the same wok, sauté the spring onions, garlic, and cardamom. Spoon the sautéed vegetables along with the reserved pork into the slow cooker.
Add in the remaining ingredients, cover with the lid and cook for 1 hour 10 minutes over low heat.

STORING

Divide the pork and vegetables between airtight containers or Ziploc bags; keep in your refrigerator for up to 3 to 5 days.
For freezing, place the pork and vegetables in airtight containers or heavy-duty freezer bags. Freeze up to 4 months. Defrost in the refrigerator. Bon appétit!

38. Ground Pork Skillet

(Ready in about 25 minutes | Servings 4)

Per serving: 349 Calories; 13g Fat; 4.4g Carbs; 45.3g Protein; 1.2g Fiber

INGREDIENTS

1 ½ pounds ground pork
2 tablespoons olive oil
1 bunch kale, trimmed and roughly chopped
1 cup onions, sliced

1/4 teaspoon black pepper, or more to taste
1/4 cup tomato puree
1 bell pepper, chopped
1 teaspoon sea salt

1 cup chicken bone broth
1/4 cup port wine
2 cloves garlic, pressed
1 chili pepper, sliced

DIRECTIONS

Heat 1 tablespoon of the olive oil in a cast-iron skillet over a moderately high heat. Now, sauté the onion, garlic, and peppers until they are tender and fragrant; reserve.
Heat the remaining tablespoon of olive oil; once hot, cook the ground pork and approximately 5 minutes until no longer pink.
Add in the other ingredients and continue to cook for 15 to 17 minutes or until cooked through.

STORING

Place the ground pork mixture in airtight containers or Ziploc bags; keep in your refrigerator for up to 3 to 4 days.
For freezing, place the ground pork mixture in airtight containers or heavy-duty freezer bags. Freeze up to 2 to 3 months. Defrost in the refrigerator. Bon appétit!

39. Keto Pork Wraps

(Ready in about 15 minutes | Servings 4)

Per serving: 281 Calories; 19.4g Fat; 5.1g Carbs; 22.1g Protein; 1.3g Fiber

INGREDIENTS

1 pound ground pork
2 garlic cloves, finely minced
1 chili pepper, deveined and finely minced

1 teaspoon mustard powder
1 tablespoon sunflower seeds
2 tablespoons champagne vinegar
1 tablespoon coconut aminos

Celery salt and ground black pepper, to taste
2 scallion stalks, sliced
1 head lettuce

DIRECTIONS

Sear the ground pork in the preheated pan for about 8 minutes. Stir in the garlic, chili pepper, mustard seeds, and sunflower seeds; continue to sauté for 1 minute longer or until aromatic.
Add in the vinegar, coconut aminos, salt, black pepper, and scallions. Stir to combine well.

STORING

Place the ground pork mixture in airtight containers or Ziploc bags; keep in your refrigerator for up to 3 to 4 days.
For freezing, place the ground pork mixture it in airtight containers or heavy-duty freezer bags. Freeze up to 2 to 3 months. Defrost in the refrigerator and reheat in the skillet.
Add spoonfuls of the pork mixture to the lettuce leaves, wrap them and serve.

40. Pork in Blue Cheese Sauce

(Ready in about 30 minutes | Servings 6)

Per serving: 348 Calories; 18.9g Fat; 1.9g Carbs; 40.3g Protein; 0.3g Fiber

INGREDIENTS

2 pounds pork center cut loin roast, boneless and cut into 6 pieces
1 tablespoon coconut aminos
6 ounces blue cheese
1/3 cup heavy cream

1/3 cup port wine
1/3 cup roasted vegetable broth, preferably homemade
1 teaspoon dried hot chile flakes
1 teaspoon dried rosemary

1 tablespoon lard
1 shallot, chopped
2 garlic cloves, chopped
Salt and freshly cracked black peppercorns, to taste

DIRECTIONS

Rub each piece of the pork with salt, black peppercorns, and rosemary.
Melt the lard in a saucepan over a moderately high flame. Sear the pork on all sides about 15 minutes; set aside.
Cook the shallot and garlic until they've softened. Add in port wine to scrape up any brown bits from the bottom.
Reduce the heat to medium-low and add in the remaining ingredients; continue to simmer until the sauce has thickened and reduced.

STORING

Divide the pork and sauce into six portions; place each portion in a separate airtight container or Ziploc bag; keep in your refrigerator for 3 to 4 days.
Freeze the pork and sauce in airtight containers or heavy-duty freezer bags. Freeze up to 4 months. Defrost in the refrigerator. Bon appétit!

41. Pork Chops with Herbs

(Ready in about 20 minutes | Servings 4)

Per serving: 192 Calories; 6.9g Fat; 0.9g Carbs; 29.8g Protein; 0.4g Fiber

INGREDIENTS

1 tablespoon butter
1 pound pork chops
2 rosemary sprigs, minced
1 teaspoon dried marjoram

1 teaspoon dried parsley
A bunch of spring onions, roughly chopped
1 thyme sprig, minced

1/2 teaspoon granulated garlic
1/2 teaspoon paprika, crushed
Coarse salt and ground black pepper, to taste

DIRECTIONS

Season the pork chops with the granulated garlic, paprika, salt, and black pepper.
Melt the butter in a frying pan over a moderate flame. Cook the pork chops for 6 to 8 minutes, turning them occasionally to ensure even cooking.
Add in the remaining ingredients and cook an additional 4 minutes.

STORING

Divide the pork chops into four portions; place each portion in a separate airtight container or Ziploc bag; keep in your refrigerator for 3 to 4 days.
Freeze the pork chops in airtight containers or heavy-duty freezer bags. Freeze up to 4 months. Defrost in the refrigerator. Bon appétit!

42. Mediterranean-Style Cheesy Pork Loin

(Ready in about 25 minutes | Servings 4)

Per serving: 476 Calories; 35.3g Fat; 6.2g Carbs; 31.1g Protein; 1.4g Fiber

INGREDIENTS

1 pound pork loin, cut into 1-inch-thick pieces
1 teaspoon Mediterranean seasoning mix
Salt and pepper, to taste
1 onion, sliced
1 teaspoon fresh garlic, smashed
2 tablespoons black olives, pitted and sliced

2 tablespoons balsamic vinegar
1/2 cup Romano cheese, grated
2 tablespoons butter, room temperature
1 tablespoon curry paste
1 cup roasted vegetable broth
1 tablespoon oyster sauce

DIRECTIONS

In a frying pan, melt the butter over a moderately high heat. Once hot, cook the pork until browned on all sides; season with salt and black pepper and set aside.
In the pan drippings, cook the onion and garlic for 4 to 5 minutes or until they've softened.
Add in the Mediterranean seasoning mix, curry paste, and vegetable broth. Continue to cook until the sauce has thickened and reduced slightly or about 10 minutes. Add in the remaining ingredients along with the reserved pork.
Top with cheese and cook for 10 minutes longer or until cooked through.

STORING

Divide the pork loin between four airtight containers; keep in your refrigerator for 3 to 5 days.
For freezing, place the pork loin in airtight containers or heavy-duty freezer bags. Freeze up to 4 to 6 months. Defrost in the refrigerator. Enjoy!

43. Old-Fashioned Goulash

(Ready in about 9 hours 10 minutes | Servings 4)

Per serving: 456 Calories; 28.7g Fat; 6.7g Carbs; 32g Protein; 3.4g Fiber

INGREDIENTS

1 ½ pounds pork butt, chopped
1 teaspoon sweet Hungarian paprika
2 Hungarian hot peppers, deveined
and minced

1 cup leeks, chopped
1 ½ tablespoons lard
1 teaspoon caraway seeds, ground
4 cups vegetable broth

2 garlic cloves, crushed
1 teaspoons cayenne pepper
2 cups tomato sauce with herbs

DIRECTIONS

Melt the lard in a heavy-bottomed pot over medium-high heat. Sear the pork for 5 to 6 minutes until just browned on all sides; set aside.
Add in the leeks and garlic; continue to cook until they have softened.
Place the reserved pork along with the sautéed mixture in your crock pot. Add in the other ingredients and stir to combine.
Cover with the lid and slow cook for 9 hours on the lowest setting.

STORING

Spoon your goulash into four airtight containers or Ziploc bags; keep in your refrigerator for up to 3 to 4 days.
For freezing, place the goulash in airtight containers. Freeze up to 4 to 6 months. Defrost in the refrigerator. Enjoy!

44. Oven-Roasted Spare Ribs

(Ready in about 3 hour 40 minutes + marinating time | Servings 6)

Per serving: 385 Calories; 29g Fat; 1.8g Carbs; 28.3g Protein; 0.1g Fiber

INGREDIENTS

2 pounds spare ribs
1 garlic clove, minced
1 teaspoon dried marjoram

1 lime, halved
Salt and ground black pepper, to taste

DIRECTIONS

Toss all ingredients in a ceramic dish.
Cover and let it refrigerate for 5 to 6 hours.
Roast the foil-wrapped ribs in the preheated oven at 275 degrees F degrees for about 3 hours 30 minutes.

STORING

Divide the ribs into six portions. Place each portion of ribs in an airtight container; keep in your refrigerator for 3 to 5 days.
For freezing, place the ribs in airtight containers or heavy-duty freezer bags. Freeze up to 4 to 6 months. Defrost in the refrigerator and reheat in the preheated oven. Bon appétit!

45. Cheesy Chinese-Style Pork

(Ready in about 20 minutes | Servings 6)

Per serving: 424 Calories; 29.4g Fat; 3.8g Carbs; 34.2g Protein; 0.6g Fiber

INGREDIENTS

1 tablespoon sesame oil
1 ½ pounds pork shoulder, cut into
strips
Himalayan salt and freshly ground
black pepper, to taste

1/2 teaspoon cayenne pepper
1/2 cup shallots, roughly chopped
2 bell peppers, sliced
1/4 cup cream of onion soup
1/2 teaspoon Sriracha sauce

1 tablespoon tahini (sesame butter)
1 tablespoon soy sauce
4 ounces gouda cheese, cut into small
pieces

DIRECTIONS

Heat he sesame oil in a wok over a moderately high flame.
Stir-fry the pork strips for 3 to 4 minutes or until just browned on all sides. Add in the spices, shallots and bell peppers and continue to cook for a further 4 minutes.
Stir in the cream of onion soup, Sriracha, sesame butter, and soy sauce; continue to cook for 3 to 4 minutes more.
Top with the cheese and continue to cook until the cheese has melted.

STORING

Place your stir-fry in six airtight containers or Ziploc bags; keep in your refrigerator for 3 to 4 days.
For freezing, wrap tightly with heavy-duty aluminum foil or freezer wrap. It will maintain the best quality for 2 to 3 months. Defrost in the refrigerator and reheat in your wok.

46. Smoked Pork Sausage Keto Bombs

(Ready in about 15 minutes + chilling time | Servings 6)

Per serving: 383 Calories; 32.7g Fat; 5.1g Carbs; 16.7g Protein; 1.7g Fiber

INGREDIENTS

3/4 pound smoked pork sausage, ground
1 teaspoon ginger-garlic paste
2 tablespoons scallions, minced

1 tablespoon butter, room temperature
1 tomato, pureed
4 ounces mozzarella cheese, crumbled
2 tablespoons flaxseed meal

8 ounces cream cheese, room temperature
Sea salt and ground black pepper, to taste

DIRECTIONS

Melt the butter in a frying pan over medium-high heat. Cook the sausage for about 4 minutes, crumbling with a spatula.
Add in the ginger-garlic paste, scallions, and tomato; continue to cook over medium-low heat for a further 6 minutes. Stir in the remaining ingredients.
Place the mixture in your refrigerator for 1 to 2 hours until firm. Roll the mixture into bite-sized balls.

STORING

Transfer the balls to the airtight containers and place in your refrigerator for up to 3 days.
For freezing, place in a freezer safe containers and freeze up to 1 month. Enjoy!

47. Breakfast Muffins with Ground Pork

(Ready in about 25 minutes | Servings 6)

Per serving: 330 Calories; 30.3g Fat; 2.3g Carbs; 19g Protein; 1.2g Fiber

INGREDIENTS

1 stick butter
3 large eggs, lightly beaten
2 tablespoons full-fat milk
1/2 teaspoon ground cardamom

3 ½ cups almond flour
2 tablespoons flaxseed meal
1 teaspoon baking powder
2 cups ground pork

Salt and pepper, to your liking
1/2 teaspoon dried basil

DIRECTIONS

In the preheated frying pan, cook the ground pork until the juices run clear, approximately 5 minutes.
Add in the remaining ingredients and stir until well combined.
Spoon the mixture into lightly greased muffin cups. Bake in the preheated oven at 365 degrees F for about 17 minutes.
Allow your muffins to cool down before unmolding and storing.

STORING

Place your muffins in the airtight containers or Ziploc bags; keep in the refrigerator for a week.
For freezing, divide your muffins among Ziploc bags and freeze up to 3 months. Defrost in your microwave for a couple of minutes. Bon appétit!

48. Easy Fall-Off-The-Bone Ribs

(Ready in about 8 hours | Servings 4)

Per serving: 192 Calories; 6.9g Fat; 0.9g Carbs; 29.8g Protein; 0.5g Fiber

INGREDIENTS

1 pound baby back ribs
4 tablespoons coconut aminos
1/4 cup dry red wine
1/2 teaspoon cayenne pepper

1 garlic clove, crushed
1 teaspoon Italian herb mix
1 tablespoon butter
1 teaspoon Serrano pepper, minced

1 Italian pepper, thinly sliced
1 teaspoon grated lemon zest

DIRECTIONS

Butter the sides and bottom of your Crock pot. Place the pork and peppers on the bottom.
Add in the remaining ingredients.
Slow cook for 9 hours on Low heat setting.

STORING

Divide the baby back ribs into four portions. Place each portion of the ribs along with the peppers in an airtight container; keep in your refrigerator for 3 to 5 days.
For freezing, place the ribs in airtight containers or heavy-duty freezer bags. Freeze up to 4 to 6 months. Defrost in the refrigerator. Reheat in your oven at 250 degrees F until heated through.

49. Brie-Stuffed Meatballs

(Ready in about 25 minutes | Servings 5)

Per serving: 302 Calories; 17.3g Fat; 1.9g Carbs; 33.4g Protein; 0.3g Fiber

INGREDIENTS

2 eggs, beaten
1 pound ground pork
1/3 cup double cream

1 tablespoon fresh parsley
Kosher salt and ground black pepper
1 teaspoon dried rosemary

10 (1-inch) cubes of brie cheese
2 tablespoons scallions, minced
2 cloves garlic, minced

DIRECTIONS

Mix all ingredients, except for the brie cheese, until everything is well incorporated.
Roll the mixture into 10 patties; place a piece of cheese in the center of each patty and roll into a ball.
Roast in the preheated oven at 380 degrees F for about 20 minutes.

STORING

Place the meatballs in airtight containers or Ziploc bags; keep in your refrigerator for up to 3 to 4 days.
Freeze the meatballs in airtight containers or heavy-duty freezer bags. Freeze up to 3 to 4 months. To defrost, slowly reheat in a saucepan.
Bon appétit!

50. Kansas-Style Meatloaf

(Ready in about 1 hour 10 minutes | Servings 8)

Per serving: 318 Calories; 14.7g Fat; 6.2g Carbs; 39.3g Protein; 0.3g Fiber

INGREDIENTS

2 pounds ground pork
2 eggs, beaten
1/2 cup onions, chopped
1/2 cup marinara sauce, bottled

8 ounces Colby cheese, shredded
1 teaspoon granulated garlic
Sea salt and freshly ground black
pepper, to taste

1 teaspoon lime zest
1 teaspoon mustard seeds
1/2 cup tomato puree
1 tablespoon Erythritol

DIRECTIONS

Mix the ground pork with the eggs, onions, marinara salsa, cheese, granulated garlic, salt, pepper, lime zest, and mustard seeds; mix to combine.
Press the mixture into a lightly-greased loaf pan. Mix the tomato paste with the Erythritol and spread the mixture over the top of your meatloaf.
Bake in the preheated oven at 365 degrees F for about 1 hour 10 minutes, rotating the pan halfway through the cook time.

STORING

Wrap your meatloaf tightly with heavy-duty aluminum foil or plastic wrap. Then, keep in your refrigerator for up to 3 to 4 days.
For freezing, wrap your meatloaf tightly to prevent freezer burn. Freeze up to 3 to 4 months. Defrost in the refrigerator. Bon appétit!

51. Ground Pork Stuffed Peppers

(Ready in about 40 minutes | Servings 4)

Per serving: 290 Calories; 20.5g Fat; 8.2g Carbs; 18.2g Protein; 1.5g Fiber

INGREDIENTS

6 bell peppers, deveined
1 tablespoon vegetable oil
1 shallot, chopped
1 garlic clove, minced

1/2 pound ground pork
1/3 pound ground veal
1 ripe tomato, chopped
1/2 teaspoon mustard seeds

Sea salt and ground black pepper, to
taste

DIRECTIONS

Parboil the peppers for 5 minutes.
Heat the vegetable oil in a frying pan that is preheated over a moderate heat. Cook the shallot and garlic for 3 to 4 minutes until they've softened.
Stir in the ground meat and cook, breaking apart with a fork, for about 6 minutes. Add the chopped tomatoes, mustard seeds, salt, and pepper.
Continue to cook for 5 minutes or until heated through. Divide the filling between the peppers and transfer them to a baking pan.
Bake in the preheated oven at 365 degrees F approximately 25 minutes.

STORING

Place the peppers in airtight containers or Ziploc bags; keep in your refrigerator for up to 3 to 4 days.
For freezing, place the peppers in airtight containers or heavy-duty freezer bags. Freeze up to 2 to 3 months. Defrost in the refrigerator.
Bon appétit!

POULTRY

52. Country-Style Chicken Stew

(Ready in about 1 hour | Servings 6)

Per serving: 280 Calories; 14.7g Fat; 2.5g Carbs; 25.6g Protein; 2.5g Fiber

INGREDIENTS

1 pound chicken thighs
2 tablespoons butter, room temperature
1/2 pound carrots, chopped
1 bell pepper, chopped

1 chile pepper, deveined and minced
1 cup tomato puree
Kosher salt and ground black pepper, to taste
1/2 teaspoon smoked paprika

1 onion, finely chopped
1 teaspoon garlic, sliced
4 cups vegetable broth
1 teaspoon dried basil
1 celery, chopped

DIRECTIONS

Melt the butter in a stockpot over medium-high flame. Sweat the onion and garlic until just tender and fragrant.
Reduce the heat to medium-low. Stir in the broth, chicken thighs, and basil; bring to a rolling boil.
Add in the remaining ingredients. Partially cover and let it simmer for 45 to 50 minutes. Shred the meat, discarding the bones; add the chicken back to the pot.

STORING

Spoon the soup into six airtight containers or Ziploc bags; keep in your refrigerator for up to 3 to 4 days.
For freezing, place the soup in airtight containers. It will maintain the best quality for about 5 months. Defrost in the refrigerator. Bon appétit!

53. Autumn Chicken Soup with Root Vegetables

(Ready in about 25 minutes | Servings 4)

Per serving: 342 Calories; 22.4g Fat; 6.3g Carbs; 25.2g Protein; 1.3g Fiber

INGREDIENTS

4 cups chicken broth
1 cup full-fat milk
1 cup double cream
1/2 cup turnip, chopped
2 chicken drumsticks, boneless and cut

into small pieces
Salt and pepper, to taste
1 tablespoon butter
1 teaspoon garlic, finely minced
1 carrot, chopped

1/2 parsnip, chopped
1/2 celery
1 whole egg

DIRECTIONS

Melt the butter in a heavy-bottomed pot over medium-high heat; sauté the garlic until aromatic or about 1 minute. Add in the vegetables and continue to cook until they've softened.
Add in the chicken and cook until it is no longer pink for about 4 minutes. Season with salt and pepper.
Pour in the chicken broth, milk, and heavy cream and bring it to a boil.
Reduce the heat to. Partially cover and continue to simmer for 20 to 25 minutes longer. Afterwards, fold the beaten egg and stir until it is well incorporated.

STORING

Spoon the soup into four airtight containers or Ziploc bags; keep in your refrigerator for up to 3 to 4 days.
For freezing, place the soup in airtight containers. It will maintain the best quality for about 4 to 6 months. Defrost in the refrigerator. Bon appétit!

54. Panna Cotta with Chicken and Bleu d' Auvergne

(Ready in about 20 minutes + chilling time | Servings 4)

Per serving: 306 Calories; 18.3g Fat; 4.7g Carbs; 29.5g Protein; 0g Fiber

INGREDIENTS

2 chicken legs, boneless and skinless
1 tablespoon avocado oil
2 teaspoons granular erythritol

3 tablespoons water
1 cup Bleu d' Auvergne, crumbled
2 gelatin sheets

3/4 cup double cream
Salt and cayenne pepper, to your liking

DIRECTIONS

Heat the oil in a frying pan over medium-high heat; fry the chicken for about 10 minutes.
Soak the gelatin sheets in cold water. Cook with the cream, erythritol, water, and Bleu d' Auvergne.
Season with salt and pepper and let it simmer over the low heat, stirring for about 3 minutes. Spoon the mixture into four ramekins.

STORING

Cover your panna cotta and chicken with plastic wrap and refrigerate for up to 5 days. Enjoy!

55. Breaded Chicken Fillets

(Ready in about 30 minutes | Servings 4)

Per serving: 367 Calories; 16.9g Fat; 6g Carbs; 43g Protein; 0.7g Fiber

INGREDIENTS

1 pound chicken fillets
3 bell peppers, quartered lengthwise
1/3 cup Romano cheese
2 teaspoons olive oil

1 garlic clove, minced
Kosher salt and ground black pepper, to taste
1/3 cup crushed pork rinds

DIRECTIONS

Start by preheating your oven to 410 degrees F.
Mix the crushed pork rinds, Romano cheese, olive oil and minced garlic. Dredge the chicken into this mixture.
Place the chicken in a lightly greased baking dish. Season with salt and black pepper to taste.
Scatter the peppers around the chicken and bake in the preheated oven for 20 to 25 minutes or until thoroughly cooked.

STORING

Place the chicken and peppers in airtight containers or Ziploc bags; keep in your refrigerator for up 1 to 2 days.
For freezing, place the chicken and peppers in airtight containers or heavy-duty freezer bags. Freeze up to 2 to 3 months. Defrost in the refrigerator or microwave. Enjoy!

56. Chicken Drumsticks with Broccoli and Cheese

(Ready in about 1 hour 15 minutes | Servings 4)

Per serving: 533 Calories; 40.2g Fat; 5.4g Carbs; 35.1g Protein; 3.5g Fiber

INGREDIENTS

1 pound chicken drumsticks
1 pound broccoli, broken into florets
2 cups cheddar cheese, shredded
1/2 teaspoon dried oregano
1/2 teaspoon dried basil

3 tablespoons olive oil
1 celery, sliced
1 cup green onions, chopped
1 teaspoon minced green garlic

DIRECTIONS

Roast the chicken drumsticks in the preheated oven at 380 degrees F for 30 to 35 minutes. Add in the broccoli, celery, green onions, and green garlic.
Add in the oregano, basil and olive oil; roast an additional 15 minutes.

STORING

Place the chicken in airtight containers or Ziploc bags; keep in your refrigerator for up to 3 to 4 days.
For freezing, place the chicken in airtight containers or heavy-duty freezer bags. Freeze up to 3 months.
Once thawed in the refrigerator, heat in the preheated oven at 375 degrees F for 20 minutes. Top with the shredded cheese and bake an additional 5 minutes until hot and bubbly.
Bon appétit!

57. Turkey Ham and Mozzarella Pate

(Ready in about 10 minutes | Servings 6)

Per serving: 212 Calories; 18.8g Fat; 2g Carbs; 10.6g Protein; 1.6g Fiber

INGREDIENTS

4 ounces turkey ham, chopped
2 tablespoons fresh parsley, roughly chopped
2 tablespoons flaxseed meal

4 ounces mozzarella cheese, crumbled
2 tablespoons sunflower seeds

DIRECTIONS

Thoroughly combine the ingredients, except for the sunflower seeds, in your food processor.
Spoon the mixture into a serving bowl and scatter the sunflower seeds over the top.

STORING

Place your pate in airtight containers or Ziploc bags; keep in your refrigerator for up to 6 days.

58. Greek-Style Saucy Chicken Drumettes

(Ready in about 50 minutes | Servings 6)

Per serving: 333 Calories; 20.2g Fat; 2g Carbs; 33.5g Protein; 0.2g Fiber

INGREDIENTS

1 ½ pounds chicken drumettes
1/2 cup port wine
1/2 cup onions, chopped

2 garlic cloves, minced
1 teaspoon tzatziki spice mix
1 cup double cream

2 tablespoons butter
Sea salt and crushed mixed peppercorns, to season

DIRECTIONS

Melt the butter in an oven-proof skillet over a moderate heat; then, cook the chicken for about 8 minutes.
Add in the onions, garlic, wine, tzatziki spice mix, double cream, salt, and pepper.
Bake in the preheated oven at 390 degrees F for 35 to 40 minutes (a meat thermometer should register 165 degrees F).

STORING

Place the chicken in airtight containers or Ziploc bags; keep in your refrigerator for up to 3 to 4 days.
For freezing, place the chicken in airtight containers or heavy-duty freezer bags. Freeze up to 3 months. Defrost in your refrigerator and reheat in the oven. Enjoy!

59. Chicken with Avocado Sauce

(Ready in about 20 minutes | Servings 4)

Per serving: 370 Calories; 25g Fat; 4.1g Carbs; 31.4g Protein; 2.6g Fiber

INGREDIENTS

8 chicken wings, boneless, cut into
bite-size chunks
2 tablespoons olive oil
Sea salt and pepper, to your liking
2 eggs

1 teaspoon onion powder
1 teaspoon hot paprika
1/3 teaspoon mustard seeds
1/3 cup almond meal
For the Sauce:

1/2 cup mayonnaise
1/2 medium avocado
1/2 teaspoon sea salt
1 teaspoon green garlic, minced

DIRECTIONS

Pat dry the chicken wings with a paper towel.
Thoroughly combine the almond meal, salt, pepper, onion powder, paprika, and mustard seeds.
Whisk the eggs in a separate dish. Dredge the chicken chunks into the whisked eggs, then in the almond meal mixture.
In a frying pan, heat the oil over a moderate heat; once hot, fry the chicken for about 10 minutes, stirring continuously to ensure even cooking.
Make the sauce by whisking all of the sauce ingredients.

STORING

Place the chicken in airtight containers or Ziploc bags; keep in your refrigerator for up to 3 to 4 days.
For freezing, place the chicken in airtight containers or heavy-duty freezer bags. Freeze up to 3 months. Defrost in your refrigerator and reheat in the oven.
Store the avocado sauce in your refrigerator for up to 3 days. Serve the warm chicken with the sauce on the side.

60. Old-Fashioned Turkey Chowder

(Ready in about 35 minutes | Servings 4)

Per serving: 350 Calories; 25.8g Fat; 5.5g Carbs; 20g Protein; 0.1g Fiber

INGREDIENTS

2 tablespoons olive oil
2 tablespoons yellow onions, chopped
2 cloves garlic, roughly chopped

1/2 pound leftover roast turkey, shredded and skin removed
1 teaspoon Mediterranean spice mix
3 cups chicken bone broth

1 ½ cups milk
1/2 cup double cream
1 egg, lightly beaten
2 tablespoons dry sherry

DIRECTIONS

Heat the olive oil in a heavy-bottomed pot over a moderate flame. Sauté the onion and garlic until they've softened.
Stir in the leftover roast turkey, Mediterranean spice mix, and chicken bone broth; bring to a rapid boil. Partially cover and continue to cook for 20 to 25 minutes.
Turn the heat to simmer. Pour in the milk and double cream and continue to cook until it has reduced slightly.
Fold in the egg and dry sherry; continue to simmer, stirring frequently, for a further 2 minutes.

STORING

Spoon the chowder into four airtight containers or Ziploc bags; keep in your refrigerator for up to 3 to 4 days.
For freezing, place the chowder in airtight containers. It will maintain the best quality for about 4 months. Defrost in the refrigerator. Bon appétit!

61. Duck and Eggplant Casserole

(Ready in about 45 minutes | Servings 4)

Per serving: 562 Calories; 49.5g Fat; 6.7g Carbs; 22.5g Protein; 2.1g Fiber

INGREDIENTS

1 pound ground duck meat
1 ½ tablespoons ghee, melted
1/3 cup double cream

1/2 pound eggplant, peeled and sliced
1 ½ cups almond flour
Salt and black pepper, to taste

1/2 teaspoon fennel seeds
1/2 teaspoon oregano, dried
8 eggs

DIRECTIONS

Mix the almond flour with salt, black, fennel seeds, and oregano. Fold in one egg and the melted ghee and whisk to combine well.
Press the crust into the bottom of a lightly-oiled pie pan. Cook the ground duck until no longer pink for about 3 minutes, stirring continuously.
Whisk the remaining eggs and double cream. Fold in the browned meat and stir until everything is well incorporated. Pour the mixture into the prepared crust. Top with the eggplant slices.
Bake for about 40 minutes. Cut into four pieces.

STORING

Slice the casserole into four pieces. Divide the pieces between four airtight containers; it will last for 3 to 4 days in the refrigerator.
For freezing, place each portion in a separate heavy-duty freezer bag. Freeze up to 2 to 3 months. Defrost in the microwave or refrigerator. Bon appétit!

62. Herbed Chicken Breasts

(Ready in about 40 minutes | Servings 8)

Per serving: 306 Calories; 17.8g Fat; 3.1g Carbs; 31.7g Protein; 0.2g Fiber

INGREDIENTS

4 chicken breasts, skinless and boneless
1 Italian pepper, deveined and thinly sliced

10 black olives, pitted
1 ½ cups vegetable broth
2 garlic cloves, pressed

2 tablespoons olive oil
1 tablespoon Old Sub Sailor
Salt, to taste

DIRECTIONS

Rub the chicken with the garlic and Old Sub Sailor; salt to taste. Heat the oil in a frying pan over a moderately high heat.
Sear the chicken until it is browned on all sides, about 5 minutes.
Add in the pepper, olives, and vegetable broth and bring it to boil. Reduce the heat simmer and continue to cook, partially covered, for 30 to 35 minutes.

STORING

Place the chicken breasts in airtight containers or Ziploc bags; keep in your refrigerator for 3 to 4 days.
For freezing, place the chicken breasts in airtight containers or heavy-duty freezer bags. It will maintain the best quality for about 4 months. Defrost in the refrigerator. Bon appétit!

63. Cheese and Prosciutto Chicken Roulade

(Ready in about 35 minutes | Servings 2)

Per serving: 499 Calories; 18.9g Fat; 5.7g Carbs; 41.6g Protein; 0.6g Fiber

INGREDIENTS

1/2 cup Ricotta cheese
4 slices of prosciutto
1 pound chicken fillet

1 tablespoon fresh coriander, chopped
Salt and ground black pepper, to taste pepper
1 teaspoon cayenne pepper

DIRECTIONS

Season the chicken fillet with salt and pepper. Spread the Ricotta cheese over the chicken fillet; sprinkle with the fresh coriander.
Roll up and cut into 4 pieces. Wrap each piece with one slice of prosciutto; secure with a kitchen twine.
Place the wrapped chicken in a parchment-lined baking pan. Now, bake in the preheated oven at 385 degrees F for about 30 minutes.

STORING

Place the chicken roulades in airtight containers or Ziploc bags; keep in your refrigerator for 3 to 4 days.
For freezing, place the chicken roulades in airtight containers or heavy-duty freezer bags. Freeze up to 4 months. Defrost in the refrigerator. Enjoy!

64. Boozy Glazed Chicken

(Ready in about 1 hour + marinating time | Servings 4)

Per serving: 307 Calories; 12.1g Fat; 2.7g Carbs; 33.6g Protein; 1.5g Fiber

INGREDIENTS

2 pounds chicken drumettes
2 tablespoons ghee, at room temperature
Sea salt and ground black pepper, to taste
1 teaspoon Mediterranean seasoning mix

2 vine-ripened tomatoes, pureed
3/4 cup rum
3 tablespoons coconut aminos
A few drops of liquid Stevia
1 teaspoon chile peppers, minced

1 tablespoon minced fresh ginger
1 teaspoon ground cardamom
2 tablespoons fresh lemon juice, plus wedges for serving

DIRECTIONS

Toss the chicken with the melted ghee, salt, black pepper, and Mediterranean seasoning mix until well coated on all sides.
In another bowl, thoroughly combine the pureed tomato puree, rum, coconut aminos, Stevia, chile peppers, ginger, cardamom, and lemon juice.
Pour the tomato mixture over the chicken drumettes; let it marinate for 2 hours. Bake in the preheated oven at 410 degrees F for about 45 minutes.
Add in the reserved marinade and place under the preheated broiler for 10 minutes.

STORING

Place the chicken drumettes in airtight containers or Ziploc bags; keep in your refrigerator for up 3 to 4 days.
To freeze the chicken drumettes, place them in airtight containers or heavy-duty freezer bags. Freeze up to 3 months. Once thawed in the refrigerator, heat in the preheated oven at 375 degrees F for 20 to 25 minutes. Bon appétit!

65. Festive Turkey Rouladen

(Ready in about 30 minutes | Servings 5)

Per serving: 286 Calories; 9.7g Fat; 6.9g Carbs; 39.9g Protein; 0.3g Fiber

INGREDIENTS

2 pounds turkey fillet, marinated and cut into 10 pieces
10 strips prosciutto
1/2 teaspoon chili powder
1 teaspoon marjoram
1 sprig rosemary, finely chopped

2 tablespoons dry white wine
1 teaspoon garlic, finely minced
1 ½ tablespoons butter, room temperature
1 tablespoon Dijon mustard
Sea salt and freshly ground black pepper, to your liking

DIRECTIONS

Start by preheating your oven to 430 degrees F.
Pat the turkey dry and cook in hot butter for about 3 minutes per side. Add in the mustard, chili powder, marjoram, rosemary, wine, and garlic.
Continue to cook for 2 minutes more. Wrap each turkey piece into one prosciutto strip and secure with toothpicks.
Roast in the preheated oven for about 30 minutes.

STORING

Wrap the turkey pieces in foil before packing them into airtight containers; keep in your refrigerator for up to 3 to 4 days.
For freezing, place them in airtight containers or heavy-duty freezer bags. Freeze up to 2 to 3 months. Defrost in the refrigerator. Bon appétit!

66. Pan-Fried Chorizo Sausage

(Ready in about 20 minutes | Servings 4)

Per serving: 330 Calories; 17.2g Fat; 4.5g Carbs; 34.4g Protein; 1.6g Fiber

INGREDIENTS

16 ounces smoked turkey chorizo
1 ½ cups Asiago cheese, grated
1 teaspoon oregano
1 teaspoon basil

1 cup tomato puree
4 scallion stalks, chopped
1 teaspoon garlic paste
Sea salt and ground black pepper, to taste

1 tablespoon dry sherry
1 tablespoon extra-virgin olive oil
2 tablespoons fresh coriander, roughly chopped

DIRECTIONS

Heat the oil in a frying pan over moderately high heat. Now, brown the turkey chorizo, crumbling with a fork for about 5 minutes.
Add in the other ingredients, except for cheese; continue to cook for 10 minutes more or until cooked through.

STORING

Place the sausage along with the sauce in four Ziploc bags; keep in the refrigerator for a week.
For freezing, divide the sausage along with sauce among Ziploc bags and freeze up to 3 to 4 months. Thaw them in the refrigerator.
Reheat the sausage and sauce in the frying pan. Top with cheese and continue to cook until cheese has melted. Enjoy!

67. Chinese Bok Choy and Turkey Soup

(Ready in about 40 minutes | Servings 8)

Per serving: 211 Calories; 11.8g Fat; 3.1g Carbs; 23.7g Protein; 0.9g Fiber

INGREDIENTS

1/2 pound baby Bok choy, sliced into quarters lengthwise
2 pounds turkey carcass

1 tablespoon olive oil
1/2 cup leeks, chopped
1 celery rib, chopped

2 carrots, sliced
6 cups turkey stock
Himalayan salt and black pepper, to taste

DIRECTIONS

In a heavy-bottomed pot, heat the olive oil until sizzling. Once hot, sauté the celery, carrots, leek and Bok choy for about 6 minutes.
Add the salt, pepper, turkey, and stock; bring to a boil.
Turn the heat to simmer. Continue to cook, partially covered, for about 35 minutes.

STORING

Spoon the soup into airtight containers or Ziploc bags; keep in your refrigerator for up to 3 to 4 days.
For freezing, place the soup in airtight containers. It will maintain the best quality for about 4 to 6 months. Defrost in your refrigerator and reheat your soup in the same way you prepared it. Bon appétit!

68. Italian-Style Turkey Wings

(Ready in about 1 hour | Servings 2)

Per serving: 488 Calories; 24.5g Fat; 2.1g Carbs; 33.6g Protein; 0.9g Fiber

INGREDIENTS

2 tablespoons sesame oil
1 pound turkey wings
1/2 cup marinara sauce

1 tablespoon Italian herb mix
2 tablespoons balsamic vinegar
1 teaspoon garlic, minced

Salt and black pepper, to taste

DIRECTIONS

Place the turkey wings, Italian herb mix, balsamic vinegar, and garlic in a ceramic dish. Cover and let it marinate for 2 to 3 hours in your refrigerator. Rub the sesame oil over turkey wings.
Grill the turkey wings on the preheated grill for about 1 hour, basting with the reserved marinade. Sprinkle with salt and black pepper to taste.

STORING

Place the turkey wings in airtight containers or Ziploc bags; keep in your refrigerator for up 3 to 4 days.
For freezing, place the turkey wings in airtight containers or heavy-duty freezer bags. Freeze up to 3 months.
Once thawed in the refrigerator, heat in the preheated oven at 375 degrees F for 20 to 25 minutes or until thoroughly warmed. Serve with marinara sauce.

69. Easy Chicken Tacos

(Ready in about 20 minutes | Servings 4)

Per serving: 535 Calories; 33.3g Fat; 4.8g Carbs; 47.9g Protein; 1.9g Fiber

INGREDIENTS

1 pound ground chicken
1 ½ cups Mexican cheese blend
1 tablespoon Mexican seasoning blend
2 teaspoons butter, room temperature

2 small-sized shallots, peeled and finely chopped
1 clove garlic, minced
1 cup tomato puree

1/2 cup salsa
2 slices bacon, chopped

DIRECTIONS

Melt the butter in a saucepan over moderately high flame. Now, cook the shallots until tender and fragrant.
Then, sauté the garlic, chicken, and bacon for about 5 minutes, stirring continuously and crumbling with a fork. Add the in Mexican seasoning blend.
Fold in the tomato puree and salsa; continue to simmer for 5 to 7 minutes over medium-low heat; reserve.
Line a baking pan with wax paper. Place 4 piles of the shredded cheese on the baking pan and gently press them down with a wide spatula to make "taco shells".
Bake in the preheated oven at 365 degrees F for 6 to 7 minutes or until melted. Allow these taco shells to cool for about 10 minutes.

STORING

Place your taco filling mixture in airtight containers or Ziploc bags; keep in your refrigerator for up to 3 to 4 days.
As for the taco shells, keep them in your refrigerator for up to 4 days.
For freezing, place it in airtight containers or heavy-duty freezer bags. Freeze up to 2 to 3 months. Defrost in the refrigerator.

70. Spicy Breakfast Sausage

(Ready in about 15 minutes | Servings 4)

Per serving: 156 Calories; 4.2g Fat; 4.1g Carbs; 16.2g Protein; 2.1g Fiber

INGREDIENTS

4 chicken sausages, sliced
1 chili pepper, minced
1 cup shallots, diced
1/4 cup dry white wine
2 teaspoons lard, room temperature

1 teaspoon garlic, minced
2 Spanish peppers, deveined and chopped
2 tablespoons fresh coriander, minced
2 teaspoons balsamic vinegar
1 cup pureed tomatoes

DIRECTIONS

In a frying pan, warm the lard over moderately high flame.
Then, sear the sausage until well browned on all sides; add in the remaining ingredients and stir to combine.
Allow it to simmer over low heat for 10 minutes or until thickened slightly.

STORING

Transfer the sausages along with the sauce to airtight containers and store in your refrigerator for up to 3 to 4 days.
For freezing, place the sausages along with the sauce in freezer safe containers or wrap tightly with heavy-duty aluminum foil; freeze up to 1 to 2 months. Defrost in the microwave for a few minutes. Enjoy!

71. Classic Chicken Salad

(Ready in about 20 minutes | Servings 4)

Per serving: 353 Calories; 23.5g Fat; 5.8g Carbs; 27.8g Protein; 2.7g Fiber

INGREDIENTS

1 medium shallot, thinly sliced
1 tablespoon Dijon mustard
1 tablespoon fresh oregano, chopped
1/2 cup mayonnaise

2 cups boneless rotisserie chicken, shredded
2 avocados, pitted, peeled and diced
Salt and black pepper, to taste
3 hard-boiled eggs, cut into quarters

DIRECTIONS

Toss the chicken with the avocado, shallots, and oregano.
Add in the mayonnaise, mustard, salt and black pepper; stir to combine.

STORING

Place the chicken salad in airtight containers and store in your refrigerator for up to 3 to 4 days.
Place the chicken salad in a freezer-safe container and store for up to three months. Defrost in the refrigerator.
Serve garnished with hard-boiled eggs and enjoy!

72. Creamed Sausage with Spaghetti Squash

(Ready in about 20 minutes | Servings 4)

Per serving: 591 Calories; 32g Fat; 4.8g Carbs; 32g Protein; 1.5g Fiber

INGREDIENTS

1 ½ pounds cheese & bacon chicken sausages, sliced
8 ounces spaghetti squash
1/2 cup green onions, finely chopped
2/3 cup double cream
1 Spanish pepper, deveined and finely minced

1 garlic clove, pressed
2 teaspoons butter, room temperature
1 ¼ cups cream of onion soup
Sea salt and ground black pepper, to taste

DIRECTIONS

Melt the butter in a saucepan over a moderate flame. Then, sear the sausages until no longer pink about 9 minutes. Reserve.
In the same saucepan, cook the green onions, pepper and garlic until they've softened.
Add in the spaghetti squash, salt, black pepper and cream of onion soup; bring to a boil.
Reduce the heat to medium-low and fold in the cream; let it simmer until the sauce has reduced slightly or about 7 minutes. Add in the reserved sausage and gently stir to combine.

STORING

Place the sausage with the spaghetti squash in four Ziploc bags; keep in the refrigerator for a week.
For freezing, divide the sausage with the spaghetti squash among four Ziploc bags and freeze up to 3 to 4 months. Defrost in your refrigerator. Reheat the sausage with the spaghetti squash in a pan. Enjoy!

73. Chicken Fajitas with Peppers and Cheese

(Ready in about 15 minutes | Servings 4)

Per serving: 301 Calories; 11.4g Fat; 5.2g Carbs; 37.9g Protein; 2.2g Fiber

INGREDIENTS

1 Habanero pepper, deveined and chopped
4 banana peppers, deveined and chopped

1 teaspoon Mexican seasoning blend
1 tablespoon avocado oil
2 garlic cloves, minced
1 cup onions, chopped

1 pound chicken, ground
1/3 cup dry sherry
Salt and black pepper, to taste
1/2 cup Cotija cheese, shredded

DIRECTIONS

In a skillet, heat the avocado oil over a moderate flame. Sauté the garlic, onions, and peppers until they are tender and aromatic or about 5 minutes.
Fold in the ground chicken and continue to cook until the juices run clear.
Add in the dry sherry, Mexican seasonings, salt and pepper. Continue to cook for 5 to 6 minutes more or until cooked through.

STORING

Place the ground chicken mixture in airtight containers or Ziploc bags; keep in your refrigerator for up to 3 to 4 days.
For freezing, place the ground chicken mixture in airtight containers or heavy-duty freezer bags. Freeze up to 2 to 3 months.
Defrost in the refrigerator and reheat in the skillet. Top with cheese and let it sit in the residual heat until the cheese has melted slightly. Enjoy!

74. Crispy Chicken Drumsticks

(Ready in about 50 minutes | Servings 4)

Per serving: 345 Calories; 14.1g Fat; 0.4g Carbs; 50.8g Protein; 0.2g Fiber

INGREDIENTS

4 chicken drumsticks
1/4 teaspoon ground black pepper, or more to the taste

1 teaspoon dried basil
1 teaspoon dried oregano
1 tablespoon olive oil

1 teaspoon paprika
Salt, to your liking

DIRECTIONS

Pat dry the chicken drumsticks and rub them with the olive oil, salt, black pepper, paprika, basil, and oregano.
Preheat your oven to 410 degrees F. Coat a baking pan with a piece of parchment paper.
Bake the chicken drumsticks until they are browned on all sides for 40 to 45 minutes.

STORING

Place the chicken drumsticks in airtight containers or Ziploc bags; keep in your refrigerator for up 3 to 4 days.
For freezing, place the chicken drumsticks in airtight containers or heavy-duty freezer bags. Freeze up to 3 months.
Once thawed in the refrigerator, heat in the preheated oven at 375 degrees F for 20 to 25 minutes or until heated through. Enjoy!

75. Chicken Fillet with Brussels Sprouts

(Ready in about 20 minutes | Servings 4)

Per serving: 273 Calories; 15.4g Fat; 4.2g Carbs; 23g Protein; 6g Fiber

INGREDIENTS

3/4 pound chicken breasts, chopped into bite-sized pieces
1/2 teaspoon ancho chile powder
1/2 teaspoon whole black peppercorns

1/2 cup onions, chopped
1 cup vegetable broth
2 tablespoons olive oil
1 ½ pounds Brussels sprouts, trimmed

and cut into halves
1/4 teaspoon garlic salt
1 clove garlic, minced
2 tablespoons port wine

DIRECTIONS

Heat 1 tablespoon of the oil in a frying pan over medium-high heat. Sauté the Brussels sprouts for about 3 minutes or until golden on all sides. Salt to taste and reserve.
Heat the remaining tablespoon of olive oil. Cook the garlic and chicken for about 3 minutes.
Add in the onions, vegetable broth, wine, ancho chile powder, and black peppercorns; bring to a boil. Then, reduce the temperature to simmer and continue to cook for 4 to 5 minutes longer.
Add the reserved Brussels sprouts back to the frying pan.

STORING

Place the chicken breasts along with the Brussels sprouts in airtight containers or Ziploc bags; keep in your refrigerator for 3 to 4 days.
For freezing, place the chicken breasts along with the Brussels sprouts in airtight containers or heavy-duty freezer bags. It will maintain the best quality for about 4 months.
Defrost in the refrigerator. Bon appétit!

76. Chicken Breasts with Mustard Sauce

(Ready in about 25 minutes | Servings 4)

Per serving: 415 Calories; 33.2g Fat; 4.5g Carbs; 24.6g Protein; 1.1g Fiber

INGREDIENTS

1/4 cup vegetable broth
1/2 cup heavy whipped cream
1/2 cup onions, chopped
2 garlic cloves, minced

1/4 cup Marsala wine
2 tablespoons brown mustard
1/2 cup fresh parsley, roughly chopped
1 tablespoon olive oil

1 pound chicken breasts, butterflied
Salt and pepper, to taste

DIRECTIONS

Heat the oil in a frying pan over a moderate flame. Cook the chicken breasts until no longer pink or about 6 minutes; season with salt and pepper to taste and reserve.

Cook the onion and garlic until it is fragrant or about 5 minutes. Add in the wine to scrape the bits that may be stuck to the bottom of your frying pan.

Pour in the broth and bring to boil. Fold in the double cream, mustard, and parsley.

STORING

Place the chicken in airtight containers or Ziploc bags; keep in your refrigerator for up 3 to 4 days.

For freezing, place the chicken in airtight containers or heavy-duty freezer bags. Freeze up to 3 months.

Once thawed in the refrigerator, heat in the preheated oven at 375 degrees F for 20 to 25 minutes or until heated through. Bon appétit!

77. Chinese-Style Cabbage with Turkey

(Ready in about 45 minutes | Servings 4)

Per serving: 293 Calories; 17.5g Fat; 9.1g Carbs; 26.2g Protein; 2.6g Fiber

INGREDIENTS

1 pound turkey, ground
2 slices smoked bacon, chopped
1 pound Chinese cabbage, finely
chopped

1 tablespoon sesame oil
1/2 cup onions, chopped
1 teaspoon ginger-garlic paste
2 ripe tomatoes, chopped

1 teaspoon Five-spice powder
Coarse salt and ground black pepper,
to taste

DIRECTIONS

Heat the oil in a wok over a moderate flame. Cook the onions until tender and translucent.

Now, add in the remaining ingredients and bring to a boil. Reduce the temperature to medium-low and partially cover.

Reduce the heat to medium-low and cook an additional 30 minutes, crumbling the turkey and bacon with a fork.

STORING

Place the Chinese cabbage with the turkey in airtight containers or Ziploc bags; keep in your refrigerator for up to 3 to 4 days.

For freezing, place the Chinese cabbage with the turkey in airtight containers or heavy-duty freezer bags. Freeze up to 2 to 3 months. Defrost in the refrigerator. Bon appétit!

78. Easy Turkey Meatballs

(Ready in about 20 minutes | Servings 4)

Per serving: 244 Calories; 13.7g Fat; 5g Carbs; 27.6g Protein; 2.2g Fiber

INGREDIENTS

For the Meatballs:
1/3 cup Colby cheese, freshly grated
3/4 pound ground turkey
1/3 teaspoon Five-spice powder
1 egg

For the Sauce:
1 1/3 cups water
1/3 cup champagne vinegar
2 tablespoons soy sauce
1/2 cup Swerve

1/2 cup tomato sauce, no sugar added
1/2 teaspoon paprika
1/3 teaspoon guar gum

DIRECTIONS

Thoroughly combine all ingredients for the meatballs. Roll the mixture into balls and sear them until browned on all sides.

In a saucepan, mix all of the sauce ingredients and cook until the sauce has thickened, whisking continuously.

Fold the meatballs into the sauce and continue to cook, partially covered, for about 10 minutes.

STORING

Place your meatballs along with the sauce in airtight containers or Ziploc bags; keep in your refrigerator for up to 3 to 4 days.

Freeze the meatballs in the sauce in airtight containers or heavy-duty freezer bags. Freeze up to 3 to 4 months. To defrost, slowly reheat in a saucepan. Bon appétit!

79. Chicken with Mediterranean Sauce

(Ready in about 15 minutes | Servings 6)

Per serving: 357 Calories; 26.2g Fat; 0.6g Carbs; 29.2g Protein; 0.2g Fiber

INGREDIENTS

1 stick butter
1 ½ pounds chicken breasts
2 teaspoons red wine vinegar
1 ½ tablespoons olive oil

1/3 cup fresh Italian parsley, chopped
2 tablespoon green garlic, finely minced
2 tablespoons red onions, finely minced

Flaky sea salt and ground black pepper, to taste

DIRECTIONS

In a cast-iron skillet, heat the oil over a moderate flame. Sear the chicken for 10 to 12 minutes or until no longer pink. Season with salt and black pepper.
Add in the melted butter and continue to cook until heated through. Stir in the green garlic, onion, and Italian parsley; let it cook for 3 to 4 minutes more.
Stir in the red wine vinegar and remove from heat.

STORING

Place the chicken along with the sauce in airtight containers or Ziploc bags; keep in your refrigerator for 3 to 4 days.
For freezing, place the chicken along with the sauce in airtight containers or heavy-duty freezer bags. It will maintain the best quality for about 4 months. Defrost in the refrigerator. Enjoy!

80. Easy Roasted Turkey Drumsticks

(Ready in about 1 hour 40 minutes | Servings 4)

Per serving: 362 Calories; 22.3g Fat; 5.6g Carbs; 34.9g Protein; 3.3g Fiber

INGREDIENTS

2 turkey drumsticks
1 ½ tablespoons sesame oil
1 tablespoon poultry seasoning

For the Sauce:
1 ounce Cottage cheese
1 ounce full-fat sour cream
1 small-sized avocado, pitted and mashed

2 tablespoons fresh parsley, finely chopped
1 teaspoon fresh lemon juice
1/3 teaspoon sea salt

DIRECTIONS

Pat the turkey drumsticks dry and sprinkle them with the poultry seasoning. Brush a baking pan with the sesame oil.
Place the turkey drumsticks on the baking pan.
Roast in the preheated oven at 350 degrees F for about 1 hour 30 minutes, rotating the pan halfway through the cooking time.
In the meantime, make the sauce by whisking all the sauce ingredients.

STORING

Wrap the turkey drumsticks in foil before packing them into an airtight container; keep in your refrigerator for up to 3 to 4 days.
As for the sauce, place it in an airtight container and keep in your refrigerator for up to 4 days.
For freezing, place the turkey drumsticks in airtight containers or heavy-duty freezer bags. Freeze up to 2 to 3 months. Defrost in the refrigerator. Bon appétit!

81. Chicken Drumettes with Leeks and Herbs

(Ready in about 30 minutes | Servings 4)

Per serving: 165 Calories; 9.8g Fat; 4.7g Carbs; 12.4g Protein; 1.3g Fiber

INGREDIENTS

4 chicken drumettes
2 tomatoes, crushed
2 tablespoons lard, room temperature
1 tablespoon coconut aminos

1 teaspoon dried marjoram
2 thyme sprigs
Salt and pepper, to taste
2 cloves garlic, minced

1/2 teaspoon fennel seeds
1 cup chicken bone broth
1/2 cup leeks, chopped
1 celery rib, sliced

DIRECTIONS

Melt the lard in a frying pan over a moderate heat. Sprinkle the chicken with salt and pepper to taste.
Then, fry the chicken until no longer pink or about 8 minutes; set aside.
In the same frying pan, cook the leeks, celery rib, and garlic for about 5 minutes, stirring continuously.
Reduce the heat to medium-low; add the remaining ingredients along with the reserved chicken drumettes. Let it simmer for about 20 minutes.

STORING

Place the chicken drumettes in airtight containers or Ziploc bags; keep in your refrigerator for up 3 to 4 days.
For freezing, place them in airtight containers or heavy-duty freezer bags. Freeze up to 3 months. Once thawed in the refrigerator, heat in the preheated oven at 375 degrees F for 20 to 25 minutes or until heated through. Enjoy!

82. Old-Fashioned Turkey Soup

(Ready in about 35 minutes | Servings 4)

Per serving: 274 Calories; 14.4g Fat; 5.6g Carbs; 26.7g Protein; 3g Fiber

INGREDIENTS

1 pound turkey drumettes
2 tablespoons olive oil
4 ½ cups vegetable broth
Salt and ground black pepper, to your liking

1/2 teaspoon hot paprika
4 dollops of sour cream
1/2 head cauliflower, broken into florets
1 rosemary sprig

1 large onion, chopped
2 garlic cloves, chopped
1 celery, chopped
1 parsnip, chopped
2 bay leaves

DIRECTIONS

Heat the oil in a heavy-bottomed pot over a moderate flame. Then, sauté the onion, garlic, celery and parsnip until they've softened. Pour in the broth and bring to a rolling boil.
Add in the cauliflower, turkey drumettes, rosemary, bay leaves, salt, black pepper and hot paprika.
Partially cover and let it simmer approximately 30 minutes. Fold in the sour cream and stir to combine well.

STORING

Spoon the soup into four airtight containers or Ziploc bags; keep in your refrigerator for up to 3 to 4 days.
For freezing, place the soup in airtight containers. It will maintain the best quality for about 4 to 6 months. Defrost in the refrigerator. Bon appétit!

83. Creamy Tomato and Chicken Chowder

(Ready in about 35 minutes | Servings 6)

Per serving: 238 Calories; 15.5g Fat; 6.1g Carbs; 36g Protein; 1.3g Fiber

INGREDIENTS

3 chicken legs, boneless and chopped
1 teaspoon ginger-garlic paste
2 cups tomato bisque
2 cups water

2 tablespoons olive oil
Sea salt and ground black pepper, to taste
1 onion, chopped

1/2 cup celery, thinly sliced
1 chili pepper, deveined and minced
1 tablespoon flax seed meal
1/2 cup Greek-style yogurt

DIRECTIONS

Heat the olive oil in a stockpot over a moderately high flame. Sear the chicken legs for about 8 minutes. Season with salt and black pepper and reserve.
In the same stockpot, cook the onion, celery, and chili pepper until they've softened.
Add in the ginger-garlic paste, tomato bisque, and water. Turn the heat to simmer and continue to cook for 30 minutes more until thoroughly cooked.
Fold in the flax seed meal and yogurt and continue to cook, stirring frequently, for 4 to 5 minutes more.

STORING

Spoon the chowder into airtight containers or Ziploc bags; keep in your refrigerator for up to 3 to 4 days.
For freezing, place the chowder in airtight containers. Freeze up to 4 to 6 months. Defrost in the refrigerator. Reheat on the stove pot and serve hot!

84. Roasted Chicken with Cashew Pesto

(Ready in about 35 minutes | Servings 4)

Per serving: 580 Calories; 44.8g Fat; 5g Carbs; 38.7g Protein; 1g Fiber

INGREDIENTS

1 cup leeks, chopped
1 pound chicken legs, skinless
Salt and ground black pepper, to taste
1/2 teaspoon red pepper flakes

For the Cashew-Basil Pesto:
1/2 cup cashews
2 garlic cloves, minced
1/2 cup fresh basil leaves

1/2 cup Parmigiano-Reggiano cheese, preferably freshly grated
1/2 cup olive oil

DIRECTIONS

Place the chicken legs in a parchnemt-lined bakign pan. Season with salt and pepper, Then, scatter the leeks around the chicken legs.
Roast in the preheated oven at 390 degrees F for 30 to 35 minutes, rotating the pan occasionally.
Pulse the cashews, basil, garlic, and cheese in your blender until pieces are small. Continue blending while adding olive oil to the mixture. Mix until the desired consistency is reached.

STORING

Place the chicken in airtight containers or Ziploc bags; keep in your refrigerator for up 3 to 4 days.
To freeze the chicken legs, place them in airtight containers or heavy-duty freezer bags. Freeze up to 3 months. Once thawed in the refrigerator, heat in the preheated oven at 375 degrees F for 20 to 25 minutes.
Store your pesto in the refrigerator for up to a week. Bon appétit!

85. Turkey Meatballs with Tangy Basil Chutney

(Ready in about 30 minutes | Servings 6)

Per serving: 390 Calories; 27.2g Fat; 1.8g Carbs; 37.4g Protein; 0.3g Fiber

INGREDIENTS

2 tablespoons sesame oil
For the Meatballs:
1/2 cup Romano cheese, grated
1 teaspoon garlic, minced
1/2 teaspoon shallot powder
1/4 teaspoon dried thyme
1/2 teaspoon mustard seeds
2 small-sized eggs, lightly beaten

1 ½ pounds ground turkey
1/2 teaspoon sea salt
1/4 teaspoon ground black pepper, or more to taste
3 tablespoons almond meal
For the Basil Chutney:
2 tablespoons fresh lime juice
1/4 cup fresh basil leaves

1/4 cup fresh parsley
1/2 cup cilantro leaves
1 teaspoon fresh ginger root, grated
2 tablespoons olive oil
2 tablespoons water
1 tablespoon habanero chili pepper, deveined and minced

DIRECTIONS

In a mixing bowl, combine all ingredients for the meatballs. Roll the mixture into meatballs and reserve.
Heat the sesame oil in a frying pan over a moderate flame. Sear the meatballs for about 8 minutes until browned on all sides.
Make the chutney by mixing all the ingredients in your blender or food processor.

STORING

Place the meatballs in airtight containers or Ziploc bags; keep in your refrigerator for up to 3 to 4 days.
Freeze the meatballs in airtight containers or heavy-duty freezer bags. Freeze up to 3 to 4 months. To defrost, slowly reheat in a frying pan.
Store the basil chutney in the refrigerator for up to a week. Bon appétit!

86. Turkey Chorizo with Bok Choy

(Ready in about 50 minutes | Servings 4)

Per serving: 189 Calories; 12g Fat; 2.6g Carbs; 9.4g Protein; 1g Fiber

INGREDIENTS

4 mild turkey Chorizo, sliced
1/2 cup full-fat milk
6 ounces Gruyère cheese, preferably freshly grated
1 yellow onion, chopped

Coarse salt and ground black pepper, to taste
1 pound Bok choy, tough stem ends trimmed
1 cup cream of mushroom soup
1 tablespoon lard, room temperature

DIRECTIONS

Melt the lard in a nonstick skillet over a moderate flame; cook the Chorizo sausage for about 5 minutes, stirring occasionally to ensure even cooking; reserve.
Add in the onion, salt, pepper, Bok choy, and cream of mushroom soup. Continue to cook for 4 minutes longer or until the vegetables have softened.
Spoon the mixture into a lightly oiled casserole dish. Top with the reserved Chorizo.
In a mixing bowl, thoroughly combine the milk and cheese. Pour the cheese mixture over the sausage.
Cover with foil and bake at 365 degrees F for about 35 minutes.

STORING

Cut your casserole into four portions. Place each portion in an airtight container; keep in your refrigerator for 3 to 4 days.
For freezing, wrap your portions tightly with heavy-duty aluminum foil or freezer wrap. Freeze up to 1 to 2 months. Defrost in the refrigerator. Enjoy!

87. Turkey Wings with Gravy

(Ready in about 6 hours | Servings 6)

Per serving: 280 Calories; 22.2g Fat; 4.3g Carbs; 15.8g Protein; 0.8g Fiber

INGREDIENTS

2 pounds turkey wings
1/2 teaspoon cayenne pepper
4 garlic cloves, sliced
1 large onion, chopped
Salt and pepper, to taste

1 teaspoon dried marjoram
1 tablespoon butter, room temperature
1 tablespoon Dijon mustard
For the Gravy:
1 cup double cream

Salt and black pepper, to taste
1/2 stick butter
3/4 teaspoon guar gum

DIRECTIONS

Rub the turkey wings with the Dijon mustard and 1 tablespoon of butter. Preheat a grill pan over medium-high heat.
Sear the turkey wings for 10 minutes on all sides.
Transfer the turkey to your Crock pot; add in the garlic, onion, salt, pepper, marjoram, and cayenne pepper. Cover and cook on low setting for 6 hours.
Melt 1/2 stick of the butter in a frying pan. Add in the cream and whisk until cooked through.
Next, stir in the guar gum, salt, and black pepper along with cooking juices. Let it cook until the sauce has reduced by half.

STORING

Wrap the turkey wings in foil before packing them into airtight containers; keep in your refrigerator for up to 3 to 4 days.
For freezing, place the turkey wings in airtight containers or heavy-duty freezer bags. Freeze up to 2 to 3 months. Defrost in the refrigerator.
Keep your gravy in refrigerator for up to 2 days.

88. Parmesan Chicken Salad

(Ready in about 20 minutes | Servings 6)

Per serving: 183 Calories; 12.5g Fat; 1.7g Carbs; 16.3g Protein; 0.9g Fiber

INGREDIENTS

2 romaine hearts, leaves separated
Flaky sea salt and ground black pepper, to taste
1/4 teaspoon chili pepper flakes
1 teaspoon dried basil

1/4 cup Parmesan, finely grated
2 chicken breasts
2 Lebanese cucumbers, sliced
For the dressing:
2 large egg yolks

1 teaspoon Dijon mustard
1 tablespoon fresh lemon juice
1/4 cup olive oil
2 garlic cloves, minced

DIRECTIONS

In a grilling pan, cook the chicken breast until no longer pink or until a meat thermometer registers 165 degrees F. Slice the chicken into strips.

STORING

Place the chicken breasts in airtight containers or Ziploc bags; keep in your refrigerator for 3 to 4 days.
For freezing, place the chicken breasts in airtight containers or heavy-duty freezer bags. It will maintain the best quality for about 4 months. Defrost in the refrigerator.
Toss the chicken with the other ingredients. Prepare the dressing by whisking all the ingredients.
Dress the salad and enjoy! Keep the salad in your refrigerator for 3 to 5 days.

89. Taro Leaf and Chicken Soup

(Ready in about 45 minutes | Servings 4)

Per serving: 256 Calories; 12.9g Fat; 3.2g Carbs; 35.1g Protein; 2.2g Fiber

INGREDIENTS

1 pound whole chicken, boneless and chopped into small chunks
1/2 cup onions, chopped
1/2 cup rutabaga, cubed
2 carrots, peeled

2 celery stalks
Salt and black pepper, to taste
1 cup chicken bone broth
1/2 teaspoon ginger-garlic paste
1/2 cup taro leaves, roughly chopped

1 tablespoon fresh coriander, chopped
3 cups water
1 teaspoon paprika

DIRECTIONS

Place all ingredients in a heavy-bottomed pot. Bring to a boil over the highest heat.
Turn the heat to simmer. Continue to cook, partially covered, an additional 40 minutes.

STORING

Spoon the soup into four airtight containers or Ziploc bags; keep in your refrigerator for up to 3 to 4 days.
For freezing, place the soup in airtight containers. It will maintain the best quality for about 5 to 6 months. Defrost in the refrigerator. Bon appétit!

90. Authentic Turkey Kebabs

(Ready in about 30 minutes | Servings 6)

Per serving: 263 Calories; 13.8g Fat; 6.7g Carbs; 25.8g Protein; 1.2g Fiber

INGREDIENTS

1 ½ pounds turkey breast, cubed
3 Spanish peppers, sliced
2 zucchinis, cut into thick slices

1 onion, cut into wedges
2 tablespoons olive oil, room temperature
1 tablespoon dry ranch seasoning

DIRECTIONS

Thread the turkey pieces and vegetables onto bamboo skewers. Sprinkle the skewers with dry ranch seasoning and olive oil.
Grill your kebabs for about 10 minutes, turning them periodically to ensure even cooking.

STORING

Wrap your kebabs in foil before packing them into airtight containers; keep in your refrigerator for up to 3 to 4 days.
For freezing, place your kebabs in airtight containers or heavy-duty freezer bags. Freeze up to 2-3 months. Defrost in the refrigerator. Bon appétit!

91. Flatbread with Chicken Liver Pâté

(Ready in about 2 hours 15 minutes | Servings 4)

Per serving: 395 Calories; 30.2g Fat; 3.6g Carbs; 17.9g Protein; 0.5g Fiber

INGREDIENTS

1 yellow onion, finely chopped
10 ounces chicken livers
1/2 teaspoon Mediterranean seasoning blend

4 tablespoons olive oil
1 garlic clove, minced
For Flatbread:
1 cup lukewarm water

1/2 stick butter
1/2 cup flax meal
1 ½ tablespoons psyllium husks
1 ¼ cups almond flour

DIRECTIONS

Pulse the chicken livers along with the seasoning blend, olive oil, onion and garlic in your food processor; reserve.
Mix the dry ingredients for the flatbread. Mix in all the wet ingredients. Whisk to combine well.
Let it stand at room temperature for 2 hours. Divide the dough into 8 balls and roll them out on a flat surface.
In a lightly greased pan, cook your flatbread for 1 minute on each side or until golden.

STORING

Wrap the chicken liver pate in foil before packing it into airtight containers; keep in your refrigerator for up to 7 days.
For freezing, place the chicken liver pate in airtight containers or heavy-duty freezer bags. Freeze up to 2 months. Defrost overnight in the refrigerator.
As for the keto flatbread, wrap them in foil before packing them into airtight containers; keep in your refrigerator for up to 4 days.
Bon appétit!

92. Italian-Style Chicken Meatballs with Parmesan

(Ready in about 20 minutes | Servings 6)

Per serving: 252 Calories; 9.7g Fat; 5.3g Carbs; 34.2g Protein; 1.4g Fiber

INGREDIENTS

For the Meatballs:
1 ¼ pounds chicken, ground
1 tablespoon sage leaves, chopped
1 teaspoon shallot powder
1 teaspoon porcini powder
2 garlic cloves, finely minced

1/3 teaspoon dried basil
3/4 cup Parmesan cheese, grated
2 eggs, lightly beaten
Salt and ground black pepper, to your liking
1/2 teaspoon cayenne pepper

For the sauce:
2 tomatoes, pureed
1 cup chicken consommé
2 ½ tablespoons lard, room temperature
1 onion, peeled and finely chopped

DIRECTIONS

In a mixing bowl, combine all ingredients for the meatballs. Roll the mixture into bite-sized balls.
Melt 1 tablespoon of lard in a skillet over a moderately high heat. Sear the meatballs for about 3 minutes or until they are thoroughly cooked; reserve.
Melt the remaining lard and cook the onions until tender and translucent. Add in pureed tomatoes and chicken consommé and continue to cook for 4 minutes longer.
Add in the reserved meatballs, turn the heat to simmer and continue to cook for 6 to 7 minutes.

STORING

Place the meatballs in airtight containers or Ziploc bags; keep in your refrigerator for up to 3 to 4 days.
Freeze the meatballs in airtight containers or heavy-duty freezer bags. Freeze up to 3 to 4 months. To defrost, slowly reheat in a saucepan.
Bon appétit!

93. Sunday Chicken with Cauliflower Salad

(Ready in about 20 minutes | Servings 2)

Per serving: 444 Calories; 36g Fat; 5.7g Carbs; 20.6g Protein; 4.3g Fiber

INGREDIENTS

1 teaspoon hot paprika
2 tablespoons fresh basil, snipped
1/2 cup mayonnaise
1 teaspoon mustard

2 teaspoons butter
2 chicken wings
1/2 cup cheddar cheese, shredded
Sea salt and ground black pepper, to taste

2 tablespoons dry sherry
1 shallot, finely minced
1/2 head of cauliflower

DIRECTIONS

Boil the cauliflower in a pot of salted water until it has softened; cut into small florets and place in a salad bowl.
Melt the butter in a saucepan over medium-high heat. Cook the chicken for about 8 minutes or until the skin is crisp and browned. Season with hot paprika salt, and black pepper.
Whisk the mayonnaise, mustard, dry sherry, and shallot and dress your salad. Top with cheddar cheese and fresh basil.

STORING

Place the chicken wings in airtight containers or Ziploc bags; keep in your refrigerator for up 3 to 4 days.
Keep the cauliflower salad in your refrigerator for up 3 days.
For freezing, place the chicken wings in airtight containers or heavy-duty freezer bags. Freeze up to 3 months. Once thawed in the refrigerator, reheat in a saucepan until thoroughly warmed.

94. Spicy Chicken Breasts

(Ready in about 30 minutes | Servings 6)

Per serving: 239 Calories; 8.6g Fat; 5.5g Carbs; 34.3g Protein; 1g Fiber

INGREDIENTS

1 ½ pounds chicken breasts
1 bell pepper, deveined and chopped
1 leek, chopped
1 tomato, pureed

2 tablespoons coriander
2 garlic cloves, minced
1 teaspoon cayenne pepper
1 teaspoon dry thyme

1/4 cup coconut aminos
Sea salt and ground black pepper, to taste

DIRECTIONS

Rub each chicken breasts with the garlic, cayenne pepper, thyme, salt and black pepper. Cook the chicken in a saucepan over medium-high heat.
Sear for about 5 minutes until golden brown on all sides.
Fold in the tomato puree and coconut aminos and bring it to a boil. Add in the pepper, leek, and coriander.
Reduce the heat to simmer. Continue to cook, partially covered, for about 20 minutes.

STORING

Place the chicken breasts in airtight containers or Ziploc bags; keep in your refrigerator for 3 to 4 days.
For freezing, place the chicken breasts in airtight containers or heavy-duty freezer bags. It will maintain the best quality for about 4 months. Defrost in the refrigerator. Bon appétit!

95. Grilled Chicken Salad with Avocado

(Ready in about 20 minutes | Servings 4)

Per serving: 408 Calories; 34.2g Fat; 4.8g Carbs; 22.7g Protein; 3.1g Fiber

INGREDIENTS

1/3 cup olive oil
2 chicken breasts
Sea salt and crushed red pepper flakes

2 egg yolks
1 tablespoon fresh lemon juice
1/2 teaspoon celery seeds

1 tablespoon coconut aminos
1 large-sized avocado, pitted and sliced

DIRECTIONS

Grill the chicken breasts for about 4 minutes per side. Season with salt and pepper, to taste.
Slice the grilled chicken into bite-sized strips.
To make the dressing, whisk the egg yolks, lemon juice, celery seeds, olive oil and coconut aminos in a measuring cup.

STORING

Place the chicken breasts in airtight containers or Ziploc bags; keep in your refrigerator for 3 to 4 days.
For freezing, place the chicken breasts in airtight containers or heavy-duty freezer bags. It will maintain the best quality for about 4 months. Defrost in the refrigerator.
Store dressing in your refrigerator for 3 to 4 days. Dress the salad and garnish with fresh avocado. Bon appétit!

96. Duck Breasts in Boozy Sauce

(Ready in about 20 minutes | Servings 4)

Per serving: 351 Calories; 24.7g Fat; 6.6g Carbs; 22.1g Protein; 0.6g Fiber

INGREDIENTS

1 ½ pounds duck breasts, butterflied
1 tablespoon tallow, room temperature
1 ½ cups chicken consommé

3 tablespoons soy sauce
2 ounces vodka
1/2 cup sour cream

4 scallion stalks, chopped
Salt and pepper, to taste

DIRECTIONS

Melt the tallow in a frying pan over medium-high flame. Sear the duck breasts for about 5 minutes, flipping them over occasionally to ensure even cooking.
Add in the scallions, salt, pepper, chicken consommé, and soy sauce. Partially cover and continue to cook for a further 8 minutes.
Add in the vodka and sour cream; remove from the heat and stir to combine well.

STORING

Place the duck breasts in airtight containers or Ziploc bags; keep in your refrigerator for up to 3 to 4 days.
For freezing, place duck breasts in airtight containers or heavy-duty freezer bags. Freeze up to 2 to 3 months. Once thawed in the refrigerator, reheat in a saucepan. Bon appétit!

97. Spicy and Cheesy Turkey Dip

(Ready in about 25 minutes | Servings 4)

Per serving: 284 Calories; 19g Fat; 3.2g Carbs; 26.7g Protein; 1.6g Fiber

INGREDIENTS

1 Fresno chili pepper, deveined and minced

1 ½ cups Ricotta cheese, creamed, 4% fat, softened

1/4 cup sour cream

1 tablespoon butter, room temperature

1 shallot, chopped

1 teaspoon garlic, pressed

1 pound ground turkey

1/2 cup goat cheese, shredded

Salt and black pepper, to taste

1 ½ cups Gruyère, shredded

DIRECTIONS

Melt the butter in a frying pan over a moderately high flame. Now, sauté the onion and garlic until they have softened.

Stir in the ground turkey and continue to cook until it is no longer pink.

Transfer the sautéed mixture to a lightly greased baking dish. Add in Ricotta, sour cream, goat cheese, salt, pepper, and chili pepper.

Top with the shredded Gruyère cheese. Bake in the preheated oven at 350 degrees F for about 20 minutes or until hot and bubbly in top.

STORING

Place your dip in an airtight container; keep in your refrigerator for up 3 to 4 days. Enjoy!

98. Authentic Aioli Baked Chicken Wings

(Ready in about 35 minutes | Servings 4)

Per serving: 562 Calories; 43.8g Fat; 2.1g Carbs; 40.8g Protein; 0.4g Fiber

INGREDIENTS

4 chicken wings

1 cup Halloumi cheese, cubed

1 tablespoon garlic, finely minced

1 tablespoon fresh lime juice

1 tablespoon fresh coriander, chopped

6 black olives, pitted and halved

1 ½ tablespoons butter

1 hard-boiled egg yolk

1 tablespoon balsamic vinegar

1/2 cup extra-virgin olive oil

1/4 teaspoon flaky sea salt

Sea salt and pepper, to season

DIRECTIONS

In a saucepan, melt the butter until sizzling. Sear the chicken wings for 5 minutes per side. Season with salt and pepper to taste.

Place the chicken wings on a parchment-lined baking pan

Mix the egg yolk, garlic, lime juice, balsamic vinegar, olive oil, and salt in your blender until creamy, uniform and smooth.

Spread the Aioli over the fried chicken. Now, scatter the coriander and black olives on top of the chicken wings.

Bake in the preheated oven at 380 degrees F for 20 to 25 minutes. Top with the cheese and bake an additional 5 minutes until hot and bubbly.

STORING

Place the chicken wings in airtight containers or Ziploc bags; keep in your refrigerator for up 3 to 4 days.

For freezing, place the chicken wings in airtight containers or heavy-duty freezer bags. Freeze up to 3 months. Once thawed in the refrigerator, heat in the preheated oven at 375 degrees F for 20 to 25 minutes or until heated through. Enjoy!

99. Spicy and Tangy Chicken Drumsticks

(Ready in about 55 minutes | Servings 6)

Per serving: 420 Calories; 28.2g Fat; 5g Carbs; 35.3g Protein; 0.8g Fiber

INGREDIENTS

3 chicken drumsticks, cut into chunks

1/2 stick butter

2 eggs

1/4 cup hemp seeds, ground

Salt and cayenne pepper, to taste

2 tablespoons coconut aminos

3 teaspoons red wine vinegar

2 tablespoons salsa

2 cloves garlic, minced

DIRECTIONS

Rub the chicken with the butter, salt, and cayenne pepper.

Drizzle the chicken with the coconut aminos, vinegar, salsa, and garlic. Allow it to stand for 30 minutes in your refrigerator.

Whisk the eggs with the hemp seeds. Dip each chicken strip in the egg mixture. Place the chicken chunks in a parchment-lined baking pan.

Roast in the preheated oven at 390 degrees F for 25 minutes.

STORING

Divide the roasted chicken between airtight containers; keep in your refrigerator for up 3 to 4 days.

For freezing, place the roasted chicken in airtight containers or heavy-duty freezer bags. Freeze up to 3 months. Defrost in the refrigerator and reheat in a pan. Enjoy!

100. Creamed Greek-Style Soup

(Ready in about 30 minutes | Servings 4)

Per serving: 256 Calories; 18.8g Fat; 5.4g Carbs; 15.8g Protein; 0.2g Fiber

INGREDIENTS

1/2 stick butter
1/2 cup zucchini, diced
2 garlic cloves, minced
4 ½ cups roasted vegetable broth

Sea salt and ground black pepper, to season
1 ½ cups leftover turkey, shredded
1/3 cup double cream
1/2 cup Greek-style yogurt

DIRECTIONS

In a heavy-bottomed pot, melt the butter over medium-high heat. Once hot, cook the zucchini and garlic for 2 minutes until they are fragrant.
Add in the broth, salt, black pepper, and leftover turkey. Cover and cook for 25 minutes, stirring periodically.
Then, fold in the cream and yogurt. Continue to cook for 5 minutes more or until thoroughly warmed.

STORING

Spoon the soup into four airtight containers or Ziploc bags; keep in your refrigerator for up to 3 to 4 days.
For freezing, place the soup in airtight containers. It will maintain the best quality for about 4 to 6 months. Defrost in the refrigerator. Enjoy!

101. White Cauliflower and Chicken Chowder

(Ready in about 30 minutes | Servings 6)

Per serving: 231 Calories; 18.2g Fat; 5.9g Carbs; 11.9g Protein; 1.4g Fiber

INGREDIENTS

1 cup leftover roast chicken breasts
1 head cauliflower, broken into small-sized florets
Sea salt and ground white pepper, to taste
2 ½ cups water
3 cups chicken consommé

1 ¼ cups sour cream
1/2 stick butter
1/2 cup white onion, finely chopped
1 teaspoon fresh garlic, finely minced
1 celery, chopped

DIRECTIONS

In a heavy bottomed pot, melt the butter over a moderate heat. Cook the onion, garlic and celery for about 5 minutes or until they've softened.
Add in the salt, white pepper, water, chicken consommé, chicken, and cauliflower florets; bring to a boil. Reduce the temperature to simmer and continue to cook for 30 minutes.
Puree the soup with an immersion blender. Fold in sour cream and stir to combine well.

STORING

Spoon your chowder into airtight containers or Ziploc bags; keep in your refrigerator for up to 3 to 4 days.
For freezing, place your chowder in airtight containers. It will maintain the best quality for about 4 to 6 months. Defrost in the refrigerator. Bon appétit!

102. Mexican-Style Turkey Bacon Bites

(Ready in about 5 minutes | Servings 4)

Per serving: 195 Calories; 16.7g Fat; 2.2g Carbs; 8.8g Protein; 0.3g Fiber

INGREDIENTS

4 ounces turkey bacon, chopped
4 ounces Neufchatel cheese
1 tablespoon butter, cold

1 jalapeno pepper, deveined and minced
1 teaspoon Mexican oregano
2 tablespoons scallions, finely chopped

DIRECTIONS

Thoroughly combine all ingredients in a mixing bowl.
Roll the mixture into 8 balls.

STORING

Divide the turkey bacon bites between two airtight containers or Ziploc bags; keep in your refrigerator for up 3 to 4 days.

FISH & SEAFOOD

103. Cheesy Tuna Pâté

(Ready in about 10 minutes | Servings 6)

Per serving: 181 Calories; 10.4g Fat; 2.1g Carbs; 19g Protein; 1g Fiber

INGREDIENTS

2 (6-ounce) cans tuna in oil, drained
1 tablespoon fresh Italian parsley, chopped
1/2 cup Cottage cheese

1 ounce sunflower seeds, ground
1 ounce sesame seeds, ground
1/2 teaspoon mustard seeds

DIRECTIONS

Add all of the above ingredients to a bowl of your blender or food processor.
Blend until everything is well combined.

STORING

Place the tuna pâté in an airtight container; keep in the refrigerator for a week.
You can freeze them in silicone molds. Once frozen, unmold and put some wax paper between each little pâté to prevent them from sticking to each other. Now, place them in a freezer-safe container for up to 3 months.
Thaw in your refrigerator and serve with keto veggie sticks.

104. Easy Cod Fritters

(Ready in about 20 minutes | Servings 5)

Per serving: 326 Calories; 21.7g Fat; 5.8g Carbs; 25.6g Protein; 1g Fiber

INGREDIENTS

2 ½ cups cod fish, cooked
1/2 cup almond flour
1/2 cup Romano cheese, preferably freshly grated
3 tablespoons olive oil

Sea salt and pepper, to taste
1 teaspoon butter, room temperature
1/2 teaspoon dried oregano
1/2 teaspoon dried thyme
1/4 cup onion, chopped

3 cups broccoli, cut into rice-sized chunks
2 eggs, whisked

DIRECTIONS

Melt the butter in a pan over medium-high flame. Once hot, cook the broccoli for 5 to 6 minutes, until crisp-tender. Let it cool completely.
Add in the cooked fish, salt, pepper, oregano, thyme, onion, eggs, almond flour, and cheese; mix until everything is well incorporated.
Form the mixture into 10 patties.
In a frying pan, heat the oil over a moderately high heat. Cook your fritters for 4 to 5 minutes per side.

STORING

Divide the fritters between airtight containers or heavy-duty freezer bags; keep in the refrigerator for a week.
For freezing, divide the fritters among heavy-duty freezer bags; freeze up to 3 months. Defrost in your microwave for a few minutes. Bon appétit!

105. Old Bay Sea Bass Chowder

(Ready in about 30 minutes | Servings 4)

Per serving: 170 Calories; 5.8g Fat; 5.7g Carbs; 20g Protein; 1.9g Fiber

INGREDIENTS

1 ¼ pounds sea bass, skin removed, cut into small chunks
2 carrots, chopped
1/4 cup port wine
1/2 cup sour cream

Sea salt and ground black pepper, to taste
1 teaspoon Old Bay seasonings
3 teaspoons olive oil
1 onion, chopped

1 celery rib, chopped
3 cups boiling water
1/2 cup fish stock

DIRECTIONS

In a heavy-bottomed pot, heat the olive oil over a moderately high flame. Once hot, cook the fish for about 10.
Stir in the onion, celery, carrot, spices, water, and fish stock and bring to a boil. Turn the heat to medium-low.
Let it simmer for 15 to 20 minutes more or until thoroughly cooked. Afterwards, add in the port wine and sour cream. Remove form the heat and stir to combine well.

STORING

Spoon the chowder into four airtight containers or Ziploc bags; keep in your refrigerator for up to 3 to 4 days.
For freezing, place the chowder in airtight containers. It will maintain the best quality for about 4 months. Defrost in the refrigerator. Bon appétit!

106. Cod Fish Fillets with French Salad

(Ready in about 15 minutes + marinating time | Servings 4)

Per serving: 425 Calories; 27.2g Fat; 6.1g Carbs; 38.3g Protein; 3g Fiber

INGREDIENTS

4 white cod fish fillets
1 tablespoon olive oil
2 tablespoons fresh lemon juice
1 teaspoon garlic, minced
2 tablespoons scallions, chopped
Salt and pepper, to taste

For French Salad:
1 cup arugula
1 head Iceberg lettuce
2 tablespoons dandelion
1/4 cup red wine vinegar
1/4 cup extra-virgin olive oil

1 cup chicory
1 cup frissee
Salt and ground black pepper, to your liking

DIRECTIONS

Toss the cod fish fillets with the olive oil, lemon juice, garlic, scallions salt, and pepper; allow it to marinate for 2 hours in your refrigerator.
Sear the fish fillets in the preheated skillet over moderately high heat; basting with the marinade.
Toss all ingredients for the salad in a salad bowl.

STORING

Place the fish fillets in airtight containers or Ziploc bags; keep in your refrigerator for up to 3 to 4 days.
For freezing, cover the airtight container and place it in the freezer; store for up to one month.
As for the salad, place it in airtight containers or Ziploc bags; keep in your refrigerator for up to 3 to 4 days.

107. Swordfish with Mashed Cauliflower

(Ready in about 35 minutes | Servings 4)

Per serving: 404 Calories; 22.2g Fat; 5.7g Carbs; 43.5g Protein; 3g Fiber

INGREDIENTS

1 ½ tablespoons extra-virgin olive oil
1 tablespoon freshly squeezed lemon juice
1 pound swordfish cutlets, about 3/4 inch thick
1/2 cup fresh basil, roughly chopped
Flaky sea salt and ground black pepper, to taste

1 ½ teaspoons Greek herb mix
1/4 cup Romano cheese, freshly grated
1 pound cauliflower, broken into florets
1/4 cup double cream
2 tablespoons butter

DIRECTIONS

Whisk the extra-virgin olive oil with the lemon juice.
Grill the fish cutlets for about 15 minutes, basting them with the lemon mixture. Season with salt, black pepper, and Greek herb mix. Reserve, keeping them warm.
Boil the cauliflower in a lightly salted water until crisp-tender. Mash the cauliflower with a potato masher.
Fold in the other ingredients and stir to combine well.

STORING

Place the grilled swordfish cutlets in airtight containers or Ziploc bags; keep in your refrigerator for up to 3 to 4 days.
For freezing, cover the airtight container and place it in the freezer; store for up to one month. Reheat in a frying pan and serve with fresh basil.
As for the mashed cauliflower, place it in airtight containers or Ziploc bags; keep in your refrigerator for up to 3 to 4 days.

108. Cheesy Salmon Dip

(Ready in about 10 minutes | Servings 10)

Per serving: 109 Calories; 6.3g Fat; 1.3g Carbs; 11.4g Protein; 0.1g Fiber

INGREDIENTS

10 ounces salmon
4 hard-boiled egg yolks, finely chopped

1/4 cup fresh scallions, chopped
5 ounces Ricotta cheese
5 ounces full-fat cream cheese

Salt and freshly ground black pepper, to your liking
1/2 teaspoon hot paprika

DIRECTIONS

Grill the salmon for about 10 minutes until browned and flakes easily with a fork. Cut into small chunks.
Mix all ingredients until everything is well incorporated.

STORING

Place the cheesy salmon dip in airtight containers or Ziploc bags; keep in your refrigerator for up to 4 days.

109. Easy Halibut Steaks

(Ready in about 35 minutes | Servings 2)

Per serving: 308 Calories; 10.9g Fat; 2g Carbs; 46.5g Protein; 0.8g Fiber

INGREDIENTS

2 halibut steaks
1 teaspoon garlic, finely minced
1/3 cup freshly squeezed lime juice
1 teaspoon dry rosemary

1 teaspoon dry thyme
4 tablespoons fresh chives, chopped
2 teaspoons sesame oil, room temperature
Flaky sea salt and white pepper, to taste

DIRECTIONS

Place the fresh lime juice, sesame oil, salt, white pepper, rosemary, thyme, chives, garlic, and halibut steak in a ceramic dish; let it marinate for about 30 minutes.
Grill the halibut steaks approximately 15 minutes, turning occasionally and basting with the reserved marinade.

STORING

Place the halibut steaks in airtight containers and keep in your refrigerator for up to 3 to 4 days.
For freezing, place them in airtight containers or wrap tightly with freezer wrap. Freeze up to 2 to 3 months. Defrost in the refrigerator. Bon appétit!

110. Cholula Shrimp Spread

(Ready in about 10 minutes + chilling time | Servings 8)

Per serving: 108 Calories; 5.4g Fat; 5g Carbs; 8.2g Protein; 0.5g Fiber

INGREDIENTS

12 ounces shrimp, canned and drained
1 tablespoon Cholula
1/2 cup mayonnaise
2 teaspoons green garlic, finely minced

Sea salt and ground black pepper, to taste
1 teaspoon cayenne pepper
1/2 teaspoon dried rosemary

DIRECTIONS

In a mixing bowl, stir all ingredients until well incorporated.
Cover and transfer to your refrigerator until thoroughly chilled.

STORING

Place the Cholula shrimp spread in an airtight container or Ziploc bag; keep in your refrigerator for 2 days.
Place the Cholula shrimp spread in freezable containers; they can be frozen for up to 3 to 4 months. Defrost in the refrigerator. Bon appétit!

111. Sherry and Butter Prawns

(Ready in about 10 minutes + marinating time | Servings 4)

Per serving: 294 Calories; 14.3g Fat; 3.6g Carbs; 34.6g Protein; 1.4g Fiber

INGREDIENTS

1 ½ pounds king prawns, peeled and deveined
2 tablespoons dry sherry
1 teaspoon dried basil
1/2 teaspoon mustard seeds

1 ½ tablespoons fresh lemon juice
1 teaspoon cayenne pepper, crushed
1 tablespoon garlic paste
1/2 stick butter, at room temperature

DIRECTIONS

Whisk the dry sherry with cayenne pepper, garlic paste, basil, mustard seeds, lemon juice and prawns. Let it marinate for 1 hour in your refrigerator.
In a frying pan, melt the butter over medium-high flame, basting with the reserved marinade.
Sprinkle with salt and pepper to taste.

STORING

Place the shrimp in airtight containers or Ziploc bags; keep in your refrigerator for up 3 to 4 days.
For freezing, arrange the cooked shrimp in a single layer on a baking tray; place in the freezer for about 15 minutes, or until it begins to harden.
Transfer the frozen shrimp to heavy-duty freezer bags. Freeze up to 3 months. Defrost in your refrigerator. Enjoy!

112. Mediterranean-Style Tuna Salad with Bocconcini

(Ready in about 10 minutes | Servings 4)

Per serving: 273 Calories; 11.7g Fat; 6.7g Carbs; 34.2g Protein; 4.1g Fiber

INGREDIENTS

1 pound tuna steak
8 ounces bocconcini
1 teaspoon sesame oil
1 teaspoon balsamic vinegar
1 tablespoon fish sauce
1/2 cup radicchio, sliced

1 tomato, diced
1/2 cup black olives, pitted and sliced
2 teaspoons tahini paste
1/2 teaspoon chili pepper, finely chopped
1 head Romaine lettuce

2 garlic cloves, minced
1/2 cup onion, thinly sliced
2 bell peppers, sliced
1 Lebanese cucumber, sliced

DIRECTIONS

Grill the tuna over medium-high heat for about 4 minutes per side. Flake the fish with a fork.
Mix the vegetables in a salad bowl. In a small mixing dish, thoroughly combine the tahini, sesame oil, vinegar, and fish sauce. Dress the salad.

STORING

Divide the tuna steak between four airtight containers; keep in your refrigerator for up to 3 to 4 days.
For freezing, place them in airtight containers or wrap tightly with freezer wrap. Freeze up to 2 to 3 months. Defrost in the refrigerator.
As for the salad, keep in your refrigerator for up to 3 to 4 days. Garnish with the bocconcini and serve well-chilled. Enjoy!

113. Super Easy Fish Cakes

(Ready in about 30 minutes | Servings 6)

Per serving: 234 Calories; 10.6g Fat; 2.5g Carbs; 31.2g Protein; 0.2g Fiber

INGREDIENTS

1 ½ pounds tilapia fish, deboned and flaked
2 tablespoons sesame oil
1/2 cup Cottage cheese, at room temperature
2 eggs, lightly beaten
1/4 cup almond meal

1/4 tablespoons flax meal
2 teaspoons brown mustard
Sea salt and pepper, to taste
2 tablespoons fresh basil, chopped

DIRECTIONS

Mix the flakes fish with the eggs, almond and flax meal, cheese, mustard, salt, pepper, and basil. Form the mixture into 12 patties.
Now, place the patties on a parchment-lined baking sheet. Spritz them with sesame oil.
Bake in the preheated oven at 395 degrees F approximately 25 minutes, rotating the pan occasionally once.

STORING

Place the fish cakes in airtight containers; it will last for 3 to 4 days in the refrigerator.
For freezing, place the fish cakes in airtight containers or heavy-duty freezer bags. Freeze up to 2 to 3 months. Defrost in the refrigerator and reheat in your oven. Bon appétit!

114. Zingy Tuna Steaks with Spinach

(Ready in about 20 minutes | Servings 6)

Per serving: 444 Calories; 38.2g Fat; 4.7g Carbs; 21.9g Protein; 1g Fiber

INGREDIENTS

2 pounds tuna steaks
3 cups spinach
1 tablespoon Dijon mustard

3 tablespoons peanut oil
Salt and pepper, to season
1/2 cup radishes, thinly sliced

1 fresh lemon, sliced
1 cup green onions, thinly sliced

DIRECTIONS

Brush each tuna steaks with peanut oil and season them with salt and pepper.
Arrange the tuna steaks on a foil-lined baking pan. Top with lemon slices, cover with foil and roast at 400 degrees F for about 10 minutes.

STORING

Divide the tuna steaks between airtight containers; keep in your refrigerator for up to 3 to 4 days.
For freezing, place the tuna steaks in airtight containers or wrap tightly with freezer wrap. Freeze up to 2 to 3 months. Defrost in the refrigerator.
Serve with spinach, green onions, radishes and mustard mixture. Bon appétit!

115. Crabmeat and Vegetable Bowl

(Ready in about 10 minutes | Servings 4)

Per serving: 232 Calories; 15.6g Fat; 6g Carbs; 18.9g Protein; 2g Fiber

INGREDIENTS

12 ounces lump legs
10 Kalamata olives, pitted and halved
1/4 cup fresh scallions, chopped
2 ounces thinly sliced bacon, chopped

4 cups spinach
1 large-sized tomato, diced
3 tablespoons olive oil
1 tablespoon peanut butter

1/2 lime, zested and juiced
Flaky sea salt and ground black pepper, to your liking
1/4 cup fresh parsley, chopped

DIRECTIONS

Start by preheating your grill to 225 degrees F for indirect cooking.
Place the crab legs on the grill grates. Close the lid and grill for about 30 minutes or until done.
To prepare the dressing, whisk the oil, peanut butter, lime juice, salt, and pepper.
Toss the remaining ingredients and dress your salad.

STORING

Divide the crab legs between airtight containers; keep in your refrigerator for up to 2 to 3 days.
For freezing, place the crab legs in airtight containers or wrap tightly with freezer wrap. Freeze up to 3 to 5 months. Defrost in the refrigerator.
Place the salad in airtight containers and keep in your refrigerator for up to 3 to 4 days. Top with crab legs and serve. Bon appétit!

116. Mackerel and Vegetable Casserole

(Ready in about 30 minutes | Servings 4)

Per serving: 301 Calories; 14g Fat; 6g Carbs; 33.3g Protein; 3.2g Fiber

INGREDIENTS

1 pound mackerel steaks, chopped
1/2 stick butter
Salt and black pepper, to your liking
1/4 cup fish consommé

1 cup goat cheese, shredded
1/2 cup fresh scallions, chopped
1/2 cup celery, thinly sliced
1 cup parsnip, thinly sliced

2 cloves garlic, thinly sliced
2 shallots, thinly sliced
2 tomatoes, thinly sliced

DIRECTIONS

In a frying pan, melt the butter in over a moderately high heat. Cook the vegetables until they are just tender and fragrant.
Add in the clam juice and tomatoes and cook for a further 5 minutes. Place the sautéed vegetables in a lightly-greased casserole dish.
Lower the mackerel steaks on top of the vegetable layer. Sprinkle with salt and pepper. Bake in the preheated oven at 420 degrees F for about 15 minutes.
Top with shredded cheese and bake for a further 5 to 6 minutes or until it is hot and bubbly.

STORING

Slice the casserole into four pieces. Divide the pieces into four airtight containers; it will last for 3 to 4 days in the refrigerator.
For freezing, place each portion in a separate heavy-duty freezer bag. Freeze up to 2 to 3 months. Defrost in the microwave or refrigerator. Bon appétit!

117. Creamed Halibut Fillets with Brown Mushrooms

(Ready in about 20 minutes | Servings 4)

Per serving: 585 Calories; 30.5g Fat; 5.5g Carbs; 66.8g Protein; 1.1g Fiber

INGREDIENTS

4 halibut fillets
1 ½ cups chicken stock
1/2 cup fresh scallions, chopped
1 cup sour cream

2 tablespoons olive oil
1 medium-sized leek, chopped
1/2 pound brown mushrooms, thinly sliced

2 garlic cloves, chopped
Sea salt and freshly ground black pepper, to taste
1 tablespoon butter

DIRECTIONS

Heat the olive oil in a saucepan over a moderately high heat. Cook the leek until tender and translucent.
Add in the mushrooms, garlic, salt, and black pepper and continue to cook for 5 minutes more or until the mushrooms release liquid.
Add in the halibut fillets and continue to cook over medium-high heat approximately 5 minutes on each side.
Add in the butter, chicken stock, and scallions; bring to a boil. Immediately reduce the heat and let it cook for 10 minutes more or until heated through.
Add in the sour cream, remove from the heat and stir to combine well.

STORING

Spoon the creamed halibut into airtight containers; it will last for 3 to 4 days in the refrigerator.
For freezing, place the creamed halibut in airtight containers or heavy-duty freezer bags. Freeze up to 4 to 6 months. Defrost in the microwave or refrigerator. Bon appétit!

118. Clams with Garlic-Tomato Sauce

(Ready in about 25 minutes | Servings 4)

Per serving: 134 Calories; 7.8g Fat; 5.9g Carbs; 8.3g Protein; 1g Fiber

INGREDIENTS

40 littleneck clams
For the Sauce:
2 tomatoes, pureed
2 tablespoons olive oil

1 shallot, chopped
Sea salt and freshly ground black pepper, to taste
1/2 teaspoon paprika

1/3 cup port wine
2 garlic cloves, pressed
1/2 lemon, cut into wedges

DIRECTIONS

Grill the clams until they are open, for 5 to 6 minutes.
In a frying pan, heat the olive oil over moderate heat. Cook the shallot and garlic until tender and fragrant.
Stir in the pureed tomatoes, salt, black pepper and paprika and continue to cook an additional 10 to 12 minutes or until thoroughly cooked.
Heat off and add in the port wine; stir to combine. Garnish with fresh lemon wedges.

STORING

Spoon the clams with sauce into four airtight containers; it will last for 3 to 4 days in the refrigerator.
For freezing, place the clams along with sauce in airtight containers or heavy-duty freezer bags. Freeze up to 3 months. Defrost in your refrigerator. Bon appétit!

119. Amberjack Fillets with Cheese Sauce

(Ready in about 20 minutes | Servings 6)

Per serving: 285 Calories; 20.4g Fat; 1.2g Carbs; 23.8g Protein; 0.1g Fiber

INGREDIENTS

6 amberjack fillets
1/4 cup fresh tarragon chopped
2 tablespoons olive oil, at room temperature

Sea salt and ground black pepper, to taste
For the Sauce:
1/3 cup vegetable broth
3/4 cup double cream

1/3 cup Romano cheese, grated
3 teaspoons butter, at room temperature
2 garlic cloves, finely minced

DIRECTIONS

In a non-stick frying pan, heat the olive oil until sizzling.
Once hot, fry the amberjack for about 6 minutes per side or until the edges are turning opaque. Sprinkle them with salt, black pepper, and tarragon. Reserve.
To make the sauce, melt the butter in a saucepan over moderately high heat. Sauté the garlic until tender and fragrant or about 2 minutes.
Add in the vegetable broth and cream and continue to cook for 5 to 6 minutes more; heat off.
Stir in the Romano cheese and continue stirring in the residual heat for a couple of minutes more.

STORING

Place the amberjack fillets in airtight containers; it will last for 3 to 4 days in the refrigerator.
For freezing, place the amberjack fillets in airtight containers or heavy-duty freezer bags. Freeze up to 2 to 3 months. Defrost in the refrigerator.
Place the sauce in glass container and wrap with a foil; it will last for 3 to 4 days in the refrigerator.
Bon appétit!

120. Middle-Eastern Salmon with Nabulsi Cheese

(Ready in about 20 minutes | Servings 6)

Per serving: 354 Calories; 20.2g Fat; 4.5g Carbs; 39.6g Protein; 0.5g Fiber

INGREDIENTS

6 salmon fillets
1 garlic clove, finely minced
1 cup Nabulsi cheese, crumbled
3 tablespoons mayonnaise

Coarse salt and black pepper, to taste
1 teaspoon Za'atar
1 cup cauliflower
1/2 cup shallots, thinly sliced

1 tablespoon fresh lemon juice
2 tablespoons sesame oil

DIRECTIONS

Toss the salmon fillets with salt, pepper, and Za'atar. Place the salmon fillets on a parchment-lined baking pan; scatter the cauliflower, shallot, and garlic around the fish fillets.
Wrap with the foil and bake in the preheated oven at 390 degrees F for 10 to 12 minutes or until the salmon fillets flake easily with a fork. Remove the foil.
Mix the Nabulsi cheese, mayonnaise, lemon juice, and sesame oil. Pour the cheese mixture over the fish and vegetables.
Bake for a further 5 minutes or until the top is hot and bubbly.

STORING

Slice the casserole into six pieces. Divide the pieces between airtight containers; it will last for 3 to 4 days in the refrigerator.
For freezing, place each portion in a separate heavy-duty freezer bag. Freeze up to 2 to 3 months. Defrost in the microwave or refrigerator.
Bon appétit!

121. Salad with Crispy-Skinned Snapper

(Ready in about 15 minutes | Servings 4)

Per serving: 507 Calories; 42.8g Fat; 6g Carbs; 24.4g Protein; 2.7g Fiber

INGREDIENTS

4 snapper fillets with skin
6 ounces Feta cheese, crumbled
Sea salt and ground black pepper, to taste
1 teaspoon ground mustard seeds
1/2 teaspoon celery seeds
2 cups arugula
2 tablespoons butter, melted

2 cups lettuce leaves, torn into pieces
1 carrot, thinly sliced
1 cup spring onions, thinly sliced
1/2 cup black olives, pitted and sliced
10 grape tomatoes, halved
For the Vinaigrette:
1/3 cup extra-virgin olive oil

1 teaspoon Dijon mustard
1 lime, juiced and zested
1 teaspoon ginger- garlic paste
1 teaspoon dried basil
2 tablespoons fresh mint, finely chopped
Sea salt and ground black pepper, to taste

DIRECTIONS

In a grill pan, melt the butter over a moderately high flame. Cook the fish for 5 to 6 minutes; flip the fish fillets over and cook them for 5 minutes more.
Toss all ingredients for the salad.
Whisk all ingredients for the vinaigrette and dress the salad.

STORING

Place the fish fillets in airtight containers or Ziploc bags; keep in your refrigerator for up to 3 to 4 days.
For freezing, cover the airtight container and place it in the freezer; store for up to one month.
As for the salad, place it in airtight containers or Ziploc bags; keep in your refrigerator for up to 3 to 4 days. Top with the fish fillets, serve, and enjoy!

122. Refreshing Prawn Salad

(Ready in about 10 minutes | Servings 6)

Per serving: 196 Calories; 8.3g Fat; 6.5g Carbs; 21.4g Protein; 1.6g Fiber

INGREDIENTS

2 pounds tiger prawns, peeled leaving tails intact
Sea salt and freshly ground black pepper, to taste
1 celery rib, sliced
1 cup white onions, chopped
1 Lebanese cucumber, chopped

1/2 head Iceberg lettuce, torn into pieces
1/4 cup fresh basil, chopped
Juice from 1 fresh lime
1/4 cup capers, drained
1/2 cup mayonnaise

DIRECTIONS

Boil the tiger prawns in a large pot of salted water for about 3 minutes. Drain well and let it cool completely.
Toss the remaining ingredients in a large bowl; toss to combine well.

STORING

Place the tiger prawns in airtight containers or Ziploc bags; keep in your refrigerator for up 3 to 4 days.
For freezing, arrange the tiger prawns in a single layer on a baking tray; place in the freezer for about 15 minutes, or until it begins to harden. Transfer the frozen tiger prawns to heavy-duty freezer bags. Freeze up to 3 months. Defrost in your refrigerator.
As for the salad, place it in airtight containers or Ziploc bags; keep in your refrigerator for up to 3 days. Top with the tiger prawns and serve immediately!

123. Halibut with Creamed Cauliflower

(Ready in about 25 minutes | Servings 4)

Per serving: 508 Calories; 22.9g Fat; 4.7g Carbs; 68.6g Protein; 1.4g Fiber

INGREDIENTS

4 halibut fillets
1 head of cauliflower, broken into florets
2 tablespoons butter

1 lemon, cut into wedges
1 cup Cheddar cheese, shredded
1/2 teaspoon dried oregano

1/2 teaspoon dried rosemary
Sea salt and ground black pepper, to taste

DIRECTIONS

Parboil the cauliflower in a pot of lightly salted water until crisp-tender.
Place in a lightly buttered baking pan; brush with melted butter, too. Season with salt and pepper to taste.
Scatter the shredded Cheddar cheese on top of the cauliflower layer and bake at 385 degrees F approximately 15 minutes.
Grill the halibut steaks until golden and crisp on top. Sprinkle with oregano and rosemary; salt to taste.

STORING

Place the grilled halibut fillets into airtight containers; it will last for 3 to 4 days in the refrigerator.
Place the creamed cauliflower in airtight containers; keep in your refrigerator for 3 to 5 days.
For freezing, place the roasted cauliflower in freezable containers; they will maintain the best quality for 10 to 12 months. Defrost in the refrigerator or microwave. Enjoy!
Place the grilled halibut fillets in airtight containers or heavy-duty freezer bags. Freeze up to 4 to 5 months. Defrost in the microwave or refrigerator. Serve with lemon wedges. Bon appétit!

124. Red Snapper Soup

(Ready in about 20 minutes | Servings 4)

Per serving: 316 Calories; 14.3g Fat; 6.6g Carbs; 32.7g Protein; 1.7g Fiber

INGREDIENTS

1 pound red snapper, chopped
1 cup tomato puree
3 cups chicken stock
1/4 cup Marsala wine

2 thyme sprigs, chopped
1/2 teaspoon dried rosemary
1/2 stick butter, melted
1 medium leek, finely chopped

2 garlic cloves, minced
1/4 cup fresh parsley, chopped
Sea salt and ground black pepper, to taste

DIRECTIONS

In a heavy-bottomed pot, melt the butter over a moderately high heat. Cook the leek and garlic for 3 to 4 minutes or until tender and fragrant.
Add in the parsley, tomato puree, chicken stock, wine, red snapper, and rosemary; bring to a rolling boil.
Turn the heat to simmer; continue to simmer until the thoroughly cooked for a further 15 to 20 minutes. Season with salt and pepper to taste.

STORING

Spoon the soup into airtight containers; keep in your refrigerator for up 3 to 4 days.
For freezing, spoon it into airtight containers or heavy-duty freezer bags. Freeze up to 4 to 6 months. Defrost in the microwave or refrigerator. Enjoy!

125. Family Seafood Bowl

(Ready in about 10 minutes | Servings 4)

Per serving: 260 Calories; 13.6g Fat; 5.9g Carbs; 28.1g Protein; 1.5g Fiber

INGREDIENTS

1 pound sea scallops, halved horizontally
1/2 cup Kalamata olives, pitted and sliced
2 cups arugula

1/2 tablespoon Dijon mustard
1 teaspoon garlic, chopped
1 cup cherry tomatoes, halved
1 Lebanese cucumber, sliced

1/4 cup extra-virgin olive oil
2 tablespoons fresh lime juice
Sea salt and pepper, to season

DIRECTIONS

Boil the scallops in a pot of a lightly salted water for about 3 minutes or until opaque; place them in a serving bowl.
To make the salad, toss the remaining ingredients until everything is well combined.

STORING

Place the cooked and chilled scallops in airtight containers or Ziploc bags; keep in your refrigerator for up 3 to 4 days.
For freezing, arrange the cooked and chilled scallops in a single layer on a baking tray; place in the freezer for about 15 minutes, or until it begins to harden.
Transfer the cooked and chilled scallops to heavy-duty freezer bags. Freeze up to 3 months. Defrost in your refrigerator.
As for the salad, place it in airtight containers or Ziploc bags; keep in your refrigerator for up to 3 days. Top with prepared scallops. Enjoy!

126. Tilapia with Spicy Dijon Sauce

(Ready in about 15 minutes + marinating time | Servings 4)

Per serving: 228 Calories; 13g Fat; 6.5g Carbs; 13.7g Protein; 1.1g Fiber

INGREDIENTS

1 tablespoon butter, room temperature
2 chili peppers, deveined and minced
1 cup heavy cream
1 teaspoon Dijon mustard

1 pound tilapia fish, cubed
Sea salt and ground black pepper, to taste
1 cup white onions, chopped

1 teaspoon garlic, pressed
1/2 cup dark rum

DIRECTIONS

Toss the tilapia with salt, pepper, onions, garlic, chili peppers and rum. Let it marinate for 2 hours in your refrigerator.
In a grill pan, melt the butter over a moderately high heat. Sear the fish in hot butter, basting with the reserved marinade.
Add in the mustard and cream and continue to cook until everything is thoroughly cooked, for 2 to 3 minutes.

STORING

Spoon the tilapia along with the sauce into airtight containers; keep in your refrigerator for 3 to 4 days.
For freezing, place the tilapia along with the sauce in airtight containers or heavy-duty freezer bags. Freeze up to 3 months. Defrost in the microwave. Bon appétit!

127. Rich and Spicy Seafood Stew

(Ready in about 25 minutes | Servings 4)

Per serving: 296 Calories; 8.6g Fat; 5.5g Carbs; 41.4g Protein; 4.3g Fiber

INGREDIENTS

1/2 pound sole, cut into 2-inch pieces
1/3 pound halibut, cut into 2-inch
pieces
1/2 cup Marsala wine

1/8 teaspoon hot sauce, or more to taste
1 tablespoon lard, room temperature
1 cup shallots, chopped
1 teaspoon garlic, smashed

Sea salt and black pepper, to taste
4 cups chicken bone broth
1 cup tomato sauce
2 thyme sprigs, chopped

DIRECTIONS

In a large-sized pot, melt the lard over medium-high heat. Cook the shallots and garlic until they've softened.
Add in the salt, black pepper, chicken bone broth, tomato sauce, and thyme and; continue to cook an additional 15 minutes.
Add in the fish, wine and hot sauce; bring to a boil. Reduce the heat to simmer. Let it simmer for 4 to 5 minutes longer, stirring periodically.

STORING

Spoon your stew into airtight containers; keep in your refrigerator for up 3 to 4 days.
For freezing, spoon your stew into airtight containers or heavy-duty freezer bags. Freeze up to 4 to 6 months. Defrost in the microwave or refrigerator. Enjoy!

128. Avocado and Herring Fat Bombs

(Ready in about 5 minutes | Servings 4)

Per serving: 316 Calories; 24.4g Fat; 5.9g Carbs; 17.4g Protein; 4.2g Fiber

INGREDIENTS

1 avocado, pitted and peeled
1/2 cup scallions, chopped
1 teaspoon capers

1 can herring
Salt and black pepper, to taste
3 ounces sunflower seeds

1/2 teaspoon hot paprika

DIRECTIONS

In a mixing bowl, combine all ingredients until well incorporated. Roll the mixture into 8 balls.

STORING

Place the fat bombs in airtight containers or Ziploc bags; keep in your refrigerator for up to 3 to 4 days.
To freeze, arrange the fat bombs on a baking tray in a single layer; freeze for about 2 hours. Transfer the frozen bombs to an airtight container. Freeze for up to 2 months. Bon appétit!

129. Saucy Tuna with Brussels Sprouts

(Ready in about 25 minutes | Servings 4)

Per serving: 372 Calories; 27.8g Fat; 5.6g Carbs; 26.5g Protein; 2.2g Fiber

INGREDIENTS

1 pound tuna
1 tablespoon fresh lemon juice
1/4 cup extra-virgin olive oil
1 tomato, chopped

Sea salt and freshly ground black
pepper, to taste
1 teaspoon dried rosemary
1/2 cup fish stock

1/2 pounds Brussels sprouts
1/4 cup parsley
2 garlic cloves, crushed
1/3 cup pine nuts, chopped

DIRECTIONS

Brush a non-stick skillet with cooking spray. Once hot, cook the tuna steaks for about 4 minutes per side; sprinkle with salt, pepper, and rosemary; set aside.
In the same skillet, cook Brussels sprouts; adding the fish stock to prevent over cooking. Then, sauté for about 5 minutes or until the Brussels sprouts are crisp-tender.
Add in the chopped tomatoes and continue to cook for 3 minutes more. Fold in the reserved tuna steaks.
Process the parsley, garlic, pine nuts, lemon juice, and olive oil in your food processor or blender until it reaches a paste consistency. Reserve.

STORING

Place the tuna steaks in airtight containers and keep in your refrigerator for up to 3 to 4 days.
Place the sauce in airtight containers and keep in your refrigerator for up to 3 to 4 days.
For freezing, place the tuna steaks in airtight containers or wrap tightly with freezer wrap. Freeze up to 2 to 3 months. Defrost in the refrigerator.
Top with the sauce and serve. Bon appétit!

130. Greek Salad with Grilled Halloumi

(Ready in about 15 minutes | Servings 4)

Per serving: 199 Calories; 10.6g Fat; 6.1g Carbs; 14.2g Protein; 1.1g Fiber

INGREDIENTS

1 pound halibut steak
1 cup cherry tomatoes, halved
1 onion, thinly sliced
1 tablespoon lemon juice

1 Lebanese cucumbers, thinly sliced
1/2 cup radishes, thinly sliced
2 tablespoons sunflower seeds
1 ½ tablespoons extra-virgin olive oil

1/2 head butterhead lettuce
1 cup Halloumi cheese
Sea salt and pepper, to taste

DIRECTIONS

Cook the halibut steak on preheated grill for 5 to 6 minutes per side. until the fish flakes easily with a fork.
Grill the halloumi cheese and slice into small pieces.
Toss the grilled halloumi cheese with the remaining ingredients and set aside.

STORING

Divide the halibut steaks between airtight containers; keep in your refrigerator for up to 3 to 4 days.
Place the Greek salad in airtight containers or Ziploc bags; keep in your refrigerator for up to 3 to 4 days.
For freezing, place the halibut steaks in airtight containers or wrap tightly with freezer wrap. Freeze up to 2 to 3 months. Defrost in the refrigerator.
Serve with chilled salad and enjoy!

131. Italian-Style Seafood Stew

(Ready in about 20 minutes | Servings 4)

Per serving: 209 Calories; 12.6g Fat; 6.6g Carbs; 15.2g Protein; 2g Fiber

INGREDIENTS

2 tablespoons lard, room temperature
1/2 teaspoon lime zest
1/2 pound shrimp
1/2 pound scallops

1 teaspoon Italian seasonings blend
Salt and ground black pepper, to taste
1 leek, chopped
2 garlic cloves, pressed

1 cup tomato puree
1 celery stalk, chopped
3 cups fish stock
2 tablespoons port wine

DIRECTIONS

Melt the lard in a large pot over a moderately high heat. Sauté the leek and garlic until they've softened.
Stir in the pureed tomatoes and continue to cook for about 10 minutes.
Add in the remaining ingredients and bring to a boil. Turn the heat to a simmer and continue to cook for 4 to 5 minutes.

STORING

Spoon your stew into airtight containers; keep in your refrigerator for up 3 to 4 days.
For freezing, spoon your stew into airtight containers or heavy-duty freezer bags. Freeze up to 4 to 6 months. Defrost in the microwave or refrigerator. Enjoy!

132. Smoky Sardine Salad

(Ready in about 10 minutes | Servings 4)

Per serving: 195 Calories; 14.7g Fat; 6g Carbs; 7.8g Protein; 3.1g Fiber

INGREDIENTS

1 head of Iceberg lettuce
1 pound fresh sardines, chopped
1 red onion, chopped
1 celery, thinly sliced

1/2 cup cucumber, thinly sliced
Sea salt and ground black pepper, to taste
3/4 cup mayonnaise

1/2 teaspoon smoked paprika
1/4 cup fresh scallions, roughly chopped

DIRECTIONS

Pat your sardines dry with a kitchen paper towel. Place your sardines in a baking dish; roast them in the preehated oven at 390 degrees F for 20 minutes.
Toss the remaining ingredients in a salad bowl.

STORING

Place the roasted sardines in airtight containers or Ziploc bags; keep in your refrigerator for up 3 to 4 days.
For freezing, arrange the roasted sardines in a single layer on a baking tray; place in the freezer for about 15 minutes, or until it begins to harden. Transfer the roasted sardines to heavy-duty freezer bags. Freeze up to 3 months. Defrost in your refrigerator.
Place the salad in airtight containers or Ziploc bags; keep in your refrigerator for up 3 to 4 days. Top your salad with the sardines and enjoy!

133. Salmon and Cheese Stuffed Peppers

(Ready in about 25 minutes | Servings 4)

Per serving: 273 Calories; 13.9g Fat; 5.1g Carbs; 28.9g Protein; 2.1g Fiber

INGREDIENTS

4 bell peppers
1 pound salmon fillets, boneless
1 onion, finely chopped
1/2 teaspoon garlic, pressed

1/3 cup mayonnaise
1/3 cup black olives, pitted and chopped
Sea salt and pepper, to taste

1/2 teaspoon dried oregano
1/2 teaspoon dried oregano
1 cup cream cheese

DIRECTIONS

Broil the bell pepper for 5 to 6 minutes until they've softened.
Now, remove the seeds and membranes and cut the peppers in half.
Cook the salmon in a lightly oiled grill pan for 5 to 6 minutes per side until the fish flakes easily with a fork. Add in the other ingredients; stir to combine well.
Divide the salmon mixture between the peppers and bake in the preheated oven at 380 degrees F for about 15 minutes or until heated through.

STORING

Place the stuffed peppers in airtight containers; keep in your refrigerator for 3 to 4 days.
Wrap each stuffed pepper tightly in several layers of plastic wrap and squeeze the air out. Place them in airtight containers; they can be frozen for up to 1 month.
Reheat the thawed stuffed peppers at 200 degrees F until they are completely warm.

134. Creole Tuna with Lemon

(Ready in about 40 minutes | Servings 4)

Per serving: 266 Calories; 11.5g Fat; 5.6g Carbs; 34.9g Protein; 0.7g Fiber

INGREDIENTS

4 tuna fillets
1/4 cup scallions, chopped
2 garlic cloves, minced

1/3 cup fresh lemon juice
1/3 cup coconut aminos
3 teaspoons olive oil

1 teaspoon lemon thyme
Salt and ground black pepper
1 teaspoon dried rosemary

DIRECTIONS

Place all ingredients in a ceramic dish; cover and let it marinate for about 30 minutes in the refrigerator.
Grill the tuna fillets for about 15 minutes, basting with the reserved marinade.

STORING

Place the tuna steaks in airtight containers and keep in your refrigerator for up to 3 to 4 days.
For freezing, place the tuna steaks in airtight containers or wrap tightly with freezer wrap. Freeze up to 2 to 3 months. Defrost in the refrigerator.

135. Pan-Seared Halibut with Herb Sauce

(Ready in about 20 minutes | Servings 4)

Per serving: 273 Calories; 19.2g Fat; 4.3g Carbs; 22.6g Protein; 0.7g Fiber

INGREDIENTS

2 tablespoons butter, at room temperature
4 halibut steaks
1 teaspoon garlic
1 ½ tablespoons extra-virgin olive oil

1/2 cup white onions, chopped
1 tablespoon fish sauce
Salt and ground black pepper, to taste
1 tablespoon soy sauce
2 cloves garlic, finely minced

3 tablespoons fish consommé
2 tablespoons fresh coriander, chopped
1/4 cup Italian parsley, finely chopped
1 tablespoon fresh lemon juice

DIRECTIONS

Melt the butter in a saucepan over medium-high heat.
Once hot, sear the halibut for 6 to 7 minutes until cooked all the way through. Reserve.
In the same pan, sauté the onions and garlic until tender and fragrant. Add in the fish consommé along with the coriander, fish sauce, and reserved halibut steaks; continue to cook, partially covered, for 5 to 6 minutes.
Whisk the remaining ingredients for the herb sauce.

STORING

Place the pan-sear halibut in airtight containers and keep in your refrigerator for up to 3 to 4 days.
Place the herb sauce in airtight containers and keep in your refrigerator for up to 3 to 4 days.
For freezing, place the pan-sear halibut in airtight containers or wrap tightly with freezer wrap. Freeze up to 2 to 3 months. Defrost in the refrigerator.

136. Pepper Boats with Herring

(Ready in about 10 minutes | Servings 4)

Per serving: 120 Calories; 5.4g Fat; 5.8g Carbs; 12.3g Protein; 1.6g Fiber

INGREDIENTS

4 pickled peppers, slice into halves
8 ounces canned herring, drained
1 teaspoon Dijon mustard

1 celery, chopped
1 cup onions, chopped

Salt and freshly ground black pepper, to taste
1 tablespoon fresh coriander, chopped

DIRECTIONS

Broil the bell pepper for 5 to 6 minutes until they've softened. Cut into halves and discard the seeds.
In a mixing bowl, thoroughly combine the herring, Dijon mustard, celery, onions, salt, black pepper, and fresh coriander.
Mix to combine well. Spoon the mixture into the bell pepper halves.

STORING

Place the stuffed peppers in airtight containers; keep in your refrigerator for 3 to 4 days.
Wrap each stuffed pepper tightly in several layers of plastic wrap and squeeze the air out. Place them in airtight containers; they can be frozen for up to 1 month.
Reheat the thawed peppers at 200 degrees F until they are completely warm. Enjoy!

137. Oven-Baked Sole Fillets

(Ready in about 30 minutes | Servings 4)

Per serving: 195 Calories; 8.2g Fat; 0.5g Carbs; 28.7g Protein; 0.6g Fiber

INGREDIENTS

2 tablespoons olive oil
1/2 tablespoon Dijon mustard
1 teaspoon garlic paste

1/2 tablespoon fresh ginger, minced
1/2 teaspoon porcini powder
Salt and ground black pepper, to taste

1/2 teaspoon paprika
4 sole fillets
1/4 cup fresh parsley, chopped

DIRECTIONS

Combine the oil, Dijon mustard, garlic paste, ginger, porcini powder, salt, black pepper and paprika.
Rub this mixture all over sole fillets. Place the sole fillets in a lightly oiled baking pan.
Bake in the preheated oven at 400 degrees F for about 20 minutes.

STORING

Place the sole fillets in airtight containers and keep in your refrigerator for up to 3 to 4 days.
For freezing, place the sole fillets in airtight containers or wrap tightly with freezer wrap. Freeze up to 2 to 3 months. Defrost in the refrigerator. Serve with fresh parsley.

138. Old-Fashioned Seafood Chowder

(Ready in about 15 minutes | Servings 5)

Per serving: 404 Calories; 30g Fat; 5.3g Carbs; 23.9g Protein; 0.3g Fiber

INGREDIENTS

1/2 stick butter
3/4 pound prawns, peeled and deveined
1/2 pound crab meat
2 tablespoons scallions, chopped
1 tablespoon tomato sauce
1 teaspoon Mediterranean spice mix

1 egg, lightly beaten
2 garlic cloves, minced
1/3 cup port wine
1 quart chicken bone broth
2 cups double cream

DIRECTIONS

In a heavy bottomed pot, melt the butter over a moderately high flame. Sauté the scallions and garlic until they've softened.
Add in the prawns, crab meat, wine, and chicken bone broth. Continue to cook until thoroughly heated for 5 to 6 minutes.
Decrease the heat to low; add in the remaining ingredients and continue to simmer for 5 minutes more.

STORING

Spoon your chowder into airtight containers; keep in your refrigerator for up 3 to 4 days.
For freezing, spoon your chowder into airtight containers or heavy-duty freezer bags. Freeze up to 4 to 6 months. Defrost in the microwave or refrigerator. Enjoy!

139. Green Salad with Crab Mayo

(Ready in about 15 minutes | Servings 4)

Per serving: 293 Calories; 27.1g Fat; 6.3g Carbs; 9.3g Protein; 3.3g Fiber

INGREDIENTS

For the Crab Mayo:
1 pound crabmeat
2 egg yolks
Coarse sea salt and ground black pepper, to season
1 teaspoon garlic, pressed

1/2 teaspoon basil
1/2 tablespoon Dijon mustard
3/4 cup extra-virgin olive oil
1/2 teaspoon Sriracha sauce
2 tablespoons fresh lime juice

For the Salad:
A bunch of scallions, chopped
1 cup radishes, sliced
1 head Romaine lettuce
1 cup Arugula
1 Spanish pepper, julienned

DIRECTIONS

Mix the egg yolks and mustard in your blender; pour in the oil in a tiny stream, and continue to blend.
Now, add in the Sriracha sauce, lime juice, salt, black pepper, garlic, basil, and crabmeat.
Toss the remaining ingredients in a salad bowl. Add in prepared crab mayo sauce and gently stir to combine.

STORING

Place your salad in airtight containers and keep in your refrigerator for up to 3 to 4 days. Serve well-chilled.

140. Parmesan Crusted Cod

(Ready in about 15 minutes | Servings 4)

Per serving: 222 Calories; 12.6g Fat; 0.9g Carbs; 27.9g Protein; 0.3g Fiber

INGREDIENTS

1 pound cod fillets, cut into 4 servings
2 tablespoons olive oil
1/2 teaspoon paprika

3/4 cup grated Parmesan cheese
Flaky sea salt and ground black pepper, to taste

DIRECTIONS

In a shallow mixing dish, combine the salt pepper, paprika, and Parmesan cheese,
Press the cod fillets into this Parmesan mixture.
Heat the olive oil in a nonstick skillet over medium-high flame. Cook the cod fillets for 12 to 15 minutes or until opaque.

STORING

Place the Parmesan crusted cod in airtight containers and keep in your refrigerator for up to 3 to 4 days.
For freezing, place the Parmesan crusted cod in airtight containers or wrap tightly with freezer wrap. Freeze up to 2 to 3 months. Defrost in the refrigerator. Bon appétit!

141. Chinese-Style Mackerel Chowder

(Ready in about 30 minutes | Servings 6)

Per serving: 165 Calories; 5.5g Fat; 4g Carbs; 25.4g Protein; 0.5g Fiber

INGREDIENTS

1 ¼ pounds mackerel, cut into small pieces
1 tablespoon peanut oil
1 chili pepper, deveined and sliced
1 tablespoon coconut aminos

1/4 cup fresh mint, chopped
2 ½ cups hot water
1 teaspoon Five-spice powder
1/2 cup white onions, sliced
1 garlic clove, smashed

1 celery rib, diced
1 bell pepper, deveined and sliced
3/4 cup heavy cream

DIRECTIONS

Heat the oil in a large pot over a moderately high heat. Cook the onion and garlic until they are just tender or about 3 minutes.
Stir in the celery, peppers, coconut aminos, water, and Five-spice powder. Reduce to a simmer, and cook, partially covered, for 15 minutes.
Fold in the fish chunks and continue to simmer an additional 15 minutes or until cooked through. Add in the heavy cream and remove from heat.

STORING

Spoon your chowder into airtight containers; keep in your refrigerator for up 3 to 4 days.
For freezing, spoon your chowder into airtight containers or heavy-duty freezer bags. Freeze up to 4 to 6 months. Defrost in the microwave or refrigerator. Serve with fresh mint leaves and enjoy!

142. Shrimp with Mignonette Sauce

(Ready in about 15 minutes | Servings 4)

Per serving: 252 Calories; 7.3g Fat; 5.3g Carbs; 36.6g Protein; 2.5g Fiber

INGREDIENTS

1 ½ tablespoons butter, melted
1 large onion, chopped
1 teaspoon garlic, minced
1 cup tomato puree
Salt and pepper, to taste

1 ½ pounds shrimp, shelled and deveined
2 tablespoons dry sherry
For Mignonette Sauce:
1/2 cup onion, chopped

1 teaspoon black pepper, coarsely ground
1/2 cup white wine vinegar

DIRECTIONS

Melt the butter in a sauté pan over a moderately high heat. Then, cook the onion and garlic until they are tender and fragrant.
Add in the tomato puree and season with salt and pepper to taste; add in shrimp and continue to cook until thoroughly cooked.
Remove from heat and add in dry sherry. Wisk all ingredients for Mignonette sauce.

STORING

Place your shrimp in airtight containers or Ziploc bags; keep in your refrigerator for up 3 to 4 days.
For freezing, arrange the cooked shrimp in a single layer on a baking tray; place in the freezer for about 15 minutes, or until it begins to harden. Transfer the frozen shrimp to heavy-duty freezer bags. Freeze up to 3 months. Defrost in your refrigerator.
Place the Mignonette sauce in airtight containers or Ziploc bags; keep in your refrigerator for up 5 days. Bon appétit!

143. Colorful Prawn Salad

(Ready in about 10 minutes + chilling time | Servings 6)

Per serving: 209 Calories; 9.5g Fat; 6.8g Carbs; 20.2g Protein; 0.4g Fiber

INGREDIENTS

1 medium-sized lemon, cut into wedges
2 pounds prawns
1/2 cup mayonnaise
1/2 cup cream cheese

1/2 teaspoon stone-ground mustard
1 tablespoon dry sherry
1 tablespoon balsamic vinegar
Salt and black pepper
4 scallion stalks, chopped

1 Italian pepper, sliced
1 cucumber, sliced
1 ½ cups radishes, sliced
1 tablespoon Sriracha sauce

DIRECTIONS

Bring a pot of a lightly salted water to a boil over high heat. Add in the lemon and prawns and cook approximately 3 minutes, until they are opaque. Drain and rinse your prawns.
In a salad bowl, toss the remaining ingredients until well combined.

STORING

Place the cooked prawns in airtight containers or Ziploc bags; keep in your refrigerator for up 3 to 4 days.
For freezing, arrange the cooked prawns in a single layer on a baking tray; place in the freezer for about 15 minutes, or until it begins to harden. Transfer the frozen prawns to heavy-duty freezer bags. Freeze up to 3 months. Defrost in your refrigerator.
Place the salad in airtight containers or Ziploc bags; keep in your refrigerator for up 3 to 4 days. Top with the prepared prawns and serve!

144. Classic Tuna and Avocado Salad

(Ready in about 20 minutes | Servings 4)

Per serving: 244 Calories; 12.7g Fat; 5.3g Carbs; 23.4g Protein; 4.4g Fiber

INGREDIENTS

1 ½ pounds tuna steaks
1 avocado, pitted, peeled and diced
Salt and ground black pepper, to taste
2 tablespoons fresh lemon juice

1 head lettuce
1/2 cup black olives, pitted and sliced
2 Italian peppers, deveined and sliced
1 cup grape tomatoes, halved

1 shallot, chopped
1/4 cup mayonnaise

DIRECTIONS

Grill the tuna steaks for about 15 minutes; cut into chunks.
In a salad bowl, mix lettuce, peppers, tomatoes, shallot, and avocado.
Then, make the dressing by mixing the mayonnaise, salt, pepper and lime juice. Dress the salad and toss to combine. Top with black olives.

STORING

Place the tuna steaks in airtight containers and keep in your refrigerator for up to 3 to 4 days.
Place the salad in airtight containers and keep in your refrigerator for up to 3 to 4 days.
For freezing, place the tuna steaks in airtight containers or wrap tightly with freezer wrap. Freeze up to 2 to 3 months. Defrost in the refrigerator.
Top your salad with the tuna chunks and serve!

145. Salmon and Ricotta Stuffed Tomatoes

(Ready in about 30 minutes | Servings 6)

Per serving: 303 Calories; 22.9g Fat; 6.8g Carbs; 17g Protein; 1.6g Fiber

INGREDIENTS

6 tomatoes, pulp and seeds removed
1 ½ cups Ricotta cheese
10 ounces salmon
1 cup scallions, finely chopped

2 garlic cloves, minced
2 tablespoons coriander, chopped
1/2 cup aioli
1 teaspoon Dijon mustard

Sea salt and ground black pepper, to taste

DIRECTIONS

Grill your salmon for about 10 minutes until browned and flakes easily with a fork. Cut into small chunks.
Thoroughly combine the salmon, scallions, garlic, coriander, aioli, mustard, salt, and pepper in a bowl.
Spoon the filling into tomatoes. Bake in the preheated oven at 390 degrees F for 17 to 20 minutes until they are thoroughly cooked.

STORING

Place the stuffed tomatoes in airtight containers; keep in your refrigerator for 3 to 4 days.
Wrap each stuffed tomato tightly in several layers of plastic wrap and squeeze the air out. Place them in airtight containers; they can be frozen for up to 1 month.
Reheat the thawed stuffed tomatoes at 200 degrees F until they are completely warm. Top with the Ricotta cheese and place under preheated broiled for 5 minutes until hot and bubbly. Enjoy!

146. Seafood Gumbo with a Twist

(Ready in about 25 minutes | Servings 4)

Per serving: 481 Calories; 26.9g Fat; 5g Carbs; 46.6g Protein; 1.3g Fiber

INGREDIENTS

2 tablespoons lard, melted
2 breakfast sausages, cut crosswise into
1/2-inch-thick slices
2 garlic cloves, finely minced

1 yellow onion, chopped
1 cup tomatoes, pureed
1 tablespoon fish sauce
3/4 cup fish consommé

1/3 cup port wine
1/2 pound tilapia, cut into chunks
20 sea scallops
2 tablespoons fresh coriander, chopped

DIRECTIONS

In a stock pot, melt the lard over medium-high heat. Cook the sausages for about 5 minutes until no longer pink; reserve.
Now, sauté the onion and garlic until they've softened; reserve.
Add in the pureed tomatoes, fish sauce, fish consommé and wine; let it simmer for another 15 minutes.
Add in the tilapia, scallops, coriander, and reserved sausages. Continue to simmer, partially covered, for 5 to 6 minutes.

STORING

Spoon your gumbo into airtight containers; keep in your refrigerator for up 3 to 4 days.
For freezing, spoon your gumbo into airtight containers or heavy-duty freezer bags. Freeze up to 4 to 6 months. Defrost in the microwave or refrigerator. Garnish with coriander and enjoy!

147. Haddock and Vegetable Skewers

(Ready in about 15 minutes | Servings 4)

Per serving: 257 Calories; 12.5g Fat; 7g Carbs; 27.5g Protein; 0.9g Fiber

INGREDIENTS

1 pound haddock, cut into small cubes
Salt and pepper, to taste
1/2 teaspoon basil

2 tablespoons olive oil
1 red onion, cut into wedges
1 zucchini, diced

1 cup cherry tomatoes
2 tablespoons coconut aminos

DIRECTIONS

Start by preheating your grill on high.
Toss the haddock and vegetables with salt, pepper, basil, olive oil, and coconut aminos.
Alternate the seasoned haddock, onion, zucchini and tomatoes on bamboo skewers.
Grill your skewers for 5 minutes for medium-rare, flipping them occasionally to ensure even cooking.

STORING

Divide the grilled skewers between four airtight containers; keep in your refrigerator for up to 3 to 4 days.
For freezing, place the grilled skewers in airtight containers or wrap tightly with freezer wrap. Freeze up to 2 to 3 months. Defrost in the refrigerator. Bon appétit!

148. Chinese-Style Mackerel

(Ready in about 35 minutes | Servings 4)

Per serving: 415 Calories; 28g Fat; 4.4g Carbs; 34.5g Protein; 1.8g Fiber

INGREDIENTS

For the Fish:
1 pound mackerel fillets
1/3 cup Shaoxing wine
Sea salt and ground black pepper, to taste
1/2 teaspoon cayenne pepper

2 tablespoons avocado oil
2 tablespoons coconut aminos
For the Mushroom Coulis:
1 ½ ounces sesame oil
1 Spanish pepper, deveined and chopped

Salt and ground black pepper, to taste
1/2 shallot, peeled and chopped
1/4 teaspoon cardamom
2 ounces button mushrooms, chopped
3 tablespoons Shaoxing wine

DIRECTIONS

In a wok, heat the avocado oil over a moderately high heat. Season the fish with salt, black pepper, and cayenne pepper.
Cook the fish for about 10 minutes until golden brown; reserve.
Add in 1/3 cup of Shaoxing wine and coconut aminos; bring to a boil. Turn the heat to simmer and continue to cook for 4 to 5 minutes.
Add the mackerel fillets back to the pan, and continue to cook for 4 minutes longer.
To make the mushroom coulis, heat sesame oil in a wok that is preheated over a moderate flame. Now, cook the shallots until tender and translucent or about 3 minutes. Turn the heat to simmer and stir in the peppers and mushrooms along with 3 tablespoons of Shaoxing wine; cook for 10 minutes longer or until the vegetables have softened. Add in salt, black pepper, and cardamom.
Puree the sautéed mixture in your blender until creamy and uniform.

STORING

Place the mackerel fillets in airtight containers and keep in your refrigerator for up to 3 to 4 days.
Place the mushroom coulis in airtight containers and keep in your refrigerator for up to 3 to 4 days.
For freezing, place the mackerel fillets in airtight containers or wrap tightly with freezer wrap. Freeze up to 2 to 3 months. Defrost in the refrigerator and serve with the mushroom coulis. Enjoy!

149. Avocado and Shrimp Salad

(Ready in about 10 minutes + chilling time | Servings 6)

Per serving: 236 Calories; 14.3g Fat; 5.3g Carbs; 16.3g Protein; 3g Fiber

INGREDIENTS

1 cup butterhead lettuce
1 avocado, pitted and sliced
1/2 cup aioli

1 pound shrimp, peeled and deveined
1/2 cup cucumber, chopped
1 shallot, thinly sliced

1 tablespoon soy sauce
2 teaspoons fresh lemon juice

DIRECTIONS

Cook your shrimp in a pot of salted water for about 3 minutes. Drain and reserve.
In a salad bowl, mix all ingredients, except for the lettuce leaves. Gently stir to combine.

STORING

Place the shrimp in airtight containers or Ziploc bags; keep in your refrigerator for up 3 to 4 days.
For freezing, arrange the cooked shrimp in a single layer on a baking tray; place in the freezer for about 15 minutes, or until it begins to harden.
Transfer the frozen shrimp to heavy-duty freezer bags. Freeze up to 3 months. Defrost in your refrigerator.
Place your salad in airtight containers or Ziploc bags; keep in your refrigerator for up 3 to 4 days. Mound the salad onto the lettuce leaves and top each portion with shrimp. Enjoy!

150. Cod Fish with Broccoli and Chutney

(Ready in about 30 minutes | Servings 4)

Per serving: 291 Calories; 9.5g Fat; 3.5g Carbs; 42.5g Protein; 3g Fiber

INGREDIENTS

1 pound broccoli, cut into florets
1 teaspoon paprika
1 ½ pounds cod fish
2 Spanish peppers, thinly sliced
1 onion, thinly sliced

2 tablespoons sesame oil
Sea salt and freshly ground black pepper, to taste

For Tomato Chutney:
1 cup tomatoes, chopped
1 teaspoon sesame oil
2 garlic cloves, sliced
Sea salt and ground black pepper, to taste

DIRECTIONS

In a frying pan, heat 2 tablespoons of sesame oil over a moderately high flame.
Stir in the broccoli florets, Spanish peppers, and onion until they've softened; season with salt, black pepper, and paprika; reserve.
In the same pan, sear the fish for 4 to 5 minutes per side.
To make the chutney, heat 1 teaspoon of sesame oil in a frying pan over a moderately high heat. Sauté the garlic until just browned or about 1 minute.
Add in the chopped tomatoes and continue to cook, stirring periodically, until cooked through. Season with salt and pepper to taste.

STORING

Place the cod fillets with sautéed broccoli mixture in airtight containers and keep in your refrigerator for up to 3 to 4 days.
For freezing, place the cod fillets with sautéed broccoli mixture in airtight containers or wrap tightly with freezer wrap. Freeze up to 2 to 3 months.
Place the tomato chutney in airtight containers or Ziploc bags; keep in your refrigerator for up 3 to 4 days.
Defrost in the refrigerator and serve with the tomato chutney. Enjoy!

151. Classic Fish Tart

(Ready in about 45 minutes | Servings 6)

Per serving: 416 Calories; 34.2g Fat; 5.5g Carbs; 19.5g Protein; 1.5g Fiber

INGREDIENTS

For the Crust:
1 teaspoon baking powder
Flaky salt, to taste
1/2 stick butter
1 cup almond meal
3 tablespoons flaxseed meal

2 teaspoons ground psyllium husk powder
2 eggs
2 tablespoons almond milk
For the Filling:
10 ounces cod fish, chopped

2 eggs
1 teaspoon Mediterranean spice mix
1 ½ cups Colby cheese, shredded
1 teaspoon stone-ground mustard
1/2 cup cream cheese
1/2 cup mayonnaise

DIRECTIONS

Thoroughly combine all the crust ingredients. Press the crust into a parchment-lined baking pan.
Bake the crust in the preheated oven at 365 degrees F for about 15 minutes.
In a mixing dish, combine the ingredients for the filling. Spread the mixture over the pie crust and bake for a further 25 minutes.

STORING

Slice your tart into six pieces; divide between airtight containers or Ziploc bags; keep in your refrigerator for up to 3 days.
For freezing, place the pieces in airtight containers or heavy-duty freezer bags. Freeze up to 3 months. Once thawed in the refrigerator, heat in the microwave until warmed through. Enjoy!

152. Spicy Fish Curry

(Ready in about 25 minutes | Servings 6)

Per serving: 270 Calories; 16.9g Fat; 5.6g Carbs; 22.3g Protein; 1.5g Fiber

INGREDIENTS

2 pounds pollock, cut into large pieces
1 teaspoon fresh garlic, minced
Salt and black pepper, to taste
1 cup coconut milk
4 Roma tomatoes, pureed

2 tablespoons sesame oil
1 cup white onions, chopped
8 fresh curry leaves
2 tablespoons fresh lime juice
2 green chilies, minced

1/2 tablespoon fresh ginger, grated
1 teaspoon mustard seeds
1 tablespoon ground coriander

DIRECTIONS

Drizzle the fish with lime juice.
Heat the sesame oil in a frying pan over a moderately high flame. Cook the onion, curry leaves and garlic for 3 to 4 minutes until tender and aromatic.
Add in the ginger, salt, pepper, tomatoes, mustard seeds, and ground coriander. Let it simmer for 12 minutes or until thoroughly cooked.
Add in the fish and coconut milk and continue to cook, partially covered, for 6 to 7 minutes longer.

STORING

Spoon the fish curry into airtight containers; it will last for 3 to 4 days in the refrigerator.
For freezing, place the fish curry in airtight containers or heavy-duty freezer bags. Freeze up to 4 to 6 months. Defrost in the microwave or refrigerator. Bon appétit!

153. Trout with Authentic Chimichurri Sauce

(Ready in about 15 minutes | Servings 6)

Per serving: 265 Calories; 20.9g Fat; 4g Carbs; 17.1g Protein; 0.7g Fiber

INGREDIENTS

2 tablespoons butter
6 trout fillets
Sea salt and ground black pepper, to taste
1/2 teaspoon curry powder

1/2 teaspoon mustard seeds
For Chimichurri Sauce:
1/3 cup apple cider vinegar
Kosher salt and pepper, to taste
2 garlic cloves, minced

1/2 cup yellow onion, finely chopped
1 chili pepper, finely chopped
1/2 cup fresh cilantro, minced
1 tablespoon fresh basil leaves, snipped
1/3 cup olive oil

DIRECTIONS

In a cast-iron skillet, melt the butter over a moderately high heat. Season the trout fillets with salt, pepper, curry powder, and mustard seeds.
Cook the trout fillets for about 5 minutes per side.
To make the Chimichurri sauce, pulse the remaining ingredients in your food processor until well mixed.

STORING

Place the trout fillets in airtight containers and keep in your refrigerator for up to 3 to 4 days.
For freezing, place the trout fillets in airtight containers or wrap tightly with freezer wrap. Freeze up to 2 to 3 months.
Place the Chimichurri sauce in airtight containers or Ziploc bags; keep in your refrigerator for up 3 to 4 days.

BEEF

154. Easy and Spicy Sloppy Joes

(Ready in about 30 minutes | Servings 6)

Per serving: 313 Calories; 20.6g Fat; 3.5g Carbs; 26.6g Protein; 2.1g Fiber

INGREDIENTS

1 ½ pounds ground beef
2 teaspoons lard, room temperature
1 large onion, chopped
2 garlic cloves, minced

Salt and ground pepper, to taste
1 teaspoon paprika
1 teaspoon mustard
1 tablespoon red wine vinegar

1/2 cup tomato sauce
1/2 teaspoon hot sauce

DIRECTIONS

Melt 1 teaspoon of the lard in a saucepan over a moderately high heat.
Once hot, sauté the onion and garlic until tender and translucent; reserve.
In the same skillet, melt another teaspoon of the lard. Cook the ground beef, breaking apart with a fork, until well browned.
Add the sautéed vegetables back to the saucepan; stir in the spices, vinegar, tomato sauce, and hot sauce. Reduce the heat to simmer and continue to cook for 17 to 20 minutes.

STORING

Place the meat mixture in airtight containers or Ziploc bags; keep in your refrigerator for up to 3 to 4 days.
For freezing, place the meat mixture in airtight containers or heavy-duty freezer bags. Freeze up to 2 to 3 months. Defrost in the refrigerator. Bon appétit!

155. Beef Brisket with Provolone Cheese

(Ready in about 6 hours | Servings 8)

Per serving: 519 Calories; 39.6g Fat; 2.7g Carbs; 34.4g Protein; 0.6g Fiber

INGREDIENTS

2 pounds beef brisket
2 tablespoons soy sauce
1/2 cup beef bone broth
2 tablespoons fresh coriander, chopped

2 garlic cloves, minced
1 rosemary springs
1 thyme sprig
2 tablespoons lard, room temperature

1 onion, cut into wedges
1/3 cup Marsala wine
Salt and pepper, to season
1 cup Provolone cheese, sliced

DIRECTIONS

Place all ingredients, except for the Provolone cheese, in your Slow Cooker.
Cook on High settings about 6 hours. Cut the beef brisket into eight portions.

STORING

Divide the beef brisket between airtight containers or Ziploc bags; keep in your refrigerator for 3 to 5 days.
For freezing, place beef brisket in airtight containers or heavy-duty freezer bags. Freeze up to 3 months. Defrost in the refrigerator.
Top the beef brisket with the slices of Provolone cheese and place under the preheated broiler for 5 to 6 minutes or until cheese melts. Enjoy!

156. Greek-Style Meatloaf

(Ready in about 55 minutes | Servings 8)

Per serving: 442 Calories; 20.6g Fat; 4.9g Carbs; 56.3g Protein; 0.7g Fiber

INGREDIENTS

2 ½ pounds ground beef
8 slices of bacon
2 teaspoons Greek seasoning mix
1 tablespoon Dijon mustard

3 teaspoons olive oil
6 ounces Halloumi cheese, crumbled
2 eggs, beaten
1 tablespoon Greek red wine

1/2 cup Greek black olives, chopped
1 red onion, finely chopped
1/4 cup half-and-half

DIRECTIONS

In a frying pan, heat the oil over a moderate flame. Once hot, cook the onion and beef until the onion is tender and the beef is no longer pink or 5 to 6 minutes.
Then, thoroughly combine half-and-half, cheese eggs, seasoning mix, mustard, wine and olives; add in sautéed mixture. Mix until everything is well combined.
Press the mixture into a loaf pan. Top the meatloaf with the bacon slices and cover with a piece of foil.
Bake in the preheated oven at 385 degrees F for 35 to 40 minutes. Remove the foil and bake for a further 13 minutes.

STORING

Wrap your meatloaf tightly with heavy-duty aluminum foil or plastic wrap. Then, keep in your refrigerator for up to 3 to 4 days.
For freezing, wrap your meatloaf tightly to prevent freezer burn. Freeze up to 3 to 4 months. Defrost in the refrigerator. Bon appétit!

157. Restaurant-Style Soup with Lime-Chili Drizzle

(Ready in about 1 hour 10 minutes | Servings 6)

Per serving: 375 Calories; 14.4g Fat; 4.8g Carbs; 47.6g Protein; 2.8g Fiber

INGREDIENTS

2 pounds beef chuck-eye roast, cubed
1 medium leek, chopped
1/2 cup green peas, frozen
1 tablespoon ghee
1/2 cup bell peppers, chopped

1 cup tomato sauce
6 cups beef bone broth
1 parsnip, chopped
1 celery with leaves, chopped
1 bay laurel

For the Lime-Chili Drizzle:
2 red chilies
2 tablespoons lime juice
1 tablespoon extra-virgin olive oil

DIRECTIONS

In a heavy-bottomed pot, melt the ghee over a moderately high heat. Sear the beef for about 5 minutes, stirring continuously, until well browned on all sides; set aside.

In the same pot, cook the leek, parsnip, celery, and peppers until they've softened. Add in the tomato sauce, beef bone broth and bay laurel; bring to a boil.

Turn the heat to simmer; partially cover and continue to cook for 45 to 50 minutes. Add in the green peas and continue to cook for about 12 minutes longer.

Make the lime-chili drizzle by whisking the ingredients.

STORING

Spoon the soup into airtight containers; keep in your refrigerator for up to 4 days.

For freezing, place the soup in airtight containers or heavy-duty freezer bags. Freeze up to 4 to 6 months. Defrost in your refrigerator. Garnish with the lime-chili drizzle and serve hot!

158. Omelet with New York Strip Steak

(Ready in about 30 minutes | Servings 6)

Per serving: 429 Calories; 27.8g Fat; 3.2g Carbs; 39.1g Protein; 0.8g Fiber

INGREDIENTS

2 tablespoons butter, at room temperature
1 ½ pounds New York strip, cut into cubes
Flaky sea salt and pepper, to season
1/2 teaspoon smoked paprika

1/2 cup scallions, chopped
2 garlic cloves, pressed
2 Spanish peppers, deveined and chopped
6 eggs

DIRECTIONS

Ina frying pan, melt the butter over a moderately high heat. Cook the beef until browned on all sided or for 10 to 12 minutes. Season with salt, pepper, and paprika; reserve.

In the same pan, cook the scallions, garlic, and pepper until just tender and aromatic.

Add in the eggs and gently stir to combine. Continue to cook, covered, for 10 minutes more or until the eggs are set.

STORING

Slice the omelet into six pieces. Place each of them in an airtight container or Ziploc bag; place in the refrigerator for up to 3 to 4 days.

To freeze, place the omelet pieces in separate Ziploc bags and freeze up to 3 months. Defrost in your microwave for a few minutes. Bon appétit!

159. Autumn Ground Chuck Casserole

(Ready in about 55 minutes | Servings 6)

Per serving: 467 Calories; 37g Fat; 4.9g Carbs; 27.1g Protein; 3.1g Fiber

INGREDIENTS

1 pound ground chuck
1 head of cabbage, cut into quarters
1 yellow onion, chopped
1/2 teaspoon mustard seeds

1 ½ cups Ricotta cheese, crumbled
8 slices Colby cheese
2 eggs
1/2 teaspoon fennel seeds

Salt and black pepper, to taste
1 cup tomato sauce
2 slices bacon, chopped
1 teaspoon dried rosemary

DIRECTIONS

Parboil the cabbage in a pot of a lightly salted water for 4 to 5 minutes; drain and reserve.

Then, cook the ground chuck for about 5 minutes until it is no longer pink. Add in the onion and bacon and continue to sauté for 4 minutes more.

Stir in the spices and tomato sauce; bring it to a boil. Turn the heat to simmer; partially cover, and continue to cook an additional 7 minutes.

Spoon 1/2 of the mixture into the bottom of a lightly oiled casserole dish. Top with a layer of the boiled cabbage leaves. Repeat the layers one more time.

Then, thoroughly combine the eggs, Ricotta cheese, and Colby cheese. Top your casserole with the cheese mixture; bake at 390 degrees F for 25 to 30 minutes or until cooked through.

STORING

Slice the casserole into six pieces. Divide the pieces into airtight containers; it will last for 3 to 4 days in the refrigerator.

For freezing, place each portion in a separate heavy-duty freezer bag. Freeze up to 2 to 3 months. Defrost in the microwave or refrigerator. Bon appétit!

160. Porterhouse Steak with Sriracha Sauce

(Ready in about 15 minutes + marinating time | Servings 4)

Per serving: 292 Calories; 14.3g Fat; 3.9g Carbs; 36.9g Protein; 0.6g Fiber

INGREDIENTS

1 ½ pounds Porterhouse steak, cubed
1/2 tablespoon lard, melted
Salt and pepper, to taste
1 teaspoon celery seeds

1/2 teaspoon dried rosemary
1/2 cup green onions, chopped
1 tablespoon fresh cilantro, chopped
2 tablespoons coconut aminos

1 teaspoon Sriracha sauce
1 tablespoon ginger-garlic paste

DIRECTIONS

In a ceramic bowl, thoroughly combine the coconut aminos, Sriracha sauce, ginger-garlic paste, salt, pepper, celery seeds, rosemary, and green onions.

Add in the cubed beef and allow it to marinate in your refrigerator for 1 hour.

Melt the lard in a frying pan over medium-high heat. Cook the Porterhouse steak for 5 to 6 minutes until it is fall-apart-tender. Add in the cilantro and remove from the heat.

STORING

Divide the Porterhouse steak between airtight containers; keep in your refrigerator for up to 3 to 4 days.

For freezing, place the Porterhouse steak in airtight containers or heavy-duty freezer bags. Freeze up to 2 to 3 months. Defrost in the refrigerator. Bon appétit!

161. Saucy Flank Steak with Leeks

(Ready in about 2 hours 15 minutes | Servings 4)

Per serving: 238 Calories; 9.2g Fat; 6.3g Carbs; 27.4g Protein; 0.6g Fiber

INGREDIENTS

1 tablespoon lard, room temperature
1 pound flank steak, thinly sliced
1 cup leeks, sliced
1 parsnip, chopped

1 heaping teaspoon garlic, thinly sliced
1/2 teaspoon cardamom
1 teaspoon fresh ginger root, minced
1/2 teaspoon paprika

1/3 cup port wine
1 ½ cups beef stock

DIRECTIONS

Melt the lard in a heavy-bottomed skillet over a moderately high heat. Cook the beef for about 12 minutes until no longer pink; reserve.

In the pan drippings, cook the leeks, parsnip and garlic approximately 3 minutes until they are tender and fragrant.

Add in the other ingredients and bring to a boil. Immediately reduce the heat to a simmer. Partially cover and continue to cook about 2 hours.

STORING

Divide the flank steak between airtight containers; keep in your refrigerator for up to 3 to 4 days.

For freezing, place the flank steak in airtight containers or heavy-duty freezer bags. Freeze up to 2 to 3 months. Defrost in the refrigerator. Enjoy!

162. Beef Tenderloin with Cabbage

(Ready in about 20 minutes + marinating time | Servings 4)

Per serving: 321 Calories; 14g Fat; 5.3g Carbs; 36.7g Protein; 1.4g Fiber

INGREDIENTS

1 pound beef tenderloin, cut into bite-sized strips
1 tablespoon fish sauce
Sea salt and pepper, to taste
1/2 teaspoon dried marjoram

1/2 teaspoon dried rosemary
1/2 teaspoon dried basil
2 tablespoons olive oil
1 red onion, chopped
1 teaspoon garlic, minced

1 cup cabbage, shredded
1 Spanish pepper, deseeded and chopped

DIRECTIONS

Toss the beef tenderloin with the fish sauce and spices. Allow it to marinate in your refrigerator for at least 2 hours.

In a Dutch oven, heat the olive oil over a moderately high heat. Cook the marinated beef for about 5 minutes, stirring periodically to ensure even cooking.

Add in the onions and garlic and cook for 2 minutes more. Now, stir in the cabbage and pepper; turn the heat to a simmer.

Continue to simmer, partially covered, for 10 to 12 minutes more.

STORING

Place the beef and cabbage in airtight containers or Ziploc bags; keep in your refrigerator for up to 3 to 5 days.

For freezing, place the beef and cabbage in airtight containers or heavy-duty freezer bags. Freeze up to 5 months. Defrost in the refrigerator. Bon appétit!

163. Spicy Ground Beef Bowl

(Ready in about 40 minutes | Servings 6)

Per serving: 361 Calories; 21.9g Fat; 6.4g Carbs; 29g Protein; 2g Fiber

INGREDIENTS

1 ½ pounds ground beef
1 teaspoon Fresno pepper, minced
1/2 teaspoon dried rosemary
1/2 teaspoon dried thyme
1/2 teaspoon red pepper flakes
1/4 teaspoon mustard seeds, ground
2 tablespoons butter, room temperature
1 bay laurel

1 onion, chopped
1 teaspoon garlic, minced
1 cup tomato puree
1/2 cup port wine
Sea salt and ground black pepper, to taste

For Ketogenic Tortillas:
1 tablespoon flaxseed meal
1/3 teaspoon baking powder
6 tablespoons water
4 egg whites
1/4 cup almond meal
1/4 teaspoon granulated Swerve
A pinch of salt

DIRECTIONS

Melt the butter in a large saucepan over a moderately high flame.
Brown the ground beef for about 5 minutes, stirring and crumbling it with a wide spatula. Stir in all seasonings, onion, garlic, and Fresno pepper. Continue to cook for a further 10 minutes.
Add in the tomato puree and port wine. Turn the heat to a simmer, partially cover, and continue to cook for 15 to 20 minutes.
To make the tortillas, whisk the eggs, almond meal, flaxseed meal, and baking powder until well combined. Add in water, Swerve and salt and whisk until everything is well combined.
Cook the tortillas in a lightly oiled skillet that is previously preheated over medium-high heat. Repeat until you run out of ingredients.

STORING

Place the ground beef mixture in airtight containers; keep in your refrigerator for 3 to 4 days.
Freeze the ground beef mixture in airtight containers or heavy-duty freezer bags. Freeze up to 2 to 3 months.
Defrost them in the refrigerator and reheat in the microwave.
Cover the tortillas with foil to prevent drying out; keep in the refrigerator for 1 to 2 days. For freezing, place a sheet of wax paper between each tortilla; then, wrap the tortillas tightly in a piece of foil; freeze up to 2 months. Enjoy!

164. Winter Beef and Beer Stew

(Ready in about 1 hour | Servings 6)

Per serving: 444 Calories; 14.2g Fat; 6.1g Carbs; 66.3g Protein; 2g Fiber

INGREDIENTS

1 ½ pounds chuck roast, cut into small chunks
1 ½ cups tomato puree
3 cups beef bone broth

1 parsnip, chopped
1 cup ale beer
1 bay leaf
1 ½ tablespoons olive oil

1/2 teaspoon mustard seeds
1/4 cup basil leaves, snipped
1 cup red onions, chopped
1 celery with leaves, chopped

DIRECTIONS

Heat the olive oil in a heavy-bottomed pot or Dutch oven over medium-high flame. Cook the chuck roast for about 6 minutes or until it is browned; set aside.
Sauté the vegetables in the same pot for about 8 minutes or until tender and fragrant, stirring occasionally.
Add in the remaining ingredients and bring to a boil. Turn the heat to a simmer and continue to cook, partially covered, for about 45 minutes.

STORING

Spoon your stew into airtight containers; keep in your refrigerator for 3 to 4 days.
For freezing, place your stew in heavy-duty freezer bags. When the bags are frozen through, stack them up like file folders to save space in the freezer. Freeze up to 3 to 4 months.
Defrost in the microwave or refrigerator. Bon appétit!

165. Mexican-Style Stuffed Tomatoes

(Ready in about 35 minutes | Servings 4)

Per serving: 244 Calories; 9.6g Fat; 6g Carbs; 28.9g Protein; 3.2g Fiber

INGREDIENTS

8 tomatoes, scoop out the pulp and chop it
3/4 cup Mexican cheese blend, crumbled
1 pound ground chuck
2 tablespoons tomato sauce

Flaky salt and pepper, to taste
1 teaspoon ancho chili powder
1/2 teaspoon caraway seeds
1 tablespoon butter

1 cup onions, chopped
2 cloves garlic, minced
1 teaspoon dried parsley flakes
1/2 cup vegetable broth

DIRECTIONS

Start by preheating your oven to 350 degrees F. Lightly grease a casserole dish with cooking spray.
In a sauté pan, melt the butter over a moderately high flame. Now, cook the onion and garlic until tender and fragrant.
Add in the ground chuck and continue to cook for 5 to 6 minutes, breaking apart with a wide spatula.
Add in the tomato sauce, salt, and pepper. Divide the filling between the prepared tomatoes.
Place the stuffed tomatoes in a lightly oiled baking dish. Mix the scooped tomato pulp with the ancho chili powder and caraway seeds; salt to taste and pour it into the baking dish.
Bake in the preheated oven at 360 degrees F for about 25 minutes until the tomatoes have softened and everything is thoroughly cooked.

STORING

Place the stuffed tomatoes in airtight containers; keep in your refrigerator for 3 to 4 days.
Wrap each stuffed tomato tightly in several layers of plastic wrap and squeeze the air out. Place them in airtight containers; they can be frozen for up to 1 month.
Reheat the thawed stuffed tomatoes at 200 degrees F until they are completely warm. Top with cheese and place under preheated broiled for 5 minutes until hot and bubbly. Enjoy!

166. Breakfast Beef Sausage Quiche

(Ready in about 45 minutes | Servings 4)

Per serving: 289 Calories; 19.7g Fat; 6.3g Carbs; 19.8g Protein; 1.4g Fiber

INGREDIENTS

1 cup cauliflower, broken into florets
1 pound beef sausages, sliced
2 Italian pepper, thinly sliced
1 onion, chopped

2 garlic cloves, minced
6 eggs
2 tablespoons Greek-style yogurt
Salt and black pepper, to taste

1 teaspoon rosemary
1/2 teaspoon caraway seeds

DIRECTIONS

In a preheated saucepan, cook the beef sausage over a moderately high flame.
Add in the peppers, onion, cauliflower, garlic, and spices; continue to sauté for 10 minutes more or until the cauliflower is crisp-tender.
Spoon the sautéed mixture into a lightly oiled casserole dish. Whisk the eggs until pale and frothy; add in yogurt and whisk to combine well.
Pour the eggs/yogurt mixture over the top and bake at 365 degrees F for 30 to 35 minutes.

STORING

Slice the quiche into four pieces; divide between airtight containers or Ziploc bags; keep in your refrigerator for up to 3 days.
For freezing, place the quiche in airtight containers or heavy-duty freezer bags. Freeze up to 3 months. Once thawed in the refrigerator, heat in the microwave until warmed through. Enjoy!

167. Zoodles with Bolognese Sauce

(Ready in about 1 hour 35 minutes | Servings 4)

Per serving: 477 Calories; 25.6g Fat; 6.3g Carbs; 41.8g Protein; 1.4g Fiber

INGREDIENTS

For Bolognese:
2 tablespoons sesame oil
1 shallot, finely chopped
1 teaspoon garlic, thinly sliced
1 cup celery with leaves, finely chopped

2 slices bacon, chopped
1 pound ground chuck
1 cup tomato puree
1/2 cup Sauvignon blanc wine
1/2 cup water

1 tablespoons Greek spice mix
Salt and ground black pepper, to taste
For Zucchini Spaghetti:
4 zucchinis, peeled and jullianed (tagliatelle shape)

DIRECTIONS

In a saucepan, heat the sesame oil over a moderately high flame. Sweat the shallot until just tender and translucent; add in the garlic and celery and continue to cook until they are just tender and fragrant.
Stir in the bacon and ground chuck; continue to cook for 6 to 7 more minutes, breaking up lumps with a fork.
Stir in the tomato puree, wine, water, and spices and continue to simmer, partially covered, for 1 hour 10 minutes.
Meanwhile, cook your zucchini in a lightly buttered wok for about 2 minutes or until they've softened.
Fold in the prepared Bolognese sauce and stir to combine well.

STORING

Place the mixture in airtight containers; keep in your refrigerator for 3 to 4 days.
Freeze the mixture in airtight containers or heavy-duty freezer bags. Freeze up to 2 to 3 months.
Defrost your Bolognese in the refrigerator and reheat in the microwave. Enjoy!

168. Cheesy Meatballs with Roasted Peppers

(Ready in about 1 hour | Servings 4)

Per serving: 348 Calories; 13.7g Fat; 5.9g Carbs; 42.8g Protein; 2.7g Fiber

INGREDIENTS

1 pound ground chuck
1 cup onions, chopped
2 garlic cloves
3 tablespoons Romano cheese, grated

1 cup tomato puree
1 egg
4 Spanish peppers, deveined and chopped
1 jalapeno pepper, deveined and minced

Salt and ground black pepper, to taste
1/2 cup Cheddar cheese, crumbled
1 ½ cups chicken broth
1/2 teaspoon mustard seeds

DIRECTIONS

Place the Spanish peppers under the preheated broiler for about 15 minutes. Peel the peppers and discard the seeds.
Thoroughly combine the jalapeno pepper, onion, garlic, Romano cheese, egg, salt, black pepper, and ground chuck; add in roasted peppers. Roll the mixture into balls.
In a lightly oiled skillet, sear the meatballs until browned on all sides about 8 to 10 minutes.
In a saucepan, heat the tomato puree, chicken broth, and mustard seeds; bring to a boil. Turn the heat to a simmer and continue to cook until cooked through. Fold in the prepared meatballs.

STORING

Place your meatballs along with the tomato sauce in airtight containers or Ziploc bags; keep in your refrigerator for up to 3 to 4 days.
Freeze your meatballs along with the tomato sauce in airtight containers or heavy-duty freezer bags. Freeze up to 3 to 4 months. To defrost, slowly reheat in a saucepan. Serve topped with Cheddar cheese. Bon appétit!

169. Grilled Flank Steak

(Ready in about 20 minutes + marinating time | Servings 6)

Per serving: 314 Calories; 11.4g Fat; 1g Carbs; 48.2g Protein; 0.7g Fiber

INGREDIENTS

2 pounds flank steak
2 garlic cloves, smashed
1 teaspoon Mediterranean spice mix
Celery salt and ground black pepper, to taste
2 tablespoons dry sherry

2 tablespoons olive oil
1 tablespoon fish sauce
1 tablespoon coconut aminos
2 tablespoons BBQ sauce

DIRECTIONS

In a ceramic bowl, thoroughly combine the fish sauce, coconut aminos, BBQ sauce, garlic, Mediterranean spice mix, salt, pepper, dry sherry, and olive oil.

Add in the flank steaks and let it marinate for 2 hours in your refrigerator.

Grill the flank steaks over direct heat for about 5 minutes per side (a meat thermometer should read 135 degrees F).

STORING

Cut the steak into six pieces; divide the pieces between six airtight containers; keep in your refrigerator for up to 3 to 4 days.

For freezing, place the steaks in airtight containers or heavy-duty freezer bags. Freeze up to 2 to 3 months. Defrost in the refrigerator. Bon appétit!

170. Beef Kabobs with Mustard Relish

(Ready in about 20 minutes | Servings 6)

Per serving: 413 Calories; 21.1g Fat; 5.8g Carbs; 45.3g Protein; 1g Fiber

INGREDIENTS

2 pounds beef shoulder, cut into cubes
2 teaspoons stone-ground mustard
3 tablespoons olive oil
2 ½ tablespoons apple cider vinegar

1 cup shallots, cut into wedges
1 large zucchini, sliced
2 garlic cloves, minced
1 jalapeno pepper, minced

2 bell peppers, sliced
Salt and ground black pepper, to taste

DIRECTIONS

Season the meat and vegetables with the salt and pepper to taste. Brush them with a nonstick cooking spray.

Thread the meat cubes and vegetables onto bamboo skewers. Grill the beef kabobs for about 10 minutes, flipping them occasionally to ensure even cooking.

Make the relish by whisking the mustard, garlic, jalapeno pepper, olive oil and apple cider vinegar.

STORING

Place your kabobs in airtight containers; keep in your refrigerator for up to 3 to 4 days.

Place the mustard relish in a glass container and cover with the lid; keep in your refrigerator for up to 3 to 4 days.

For freezing, place your kabobs in airtight containers or heavy-duty freezer bags. Freeze up to 2 to 3 months. Defrost in the refrigerator. Bon appétit!

171. Thai Steak Salad

(Ready in about 15 minutes | Servings 4)

Per serving: 288 Calories; 21.5g Fat; 8.6g Carbs; 15.8g Protein; 5g Fiber

INGREDIENTS

1/2 pound flank steak, trimmed
1 bunch fresh Thai basil
2 tablespoons white wine
1 garlic clove, minced

1 avocado, pitted, peeled and sliced
1 bell pepper, sliced
1 teaspoon coconut aminos
2 tablespoons olive oil

1 cup scallions, chopped
1 Bird's eye chili, minced
1/4 cup sunflower seeds
Salt and black pepper, to season

DIRECTIONS

Toss the flank steak with the salt, pepper and coconut aminos.

In a frying pan, heat 1 tablespoon of olive oil over a moderate heat. Cook the scallions and garlic until tender for 3 to 4 minutes; reserve.

In the same pan, heat another tablespoon of olive oil. Once hot, cook the flank steak for about 5 minutes per side; add in the sautéed mixture.

Toss the remaining ingredients in a nice salad bowl; toss to combine well.

STORING

Cut the steak into thin pieces using a knife, slicing against the grain; divide the pieces between four airtight containers; keep in your refrigerator for up to 3 to 4 days.

Place the salad in airtight containers; keep in your refrigerator for up to 3 to 4 days.

For freezing, place the steaks in airtight containers or heavy-duty freezer bags. Freeze up to 2 to 3 months. Defrost in the refrigerator.

Serve the flank steak on top of the salad and enjoy!

172. Swiss Cheese and Beef Dipping Sauce

(Ready in about 20 minutes | Servings 8)

Per serving: 333 Calories; 29.2g Fat; 2.9g Carbs; 14.7g Protein; 0.1g Fiber

INGREDIENTS

1 ½ cups beef sausages, crumbled
1 tablespoon olive oil
1 shallot, chopped

2 garlic cloves, minced
2 tablespoons fresh Italian parsley, roughly chopped

1 ½ cups Swiss cheese, shredded
1 cup Ricotta cheese, at room temperature

DIRECTIONS

In a saucepan, heat the olive oil over a moderately high flame. Cook the shallot until tender and translucent or about 4 minutes.
Stir in the garlic and continue to cook for 30 seconds more until fragrant. Add in the sausage, cheese and parsley.
Bake in the preheated oven at 320 degrees F for 15 to 18 minutes.

STORING

Place the cheese and beef dipping sauce in an airtight container; keep in your refrigerator for up 3 to 4 days. Enjoy!

173. Beef and Tomato Casserole

(Ready in about 25 minutes | Servings 4)

Per serving: 509 Calories; 29.6g Fat; 6.1g Carbs; 45.2g Protein; 1.6g Fiber

INGREDIENTS

2 tablespoons sun-dried tomatoes, chopped
1 cup Colby cheese, grated
1 tablespoon lard, room temperature

1 pound ground chuck
2 garlic cloves, minced
1/2 cup onions, finely chopped
2 tomatoes, chopped

1/2 tablespoon dill relish
Sea salt and ground black pepper to taste
1/2 teaspoon mustard powder
3/4 cup Ricotta cream

DIRECTIONS

Start by preheating your oven to 395 degrees F.
Melt the lard in a saucepan over medium-high flame. Once hot, brown the ground chuck, breaking apart with a spatula.
Add in the garlic and onions and cook until they are tender and aromatic. Stir in the tomatoes, dill relish and seasonings.
Spoon the sautéed mixture into a lightly-oiled baking dish. Top with the cheese. Bake in the preheated oven for about 20 minutes.

STORING

Slice your casserole into four pieces; divide between airtight containers or Ziploc bags; keep in your refrigerator for up to 3 days.
For freezing, place your casserole in airtight containers or heavy-duty freezer bags. Freeze up to 3 months. Once thawed in the refrigerator, heat in the microwave until warmed through. Enjoy!

174. Beef Sausage with Aioli Sauce

(Ready in about 15 minutes | Servings 4)

Per serving: 549 Calories; 49.3g Fat; 4.7g Carbs; 16.2g Protein; 0.8g Fiber

INGREDIENTS

1 pound beef sausage, crumbled
Kosher salt and pepper, to taste
2 tablespoons coriander
1 tablespoon olive oil

1/2 cup onion, chopped
1 teaspoon garlic, finely minced
For the Sauce:
1/4 cup aioli

1 teaspoon paprika
1 ½ teaspoon mustard

DIRECTIONS

In a frying pan, heat the olive oil over a moderate heat. Stir in the onion and garlic and continue to cook for 2 to 3 minutes or until they've softened.
Stir in the beef sausage; continue to cook for 3 to 4 minutes or until no longer pink. Add in the salt, pepper, and coriander and stir to combine well.
Make the sauce by whisking all the sauce ingredients.

STORING

Place the sausage in four Ziploc bags; keep in your refrigerator for a week.
Place the sauce in an airtight container; keep in your refrigerator for a week.
For freezing, divide your sausage among Ziploc bags and freeze up to 3 to 4 months. Thaw them in the refrigerator. You can reheat the sausage in a pan. Enjoy!

175. Tender and Spicy Flank Steak

(Ready in about 1 hour 20 minutes + marinating time | Servings 4)

Per serving: 326 Calories; 11.1g Fat; 1.6g Carbs; 52g Protein; 0g Fiber

INGREDIENTS

1 ½ pounds flank steak
1/2 teaspoon ancho chile powder

1 teaspoon fresh ginger root, minced
Sea salt and black pepper, to taste

1 teaspoon celery seeds

DIRECTIONS

Place all ingredients in a ceramic dish and let it marinate for 1 hour in your refrigerator.
Preheat your grill to medium-high.
Then, grill the flank steak for about 15 minutes, basting them with the reserved marinade.

STORING

Cut the steak into four pieces; divide the pieces between six airtight containers; keep in your refrigerator for up to 3 to 4 days.
For freezing, place the steaks in airtight containers or heavy-duty freezer bags. Freeze up to 2 to 3 months. Defrost in the refrigerator. Bon appétit!

176. Old-Fashioned Beef Mélange

(Ready in about 1 hour 35 minutes | Servings 6)

Per serving: 375 Calories; 13.3g Fat; 5.6g Carbs; 55.1g Protein; 1.2g Fiber

INGREDIENTS

2 pounds beef rib-eye steak, cubed
1 bay laurel
Salt and pepper, to taste
1 cup leeks, chopped
3 teaspoons lard, room temperature

1 teaspoon ginger-garlic paste
1 teaspoon dried parsley flakes
6 cups roasted vegetable broth
1 tablespoon oyster sauce
2 vine-ripened tomatoes, pureed

1 tablespoon paprika
1 teaspoon celery seeds, crushed
1/2 teaspoon mustard seeds

DIRECTIONS

Melt 1 teaspoon of lard in a large stock pot over a moderately high heat. Now, brown the rib-eye steak until it is no longer pink or about 6 minutes.
Season with salt and pepper to taste; reserve.
Heat the remaining 2 teaspoons of lard and sauté the leeks until tender and fragrant.
Now, add in the remaining ingredients. Continue to cook, partially covered, for 1 hour 20 minutes.

STORING

Spoon your mélange into six airtight containers; keep in your refrigerator for up to 4 days.
For freezing, place your mélange in airtight containers or heavy-duty freezer bags. Freeze up to 4 to 6 months. Defrost in the microwave or refrigerator. Bon appétit!

177. Hearty Winter Beef Stew

(Ready in about 40 minutes | Servings 6)

Per serving: 259 Calories; 10.1g Fat; 4.1g Carbs; 35.7g Protein; 0.5g Fiber

INGREDIENTS

1 ½ pounds beef shoulder, cubed
1 tablespoon olive oil
1 tablespoon white mushrooms, thinly sliced

1 teaspoon dried caraway seeds
1/4 teaspoon hot paprika
1 bay leaf
4 cups beef bone broth

1 egg, lightly whisked
1 cup onions, thinly sliced
1 teaspoon garlic, chopped
Salt and pepper, to taste

DIRECTIONS

In a heavy-bottomed pot, heat the olive oil over a moderately high flame.
Sear the beef for about 7 minutes until it's just browned; reserve.
In the same pot, cook the onions for about 3 minutes or until fragrant. Stir in the garlic and mushrooms and continue to cook for a minute or so.
Stir in the remaining ingredients, cover, and cook for 35 minutes more. Add in the egg, remove from the heat, and stir to combine.

STORING

Spoon your stew into airtight containers; keep in your refrigerator for up to 4 days.
For freezing, place your stew in airtight containers or heavy-duty freezer bags. Freeze up to 4 to 6 months. Defrost in the microwave or refrigerator. Bon appétit!

178. Authentic Hungarian Beef Paprikash

(Ready in about 1 hour 25 minutes | Servings 4)

Per serving: 357 Calories; 15.8g Fat; 5g Carbs; 40.2g Protein; 2.2g Fiber

INGREDIENTS

1 ¼ pounds beef roast, diced
1 tablespoon Hungarian paprika
4 cups beef broth
1 celery with leaves, chopped

2 bell pepper, deveined and chopped
1 tablespoon flaxseed meal
1 cup leeks, peeled and chopped
Salt and pepper, to taste

2 tablespoons lard, room temperature
1/2 cup dry white wine

DIRECTIONS

In a heavy-bottomed pot, melt the lard over moderate heat. Cook the beef and leeks for about 5 minutes. Sprinkle with salt, pepper, and Hungarian paprika.
Add in wine to deglaze the bottom of your pot. Add in the beef broth, celery, and peppers. Turn the heat to a simmer and continue to cook for a further 1 hour 10 minutes.
Stir in the flaxseed meal; continue stirring for about 4 minutes to thicken the liquid.

STORING

Spoon the Hungarian paprikash into airtight containers; keep in your refrigerator for up to 4 days.
For freezing, place the Hungarian paprikash in airtight containers or heavy-duty freezer bags. Freeze up to 4 to 6 months. Defrost in the microwave or refrigerator. Bon appétit!

179. Family Sausage and Vegetable Casserole

(Ready in about 30 minutes | Servings 4)

Per serving: 424 Calories; 32.4g Fat; 6g Carbs; 23.7g Protein; 1.6g Fiber

INGREDIENTS

4 beef sausages, sliced
2 Spanish peppers, sliced
1 tablespoon butter
2 garlic cloves, finely chopped

1 teaspoon dry chili pepper, crushed
Salt and pepper, to taste
1 teaspoon paprika
1 ½ cups vegetable broth

1 yellow onion, sliced
1 cup cauliflower, broken into small florets
1 celery stalk, chopped

DIRECTIONS

In a frying pan, melt the butter over a moderately high heat. Brown the sausage until browned on all sides or about 5 minutes; reserve.
Sauté the onion, cauliflower, peppers, celery, and garlic for about 8 minutes or until the vegetables have softened.
Place the sautéed vegetables in a lightly buttered baking dish. Season with salt, pepper, and paprika. Nestle the reserved sausages within the vegetables.
Pour in the vegetable broth and bake in the preheated oven at 360 degrees F for 10 to 12 minutes.

STORING

Slice your casserole into four pieces; divide between airtight containers or Ziploc bags; keep in your refrigerator for up to 3 days.
For freezing, place your casserole in airtight containers or heavy-duty freezer bags. Freeze up to 3 months. Once thawed in the refrigerator, heat in the microwave until warmed through. Enjoy!

180. The Best Keto Lasagna Ever

(Ready in about 1 hour 30 minutes | Servings 6)

Per serving: 494 Calories; 41g Fat; 3.8g Carbs; 24.1g Protein; 1.1g Fiber

INGREDIENTS

For the Lasagna Sheets:
1 1/2 cup Romano cheese, grated
1/2 teaspoon dried Mediterranean spice mix
3 eggs, whisked
6 ounces cream cheese, at room temperature

For the Filling:
1 ½ pounds ground beef
1 cup marinara sauce
2 cups cream cheese
1 cup Cheddar cheese

1 onion, chopped
1 tablespoon butter, room temperature
1 teaspoon fresh garlic, smashed
2 slices bacon, chopped

DIRECTIONS

Begin by preheating your oven to 365 degrees F. Line a baking sheet with parchment paper.
Combine the eggs and 6 ounces of cream cheese with a hand mixer. Stir in the remaining ingredients for the lasagna sheets and continue to mix until everything is well combined.
Spread the mixture onto a baking sheet and bake in the preheated oven for 17 to 20 minutes. Let it cool and then, place in your refrigerator for about 30 minutes. Slice into lasagna sheets and reserve.
In a saucepan, melt the butter over a moderately high heat. Cook the ground beef for about 4 minutes or until no longer pink.
Stir in the onion, garlic and bacon; continue to cook an additional 4 minutes. Add in the marinara sauce and continue to simmer an additional 12 minutes.
Pour 1/4 cup of the beef sauce into the bottom of a lightly greased baking dish. Top with the first lasagna sheet. Repeat until you run out of ingredients, ending with the sauce layer.
Bake for about 20 minutes or until heated through.

STORING

Place your lasagna in airtight container and keep in your refrigerator for up to 3 days.
For freezing, place your lasagna in airtight containers or heavy-duty freezer bags. Freeze up to 3 months. Once thawed in the refrigerator, heat in the microwave until warmed through.
Top with the cheese and place under the preheated broiled for 6 to 7 minutes or until the top is hot and bubbly. Enjoy!

181. Summer Cold Steak Salad

(Ready in about 20 minutes | Servings 6)

Per serving: 315 Calories; 13.8g Fat; 6.4g Carbs; 37.5g Protein; 0.9g Fiber

INGREDIENTS

1 ½ pounds rib-eye steak, 1-inch thick piece

1 head of butter lettuce, leaves separated and torn into pieces

1 Serrano pepper, thinly sliced

1 onion, peeled and thinly sliced

1 cup cherry tomatoes, halved

1 Lebanese cucumber, sliced

2 bell peppers, thinly sliced

2 tablespoons fresh lime juice

1/4 cup extra-virgin olive oil

Salt and pepper, to taste

1/2 teaspoon dried Mediterranean spice mix

DIRECTIONS

Brush a frying pan with a nonstick cooking spray. One hot, cook the steak for about 3 to 4 minutes on each side for medium rare. After that, thinly slice the steak across the grain.

In a salad bowl, mix the remaining ingredients; toss to coat.

STORING

Place the steak in an airtight container and keep in your refrigerator for up to 3 to 4 days.

Place the salad in an airtight container and keep in your refrigerator for up to 2 days.

For freezing, place the steak in airtight containers or heavy-duty freezer bags. Freeze up to 2 to 3 months. Defrost in the refrigerator.

Place the steak on the top of your salad and serve. Bon appétit!

182. Beef and Broccoli Skillet

(Ready in about 20 minutes | Servings 4)

Per serving: 241 Calories; 7.6g Fat; 6g Carbs; 36g Protein; 3.9g Fiber

INGREDIENTS

1 pound ground beef

1 head broccoli, cut into small florets

2 garlic cloves, minced

1/2 teaspoon red pepper flakes, crushed

1/2 cup vegetable broth

2 teaspoons olive oil

1/2 teaspoon curry paste

1 large onion, sliced

Kosher salt and black pepper, to season

DIRECTIONS

In a cast-iron skillet, heat 1 teaspoon of the olive oil over a moderately high flame. Cook the broccoli for 3 to 4 minutes until crisp-tender. Stir in the garlic and onion and continue to cook for 2 to 3 minutes more until tender and aromatic. Reserve.

In the same skillet, heat another teaspoon of the oil and cook the beef until it is well browned, crumbling with a fork.

Add in the sauteed broccoli mixture, turn the heat to a simmer, and stir in the other ingredients. Cover and continue to cook for 12 minutes more.

STORING

Place the beef along with broccoli in airtight containers or Ziploc bags; keep in your refrigerator for up to 3 to 4 days.

For freezing, place the beef along with the broccoli in airtight containers or heavy-duty freezer bags. Freeze up to 2 to 3 months. Defrost in the refrigerator. Bon appétit!

183. Easy Roasted Skirt Steak

(Ready in about 25 minutes + marinating time | Servings 6)

Per serving: 343 Calories; 27.3g Fat; 3g Carbs; 20.1g Protein; 0.9g Fiber

INGREDIENTS

1 ½ pounds skirt steak

1 tablespoon stone-ground mustard

Sea salt and black pepper, to taste

2 tablespoons green garlic, chopped

1/2 cup dry red wine

1 tablespoon olive oil

DIRECTIONS

Remove the connective tissue from one side of your steak using a knife.

Place the skirt steak, mustard, salt, black pepper, green garlic, and red wine in a ceramic dish. Let it marinate in your refrigerator at least 1 hour.

Brush the marinated steak with olive oil and place on a parchment-lined baking pan. Bake in the preheated oven at 360 degrees F for about 20 minutes, basting with the reserved marinade.

STORING

Cut the steak into thin pieces using a knife, slicing against the grain; divide the pieces between six airtight containers; keep in your refrigerator for up to 3 to 4 days.

For freezing, place the steaks in airtight containers or heavy-duty freezer bags. Freeze up to 2 to 3 months. Defrost in the refrigerator. Bon appétit!

184. French Beef Soup with Ventrèche

(Ready in about 2 hours 10 minutes | Servings 4)

Per serving: 340 Calories; 19.6g Fat; 6.5g Carbs; 30.2g Protein; 2g Fiber

INGREDIENTS

1 pound beef stew meat, cubed
2 tablespoons butter
4 ounces ventrèche, chopped
4 cups vegetable broth
1 yellow onion, chopped

2 cloves garlic, minced
1 bell pepper, deveined and chopped
1 small-sized ripe tomato, crushed
2 tablespoons fresh chives, chopped
1 tablespoon cider vinegar

2 tablespoons dry red wine
1 celery rib, chopped
2 sprigs rosemary
1 tablespoon flaxseed meal, dissolved
in 2 tablespoons of cold water

DIRECTIONS

In a heavy-bottomed pot, melt 1 tablespoon of butter over a moderate heat. Cook the ventrèche for about 4 minutes and reserve.
Melt another tablespoon of butter. Once hot, sauté the onions, garlic, pepper, and celery for 3 to 4 minutes until they have softened. Add in the beef and continue to cook until browned.
Stir in the rosemary, tomato, vinegar, red wine, and broth. Turn the heat to a simmer, cover and continue to cook for a further 2 hours.
Add in the flaxseed slurry and continue to cook an additional 3 to 4 minutes or until thoroughly cooked. Add in the reserved ventrèche.

STORING

Spoon your soup into airtight containers; keep in your refrigerator for up to 4 days.
For freezing, place your soup in airtight containers or heavy-duty freezer bags. Freeze up to 4 to 6 months. Defrost in the microwave or refrigerator.
Serve with fresh chives. Bon appétit!

185. Finger-Lickin' Good Filet Mignon

(Ready in about 3 hours 30 minutes | Servings 8)

Per serving: 219 Calories; 7.2g Fat; 0.6g Carbs; 34.6g Protein; 0.3g Fiber

INGREDIENTS

2 pounds filet mignon
1 teaspoon porcini powder
1 teaspoon dried thyme

1/4 cup Marsala wine
1 tablespoon brown mustard
1 heaping teaspoon garlic, sliced

Sea salt and pepper, to taste

DIRECTIONS

Rub the filet mignon with mustard and garlic. Toss with spices and place on a lightly oiled baking pan. Pour in Marsala wine.
Roast in the preheated oven at 370 degrees F for 1 hour 30 minutes.
Turn the oven temperature to 310 degrees F and roast an additional 2 hours.

STORING

Place the filet mignon in airtight containers and keep in your refrigerator for up to 3 to 4 days.
For freezing, place the filet mignon in airtight containers or heavy-duty freezer bags. Freeze up to 2 to 3 months. Defrost in the refrigerator.
Bon appétit!

186. Spicy Beef Medley

(Ready in about 2 hours 10 minutes | Servings 4)

Per serving: 467 Calories; 18.7g Fat; 3.7g Carbs; 58g Protein; 2.1g Fiber

INGREDIENTS

1 ½ pounds chuck roast, cut into small
chunks
1 teaspoon garlic, minced
2 tablespoons butter
1 Serrano pepper, finely minced

1 celery with leaves, chopped
4 cups vegetable broth
1 tablespoon flaxseed meal, dissolved
in 2 tablespoons of water
1 large onion, chopped

2 bell peppers, chopped
Salt and pepper, to taste
1 teaspoon mustard seeds
1/4 teaspoon cardamom, ground

DIRECTIONS

In a Dutch oven, melt 1 tablespoon of butter and brown the beef, breaking apart with a fork; set aside.
Then, melt the remaining tablespoon of butter and sauté the vegetables until they've softened.
Add the reserved beef to the Dutch oven along with the vegetable broth. Add the seasonings and bring to a boil.
Reduce the heat to a simmer and continue to cook approximately 2 hours.
Stir in the flaxseed slurry. Let it cook, stirring continuously, until the cooking liquid has thickened about 2 minutes.

STORING

Spoon the beef medley into airtight containers; keep in your refrigerator for up to 4 days.
For freezing, place the beef medley in airtight containers or heavy-duty freezer bags. Freeze up to 4 to 6 months. Defrost in the microwave or refrigerator. Bon appétit!

187. Winter Sausage and Vegetable Bowl

(Ready in about 40 minutes | Servings 4)

Per serving: 250 Calories; 17.5g Fat; 5.4g Carbs; 6.8g Protein; 2.8g Fiber

INGREDIENTS

4 beef sausages, sliced
2 Italian peppers, deveined and chopped
1 large onion, chopped
2 tablespoons olive oil

1 celery rib, chopped
Salt and pepper, to taste
1 teaspoon fresh garlic, smashed
1 cup tomato sauce

1 teaspoon dried parsley flakes
1 ½ cups vegetable broth
1/4 cup dry red wine
2 rosemary sprigs

DIRECTIONS

In a saucepan, heat the oil over a moderately high heat. Brown the sausage for about 3 minutes, stirring periodically to ensure even cooking. Stir in the onion, garlic, peppers, and celery rib; season with salt and pepper to taste. Continue to cook for 6 to 7 minutes or until they've softened. Add in the other ingredients, bringing it to a rolling boil. Turn the heat to a simmer and continue to cook for 20 to 25 minutes or until heated through.

STORING

Place the sausage along with vegetables in four Ziploc bags; keep in your refrigerator for a week.
For freezing, divide your sausage along with vegetables among Ziploc bags and freeze up to 3 to 4 months. Thaw them in the refrigerator. You can reheat the sausage in a saucepan. Enjoy!

188. Easy Pan-Fried Skirt Steak

(Ready in about 20 minutes + marinating time | Servings 6)

Per serving: 350 Calories; 17.3g Fat; 2.1g Carbs; 42.7g Protein; 0.8g Fiber

INGREDIENTS

2 pounds skirt steak
1/2 cup onions, chopped
1/4 cup Pinot Noir

2 tablespoons sesame oil
2 tablespoons coconut aminos
2 garlic cloves, minced

1 teaspoon dried parsley flakes
1 teaspoon dried marjoram
Salt and pepper, to taste

DIRECTIONS

Place the skirt steak along with other ingredients in a ceramic dish. Let it marinate in your refrigerator overnight.
Preheat a lightly oiled frying pan over a moderately high heat. Cook your skirt steaks for 8 to 10 minutes per side. Bon appétit!

STORING

Cut the steak into thin pieces using a knife, slicing against the grain; divide the pieces between six airtight containers; keep in your refrigerator for up to 3 to 4 days.
For freezing, place the steaks in airtight containers or heavy-duty freezer bags. Freeze up to 2 to 3 months. Defrost in the refrigerator. Bon appétit!

189. Cheeseburger Soup with Herbs

(Ready in about 25 minutes | Servings 4)

Per serving: 326 Calories; 20.5g Fat; 4.5g Carbs; 26.8g Protein; 0.7g Fiber

INGREDIENTS

1/2 pound ground chuck
1 cup cream cheese
1 cup scallions, chopped

2 tablespoons butter, softened
1 celery with leaves, chopped
4 cups chicken broth

1/2 cup sour cream
1 tablespoon fresh parsley, chopped
1 tablespoon fresh basil, chopped

DIRECTIONS

Ina heavy-bottomed pot, melt the butter over a moderately high heat. Cook the ground chuck for about 5 minutes, crumbling with a fork; set aside.
Add in the scallions and celery and continue to cook for a further 4 minutes, adding a splash of broth if needed.
Add in parsley, basil, and broth; bring to a boil. Immediately reduce heat to a simmer. Add the cooked meat back to the pot, partially cover, and continue to cook for 8 to 10 minutes.
Add in the sour cream and let it cook for 3 minutes more until cooked through.

STORING

Spoon the soup into four airtight containers or Ziploc bags; keep in your refrigerator for up to 3 to 4 days.
For freezing, place the soup in airtight containers. It will maintain the best quality for about 4 to 6 months. Defrost in the refrigerator.
Add in the cheese and reheat in your pot for 5 to 6 minutes until the cheese has melted completely. Serve in individual bowls. Bon appétit!

190. Bacon-Wrapped Meatballs

(Ready in about 30 minutes | Servings 6)

Per serving: 399 Calories; 27g Fat; 1.8g Carbs; 37.7g Protein; 0.9g Fiber

INGREDIENTS

For the Meatballs:
1 ½ pounds ground chuck
6 slices bacon, cut into thirds lengthwise
1 egg, beaten
Sea salt and ground black pepper, to your liking

1 ½ tablespoons sesame oil
1/2 cup crushed pork rinds
1/2 cup onion, chopped
2 cloves garlic, smashed

For the Parsley Sauce:
1 cup fresh Italian parsley
Flaky salt, to taste
2 tablespoons sunflower seeds, soaked
1/2 tablespoon olive oil

DIRECTIONS

Thoroughly combine all ingredients for the meatballs. Roll the mixture into 18 balls and wrap each of them with a slice of bacon; secure with a toothpick.
Bake the meatballs in the preheated oven at 385 degrees F for about 30 minutes, rotating the pan once or twice.
Pulse all ingredients for the parsley sauce in your blender or food processor until your desired consistency is reached.

STORING

Place your meatballs in airtight containers or Ziploc bags; keep in your refrigerator for up to 3 to 4 days.
Place the parsley sauce in airtight containers and keep in your refrigerator for up to 7 days.
Freeze the meatballs in airtight containers or heavy-duty freezer bags. Freeze up to 3 to 4 months. To defrost, slowly reheat in a saucepan. Serve with the parsley sauce on the side. Bon appétit!

191. Slow Cooker Beef Shoulder

(Ready in about 6 hours + marinating time | Servings 6)

Per serving: 296 Calories; 12g Fat; 5g Carbs; 35.2g Protein; 0.6g Fiber

INGREDIENTS

1 ½ pounds beef shoulder
2 tablespoons coconut aminos
2 tablespoons olive oil
1 large-sized leek, chopped

2 celery stalks, chopped
1 cup chicken stock
1 teaspoon garlic, smashed
1 teaspoon Dijon mustard

Salt and black pepper, to taste
2 tablespoons Marsala wine

DIRECTIONS

Rub the beef shoulder with the garlic, mustard, salt, and black pepper. Add in Marsala wine and coconut aminos. Let it marinate for 3 hours in your refrigerator.
Heat the olive oil in your slow cooker and sauté the leeks until they've softened.
Then, cook the beef shoulder until it is golden-brown on top. Add in the celery and stock and stir to combine.
Cover with the lid and cook on Low heat setting for 5 to 6 hours.

STORING

Cut the beef shoulder into thin pieces using a knife, slicing against the grain; divide the pieces between six airtight containers; keep in your refrigerator for up to 3 to 4 days.
For freezing, place the beef shoulder in airtight containers or heavy-duty freezer bags. Freeze up to 2 to 3 months. Defrost in the refrigerator. Bon appétit!

192. Mexican-Style Keto Tacos

(Ready in about 30 minutes | Servings 4)

Per serving: 258 Calories; 19.3g Fat; 5g Carbs; 16.3g Protein; 1.9g Fiber

INGREDIENTS

1 ½ cups ground beef
6 slices bacon, chopped
2 teaspoon white vinegar
2 chili peppers, minced

Salt and pepper, to taste
1/2 teaspoon shallot powder
1/2 teaspoon ground cumin
1 cup tomato puree

1/2 cup cream of onion soup
1 ½ cups Mexican cheese blend, shredded

DIRECTIONS

Place 6 piles of the Mexican cheese on a parchment-lined baking pan; bake in the preheated oven at 385 degrees F for 13 to 15 minutes and let them cool slightly.
Then, in a frying pan, cook the ground beef until no longer pink or about 5 minutes. Add in the tomato puree, salt, pepper, shallot powder, and ground cumin; continue to cook for 5 minutes more.
In another pan, cook the bacon along with the remaining ingredients for about 3 minutes or until cooked through.

STORING

Place the meat mixture in airtight containers or Ziploc bags; keep in your refrigerator for up to 3 to 4 days.
Place the bacon sauce in airtight containers or Ziploc bags; keep in your refrigerator for up to 3 to 4 days.
Place the cheese tacos in airtight containers and keep in your refrigerator for up to 3 to 4 days.
For freezing, place the meat mixture in airtight containers or heavy-duty freezer bags. Freeze up to 2 to 3 months. Defrost in the refrigerator. Bon appétit!
Assemble your tacos. Divide the meat mixture among the 6 taco shells; top with the bacon sauce. Enjoy!

193. Beef Stuffed Avocado

(Ready in about 20 minutes | Servings 6)

Per serving: 407 Calories; 28.8g Fat; 16.4g Carbs; 23.4g Protein; 6.1g Fiber

INGREDIENTS

3 ripe avocados, pitted and halved
1 tablespoon butter, room temperature
1/2 cup onions, sliced
3/4 cup Swiss cheese, shredded

3 tablespoons green olives, pitted and sliced
3/4 pound ground chuck
1/3 cup vegetable broth

1/2 cup mayonnaise
1 large tomato, chopped
Salt and pepper, to taste

DIRECTIONS

Melt the butter in a nonstick skillet a moderate heat; cook the ground chuck for about 3 minutes, crumbling it with a fork.

Add in the broth and onions. Continue to sauté until the onions are tender translucent. Season with salt and pepper to taste.

Scoop out some of the middle of your avocados. Combine the avocado flash with the chopped tomatoes and green olives. Add in the reserved beef mixture and stuff your avocado.

Place the stuffed avocado in a parchment-lined baking pan. Bake in the preheated oven at 350 degrees F for about 10 minutes.

STORING

Place the stuffed avocado in airtight containers; keep in your refrigerator for 3 to 4 days.

Top with the Swiss cheese and place under the preheated broiler for about 5 minutes or until the cheese is hot and bubbly. Serve with mayonnaise. Bon appétit!

194. Rustic Hamburger and Cabbage Soup

(Ready in about 35 minutes | Servings 4)

Per serving: 307 Calories; 23.6g Fat; 5.4g Carbs; 14.8g Protein; 2.9g Fiber

INGREDIENTS

3/4 pound ground beef
1 cup tomato sauce
4 cups vegetable broth
1 sprig thyme

1/2 cup onions, chopped
1 bell pepper, diced
1 ½ tablespoons tallow, room temperature
1 cup green cabbage, shredded

1 celery with leaves, diced
Salt and pepper, to taste
2 cloves garlic, minced
1 cup sour cream

DIRECTIONS

In a large soup pot, melt the tallow until sizzling. Once hot, cook the ground beef for about 5 minutes, falling apart with a fork; reserve.

Add in the onions, garlic, bell pepper, cabbage, and celery and continue to cook for 5 to 6 minutes more or until the vegetables have softened.

Stir in the remaining ingredients along with the reserved ground beef; bring to a boil. Reduce the heat to a simmer and continue to cook an additional 20 minutes until everything is thoroughly cooked.

STORING

Spoon the soup into four airtight containers or Ziploc bags; keep in your refrigerator for up to 3 to 4 days.

For freezing, place the soup in airtight containers. It will maintain the best quality for about 4 to 6 months. Defrost in the refrigerator.

Reheat in a soup pot and serve dolloped with chilled sour cream. Enjoy!

195. Porterhouse Steak in Red Wine Sauce

(Ready in about 1 hour 40 minutes | Servings 6)

Per serving: 339 Calories; 21.7g Fat; 5.2g Carbs; 35g Protein; 1.5g Fiber

INGREDIENTS

1 ½ pounds Porterhouse steak, cut into 6 serving-size pieces
1/2 teaspoon dried oregano
1 tablespoon dried marjoram
1 red onion, chopped
1/2 teaspoon fresh garlic, minced

1 ½ cups Brussels sprouts, quartered
Kosher salt and black pepper, to taste
1 cup roasted vegetable broth
2 tablespoons olive oil

For the Sauce:
1/2 cup dry red wine
3/4 teaspoon yellow mustard
1 cup heavy cream
1/2 cup roasted vegetable broth
1/4 teaspoon ground cardamom

DIRECTIONS

Heat the olive oil in an oven-proof skillet over medium-high flame. Sear the steak until just browned, 4 to 5 minutes per side; reserve.

In the same skillet, cook the onion and garlic until they've softened. Add in the Brussels sprouts and continue to cook until just tender.

Add the Porterhouse steak back to the skillet. Add all spices along with 1 cup of vegetable broth. Cover with foil and roast at 350 degrees F for 1 hour 15 minutes. Reserve.

Add the remaining ingredients to the pan and continue to simmer for about 15 minutes until the sauce has thickened and reduced.

STORING

Divide the Porterhouse steak along with the sauce between airtight containers; keep in your refrigerator for up to 3 to 4 days.

For freezing, place the Porterhouse steak along with the sauce in airtight containers or heavy-duty freezer bags. Freeze up to 2 to 3 months. Defrost in the refrigerator. Bon appétit!

196. Tender Chuck Short Ribs

(Ready in about 2 hours 35 minutes | Servings 8)

Per serving: 231 Calories; 8.9g Fat; 1.3g Carbs; 34.7g Protein; 0.2g Fiber

INGREDIENTS

2 pounds chuck short ribs
1 vine-ripened tomato
2 garlic cloves, minced
1/2 teaspoon red pepper flakes

1 tablespoon butter, at room temperature
1/2 cup dry red wine
Sea salt and black pepper, to taste

DIRECTIONS

Start by preheating your oven to 325 degrees F.
Toss the beef ribs with salt, pepper and red pepper flakes until well coated.
In a large frying pan, melt the butter over medium-high heat. Sear the short ribs until browned, about 9 minutes.
Place the ribs in a lightly-oiled baking pan. Add in the remaining ingredients.
Cover with foil and roast in the preheated oven at 330 degrees F for 2 hours. Remove the foil and roast an additional 30 minutes.

STORING

Divide the ribs into portions. Place each portion in an airtight container; keep in your refrigerator for 3 to 5 days.
For freezing, place the ribs in airtight containers or heavy-duty freezer bags. Freeze up to 4 to 6 months. Defrost in the refrigerator. Reheat in your oven at 250 degrees F until heated through. Bon appétit!

197. German Szegediner Gulasch (Beef with Sauerkraut)

(Ready in about 20 minutes | Servings 4)

Per serving: 342 Calories; 22g Fat; 7.7g Carbs; 29.4g Protein; 4.3g Fiber

INGREDIENTS

18 ounces sauerkraut, rinsed and well drained
1 ¼ pounds ground chuck roast

1 teaspoon hot paprika
1 teaspoon celery powder
1 tablespoon lard, melted

1 medium leek, chopped
1 teaspoon fresh garlic, minced
1 bay laurel

DIRECTIONS

In a saucepan, melt the lard over a moderately high heat. Sauté the leek and garlic until tender and fragrant.
Add in the ground chuck and continue to cook until slightly browned or about 5 minutes.
Add in the remaining ingredients. Reduce the heat to a simmer. Cover and continue to cook for a further 7 minutes until everything is cooked through.

STORING

Divide the beef with sauerkraut between four airtight containers or Ziploc bags; keep in your refrigerator for up to 3 to 5 days.
For freezing, place the beef with sauerkraut in airtight containers or heavy-duty freezer bags. Freeze up to 5 months. Defrost in the refrigerator. Bon appétit!

198. Grandma's Blead Roast with Goat Cheese

(Ready in about 8 hours | Servings 6)

Per serving: 439 Calories; 33.4g Fat; 4.2g Carbs; 25.5g Protein; 0.6g Fiber

INGREDIENTS

1 ½ pounds blade roast
1 ¼ cups water
2 tablespoons butter, room temperature

1 large onion, chopped
2 cloves garlic, minced
1 Italian pepper, deveined, and sliced
6 ounces goat cheese, crumbled

2 tablespoons coconut aminos
1 tablespoon red wine vinegar
1/3 teaspoon ground mustard seeds

DIRECTIONS

Brush the sides and bottom of your Crock pot with a nonstick spray.
Melt the butter in a large saucepan over a moderate heat. Now, sauté the onion, garlic, and pepper until they've softened.
Transfer the sautéed mixture to your Crock pot. Add in the blade roast coconut aminos, vinegar, mustard seeds, and water.
Cover with the lid; cook on Low heat setting for 7 hours.

STORING

Place the blade roast along with cooking juices in airtight containers or Ziploc bags; keep in your refrigerator for 3 to 5 days.
For freezing, place the blade roast along with cooking juices in airtight containers or heavy-duty freezer bags. Freeze up to 3 months. Defrost in the refrigerator.
Top with cheese and place under the preheated broiler for 6 to 7 minutes or until thoroughly warmed. Enjoy!

199. Italian-Style Herbed Meatloaf

(Ready in about 50 minutes | Servings 6)

Per serving: 163 Calories; 8.4g Fat; 5.6g Carbs; 12.2g Protein; 1.9g Fiber

INGREDIENTS

2 garlic cloves, minced
1/3 cup almond meal
2 tablespoons flaxseed meal
1 tablespoon yellow mustard
1 ½ teaspoons coconut aminos

1/3 cup heavy cream
2 pounds ground beef
1 egg, slightly beaten
1 large onions, chopped
1 teaspoon Italian seasoning mix

For the Tomato Sauce:
2 vine-ripened tomatoes, pureed
1 tablespoon dried parsley flakes
Salt and pepper, to taste

DIRECTIONS

In a mixing bowl, combine all ingredients for the meatloaf. Press the meatloaf mixture into a lightly greased loaf pan.
In a saucepan, over a moderate heat, cook all ingredients for the sauce until reduced slightly, about 4 minutes. Pour the sauce over the top of your meatloaf.
Bake at 365 degrees F for 40 to 45 minutes.

STORING

Wrap your meatloaf tightly with heavy-duty aluminum foil or plastic wrap. Then, keep in your refrigerator for up to 3 to 4 days.
For freezing, wrap your meatloaf tightly to prevent freezer burn. Freeze up to 3 to 4 months. Defrost in the refrigerator. Bon appétit!

200. Perfect Roast Beef with Horseradish Sauce

(Ready in about 2 hours + marinating time | Servings 6)

Per serving: 493 Calories; 39.4g Fat; 2.9g Carbs; 27.9g Protein; 0.5g Fiber

INGREDIENTS

1 ½ pounds top sirloin roast
1 ½ tablespoons Dijon mustard
1/2 teaspoon paprika
1/3 cup Merlot
1 sprig thyme

1 sprig rosemary
1 teaspoon dried marjoram
1/4 cup olive oil
1 garlic clove, minced

For the Sauce:
2 tablespoons prepared horseradish
2 tablespoons mayonnaise
1/4 cup cream cheese

DIRECTIONS

Place all ingredients for the roast beef in a ceramic bowl; let it marinate in your refrigerator for 3 to 4 hours.
Transfer the top sirloin roast along with the marinade to a lightly oiled baking pan.
Wrap with the foil and bake in the preheated oven at 370 degrees F approximately 1 hour. Rotate the pan and continue to roast for 1 hour longer (a meat thermometer should register 125 degrees F).
Whisk all ingredients for the horseradish sauce.

STORING

Divide the top sirloin roast into six portions; place each portion in an airtight container or Ziploc bag; keep in your refrigerator for 3 to 4 days.
Place the horseradish sauce in an airtight container; keep in your refrigerator for 3 to 5 days.
For freezing, place the top sirloin roast in airtight containers or heavy-duty freezer bags. Freeze up to 2 to 3 months. Defrost in the refrigerator. Bon appétit!

201. Saucy Mediterranean Tenderloin

(Ready in about 30 minutes | Servings 4)

Per serving: 451 Calories; 34.4g Fat; 3.6g Carbs; 29.7g Protein; 1.1g Fiber

INGREDIENTS

1 ½ pounds tenderloin
1 teaspoon Mediterranean seasoning mix
2 tablespoons olive oil

1 cup red onions, chopped
1/2 cup dry red wine
2 garlic cloves, minced

1 tablespoon Dijon mustard
Kosher salt and black pepper, to taste
1 Italian pepper, deveined and chopped

DIRECTIONS

Rub the tenderloin steak with the mustard, salt, pepper, and Mediterranean seasoning mix.
Heat the olive oil in a nonstick skillet over moderately high heat. Cook the tenderloin steak for 9 to 10 minutes per side.
Sauté the onion, garlic, and Italian pepper for 3 to 4 minutes more until they've softened. Add in red wine to scrape up any browned bits from the bottom of the skillet.
Continue to cook until the cooking liquid has thickened and reduced by half.

STORING

Divide the tenderloin steaks along with the sauce between airtight containers; keep in your refrigerator for up to 3 to 4 days.
For freezing, place the tenderloin steaks along with the sauce in airtight containers or heavy-duty freezer bags. Freeze up to 2 to 3 months. Defrost in the refrigerator. Bon appétit!

202. Beef Sirloin with Tangy Mustard Sauce

(Ready in about 20 minutes | Servings 4)

Per serving: 321 Calories; 13.7g Fat; 1g Carbs; 45g Protein; 0.4g Fiber

INGREDIENTS

1 tablespoon olive oil
4 (1 ½-inch) thick sirloin steaks
Seasoned salt and black pepper, to taste
1 tablespoon deli mustard

1 sprig rosemary, chopped
1/3 cup cream cheese, room temperature
1 tablespoon fresh basil, finely chopped

DIRECTIONS

Season the sirloin steaks with salt, pepper, and rosemary. Heat olive oil in a large grill pan over medium-high flame.
Sear the sirloin steaks in the grill pan for 5 minutes; flip them over and cook for 4 to 5 minutes on the other side.
Combine together the cream cheese, mustard, and basil. Place in your refrigerator until ready to serve.

STORING

Divide the sirloin steaks between airtight containers; keep in your refrigerator for up to 3 to 4 days.
Place the tangy mustard sauce in an airtight container; keep in your refrigerator for 4 days.
For freezing, place the sirloin steaks in airtight containers or heavy-duty freezer bags. Freeze up to 2 to 3 months. Defrost in the refrigerator.
Bon appétit!

203. Cheeseburger Chowder with Tomatoes and Plum Vinegar

(Ready in about 30 minutes | Servings 6)

Per serving: 238 Calories; 12.6g Fat; 5.6g Carbs; 25.1g Protein; 0.9g Fiber

INGREDIENTS

1 ½ pounds ground beef
1 tablespoon butter, room temperature
2 Roma tomatoes, pureed
1 bay laurel

1 leek, chopped
2 garlic cloves, chopped
2 cups vegetable broth
1 cup Cheddar cheese, shredded

2 tablespoons plum vinegar
Salt and pepper, to your liking

DIRECTIONS

Melt the butter in a soup pot over a moderately-high flame. Cook the beef until it is no longer pink, breaking apart with a fork. Reserve.
In the pan drippings, cook the leeks and garlic until they've softened, for 5 to 6 minutes.
Add in the vegetable broth, tomatoes, salt, pepper, and bay laurel. Cover and continue to cook for 18 to 20 minutes more.

STORING

Spoon the soup into airtight containers or Ziploc bags; keep in your refrigerator for up to 3 to 4 days.
For freezing, place the soup in airtight containers. It will maintain the best quality for about 4 to 6 months. Defrost in the refrigerator.
Add in the cheese and reheat in your pot for 5 to 6 minutes until the cheese has melted completely. Serve in individual bowls garnished with plum vinegar. Bon appétit!

204. Mini Meatloaf Muffins

(Ready in about 40 minutes | Servings 6)

Per serving: 404 Calories; 22.8g Fat; 6.2g Carbs; 44g Protein; 1.3g Fiber

INGREDIENTS

1 ¼ pounds ground chuck
1 shallot, chopped
3/4 cup mozzarella cheese, grated
1/2 cup pork rinds, crushed

Salt and pepper, to taste
1 tablespoon lard, room temperature
2 garlic cloves, minced
2 eggs, lightly beaten

1/4 cup almond meal
1/2 pound button mushrooms, chopped
1/2 cup tomato puree

DIRECTIONS

Melt the lard in a saucepan over a moderately high flame. Sauté the shallot and mushrooms until they are just tender and aromatic.
Add in the remaining ingredients and mix to combine well.
Press the mixture into a lightly greased muffin pan. Bake in the preheated oven at 380 degrees F for 25 to 30 minutes.

STORING

Wrap the mini meatloaves with heavy-duty aluminum foil or plastic wrap. Then, keep in your refrigerator for up to 3 to 4 days.
For freezing, wrap the mini meatloaves to prevent freezer burn. Freeze up to 3 to 4 months. Defrost in the refrigerator and reheat in your oven. Bon appétit!

EGGS & DAIRY

205. Italian-Style Egg Muffins

(Ready in about 10 minutes | Servings 3)

Per serving: 423 Calories; 34.1g Fat; 2.2g Carbs; 26.5g Protein; 0g Fiber

INGREDIENTS

6 eggs
1 pound beef sausages, chopped
1 tablespoon olive oil

1 cup Romano cheese, freshly grated
Sea salt and black pepper, to season
1/2 teaspoon cayenne pepper

DIRECTIONS

Whisk the eggs until pale and frothy. Add in the remaining ingredients and stir to combine.
Pour the mixture into a lightly greased muffin pan. Bake in the preheated oven at 400 degrees F for 5 to 6 minutes.

STORING

Place your muffins in the airtight containers or Ziploc bags; keep in the refrigerator for a week.
For freezing, divide your muffins among three Ziploc bags and freeze up to 3 months. Defrost in your microwave for a couple of minutes.
Bon appétit!

206. Autumn Cheese and Pepper Dip

(Ready in about 35 minutes | Servings 10)

Per serving: 228 Calories; 17.2g Fat; 5.7g Carbs; 10.2g Protein; 0.5g Fiber

INGREDIENTS

1 jar (17-ounce) roasted red peppers, drained and chopped
1 teaspoon deli mustard
1 ¼ cups Colby cheese, grated

10 ounces cream cheese, room temperature
1 cup mayonnaise
Salt and black pepper, to taste

DIRECTIONS

In a mixing bowl, combine the ingredients until everything is well combined.
Spoon the mixture into a lightly greased baking pan.
Bake in the preheated oven at 355 degrees F for about 30 minutes, rotating the baking pan halfway through the cook time.

STORING

Place your dip in an airtight container; keep in your refrigerator for up 3 to 4 days. Enjoy!

207. Cheese and Sardine Stuffed Avocado

(Ready in about 25 minutes | Servings 4)

Per serving: 286 Calories; 23.9g Fat; 6g Carbs; 11.2g Protein; 6g Fiber

INGREDIENTS

2 ounces canned sardines, flaked
2 tablespoons chives, chopped
Salt and pepper, to taste
2 tablespoons fresh parsley, chopped

1/2 cup cucumbers, diced
2 large-sized avocados, halved and pitted
4 ounces Asiago cheese, grated

DIRECTIONS

In a mixing bowl, combine the sardines, chives, salt, pepper, parsley, and cucumber. Stuff your avocado halves.
Place the stuffed avocado in a parchment-lined baking pan. Bake in the preheated oven at 355 degrees F for about 20 minutes.

STORING

Place the stuffed avocado in airtight containers; keep in your refrigerator for 3 to 4 days.
Top with Asiago cheese and place under the preheated broiler for about 5 minutes or until the the cheese is hot and bubbly. Bon appétit!

208. Classic Spicy Egg Salad

(Ready in about 15 minutes | Servings 8)

Per serving: 174 Calories; 13g Fat; 5.7g Carbs; 7.4g Protein; 0.8g Fiber

INGREDIENTS

10 eggs
1/2 cup onions, chopped
1/2 cup celery with leaves, chopped
2 cups butterhead lettuce, torn into pieces
3/4 cup mayonnaise

1 teaspoon hot sauce
1 tablespoon Dijon mustard
1/2 teaspoon fresh lemon juice
Kosher salt and black pepper, to taste

DIRECTIONS

Place the eggs in a saucepan and cover them with water by 1 inch. Cover and bring the water to a boil over high heat. Boil for 6 to 7 minutes over medium-high heat.
Peel the eggs and chop them coarsely. Add in the remaining ingredients and toss to combine.

STORING

Place the egg salad in an airtight container or Ziploc bag; transfer to your refrigerator; it should be consumed within two days. Bon appétit!

209. Breakfast Eggs in a Mug

(Ready in about 5 minutes | Servings 2)

Per serving: 197 Calories; 13.8g Fat; 2.7g Carbs; 15.7g Protein; 0.1g Fiber

INGREDIENTS

4 eggs
1 garlic clove, minced
1/4 teaspoon turmeric powder

1/4 cup milk
1/4 cup Swiss cheese, freshly grated
Salt and pepper, to taste

DIRECTIONS

Combine the ingredients until well incorporated.
Brush 2 microwave-safe mugs with a nonstick cooking spray (butter-flavored). Spoon the egg mixture into the mugs.
Microwave for about 40 seconds. Stir and microwave for 1 minute more or until they're done.

STORING

Place the eggs in airtight containers; keep in the refrigerator for 3 to 4 days.
For freezing, divide the eggs among two Ziploc bags and freeze up to 3 months. Defrost in your microwave for a couple of minutes. Enjoy!

210. Cheese and Prosciutto Stuffed Avocado

(Ready in about 15 minutes | Servings 6)

Per serving: 308 Calories; 27g Fat; 6.4g Carbs; 8.8g Protein; 4.9g Fiber

INGREDIENTS

2/3 cup Ricotta cheese
1 teaspoon stone-ground mustard
Salt and pepper, to taste
1 teaspoon hot paprika

1/3 cup Queso Fresco, crumbled
1 cup prosciutto, chopped
3 avocados, cut into halves and pitted

DIRECTIONS

Scoop out the avocados; combine avocado flesh with the remaining ingredients; stir until everything is well incorporated.
Spoon the mixture into the avocado halves.

STORING

Place the stuffed avocado in airtight containers; keep in your refrigerator for 3 to 4 days.
Place under the preheated broiler for about 5 minutes or until the cheese is hot and bubbly. Bon appétit!

211. Asiago, Pepperoni, and Pepper Casserole

(Ready in about 35 minutes | Servings 4)

Per serving: 334 Calories; 23g Fat; 6.2g Carbs; 25.5g Protein; 4.9g Fiber

INGREDIENTS

8 eggs
Salt and pepper, to taste
1 cup Asiago cheese, grated

1/2 cup cream cheese
1 bell pepper, chopped
1 chili pepper, deveined and chopped

1 teaspoon yellow mustard
8 slices pepperoni, chopped

DIRECTIONS

In a mixing bowl, combine the eggs, salt, pepper, and cheese; spoon the mixture into a lightly greased baking dish.
Add in the other ingredients. Bake in the preheated oven at 365 degrees F for about 30 minutes or until cooked through.

STORING

Slice the casserole into four pieces. Divide the pieces between three airtight containers; it will last for 3 to 4 days in the refrigerator.
For freezing, place each portion in a separate heavy-duty freezer bag. Freeze up to 2 to 3 months. Defrost in the microwave or refrigerator.
Bon appétit!

212. Simple and Quick Egg Muffins

(Ready in about 5 minutes | Servings 2)

Per serving: 244 Calories; 17.5g Fat; 2.9g Carbs; 19.2g Protein; 0.9g Fiber

INGREDIENTS

2 tablespoons onions, chopped
4 tablespoons Greek-style yogurt
1/4 cup Feta cheese, crumbled

4 eggs
Salt and pepper, to taste

DIRECTIONS

Mix all of the above ingredients in a bowl.
Spoon the mixture into lightly greased mugs.
Microwave for about 70 seconds.

STORING

Place the muffins in airtight containers and refrigerate for a week.
To freeze, place the muffins on a baking tray and freeze for 2 hours. Now, place them in airtight containers. They can be frozen for 2 to 3 months. Bon appétit!

213. Cheese Sticks with Peppery Dipping Sauce

(Ready in about 40 minutes | Servings 8)

Per serving: 200 Calories; 16.9g Fat; 3.7g Carbs; 9.4g Protein; 1.1g Fiber

INGREDIENTS

2 eggs
3 tablespoons almond meal
1 teaspoon baking powder
Salt and red pepper flakes, to serve
1/3 teaspoon cumin powder
1/3 teaspoon dried rosemary
2 (8-ounce) packages Colby cheese, cut into sticks
3/4 cup Romano cheese, grated

For Roasted Red Pepper Dip:
3/4 cup roasted red peppers, drained and chopped
1 tablespoon yellow mustard
1 cup Ricotta cheese
1/3 cup sour cream
1 teaspoon fresh garlic, minced
Black pepper to taste

DIRECTIONS

In a shallow bowl, whisk the eggs until pale and frothy. In a separate shallow bowl, mix the Romano cheese, almond meal, baking powder, and spices.
Dip the cheese stick into the eggs, and then dredge them into dry mixture. Place in your freezer for about 30 minutes.
Deep fry the cheese sticks for 5 to 6 minutes. Prepare the sauce by whisking the ingredients.

STORING

Divide the cheese sticks between airtight containers or Ziploc bags; keep in your refrigerator for up to 4 days.
Place the dipping sauce in airtight containers; keep in your refrigerator for 3 to 4 days.
To freeze, divide the cheese sticks between airtight containers. Freeze up to 2 months. Defrost and reheat in your oven until it is crisp.
Enjoy!

214. Festive Zucchini Boats

(Ready in about 35 minutes | Servings 3)

Per serving: 506 Calories; 41g Fat; 4.5g Carbs; 27.5g Protein; 0.3g Fiber

INGREDIENTS

3 medium-sized zucchinis, cut into halves and scoop out the
pulp
6 eggs
1 tablespoon Dijon mustard

2 sausages, cooked and crumbled
Salt and pepper, to taste
1/2 teaspoon dried basil

DIRECTIONS

Place the zucchini boats on a lightly oiled baking sheet. Mix the Dijon mustard, sausages, salt, pepper, and basil.
Spoon the sausage mixture into the zucchini shells. Crack an egg in each zucchini shell.
Bake in the preheated oven at 390 degrees F for 30 to 35 minutes or until tender and cooked through.

STORING

Place the zucchini boats in airtight containers or Ziploc bags; keep in your refrigerator for 3 to 4 days.
Wrap each zucchini boat tightly in several layers of plastic wrap and squeeze the air out. Place them in a freezable container; they can be frozen for up to 1 month.
Bake the thawed zucchini at 200 degrees F until they are completely warm. Enjoy!

215. Mediterranean-Style Fat Bombs

(Ready in about 5 minutes | Servings 6)

Per serving: 217 Calories; 18.7g Fat; 2.1g Carbs; 9.9g Protein; 0.4g Fiber

INGREDIENTS

4 ounces salami, chopped
2 tablespoons cilantro, finely chopped
1/2 cup black olives, pitted and chopped

1/2 teaspoon paprika
4 ounces Feta cheese, crumbled
1/4 cup mayonnaise

DIRECTIONS

In a mixing bowl, thoroughly combine all of the above ingredients.
Roll the mixture into 10 to 12 balls

STORING

Place the fat bombs in airtight containers or Ziploc bags; keep in your refrigerator for up to 3 to 4 days.
For freezing, place the fat bombs in airtight containers. Freeze up to 1 month. Defrost in the refrigerator. Enjoy!

216. Movie Night Cheese Crisps

(Ready in about 10 minutes | Servings 4)

Per serving: 205 Calories; 15g Fat; 2.9g Carbs; 14.5g Protein; 0g Fiber

INGREDIENTS

1 thyme sprig, minced
2 cups Monterey-Jack cheese, shredded
1/2 teaspoon garlic powder

1/4 teaspoon onion powder
1/2 teaspoon ancho chili powder

DIRECTIONS

Begin by preheating your oven to 390 degrees F. Line baking sheets with Silpat mat.
Place small piles of the cheese mixture on the prepared baking sheets.
Bake for 6 to 7 minutes; then, let them cool at room temperature.

STORING

Divide the crisps between two airtight containers or Ziploc bags; keep in your refrigerator for up to 4 days.
To freeze, divide the crisps between two airtight containers. Freeze up to 2 months. Defrost and reheat in your oven until it is crisp. Enjoy!

217. Nana's Pickled Eggs

(Ready in about 20 minutes | Servings 5)

Per serving: 145 Calories; 9g Fat; 2.8g Carbs; 11.4g Protein; 0.9g Fiber

INGREDIENTS

2 clove garlic, sliced
1 cup white vinegar
10 eggs
1 tablespoon yellow curry powder
1/2 cup onions, sliced

1 teaspoon fennel seeds
1 teaspoon mustard seeds
1 tablespoon sea salt
1 ¼ cups water

DIRECTIONS

Place the eggs in a saucepan and cover them with water by 1 inch. Cover and bring the water to a boil over high heat. Boil for 6 to 7 minutes over medium-high heat.
Peel the eggs and add them to a large-sized jar.
Cook the other ingredients in a saucepan pan over moderately-high heat; bring to a boil.
Immediately turn the heat to medium-low and continue to simmer for 5 to 6 minutes. Pour the mixture into the prepared jar.

STORING

Keep the pickled eggs in your refrigerator for 2 to 3 weeks. Bon appétit!

218. Pickle, Cheese, and Broccoli Bites

(Ready in about 15 minutes | Servings 6)

Per serving: 407 Calories; 26.8g Fat; 5.8g Carbs; 33.4g Protein; 1.1g Fiber

INGREDIENTS

1/4 teaspoon dried dill weed
1/2 teaspoon onion powder
4 cups broccoli, grated
1/2 pound salami, chopped
12 ounces Cottage cheese curds
1 cup Swiss cheese, freshly grated

1 teaspoon garlic, minced
1/2 teaspoon mustard seeds
1/2 cup dill pickles, chopped and thoroughly squeezed
Salt and black pepper, to taste
1 cup crushed pork rinds
1 teaspoon smoked paprika

DIRECTIONS

Thoroughly combine all ingredients, except for the pork rinds and paprika. Roll the mixture into 18 balls.
In a shallow dish, mix the pork rinds with the smoked paprika.
Roll each ball over the paprika mixture until completely coated. Fry these balls in a preheated skillet for 5 to 6 minutes.

STORING

Divide the broccoli balls between airtight containers or Ziploc bags; keep in your refrigerator for up to 3 to 4 days.
For freezing, place the broccoli balls in airtight containers. Freeze up to 1 month. Defrost in the refrigerator. Enjoy!

219. Mushroom and Cheese Wraps

(Ready in about 20 minutes | Servings 4)

Per serving: 172 Calories; 14g Fat; 3.4g Carbs; 9.5g Protein; 1g Fiber

INGREDIENTS

For the Wraps:
2 tablespoons cream cheese
6 eggs, separated into yolks and whites
1 tablespoon butter, room temperature
Sea salt, to taste

For the Filling:
1 cup Cremini mushrooms, chopped
4 slices of Swiss cheese
Salt and pepper, to taste
6-8 fresh arugula

1 teaspoon olive oil
1 large vine-ripened tomatoes, chopped

DIRECTIONS

Mix all ingredients for the wraps until well combined. Prepare four wraps in a frying pan and set them aside.
Next, heat 1 teaspoon of olive oil over a moderate heat. Cook the mushrooms until they release the liquid; season with salt and pepper.

STORING

Place your wraps in airtight containers and keep in your refrigerator for up to 3 to 4 days.
Place the filling in airtight containers and keep in your refrigerator for up to 3 to 4 days. Assemble the wraps. Divide the sautéed mushrooms, arugula, cheese, and tomatoes between the warm wraps.

220. Cheese and Basil Keto Balls

(Ready in about 10 minutes | Servings 10)

Per serving: 105 Calories; 7.2g Fat; 2.8g Carbs; 7.5g Protein; 0.2g Fiber

INGREDIENTS

1/3 cup black olives, pitted and chopped
1 ½ cups Cottage cheese, at room temperature
18 fresh basil leaves, snipped
1 ½ cups Colby cheese, shredded

1 ½ tablespoons tomato ketchup, no sugar added
1 teaspoon red pepper flakes
Salt and freshly ground black pepper

DIRECTIONS

Mix all of the above ingredients until well combined.
Roll the mixture into 18 to 20 balls.

STORING

Divide the keto balls between airtight containers or Ziploc bags; keep in your refrigerator for up to 3 to 4 days.
For freezing, place the keto balls in airtight containers. Freeze up to 1 month. Defrost in the refrigerator. Enjoy!

221. Mediterranean Eggs with Aioli

(Ready in about 20 minutes | Servings 8)

Per serving: 285 Calories; 22.5g Fat; 1.8g Carbs; 19.5g Protein; 0.3g Fiber

INGREDIENTS

1/2 Feta cheese, crumbled
1/3 cup Greek-style yogurt
1/2 cup scallions, finely chopped
8 eggs
2 cans anchovies, drained
1 cup butterhead lettuces, torn into pieces
1/2 tablespoon deli mustard

For Aioli:
1 egg
1/2 cup olive oil
2 medium cloves garlic, minced
1 tablespoon fresh lime juice
Salt, to taste

DIRECTIONS

Place the eggs in a saucepan and cover them with water by 1 inch. Cover and bring the water to a boil over high heat. Boil for 6 to 7 minutes over medium-high heat.
Peel and chop the eggs. Add in the anchovies, lettuce, scallions, Feta cheese, Greek-style yogurt, mustard.
To make the aioli, blend the egg, garlic, and lemon juice until well combined. Gradually pour in the oil and continue to blend until everything is well incorporated. Salt to taste.
Toss the salad with the prepared aioli.

STORING

Place the egg salad in an airtight container or Ziploc bag; transfer to your refrigerator; it should be consumed within 3 days. Enjoy!

222. Egg Drop Soup with Tofu

(Ready in about 15 minutes | Servings 3)

Per serving: 153 Calories; 9.8g Fat; 2.7g Carbs; 15g Protein; 0.5g Fiber

INGREDIENTS

2 eggs, beaten
1/2 teaspoon curry paste
1/2 pound extra-firm tofu, cubed
2 cups vegetable broth

1 tablespoon coconut aminos
1 teaspoon butter, softened
1/4 teaspoon cayenne pepper
Salt and ground black ground, to taste

DIRECTIONS

In a heavy-bottomed pot, cook the broth, coconut aminos and butter over high heat; bring to a boil.
Immediately turn the heat to a simmer. Stir in the eggs and curry paste, whisking constantly, until well incorporated.
Add in the salt, black pepper, cayenne pepper, and tofu. Partially cover and continue to simmer approximately 2 minutes.

STORING

Place the soup in three airtight containers or Ziploc bag; transfer to your refrigerator; it should be consumed within 3 days. Enjoy!

223. Old-Fashioned Stuffed Peppers

(Ready in about 45 minutes | Servings 4)

Per serving: 359 Calories; 29.7g Fat; 6.7g Carbs; 17.7g Protein; 2.5g Fiber

INGREDIENTS

4 bell peppers
12 ounces Cottage cheese, room temperature
1/2 cup pork rinds, crushed

1 teaspoon garlic, smashed
1 ½ cups pureed tomatoes
1 teaspoon Italian herb mix

DIRECTIONS

Parboil the peppers in salted water for about 5 minutes.
In a mixing bowl, combine the cheese, pork rinds, and garlic until everything is well incorporated. Divide the filling among bell peppers.
Whisk the pureed tomatoes with the Italian herb mix until well combined. Pour the tomato mixture over the stuffed pepper.
Bake in the preheated oven at 350 degrees F for 35 to 40 minutes.

STORING

Place the stuffed peppers in airtight containers; keep in your refrigerator for 3 to 4 days.
Wrap each stuffed pepper tightly in several layers of plastic wrap and squeeze the air out. Place them in airtight containers; they can be frozen for up to 1 month.
Bake the thawed stuffed peppers at 200 degrees F until they are completely warm.

224. Egg and Bacon Salad

(Ready in about 20 minutes | Servings 4)

Per serving: 284 Calories; 21.3g Fat; 6.8g Carbs; 16.7g Protein; 0.7g Fiber

INGREDIENTS

8 eggs
1/2 cup bacon bits
1 ½ teaspoons fresh lemon juice
Salt and pepper, to taste

1/3 cup mayonnaise
1 tablespoon scallions, chopped
1/2 teaspoon deli mustard
2 cups Iceberg lettuce leaves

DIRECTIONS

Place the eggs in a saucepan and cover them with water by 1 inch. Cover and bring the water to a boil over high heat. Boil for 6 to 7 minutes over medium-high heat.
Peel and chop the eggs. Add in the remaining ingredients; gently stir to combine.

STORING

Place the egg salad in an airtight container or Ziploc bag; transfer to your refrigerator; it should be consumed within two days. Bon appétit!

225. Cauliflower "Mac" and Cheese Casserole

(Ready in about 15 minutes | Servings 4)

Per serving: 357 Calories; 32.5g Fat; 6.9g Carbs; 8.4g Protein; 1.3g Fiber

INGREDIENTS

1 large-sized head cauliflower, broken into florets
1 cup Cottage cheese
1/2 cup milk
1/2 cup double cream
2 tablespoons olive oil

1 teaspoon garlic powder
1/2 teaspoon shallot powder
1 teaspoon dried parsley flakes
Salt and pepper, to taste

DIRECTIONS

Start by preheating your oven to 420 degrees F.
In a lightly oiled baking dish, toss the cauliflower florets with the olive oil, salt, and pepper. Bake in the preheated oven for about 15 minutes.
In a mixing dish, whisk the milk, cream, cheese, and spices. Pour the mixture over the cauliflower layer in the baking dish.
Bake for another 10 minutes, until the top is hot and bubbly.

STORING

Slice the casserole into four pieces. Divide the pieces between four airtight containers; it will last for 3 to 4 days in the refrigerator.
For freezing, place each portion in a separate heavy-duty freezer bag. Freeze up to 2 to 3 months. Defrost in the microwave or refrigerator.
Bon appétit!

226. Pepperoni and Vegetable Frittata

(Ready in about 25 minutes | Servings 4)

Per serving: 310 Calories; 26.2g Fat; 3.9g Carbs; 15.4g Protein; 0.8g Fiber

INGREDIENTS

8 pepperoni slices
8 eggs, whisked
1 habanero pepper, chopped

1 celery rib, chopped
1/2 stick butter, at room temperature
1/2 cup onions, chopped

2 garlic cloves, minced
Salt and pepper, to season

DIRECTIONS

In a skillet, melt the butter over a moderately high flame. Sauté the onions and garlic for about 3 minutes, stirring continuously to ensure even cooking.
Add in the habanero pepper and celery, and continue to cook for 4 to 5 minutes longer or until just tender and fragrant.
Spoon the mixture into a lightly greased baking dish. Top with the pepperoni slices.
Pour the whisked eggs over the pepperoni layer; season with salt and pepper to taste. Bake for 15 to 18 minutes.

STORING

Cut your frittata into four wedges. Place each of them in an airtight container; place in the refrigerator for up 3 to 4 days.
To freeze, place in separate Ziploc bags and freeze up to 3 months. To defrost, place in your microwave for a few minutes. Enjoy!

227. Baked Avocado Boats

(Ready in about 20 minutes | Servings 4)

Per serving: 342 Calories; 30.4g Fat; 6.5g Carbs; 11.1g Protein; 4.8g Fiber

INGREDIENTS

2 avocados, halved and pitted, skin on
2 eggs, beaten
Salt and pepper, to taste
1/2 teaspoon garlic powder

1 tablespoon fresh parsley, coarsely chopped
2 ounces goat cheese, crumbled
2 ounces Swiss cheese, grated

DIRECTIONS

Start by preheating your oven to 355 degrees F. Place the avocado halves in a baking dish.
In a mixing dish, thoroughly combine the eggs with cheese, salt, pepper, garlic powder, and parsley. Spoon the mixture into the avocado halves.
Bake for about 18 minutes or until everything is cooked through.

STORING

Place the stuffed avocado in airtight containers; keep in your refrigerator for 3 to 4 days. Bon appétit!

228. Keto Salad with Cheese Balls

(Ready in about 20 minutes | Servings 6)

Per serving: 234 Calories; 16.7g Fat; 5.9g Carbs; 12.4g Protein; 4.3g Fiber

INGREDIENTS

For the Cheese Balls:
3 eggs
1 cup almond meal
1 teaspoon baking powder
Salt and pepper, to taste
1 cup blue cheese, crumbled
1/2 cup Romano cheese, shredded

For the Salad:
1 cup grape tomatoes, halved
1/3 cup mayonnaise
1 teaspoon Mediterranean seasoning blend
1/2 cup scallions, thinly sliced
1/2 cup radishes, thinly sliced
1 head Iceberg lettuce

DIRECTIONS

Thoroughly combine all ingredients for the cheese balls. Roll the mixture into bite-sized balls. Bake the cheese balls in the preheated oven at 380 degrees F for 8 to 10 minutes.
Toss all the salad ingredients in a large bowl.

STORING

Divide the cheese balls between airtight containers or Ziploc bags; keep in your refrigerator for up to 3 to 4 days.
Place your salad in an airtight container and keep in your refrigerator for 3 to 4 days.
For freezing, place the cheese balls in airtight containers. Freeze up to 1 month. Defrost in the refrigerator.
Serve on your salad and enjoy!

229. Baked Cheese-Stuffed Tomatoes

(Ready in about 45 minutes | Servings 5)

Per serving: 306 Calories; 27.5g Fat; 4.4g Carbs; 11.3g Protein; 1.3g Fiber

INGREDIENTS

2 teaspoons olive oil
1/4 cup Greek-style yogurt
1 egg, whisked
1 tablespoon fresh green garlic, minced
4 tablespoons fresh shallots, chopped

1 cup Ricotta cheese, at room temperature
1 ½ cups Swiss cheese, shredded
5 vine-ripened tomatoes, cut into halves and scoop out the pulp
Salt and ground black pepper, to taste

DIRECTIONS

Start by preheating your oven to 355 degrees F.
Then, thoroughly combine the cheese, yogurt, egg, green garlic, shallots, salt, and pepper. Stuff the tomato halves with this filling.
Brush the stuffed tomatoes with olive oil. Bake in the preheated oven for about 30 minutes.

STORING

Place the stuffed tomatoes in airtight containers or Ziploc bags; keep in your refrigerator for 3 to 4 days.
Wrap each stuffed tomato tightly in several layers of plastic wrap and squeeze the air out. Place them in a freezable container; they can be frozen for up to 1 month.
Bake the thawed stuffed tomatoes in your oven at 210 degrees F until they are warmed through.

230. Decadent Scrambled Eggs

(Ready in about 15 minutes | Servings 4)

Per serving: 495 Calories; 45g Fat; 6.3g Carbs; 19.5g Protein; 0.3g Fiber

INGREDIENTS

8 eggs, well beaten
1/4 cup milk
2 tablespoons butter
Salt, to taste

For the Swiss Chard Pesto:
1/2 cup olive oil
1 cup Pecorino Romano cheese, grated
2 tablespoons fresh lime juice

1 teaspoon garlic, minced
2 cups Swiss chard
A pinch of ground cloves

DIRECTIONS

Melt the butter in a cast-iron skillet over moderately-high flame. Beat the eggs with the milk; salt to taste.
When the butter is just hot, cook the egg mixture, gently stirring to create large soft curds. Cook until the eggs are barely set.
Add all the ingredients for the pesto, except the olive oil, to your blender.
Pulse until your ingredients are coarsely chopped. With the machine running, gradually pour in the olive oil and blend until creamy and uniform.

STORING

Divide the scrambled eggs between four airtight containers or Ziploc bags. Refrigerate for up to 3 days.
Put the prepared pesto into a separate container and keep in your refrigerator for a week.
For freezing, place the scrambled eggs in four Ziploc bags and freeze up to 6 months. Defrost in your refrigerator or microwave.

231. Spicy Cheese Omelet with Chervil

(Ready in about 15 minutes | Servings 2)

Per serving: 490 Calories; 44.6g Fat; 4.5g Carbs; 22.7g Protein; 0.8g Fiber

INGREDIENTS

4 eggs, beaten
1/2 cup Cheddar cheese, grated
2 tablespoons olive oil
1/2 teaspoon habanero pepper, minced

1/2 cup queso fresco cheese, crumbled
2 tablespoons fresh chervil, roughly chopped
Salt and pepper, to taste

DIRECTIONS

In a frying pan, heat the oil over a moderately high heat. Cook the eggs until the edges barely start setting.
Add in the salt, pepper, habanero pepper, and cheese and cook an additional 4 minutes.

STORING

Slice the omelet into two pieces. Place each of them in an airtight container or Ziploc bag; place in the refrigerator for up to 3 to 4 days.
To freeze, place in separate Ziploc bags and freeze up to 3 months. Defrost in your microwave for a few minutes.
Serve with fresh chervil. Bon appétit!

232. Curried Asparagus Frittata

(Ready in about 20 minutes | Servings 4)

Per serving: 248 Calories; 17.1g Fat; 6.2g Carbs; 17.6g Protein; 1.6g Fiber

INGREDIENTS

8 eggs, beaten
1 cup asparagus spears, chopped
1/2 teaspoon Fresno pepper, minced

1 teaspoon curry paste
Salt and pepper, to your liking
3/4 cup Cheddar cheese, grated

1/4 cup fresh parsley, to serve
2 tablespoons olive oil
1/2 cup onions, chopped

DIRECTIONS

Begin by preheating your oven to 370 degrees F.
In an oven-proof skillet, heat the oil over a medium heat. Sauté the onions until they are tender and caramelized.
Add in the asparagus and cook until they've softened.
Stir in the eggs, Fresno pepper, curry paste, salt, and pepper. Cook the eggs until the edges barely start setting.
Scatter the cheese over the top of your frittata. Bake your frittata in the preheated oven for about 15 minutes.

STORING

Cut your frittata into four wedges. Place each of them in an airtight container; place in the refrigerator for up 3 to 4 days.
To freeze, place your frittata in separate Ziploc bags and freeze up to 3 months. To defrost, place in your microwave for a few minutes.
Serve with fresh parsley and enjoy!

233. Scrambled Eggs with Crabmeat

(Ready in about 15 minutes | Servings 3)

Per serving: 334 Calories; 26.2g Fat; 4.4g Carbs; 21.1g Protein; 0.4g Fiber

INGREDIENTS

6 eggs, whisked
1 can crabmeat, flaked
1/2 teaspoon rosemary
1/2 teaspoon basil

1 tablespoon butter, room temperature
For the Sauce:
1/2 teaspoon garlic, minced
3/4 cup cream cheese

1/2 cup onions, white and green parts,
chopped
3 tablespoons mayonnaise
Salt and black pepper, to taste

DIRECTIONS

In a frying pan, melt the butter over a moderately high flame. Cook the eggs, gently stirring to create large soft curds. Cook until the eggs are barely set.
Add in the crabmeat, rosemary and basil, and continue to cook, stirring frequently, until cooked through. Salt to taste.
Make the sauce by whisking all ingredients.

STORING

Divide the scrambled eggs between three airtight containers or Ziploc bags. Refrigerate for up to 3 days.
Put the prepared sauce into a separate container and keep in your refrigerator for a week.
For freezing, place the scrambled eggs in four Ziploc bags and freeze up to 6 months. Defrost in your refrigerator or microwave.

234. Black Pepper, Tomato and Cheese Omelet

(Ready in about 15 minutes | Servings 2)

Per serving: 307 Calories; 25g Fat; 2.5g Carbs; 18.5g Protein; 1g Fiber

INGREDIENTS

4 eggs
1/4 cup goat cheese, crumbled
1/4 cup Appenzeller cheese, shredded
1 tablespoon olive oil

1/4 teaspoon black peppercorns, crushed
1 cup cherry tomatoes, halved
Salt, to taste

DIRECTIONS

In a frying pan, heat the olive oil over a moderate heat. Pour in the eggs; swirl the eggs around using a spatula. Season the eggs with salt and black pepper.
When the eggs are just set and no visible liquid egg remains, top them with the cheese. Fold gently in half with the spatula.

STORING

Slice the omelet into two pieces. Place each of them in an airtight container or Ziploc bag; place in the refrigerator for up to 3 to 4 days.
To freeze, place in separate Ziploc bags and freeze up to 3 months. Defrost in your microwave for a few minutes.
Serve with cherry tomatoes. Bon appétit!

235. Genoa Salami and Goat Cheese Waffles

(Ready in about 20 minutes | Servings 2)

Per serving: 470 Calories; 40.3g Fat; 2.9g Carbs; 24.4g Protein; 0.6g Fiber

INGREDIENTS

2 tablespoons olive oil
Salt and black pepper, to your liking
1/2 teaspoon chili pepper flakes

4 eggs
1/2 cup goat cheese, crumbled
4 slices Genoa salami, chopped

DIRECTIONS

Strat by preheating your waffle iron and brush it with a nonstick cooking oil.
Mix all ingredients until everything is well combined.
Pour the batter into waffle iron and cook until golden and cooked through. Repeat until all the batter is used.

STORING

Place the waffles in separate airtight containers; keep in the refrigerator for a week.
For freezing, divide the waffles among two airtight containers or heavy-duty freezer bags and freeze up to 3 months. Defrost in your microwave for a couple of minutes. Enjoy!

236. Blue Cheese and Soppressata Balls

(Ready in about 15 minutes | Servings 8)

Per serving: 168 Calories; 13g Fat; 2.5g Carbs; 10.3g Protein; 0.2g Fiber

INGREDIENTS

6 slices Soppressata, chopped
6 ounces Parmigiano-Reggiano cheese, grated
1 teaspoon baking powder
1 teaspoon garlic, minced
1 egg, whisked

1/2 teaspoon dried basil
1/2 teaspoon dried oregano
6 ounces cream cheese
Salt and pepper, to taste
1/4 cup almond meal

DIRECTIONS

Thoroughly combine all ingredients until well combined.
Roll the mixture into bite-sized balls and arrange them on a parchment-lined cookie sheet.
Bake in the preheated oven at 400 degrees F approximately 15 minutes or until they are golden and crisp.

STORING

Wrap the Cheese and Soppressata balls tightly in a plastic wrap. Keep in your refrigerator for up to 3 to 4 days.
For freezing, wrap the Cheese and Soppressata balls tightly in a resealable freezer bag. Freeze up to 2 months. To defrost, remove from freezer the morning before you want to serve.

237. Eggs with Prosciutto di Parma and Cheese

(Ready in about 10 minutes | Servings 2)

Per serving: 431 Calories; 33.1g Fat; 2.7g Carbs; 30.3g Protein; 0.3g Fiber

INGREDIENTS

4 slices Prosciutto di Parma, chopped
4 eggs, beaten
1 teaspoon Italian herb mix

Sea salt and black pepper, to season
4 ounces Asiago cheese, grated

DIRECTIONS

Preheat a slightly greased frying pan over medium-high heat.
Add in the eggs, Italian herb mix, salt, and black pepper. When the eggs are just set and no visible liquid egg remains, top with Asiago cheese. Fold gently in half with the spatula.
Cook an additional 1 to 2 minutes or until cooked through.

STORING

Slice the omelet into two pieces. Place each of them in an airtight container or Ziploc bag; place in the refrigerator for up to 3 to 4 days.
To freeze, place in separate Ziploc bags and freeze up to 3 months. Defrost in your microwave for a few minutes. Bon appétit!

238. Alfredo Cheese Dip

(Ready in about 30 minutes | Servings 12)

Per serving: 154 Calories; 13g Fat; 3.3g Carbs; 6.2g Protein; 0.1g Fiber

INGREDIENTS

2 tablespoons butter
2 cloves garlic, chopped
1 ½ cups Swiss chard, chopped
1/2 cup Swiss cheese, grated
1 ½ cups Ricotta cheese, softened

1/2 cup Prosciutto, roughly chopped
6 ounces double cream
2 egg yolks
Salt and pepper, to taste

DIRECTIONS

Strat by preheating your oven to 355 degrees F.
In a saucepan, melt the butter over medium-low heat. Cook the cream, salt and pepper for about 3 minutes.
Add in the egg yolks and continue to cook for 4 to 5 minutes more, stirring continuously. Spoon the mixture into a baking dish.
Add in the remaining ingredients and stir to combine. Bake in the preheated oven for 18 to 20 minutes.

STORING

Place your dip in an airtight container and keep in your refrigerator for 3 to 4 days. Enjoy!

239. Goat Cheese Deviled Eggs

(Ready in about 20 minutes | Servings 5)

Per serving: 177 Calories; 12.7g Fat; 4.6g Carbs; 11.4g Protein; 0.4g Fiber

INGREDIENTS

10 eggs
2 tablespoons bell peppers, minced
2 tablespoons goat cheese, crumbled
1/4 cup mayonnaise

2 tablespoons shallot, finely chopped
2 tablespoons celery, finely chopped
1/2 teaspoon red pepper flakes
Salt and black pepper, to taste

DIRECTIONS

Place the eggs in a saucepan and cover them with water by 1 inch. Cover and bring the water to a boil over high heat. Boil for 6 to 7 minutes over medium-high heat.
Peel the eggs and slice them in half lengthwise; mix the yolks with the remaining ingredients.
Divide the mixture between the egg whites and arrange the deviled eggs on a nice serving platter.

STORING

Place the deviled eggs in an airtight container or Ziploc bag; transfer to your refrigerator; they should be consumed within 2 days.
For freezing, spoon out the yolk mixture from the deviled eggs. Add the egg yolk mixture to an airtight container or Ziploc bag.
Place the container in the freezer for up to 3 months. To defrost, let them sit overnight in the refrigerator until they are fully thawed out.

240. Genovese Salami and Egg Fat Bombs

(Ready in about 5 minutes | Servings 6)

Per serving: 156 Calories; 12.2g Fat; 1.6g Carbs; 9.7g Protein; 0g Fiber

INGREDIENTS

6 ounces Genovese salami, chopped
2 hard-boiled eggs, chopped
1 ½ tablespoons fresh cilantro, chopped

6 ounces cream cheese
Salt and pepper, to taste

DIRECTIONS

Thoroughly combine all ingredients until well incorporated. Shape into 12 balls.

STORING

Divide the fat bombs between airtight containers or Ziploc bags; keep in your refrigerator for up to 3 to 4 days.
For freezing, place the fat bombs in airtight containers. Freeze up to 1 month. Defrost in the refrigerator. Enjoy!

241. Spanish-Style Sausage and Eggs

(Ready in about 20 minutes | Servings 2)

Per serving: 462 Calories; 40.6g Fat; 7.1g Carbs; 16.9g Protein; 2.1g Fiber

INGREDIENTS

6 ounces Chorizo sausage, crumbled
4 eggs, whisked
1/2 cup Hojiblanca olives, pitted and sliced
1 teaspoon garlic paste
1 teaspoon ancho chili pepper, deveined and minced

2 tablespoons canola oil
1/2 cup red onions, chopped
2 rosemary sprigs, leaves picked and chopped
Salt and black pepper to the taste

DIRECTIONS

In a frying pan, heat the oil over a moderate flame; cook red onions until just tender and fragrant, about 4 to 5 minutes.
Add in the garlic, pepper, salt, black pepper, sausage, and olives; continue to cook, stirring constantly, for 7 to 8 minutes.
Stir in the eggs and rosemary leaves; cook for 4 to 5 minutes, lifting and folding the eggs until thickened.

STORING

Divide the eggs between two airtight containers or Ziploc bags. Refrigerate for up to 3 days.
For freezing, place the eggs in two Ziploc bags and freeze up to 6 months. Defrost in your refrigerator or microwave. Enjoy!

242. Greek-Style Egg and Apple Muffins

(Ready in about 20 minutes | Servings 6)

Per serving: 81 Calories; 3.5g Fat; 6.7g Carbs; 5.5g Protein; 2.1g Fiber

INGREDIENTS

1/4 cup Greek-style yogurt
3 eggs, beaten
1 apple, sliced
3/4 Feta cheese

2 tablespoons ground almonds
4 tablespoons Swerve
1/2 teaspoon vanilla paste

DIRECTIONS

Begin by preheating an oven to 365 degrees F.
Thoroughly combine all ingredients until well mixed. Spoon the batter into lightly buttered muffin cups.
Bake in the preheated oven for about 15 minutes. Place on a wire rack before unmolding.

STORING

Divide the muffins between three airtight containers; keep in the refrigerator for a week.
For freezing, divide the muffins among three Ziploc bags and freeze up to 3 months. Defrost in your microwave for a couple of minutes.
Enjoy!

243. Keto Belgian Waffles

(Ready in about 30 minutes | Servings 6)

Per serving: 316 Calories; 25g Fat; 1.5g Carbs; 20.2g Protein; 0.1g Fiber

INGREDIENTS

3 smoked Belgian sausages, crumbled
1 cup Limburger cheese, shredded
1/2 teaspoon ground cloves

6 eggs
6 tablespoons milk
Sea salt and pepper, to taste

DIRECTIONS

Whisk the eggs with the milk and spices until pale and frothy.
Add in the crumbled Belgian sausage and Limburger cheese. Mix until everything is well combined.
Brush a waffle iron with a nonstick cooking spray.
Pour the batter into waffle iron and cook until golden and cooked through. Repeat until all the batter is used.

STORING

Place the waffles in separate airtight containers; keep in the refrigerator for a week.
For freezing, divide the waffles among two airtight containers or heavy-duty freezer bags and freeze up to 3 months. Defrost in your microwave for a couple of minutes. Enjoy!

244. The Best Cauliflower Fritters Ever

(Ready in about 35 minutes | Servings 6)

Per serving: 199 Calories; 13.8g Fat; 6.8g Carbs; 13g Protein; 2.8g Fiber

INGREDIENTS

1 ½ tablespoons butter, room temperature

1 small onion, chopped

1 garlic clove, minced

1 pound cauliflower, grated

4 tablespoons almond meal

2 tablespoons ground flaxseed

1/2 cup Colby cheese, shredded

1 cup Romano cheese

2 eggs, beaten

Sea salt and pepper, to taste

DIRECTIONS

Begin by preheating your oven to 390 degrees F.

Melt the butter in a nonstick skillet over medium heat. Cook the onion and garlic until they are tender and fragrant.

Add in the remaining ingredients and stir until well combined. Form the mixture into patties.

Bake in the preheated for about 30 minutes, flipping them halfway through the cook time.

STORING

Divide your fritters between three airtight containers or heavy-duty freezer bags; keep in the refrigerator for a week.

For freezing, divide the fritters among three heavy-duty freezer bags; freeze up to 3 months. Defrost in your microwave for a few minutes.

Bon appétit!

245. Scotch Eggs with Ground Pork

(Ready in about 20 minutes | Servings 8)

Per serving: 247 Calories; 11.4g Fat; 0.6g Carbs; 33.7g Protein; 0.1g Fiber

INGREDIENTS

8 eggs

1 ½ pounds ground pork

1/2 cup Romano cheese, freshly grated

1 teaspoon garlic, smashed

1/2 teaspoon onion powder

1/2 teaspoon red pepper flakes, crushed

1 teaspoon Italian seasoning mix

DIRECTIONS

Place the eggs in a saucepan and cover them with water by 1 inch. Cover and bring water to a boil over high heat. Boil for 6 to 7 minutes over medium-high heat; peel the eggs and rinse them under running water.

Thoroughly combine the remaining ingredients. Divide the mixture into 8 pieces; now, using your fingers, shape the meat mixture around the eggs.

Bake in the preheated oven at 365 degrees F for 20minutes until golden brown.

STORING

Place the scotch eggs in airtight containers or Ziploc bags; keep in the refrigerator for up to 1 week.

For freezing, divide the scotch eggs between Ziploc bags; they can be frozen for up to 2 months. Defrost overnight and place in the oven at 175 degrees F for 10 minutes.

246. Mediterranean-Style Panna Cotta

(Ready in about 40 minutes | Servings 8)

Per serving: 155 Calories; 12.7g Fat; 6.2g Carbs; 4.6g Protein; 0.4g Fiber

INGREDIENTS

1 ½ cups double cream

1 cup chive cream cheese

2 teaspoons powdered gelatin

4 bell peppers, sliced

1 tablespoon olive oil, room temperature

1/4 cup fresh parsley, chopped

Salt and pepper, to taste

1/2 teaspoon mustard seeds

1/2 teaspoon paprika

DIRECTIONS

Strat by preheating your oven to 450 degrees F.

Brush the bell peppers with olive oil and roast them for about 30 minutes, until the skin is charred in spots.

Peel the peppers and chop them.

In the meantime, cook the remaining ingredients for about 10 minutes until thoroughly warmed.

Fold in the chopped peppers and stir to combine. Divide the mixture between eight lightly oiled ramekins. Place in your refrigerator overnight.

STORING

Cover each ramekin with plastic wrap and refrigerate for up to 5 days. Enjoy!

247. Chipotle Cheese Frittata

(Ready in about 25 minutes | Servings 6)

Per serving: 225 Calories; 17g Fat; 5.1g Carbs; 13.2g Protein; 0.9g Fiber

INGREDIENTS

1/3 cup Crema Mexicana
1 Spanish pepper, chopped
1 teaspoon chipotle paste
1 ½ cups spinach

1 tablespoon butter, room temperature
1 large onion, chopped
2 garlic cloves, minced
10 eggs

Salt and black pepper, to taste
1/2 cup Mexican cheese blend, shredded

DIRECTIONS

Preheat your oven to 365 degrees F.
In an oven-proof skillet, melt the butter over a moderately high flame. Sauté the onion until caramelized and fragrant.
Add in the garlic, Spanish peppers, and chipotle paste, and continue to cook for about 4 minutes more.
Add in the spinach and continue to cook for 2 minutes or until it wilts. Whisk the eggs, salt, pepper and Crema Mexicana.
Spoon the egg/cheese mixture into the skillet.
Bake in the preheated oven for 8 to 10 minutes or until your frittata is golden on top.
Top with the Mexican cheese blend and bake an additional 5 minutes or until the cheese is hot and bubbly.

STORING

Cut the frittata into six wedges. Place each of them in an airtight container; place in the refrigerator for up 3 to 4 days.
To freeze, place in separate Ziploc bags and freeze up to 3 months. To defrost, place in your microwave for a few minutes.

248. Easy Mini Frittatas

(Ready in about 40 minutes | Servings 5)

Per serving: 261 Calories; 16g Fat; 6.6g Carbs; 21.1g Protein; 0.9g Fiber

INGREDIENTS

8 eggs, whisked
1 cup Asiago cheese, shredded
1/2 teaspoon chipotle powder
1 tablespoon olive oil

1 onion, chopped
1 Italian pepper, chopped
1 cup spinach, torn into pieces
3 slices bacon, chopped

Salt and pepper, to taste
1 tablespoon fresh coriander, chopped

DIRECTIONS

Begin by preheating your oven to 380 degrees F.
Heat the oil in frying pan over medium-high heat; cook the onion for about 6 minutes or until caramelized.
Add in the pepper and spinach, and continue to sauté for 4 to 5 minutes.
Add in the bacon and continue to cook for 3 to 4 minutes. Stir in the remaining ingredients. Spoon the mixture into a lightly oiled muffin pan.
Bake in the preheated oven for about 22 minutes.

STORING

Place the mini frittatas in the airtight containers or Ziploc bags; keep in the refrigerator for a week.
For freezing, divide the mini frittatas between two Ziploc bags and freeze up to 3 months. Defrost in your microwave for a couple of minutes. Bon appétit!

249. Nutty Cheese Logs

(Ready in about 10 minutes + chilling time | Servings 15)

Per serving: 209 Calories; 18.9g Fat; 3.7g Carbs; 6.6g Protein; 0.3g Fiber

INGREDIENTS

1 tablespoon Mediterranean spice mix
1 teaspoon lemon juice
14 ounces Ricotta cheese, at room temperature

14 ounces Swiss cheese, grated
1/2 cup mayonnaise
1/2 cup pine nuts, finely chopped

DIRECTIONS

Combine all ingredients, except for the pine nut, in a mixing bowl. Place the mixture in your refrigerator for about 4 hours or until firm.
Shape the mixture into two logs and roll them over chopped pine nuts.

STORING

Place the cheese logs in airtight containers or Ziploc bags; keep in your refrigerator for up to 3 to 4 days.
For freezing, place the cheese logs in airtight containers. Freeze up to 1 month. Defrost in the refrigerator. Enjoy!

250. Spanish-Style Cheese Crisps

(Ready in about 18 minutes | Servings 2)

Per serving: 100 Calories; 8g Fat; 0g Carbs; 7g Protein; 0.4g Fiber

INGREDIENTS

3 cups Manchego cheese, grated
1 teaspoon dried Perejil
1/2 teaspoon Spanish pimentón

Sea salt and black pepper, to taste
1/2 teaspoon granulated garlic

DIRECTIONS

Start by preheating your oven to 410 degrees F.
Mix all of the above ingredients. Place about 2 tablespoons of the mixture into small mounds on a parchment-lined baking sheet.
Bake for 13 to 15 minutes or until golden and crisp.

STORING

Divide the crisps between two airtight containers or Ziploc bags; keep in your refrigerator for up to 4 days.
To freeze, divide the crisps between two airtight containers. Freeze up to 2 months. Defrost and reheat in your oven until it is crisp. Enjoy!

251. Vegetarian Tacos with Guacamole

(Ready in about 10 minutes | Servings 6)

Per serving: 370 Calories; 30g Fat; 4.9g Carbs; 19.5g Protein; 4g Fiber

INGREDIENTS

1 pound Monterey-Jack cheese, grated
1 teaspoon taco seasoning mix
1 ½ cups guacamole

1 cup cream cheese
2 cups arugula

DIRECTIONS

Thoroughly combine the cheese and taco seasoning mix.
On a parchment-lined baking sheet, place 1/4 cup piles of cheese 2 inches apart. Press the cheese down lightly.
Bake at 350 degrees F for about 7 minutes or until the edges of your tacos are brown.

STORING

Place the cheese tacos in airtight containers and keep in your refrigerator for up to 3 to 4 days.
Assemble your tacos. Top with the guacamole, cream cheese and arugula. Enjoy!

252. Baked Eggs Provencal

(Ready in about 20 minutes | Servings 5)

Per serving: 444 Calories; 35.3g Fat; 2.7g Carbs; 29.8g Protein; 1g Fiber

INGREDIENTS

1 teaspoon Herbes de Provence
1/4 cup chicken broth
5 eggs
1 ½ cups Comté cheese, shredded
4 slices Bayonne ham, chopped

1/2 cup onions, chopped
1/2 cup fire-roasted tomatoes, diced
1 clove garlic, minced
1 tablespoon butter

DIRECTIONS

In an oven-proof pan, melt the butter over medium-high heat. Now, cook the Bayonne ham for about 5 minutes until crisp; reserve.
Then, sauté the onions in the pan drippings. Add in the tomatoes, garlic, Herbes de Provence, and broth; continue to cook for 5 to 6 minutes more.
Now, create 5 holes in the vegetable mixture. Crack an egg into each hole.
Bake in the preheated oven at 350 degrees F for about 18 minutes until the egg whites are completely cooked through. Top with reserved Bayonne ham.

STORING

Place the Eggs Provencal in airtight containers or Ziploc bags; keep in your refrigerator for 3 to 4 days.
Place the Eggs Provencal in a freezable container; they can be frozen for up to 1 month.
Top with the cheese. Bake the thawed Eggs Provencal at 200 degrees F until they are completely warm. Enjoy!

253. Dad's Cheeseburger Quiche

(Ready in about 45 minutes | Servings 6)

Per serving: 310 Calories; 18.3g Fat; 3.8g Carbs; 30.7g Protein; 0.6g Fiber

INGREDIENTS

1 Italian pepper, chopped
1/2 pound ground beef
1/2 ground pork
1 medium leek, chopped

1 garlic clove, chopped
2 zucchinis, thinly sliced
2 tomatoes, thinly sliced
1/4 cup double cream

8 eggs
1/2 cup Colby cheese, grated
Salt and pepper, to taste

DIRECTIONS

Preheat a lightly greased nonstick skillet over medium-high heat. Now, brown the ground meat, leek, garlic and Italian pepper for about 5 minutes, stirring periodically. Season with salt and pepper to taste.
Spoon the meat layer on the bottom of a lightly greased baking pan. Place the zucchini slices on top. Top with tomato slices.
Beat the cream, eggs and cheese in a mixing dish. Spread this mixture on the top of the vegetables.
Bake in the preheated oven at 360 degrees F for about 45 minutes or until cooked through.

STORING

Slice the quiche into six pieces; divide between airtight containers or Ziploc bags; keep in your refrigerator for up to 3 days.
For freezing, place the quiche in airtight containers or heavy-duty freezer bags. Freeze up to 3 months. Once thawed in the refrigerator, heat in the microwave until warmed through. Enjoy!

254. French-Style Gorgonzola Cheese Soup

(Ready in about 20 minutes | Servings 4)

Per serving: 296 Calories; 14.1g Fat; 6.4g Carbs; 14.2g Protein; 1.5g Fiber

INGREDIENTS

6 ounces Gorgonzola cheese, shredded
1 ½ cups milk
1 celery stalk, chopped
1 chili pepper, finely chopped

1 teaspoon ginger-garlic paste
1 ½ tablespoons flaxseed meal
2 cups water
2 tablespoons butter

1/2 cup white onions, chopped
Salt and pepper, to taste

DIRECTIONS

Melt the butter in a heavy-bottomed pot over a moderately high heat. Sauté the onions, celery and pepper until tender and fragrant.
Add in the garlic paste, flaxseed meal, water, and milk and bring to a boil; immediately, turn the heat to medium-low. Partially cover, and continue to simmer for 8 to 10 minutes.
Fold in the Gorgonzola cheese and remove from the heat. Season with salt and pepper.

STORING

Spoon the soup into four airtight containers; keep in your refrigerator for up to 4 days.

255. Italian Burgers with Mushrooms

(Ready in about 20 minutes | Servings 4)

Per serving: 370 Calories; 30g Fat; 4.7g Carbs; 16.8g Protein; 2.2g Fiber

INGREDIENTS

1/2 stick butter, softened
1 teaspoon garlic, minced
2 cups Cremini mushrooms, chopped

6 tablespoons blanched almond flour
6 tablespoons ground flax seeds
1 tablespoon Italian seasoning mix

1 teaspoon Dijon mustard
2 eggs, whisked
1/2 cup Romano cheese, grated

DIRECTIONS

In a frying pan, melt 1 tablespoon of butter over medium-high heat. Sauté the garlic and mushrooms until just tender and fragrant; drain excess water.
Add in the remaining ingredients and mix to combine well.
Shape the mixture into 4 patties.
In the same frying pan, melt the remaining butter; once hot, fry the patties for 6 to 7 minutes per side.

STORING

Divide your burgers between four airtight containers or heavy-duty freezer bags; keep in the refrigerator for a week.
For freezing, divide your burgers among four heavy-duty freezer bags; freeze up to 3 months. Defrost in your microwave for a few minutes.
Bon appétit!

VEGETABLES & SIDE DISHES

256. Tangy Cabbage Soup

(Ready in about 25 minutes | Servings 4)

Per serving: 185 Calories; 16.6g Fat; 2.4g Carbs; 2.9g Protein; 1.9g Fiber

INGREDIENTS

2 cups cabbage, shredded
1 cup sour cream
1 bell pepper, chopped

4 cups roasted vegetable broth
1 ½ tablespoons olive oil
1 yellow onion, chopped

2 garlic cloves, minced
1 celery, chopped

DIRECTIONS

In a heavy-bottomed pot, heat olive oil over a moderate flame. Sauté the onion and garlic until just tender and aromatic.
Add in the celery, cabbage, and pepper and continue to cook for about 6 minutes, stirring occasionally to ensure even cooking.
Pour in the roasted vegetable broth and cook, partially covered, for 10 to 12 minutes longer.
Puree the mixture with an immersion blender. Stir in the sour cream; and remove from heat; stir to combine well.

STORING

Spoon the soup into four airtight containers; keep in your refrigerator for up to 4 days.
For freezing, place the soup in heavy-duty freezer bags. When the bags are frozen through, stack them up like file folders to save space in the freezer. Enjoy!

257. Summer Cheese Ball

(Ready in about 25 minutes | Servings 2)

Per serving: 133 Calories; 9.9g Fat; 6.8g Carbs; 6g Protein; 0.7g Fiber

INGREDIENTS

1 Lebanese cucumber, chopped
2 tablespoons pine nuts, chopped

1 teaspoon salt
1 ounce Feta cheese

1 ounce Neufchatel
1 tablespoon fresh basil, chopped

DIRECTIONS

Salt the chopped cucumber and place it in a colander. Let it stand for 30 minutes; press the cucumber to drain away the excess liquid and transfer to a mixing bowl.
Mix in the cheese and basil. Shape the mixture into a ball and top with chopped nuts.

STORING

Place the cheese ball in an airtight container or Ziploc bags; keep in your refrigerator for up to 3 to 4 days.
For freezing, place the cheese ball in an airtight container. Freeze up to 1 month. Defrost in the refrigerator. Enjoy!

258. Ground Chicken-Stuffed Tomatoes

(Ready in about 25 minutes | Servings 4)

Per serving: 366 Calories; 23.2g Fat; 6.8g Carbs; 23.2g Protein; 2.1g Fiber

INGREDIENTS

4 tomatoes, scoop out the pulp
Seasoned salt and pepper, to taste
1/2 cup cream of celery soup
1 ½ cups Parmesan cheese, grated

1/2 cup onions, chopped
1 garlic clove, smashed
1 tablespoon canola oil
1/2 pound ground chicken

1 tablespoon fresh coriander, chopped
1 teaspoon oregano, chopped

DIRECTIONS

In a frying pan, heat the oil over a moderately-high heat. Cook ground chicken, onion, and garlic for about 4 minutes, stirring periodically to ensure even cooking; set aside.
Add in the tomato pulp, coriander, oregano, salt, and pepper. Divide this filling between tomatoes.
Place the stuffed tomatoes in a lightly oiled casserole dish.
Pour the cream of celery soup around stuffed tomatoes; bake in the preheated oven at 365 degrees F for about 20 until heated through.

STORING

Place the stuffed tomatoes in airtight containers; keep in your refrigerator for 3 to 4 days.
Wrap each stuffed tomato tightly in several layers of plastic wrap and squeeze the air out. Place them in airtight containers; they can be frozen for up to 1 month.
Reheat the thawed stuffed tomatoes at 200 degrees F until they are completely warm. Top with Parmesan cheese and place under preheated broiled for 5 minutes until hot and bubbly. Enjoy!

259. Greek-Style Roasted Asparagus

(Ready in about 15 minutes | Servings 6)

Per serving: 128 Calories; 9.4g Fat; 2.9g Carbs; 6.4g Protein; 2.9g Fiber

INGREDIENTS

1 cup Halloumi cheese, crumbled
1 red onion, chopped
2 garlic cloves, minced

1 ½ pounds asparagus spears
2 tablespoons extra-virgin olive oil
Salt and black pepper, to the taste

DIRECTIONS

Brush your asparagus with extra-virgin olive oil. Toss with the onion, garlic, salt, and black pepper.
Roast in the preheated oven at 395 degrees F for about 15 minutes.

STORING

Place the roasted asparagus in airtight containers; keep in your refrigerator for 3 to 5 days.
For freezing, place the roasted asparagus in a freezable container; they can be frozen for 10 to 12 months.
Top the roasted asparagus with cheese and place under the preheated broiler for 5 to 6 minutes or until cheese melts. Enjoy!

260. Pasta with Alfredo Sauce

(Ready in about 30 minutes | Servings 4)

Per serving: 614 Calories; 55.9g Fat; 3.6g Carbs; 25.6g Protein; 0g Fiber

INGREDIENTS

1 stick butter
1 cup double cream
1 garlic clove, minced
2 cups Romano cheese, grated

2 ounces Ricotta cheese, room temperature
3 eggs, room temperature
1/2 teaspoon wheat gluten
1 teaspoon Italian spice mix

DIRECTIONS

Mix the Ricotta cheese, eggs, and gluten until creamy. Press this mixture into a parchment-lined baking sheet.
Bake at 310 degrees F for about 6 minutes. Let it cool for about 10 minutes and cut into strips using a sharp knife.
Cook this the pasta in a lightly salted water for 3 to 4 minutes.
In a saucepan, melt the butter over low heat. Cook the garlic and cream until warmed; stir in Romano cheese and Italian spice mix; heat off.
Fold in the reserved pasta. Gently stir to combine.

STORING

Place the pasta with the alfredo sauce in airtight containers; keep in your refrigerator for 3 to 4 days.

261. Goat Cheese, Ham, and Spinach Muffins

(Ready in about 25 minutes | Servings 6)

Per serving: 275 Calories; 15.8g Fat; 2.2g Carbs; 21.6g Protein; 1.2g Fiber

INGREDIENTS

10 ounces baby spinach, cooked and drained
1/2 pound smoked ham, chopped
1 teaspoon Mediterranean seasoning mix
1 ½ cups goat cheese, crumbled

5 eggs
1/2 cup milk
Salt and pepper, to taste

DIRECTIONS

Thoroughly combine all ingredients in a mixing bowl. Spoon the batter into a lightly oiled muffin tin.
Bake in the preheated oven at 350 degrees F for about 25 minutes.

STORING

Place these muffins in airtight containers or Ziploc bags; keep in the refrigerator for a week.
For freezing, divide the muffins among Ziploc bags and freeze up to 3 months. Defrost in your microwave for a couple of minutes. Enjoy!

262. Cheddar and Mushroom-Stuffed Peppers

(Ready in about 30 minutes | Servings 6)

Per serving: 319 Calories; 18.8g Fat; 5.6g Carbs; 10.3g Protein; 1.9g Fiber

INGREDIENTS

6 bell peppers, seeds and tops removed
1/2 cup Cheddar cheese, grated
1/2 cup tomato puree
3/4 pound Cremini mushrooms, chopped
2 tablespoons olive oil

1 onion, chopped
1 teaspoon garlic, minced
2 tablespoons fresh cilantro, chopped
1 teaspoon mustard seeds
Salt to taste

DIRECTIONS

In a frying pan, heat the olive oil over a moderately-high flame. Sauté the onion and garlic until they are tender and aromatic.
Add in the Cremini mushrooms and continue to cook for a further 5 minutes or until the mushrooms release the liquid.
Add in the cilantro, mustard seeds, and salt; stir to combine. Divide this filling between bell peppers. Place the peppers in a lightly greased casserole dish.
Pour the tomato sauce around stuffed peppers. Bake at 385 degrees F for about 22 minutes or until heated through.

STORING

Place the stuffed peppers in airtight containers; keep in your refrigerator for 3 to 4 days.
Wrap each stuffed pepper tightly in several layers of plastic wrap and squeeze the air out. Place them in airtight containers; they can be frozen for up to 1 month.
Top with Cheddar cheese. Bake the thawed stuffed peppers at 300 degrees F until cheese melts.

263. Aromatic Prawns with Bok Choy

(Ready in about 15 minutes | Servings 4)

Per serving: 171 Calories; 8.4g Fat; 5.8g Carbs; 18.9g Protein; 1.9g Fiber

INGREDIENTS

10 ounces prawns, peeled and deveined
1 ½ pounds Bok choy, trimmed and thinly sliced
1 (1/2-inch) piece ginger, freshly grated
1 tablespoon fish sauce

2 tablespoons peanut oil
1 teaspoon garlic, minced
Salt and pepper, to taste

DIRECTIONS

Heat 1 tablespoon of the peanut oil in a frying pan over a moderately-high heat. Sauté the garlic until tender and aromatic.
Stir in the Bok choy, ginger, fish sauce, salt, and pepper; cook for 5 to 6 minutes, stirring periodically to ensure even cooking.
In the same pan, heat the remaining tablespoon of oil and cook the prawns until opaque, about 4 minutes.
Serve your prawns with the reserved Bok choy.

STORING

Place the prawns and Bok choy in airtight containers or Ziploc bags; keep in your refrigerator for up 3 to 4 days.
For freezing, place your prawns and Bok choy in heavy-duty freezer bags. Freeze up to 3 months. Defrost in your refrigerator. Enjoy!

264. Creole Cheesy Spinach

(Ready in about 10 minutes | Servings 4)

Per serving: 208 Calories; 13.5g Fat; 6g Carbs; 14.5g Protein; 5.1g Fiber

INGREDIENTS

2 pounds spinach, torn into pieces
1/2 stick butter
Sea salt and pepper, to taste

1/4 teaspoon caraway seeds
1 cup Creole cream cheese
1 teaspoon garlic, pressed

DIRECTIONS

Melt the butter in a saucepan over medium-high heat; now, sauté the garlic until tender and fragrant.
Add the spinach, salt, pepper, and caraway seeds; continue to cook for about 6 minutes until warmed through.

STORING

Place your spinach in airtight containers; keep in your refrigerator for 3 to 5 days.
For freezing, place your spinach in a freezable container; they can be frozen for 4 to 5 months. Top with the cheese and reheat in the saucepan until cheese melts completely. Enjoy!

265. Brown Mushroom Stew

(Ready in about 30 minutes | Servings 4)

Per serving: 133 Calories; 3.7g Fat; 5.7g Carbs; 14g Protein; 3.1g Fiber

INGREDIENTS

1/2 pound brown mushrooms, chopped
1 tablespoon butter, room temperature
1 cup onions, chopped
1 bay laurel
1 celery, chopped

2 ½ cups vegetable broth
1/4 cup dry white wine
1 cup tomato puree
Salt and ground black pepper, to taste
1/4 teaspoon ground allspice

1 teaspoon jalapeno pepper, deveined and minced
1 bell pepper, deveined and chopped
2 garlic cloves, pressed
1/4 cup fresh parsley, chopped

DIRECTIONS

In Dutch oven, melt the butter over a moderate heat. Cook the onion, peppers, garlic, and celery for about 7 minutes.
Add in the mushrooms and cook an additional 2 to 3 minutes. Add in the vegetable broth, wine, tomato puree, and seasonings; bring to a boil.
Turn the heat to a simmer; let it simmer for about 20 minutes or until cooked through.

STORING

Spoon the stew into four airtight containers or Ziploc bags; keep in your refrigerator for up to 3 to 4 days.
For freezing, place the stew in airtight containers. Freeze up to 4 to 6 months. Defrost in the refrigerator. Bon appétit!

266. Spicy and Aromatic Chinese Cabbage

(Ready in about 15 minutes | Servings 4)

Per serving: 53 Calories; 3.7g Fat; 3.2g Carbs; 1.7g Protein; 2.1g Fiber

INGREDIENTS

3/4 pound Chinese cabbage, cored and cut into chunks
1 teaspoon Chinese Five-spice powder
Salt and Sichuan pepper, to taste
1 tablespoon sesame oil

1 shallot, sliced
1/2 teaspoon chili sauce, sugar-free
2 tablespoons rice wine
1 tablespoon soy sauce

DIRECTIONS

Heat the sesame oil in a wok a moderately-high heat. Sauté the shallot until tender and translucent. Add in the Chinese cabbage and continue to cook for about 3 minutes.
Partially cover and add in the remaining ingredients; continue to cook for 5 minutes more.

STORING

Place the Chinese cabbage in airtight containers or Ziploc bags; keep in your refrigerator for 3 to 5 days.
Place the Chinese cabbage in freezable containers; they can be frozen for up to 10 months. Defrost in the refrigerator or microwave. Bon appétit!

267. Roasted Tomatoes with Cheese

(Ready in about 25 minutes | Servings 4)

Per serving: 247 Calories; 19.8g Fat; 5.3g Carbs; 11g Protein; 1.8g Fiber

INGREDIENTS

1 ½ pounds tomatoes, sliced
1/4 cup extra-virgin olive oil
1 tablespoon balsamic vinegar
2 garlic cloves, pressed

Sea salt and pepper, to taste
1 teaspoon Mediterranean spice mix
1 cup Caciocavallo cheese, shredded

DIRECTIONS

Start by preheating your oven to 390 degrees F.
Toss your tomatoes with olive oil, vinegar, garlic, salt, pepper, and Mediterranean spice mix. Place tomatoes on a lightly oiled baking sheet.
Roast in the preheated oven for about 20 minutes until your tomatoes begin to caramelize.

STORING

Place the roasted tomatoes in airtight containers or Ziploc bags; keep in your refrigerator for 3 to 4 days.
Place the roasted tomatoes in freezable containers; they can be frozen for up to 1 month.
Top the thawed tomatoes with Caciocavallo cheese and place under the preheated broiler until the cheese is hot and bubbly. Enjoy!

268. Old-Fashioned Cabbage with Bacon and Eggs

(Ready in about 15 minutes | Servings 4)

Per serving: 173 Calories; 10.6g Fat; 5.6g Carbs; 14.2g Protein; 1.6g Fiber

INGREDIENTS

2 cups cabbage, shredded
2 teaspoons red wine
4 eggs
4 rashers of bacon, chopped
1 cup red onions, minced

1 teaspoon garlic, smashed
1 bay laurel
1 thyme sprig
1 rosemary sprig
Kosher salt and black pepper, to taste

DIRECTIONS

Cook the bacon in a nonstick skillet over medium-high heat; reserve. Sauté the red onions and garlic in 1 tablespoon of bacon grease.
Add in the cabbage and continue to cook, stirring frequently, until it has softened or about 4 minutes.
Add a splash of wine to deglaze the pan. Add in the spices and continue to cook for a further 2 minutes.
Fry the eggs in 1 tablespoon of bacon grease. Add in the reserved bacon and top with fried eggs.

STORING

Place your cabbage in airtight containers or Ziploc bags; keep in your refrigerator for 3 to 5 days.
Place your cabbage in freezable containers; they can be frozen for up to 10 months. Defrost in the refrigerator or microwave. Bon appétit!

269. Mixed Greens with Caciocavallo Cheese

(Ready in about 25 minutes | Servings 5)

Per serving: 160 Calories; 10g Fat; 5.1g Carbs; 11g Protein; 4.6g Fiber

INGREDIENTS

2 pounds mixed greens, fresh or frozen, torn into pieces
1 tablespoon olive oil
1/4 cup cream of celery soup
1 tablespoon balsamic vinegar

Sea salt and pepper, to taste
1 cup Caciocavallo cheese, shredded
1 teaspoon garlic, chopped
1/2 cup shallot

DIRECTIONS

Het the olive oil in a Dutch oven over a moderately-high heat. Cook the garlic and shallot for 2 to 3 minutes or until tender and fragrant.
Add in the mixed greens and cream of celery soup; continue to cook, partially covered, for about 15 minutes until greens are wilted.
Add in the vinegar, salt, and pepper; heat off.

STORING

Place the sautéed greens in airtight containers; keep in your refrigerator for 3 to 5 days.
For freezing, place the sautéed greens in a freezable container; they can be frozen for 4 to 5 months. Top with cheese and reheat in the saucepan until cheese melts completely. Enjoy!

270. Cabbage Noodles with Meat Sauce

(Ready in about 20 minutes | Servings 4)

Per serving: 236 Calories; 8.3g Fat; 5.1g Carbs; 29.9g Protein; 2.9g Fiber

INGREDIENTS

1 pound green cabbage, spiralized
1/2 teaspoon garlic, chopped
3/4 pound ground chuck
1/2 teaspoon chili pepper, minced

2 slices pancetta, chopped
1/2 cup onion, thinly sliced
2 bay leaves
Sea salt and black pepper, to taste

DIRECTIONS

Parboil the cabbage in a pot of lightly salted water for 3 to 4 minutes; drain.
Cook the pancetta over a moderately-high heat for about 4 minutes, breaking apart with a fork and reserve.
Cook the onion and garlic in the bacon grease until they've softened. Add in the ground chuck, chili pepper, salt and black pepper; continue to cook until ground beef is no longer pink.
Add the pancetta back to the pan. Top with the cabbage noodles.

STORING

Place the cabbage noodles in airtight containers or Ziploc bags; keep in your refrigerator for 3 to 5 days.
Place the cabbage noodles in freezable containers; they can be frozen for up to 10 months. Defrost in the refrigerator or microwave. Bon appétit!

271. Greek-Style Zucchini Patties

(Ready in about 15 minutes | Servings 6)

Per serving: 153 Calories; 11.8g Fat; 6.6g Carbs; 6.4g Protein; 1.1g Fiber

INGREDIENTS

1 pound zucchinis, shredded
1 cup Halloumi cheese, shredded
1/2 cup onion, finely chopped
1 teaspoon garlic, finely minced
2 tablespoons butter

1 egg, whisked
2 celery stalks, shredded
2 tablespoons cilantro, chopped
Sea salt and pepper, to taste

DIRECTIONS

Thoroughly combine all ingredients in a mixing bowl.
Form the mixture into 12 patties and arrange them on a parchment-lined baking sheet.
Bake in the preheated oven at 365 degrees F for 12 minutes, rotating the pan once or twice.

STORING

Place the zucchini patties in airtight containers or Ziploc bags; keep in your refrigerator for 3 to 5 days.
Place the zucchini patties in a freezable container; they can be frozen for up to 10 to 12 months. Bake the thawed zucchini at 200 degrees F. Enjoy!

272. Roman-Style Chicory with Pine Nuts

(Ready in about 10 minutes | Servings 4)

Per serving: 65 Calories; 4.7g Fat; 5.7g Carbs; 2.1g Protein; 1.5g Fiber

INGREDIENTS

3 teaspoons butter
2 heads chicory, cut into chunks
1/4 cup pine nuts

2 garlic cloves, crushed
1 shallot, chopped
Salt and pepper, to taste

DIRECTIONS

Parboil the chicory in a pot of lightly salted water for 5 to 6 minutes; drain.
Melt the butter over moderately-high heat and sauté the chicory with garlic and shallots.
Season with salt and pepper. Top with pine nuts.

STORING

Place the sautéed chicory in airtight containers; keep in your refrigerator for 3 to 5 days.
For freezing, place the sautéed chicory in a freezable container; they can be frozen for 4 to 5 months. Enjoy!

273. Spicy Salad with Macadamia Nuts

(Ready in about 5 minutes | Servings 4)

Per serving: 184 Calories; 16.8g Fat; 4g Carbs; 2.1g Protein; 1.4g Fiber

INGREDIENTS

1 cup radishes, thinly sliced
2 cups butterhead lettuce, torn into bite-sized pieces
1 Lebanese cucumber, sliced
1 bell pepper, sliced
1 white onion, sliced
1 ounce macadamia nuts, chopped

Sea salt, to season
1 tablespoon sunflower seeds
1/2 lemon, freshly squeezed
3 tablespoons olive oil
1/2 teaspoon Sriracha sauce

DIRECTIONS

In a mixing bowl, toss all ingredients until well combined.
Taste and adjust seasonings.
Storing
Place your salad in airtight containers and keep in your refrigerator for up to 3 days.

274. Caciocavallo Cheese and Spinach Muffins

(Ready in about 30 minutes | Servings 6)

Per serving: 252 Calories; 19.7g Fat; 3g Carbs; 16.1g Protein; 0.2g Fiber

INGREDIENTS

1 cup spinach, chopped
2 tablespoons butter, melted
Sea salt and black pepper, to taste

8 eggs
1 cup full-fat milk
1 ½ cups Caciocavallo cheese, shredded

DIRECTIONS

Start by preheating your oven to 360 degrees F. Brush muffin cups with a nonstick spray.
Whisk the eggs and milk until pale and frothy; add in the butter, salt, pepper, and spinach. Fold in the cheese.
Bake in the preheated oven for 20 to 22 minutes or until a tester comes out dry and clean.

STORING

Wrap the muffins tightly with heavy-duty aluminum foil or plastic wrap. Then, keep in your refrigerator for up to 3 to 4 days.
For freezing, wrap the muffins tightly to prevent freezer burn. Freeze up to 3 to 4 months. Defrost in the refrigerator. Bon appétit!

275. Cream of Cauliflower Soup

(Ready in about 20 minutes | Servings 4)

Per serving: 260 Calories; 22.5g Fat; 4.1g Carbs; 7.2g Protein; 4.2g Fiber

INGREDIENTS

3 cups cauliflower, cut into florets
1 cup avocado, pitted and chopped
Salt and pepper, to taste

1 thyme sprig
1 cup coconut milk, unsweetened
3 cups roasted vegetable broth

DIRECTIONS

In a heavy-bottomed pot, simmer the vegetable broth over medium-high heat. Add in the cauliflower and continue to simmer for 10 to 15 minutes more.
Add in the coconut milk, avocado, salt, pepper, and thyme. Partially cover and continue to cook for a further 5 minutes.
Puree the mixture in your blender.

STORING

Spoon the soup into airtight containers; keep in your refrigerator for up 3 to 4 days.
For freezing, place the soup in airtight containers or heavy-duty freezer bags. Freeze up to 4 to 6 months. Defrost in the microwave or refrigerator. Enjoy!

276. Kapusta (Polish Braised Cabbage)

(Ready in about 20 minutes | Servings 6)

Per serving: 259 Calories; 18.1g Fat; 3.6g Carbs; 15.5g Protein; 1.8g Fiber

INGREDIENTS

1 pound cabbage, shredded
1 bell pepper, finely chopped
1/2 cup vegetable broth

3 strips bacon, diced
1/2 teaspoon red pepper flakes, crushed

DIRECTIONS

In a Dutch oven, fry the bacon for 5 to 6 minutes. Add in the cabbage and pepper and continue to cook until they've softened.
Add in the broth and red pepper flakes and cover the pan. Turn the heat to medium-low and let it simmer for 10 to 13 minutes or until cooked through.
Taste and adjust the seasonings.

STORING

Place the roasted cabbage in airtight containers or Ziploc bags; keep in your refrigerator for 3 to 5 days.
Place the cabbage in freezable containers; they can be frozen for up to 10 months. Defrost in the refrigerator or microwave. Bon appétit!

277. Kohlrabi with Garlic-Mushroom Sauce

(Ready in about 15 minutes | Servings 4)

Per serving: 220 Calories; 20g Fat; 5.3g Carbs; 4g Protein; 3.8g Fiber

INGREDIENTS

3/4 pound kohlrabi, trimmed and thinly sliced
1/2 pound button mushrooms, sliced
1 ½ cups sour cream
3 tablespoons olive oil

1/2 cup white onions, chopped
1/2 teaspoon garlic, chopped
Kosher salt and ground black pepper, to taste

DIRECTIONS

In a large pot of salted water, place the kohlrabi and parboil over medium-high heat for about 8 minutes. Drain.
In a saucepan, heat the oil over medium-high heat. Sauté the onions, mushrooms, and garlic until they've softened.
Season with salt and pepper to taste. Add in the sour cream and stir to combine well.

STORING

Transfer the vegetables to the airtight containers and place in your refrigerator for up to 3 to 5 days.
For freezing, place the vegetables in freezer safe containers and freeze up to 8 to 10 months. Defrost in the microwave for a few minutes.
Bon appétit!

278. Greek-Style Vegetables

(Ready in about 15 minutes | Servings 4)

Per serving: 318 Calories; 24.3g Fat; 5.1g Carbs; 15.4g Protein; 1.7g Fiber

INGREDIENTS

1/2 pound brown mushrooms, chopped
1 cup broccoli, cut into small florets
1 medium-sized zucchini, chopped
8 ounces feta cheese, cubed
1 teaspoon Greek seasoning mix

2 tablespoons olive oil
1 onion, chopped
1 teaspoon garlic, minced
1 vine-ripened tomato, pureed
1/4 cup white wine

DIRECTIONS

In a medium pot, heat the oil over a moderately-high heat. Sauté the onion and garlic for about 5 minutes, adding a splash of water if needed, until tender and aromatic.
Add in the mushrooms, broccoli, zucchini, Greek seasoning mix, tomato puree, and white wine. Continue to cook for 4 to 5 minutes or until they've softened.

STORING

Place the Greek vegetables in airtight containers or Ziploc bags; keep in your refrigerator for 3 to 5 days.
Place the Greek vegetables in freezable containers; they can be frozen for up to 10 months. Defrost in the refrigerator or microwave. Serve with cubed feta cheese. Enjoy!

279. Easy Keto Broccoli Pilaf

(Ready in about 20 minutes | Servings 4)

Per serving: 126 Calories; 11.6g Fat; 5.4g Carbs; 1.3g Protein; 2.7g Fiber

INGREDIENTS

1 head broccoli, broken into a rice-like chunks
1 Italian pepper, chopped
1 habanero pepper, minced
1/2 shallots, chopped

1/2 teaspoon garlic, smashed
1 celery rib, chopped
1/2 stick butter
Salt and pepper, to your liking

DIRECTIONS

In a saucepan, melt the butter over a moderately-high heat. Saute the shallot, garlic, and peppers for about 3 minutes.
Stir in the broccoli and celery; continue to cook for 4 to 5 minutes or until tender and aromatic. Season with salt and pepper to taste.
Continue to cook for 5 to 6 minutes or until everything is cooked through.

STORING

Spoon the broccoli pilaf into four airtight containers; keep in your refrigerator for 3 to 5 days.
For freezing, place the broccoli pilaf in airtight containers or heavy-duty freezer bags. Freeze up to 10 to 12 months. Defrost in the microwave. Bon appétit!

280. Provençal-Style Green Beans

(Ready in about 15 minutes | Servings 4)

Per serving: 183 Calories; 16.1g Fat; 4.4g Carbs; 3.2g Protein; 4g Fiber

INGREDIENTS

1 pound green beans
1/2 teaspoon fresh garlic, minced
1/2 teaspoon red pepper flakes
Salt and pepper, to taste

1 tablespoon butter, melted
1 celery stalk, shredded
For Tapenade:
1 ½ tablespoons capers

2 anchovy fillets
1 tablespoon fresh lime juice
1/2 cup black olives
3 tablespoons extra-virgin olive oil

DIRECTIONS

Steam the green beans approximately 4 minutes or until crisp-tender.
In a saucepan, melt the butter over a moderately-high heat. Sauté the celery and garlic for 4 to 5 minutes or until they are tender and fragrant. Add in green beans and stir to combine.
Season with red pepper, salt, and black pepper.
To make the tapenade, pulse all ingredients until well combined.

STORING

Place the green beans in airtight containers and keep in your refrigerator for 3 to 4 days.
Place the tapenade in airtight containers and keep in your refrigerator for up to a week.
Spread the chilled green beans in a single layer on a baking sheet. Freeze for about 2 hours. Place the frozen green beans in freezer bags and keep for about 3 months. Reheat in a saucepan and enjoy!

281. Chanterelle with Eggs and Enchilada Sauce

(Ready in about 15 minutes | Servings 4)

Per serving: 290 Calories; 21.7g Fat; 6.5g Carbs; 10.6g Protein; 5.5g Fiber

INGREDIENTS

1 pound Chanterelle mushroom, sliced
1/4 cup enchilada sauce
2 tablespoons butter, room temperature

1 yellow onion, chopped
4 eggs
1/2 teaspoon ginger-garlic paste
Kosher salt and black pepper, to taste

2 tomatillos, chopped
1 medium-sized avocado, pitted and mashed

DIRECTIONS

Melt the butter in a saucepan over a moderately-high flame. Cook the onion until tender and translucent.
Add in the ginger-garlic paste, mushrooms, salt, black pepper, and chopped tomatillos. Add in the eggs and scramble them well.

STORING

Divide the mushroom mixture between four airtight containers or Ziploc bags. Refrigerate for up to 3 days.
For freezing, place the mushroom mixture in four Ziploc bags and freeze up to 6 months. Defrost in your refrigerator or microwave.
Serve with enchilada sauce and avocado. Enjoy!

282. Broccoli with Gruyère Cheese Sauce

(Ready in about 30 minutes | Servings 6)

Per serving: 159 Calories; 12.3g Fat; 7.2g Carbs; 5.7g Protein; 5.5g Fiber

INGREDIENTS

2 pounds broccoli, cut into small florets
1/4 teaspoon turmeric powder
Sea salt and black pepper, to taste

1 ½ tablespoons olive oil
1/4 cup scallions, chopped
2 tablespoons green garlic, minced

For the Sauce:
1/3 cup sour cream
1/2 cup Gruyère cheese, shredded
1 ½ tablespoons butter

DIRECTIONS

Parboil the broccoli florets in a large pot of boiling water for about 3 minutes until crisp-tender. Drain.
Heat the oil in a frying pan over a moderately-high heat. Once hot, cook the scallions and green garlic for about 2 minutes or until tender and aromatic.
Add in the curry turmeric powder, salt, pepper and continue to sauté for 3 minutes more or until aromatic.
Add a splash of vegetable broth, partially cover, and continue to cook for 6 to 7 minutes. Add the reserved broccoli back to the pan.
In another pan, melt the butter over a moderately-high heat. Add in the sour cream and cheese and stir over low heat for 2 to 3 minutes.

STORING

Spoon the cooked broccoli into airtight containers; keep in your refrigerator for 3 to 5 days.
Place the sauce in airtight containers and keep in your refrigerator for up to 5 days.
For freezing, place the cooked broccoli in airtight containers or heavy-duty freezer bags. Freeze up to 10 to 12 months. Defrost in the microwave. Bon appétit!

283. Celery with Peppercorn Sauce

(Ready in about 40 minutes | Servings 6)

Per serving: 183 Calories; 14.2g Fat; 6.5g Carbs; 2.6g Protein; 2.2g Fiber

INGREDIENTS

Kosher salt and white pepper, to taste
2 tablespoons balsamic vinegar
1 ½ pounds celery, trimmed and halved lengthwise

2 tablespoons ghee, room temperature
1 teaspoon garlic, smashed
For the Sauce:
1 ½ cups cream of celery soup

3 tablespoons rum
2 tablespoons ghee
1/2 cup onions, minced
1 cup double cream

DIRECTIONS

Start by preheating your oven to 410 degrees F.
Toss your celery with 2 tablespoons of ghee, salt, white pepper, balsamic vinegar, and garlic.
Roast the celery in the preheated oven for about 30 minutes.
In the meantime, melt the 2 tablespoons of ghee in a cast-iron skillet over a moderately-high heat. Once hot, cook the onions for 2 to 3 minutes until tender and translucent.
Add the rum and cream of celery soup; bring it to a boil. Continue to cook for 4 to 5 minutes. Turn the heat to a simmer.
Add in the double cream and continue to simmer until the sauce has thickened and reduced.

STORING

Place the roasted celery in airtight containers or Ziploc bags; keep in your refrigerator for up to 3 to 5 days.
Place the roasted celery in airtight containers or Ziploc bags; keep in your refrigerator for up to 4 days.
To freeze, arrange the roasted celery on a baking sheet in a single layer; freeze for about 2 hours. Transfer the roasted celery to freezer storage bags. Freeze for up to 12 months. Bon appétit!

284. Mushroom and Cauliflower Quiche

(Ready in about 35 minutes | Servings 4)

Per serving: 275 Calories; 21.3g Fat; 5.3g Carbs; 14g Protein; 3g Fiber

INGREDIENTS

1 pound cauliflower florets
1/2 pound brown mushrooms, thinly sliced
1 1/2 cup cream cheese

1 cup Gruyère cheese
1 cup cream of mushroom soup
1 teaspoon Italian herb mix
2 tablespoons butter

4 eggs, lightly beaten
1 teaspoon Dijon mustard

DIRECTIONS

Melt the butter in a saucepan over medium-high heat. Now, cook the mushrooms until they release the liquid. Add in the cream of mushrooms soup, Italian herb mix, and cauliflower.
Continue to sauté until the cauliflower has softened. Spoon the cauliflower mixture into a buttered casserole dish.
In a mixing bowl, whisk the eggs, cheese, and Dijon mustard. Spoon the sauce over the top of your casserole.
Bake in the preheated oven at 365 degrees F for about 30 minutes or until the top is hot and bubbly.

STORING

Slice your casserole into four pieces. Divide the pieces between airtight containers; it will last for 3 to 4 days in the refrigerator.
For freezing, place each portion in a separate heavy-duty freezer bag. Freeze up to 2 to 3 months. Defrost in the microwave or refrigerator. Bon appétit!

285. Oven-Baked Avocado

(Ready in about 25 minutes | Servings 6)

Per serving: 255 Calories; 21g Fat; 3.3g Carbs; 10.8g Protein; 4.8g Fiber

INGREDIENTS

3 medium-sized ripe avocados, halved and pitted

3 ounce Pancetta, chopped
2 eggs, beaten

3 ounces chive cream cheese
Salt and pepper, to taste

DIRECTIONS

Begin by preheating an oven to 380 degrees F. Place the avocado halves in a baking pan.
Thoroughly combine the eggs, cheese, Pancetta, salt, and pepper. Spoon the mixture into avocado halves.
Bake in the preheated oven for 18 to 20 minutes.

STORING

Place the stuffed avocado in airtight containers; keep in your refrigerator for 3 to 4 days.

286. Cauliflower and Oyster Mushroom Medley

(Ready in about 20 minutes | Servings 4)

Per serving: 300 Calories; 27.9g Fat; 8.6g Carbs; 5.2g Protein; 2.6g Fiber

INGREDIENTS

1/2 head cauliflower, cut into small florets
Salt and pepper, to taste
2 tablespoons Romano cheese, grated

10 ounces Oyster mushrooms, sliced
2 garlic cloves, minced
1/2 stick butter, room temperature
1/3 cup cream of celery soup

1/3 cup double cream
1/4 cup mayonnaise, preferably home-made

DIRECTIONS

In a saucepan, melt the butter over a moderate heat. Once hot, sauté the cauliflower and mushrooms until softened.
Add in the garlic and continue to sauté for a minute or so or until aromatic.
Stir in the cream of celery soup, double cream, salt, and pepper. Continue to cook, covered, for 10 to 12 minutes, until most of the liquid has evaporated.
Fold in the Romano cheese and stir to combine well.

STORING

Divide your medley between four airtight containers or Ziploc bags. Refrigerate for up to 3 days.
For freezing, place your medley in four Ziploc bags and freeze up to 6 months. Defrost in your refrigerator or microwave. Serve with mayonnaise and enjoy!

287. Japanese-Style Eringi Mushrooms

(Ready in about 15 minutes | Servings 3)

Per serving: 103 Calories; 6.7g Fat; 5.9g Carbs; 2.7g Protein; 3.3g Fiber

INGREDIENTS

8 ounces Eringi mushrooms, trim away about 1-inch of the root section
Salt and Sansho pepper, to season

1 ½ tablespoons butter, melted
1 cup onions, finely chopped
2 cloves garlic, minced

2 tablespoons mirin
1/2 cup dashi stock
1 tablespoon lightly toasted sesame seeds

DIRECTIONS

Melt the butter in a large pan over a moderately-high flame. Cook the onions and garlic for about 4 minutes, stirring continuously to ensure even cooking.
Add in the Eringi mushrooms and continue to cook an additional 3 minutes until they are slightly shriveled.
Season to taste and add in the mirin and dashi stock; continue to cook an additional 3 minutes.

STORING

Place the Eringi mushrooms in airtight containers; keep in your refrigerator for 3 to 5 days.
Place the Eringi mushrooms on the parchment-lined baking sheet, about 1-inch apart from each other; freeze for about 2 to 3 hours. Remove the Eringi mushrooms to a freezer bag for long-term storage; they will maintain the best quality for 10 to 12 months. Garnish with sesame seeds. Enjoy!

288. Mediterranean Creamy Broccoli Casserole

(Ready in about 25 minutes | Servings 3)

Per serving: 195 Calories; 12.7g Fat; 6.7g Carbs; 11.6g Protein; 3.2g Fiber

INGREDIENTS

3/4 pound broccoli, cut into small florets
1 teaspoon Mediterranean spice mix

2 ounces Colby cheese, shredded
3 tablespoons sesame oil
1 red onion, minced

2 garlic cloves, minced
3 eggs, well-beaten
1/2 cup double cream

DIRECTIONS

Begin by preheating your oven to 320 degrees F. Brush the sides and bottom of a casserole dish with a nonstick cooking spray.
In a frying pan, heat the sesame oil over a moderately-high heat. Sauté the onion and garlic until just tender and fragrant.
Add in the broccoli and continue to cook until crisp-tender for about 4 minutes. Spoon the mixture into the preparade casserole dish.
Whisk the eggs with double cream and Mediterranean spice mix. Spoon this mixture over the broccoli layer.
Bake in the preheated oven for 18 to 20 minutes.

STORING

Slice the casserole into three pieces. Divide the pieces between three airtight containers; it will last for 3 to 4 days in the refrigerator.
For freezing, place each portion in a separate heavy-duty freezer bag. Freeze up to 2 to 3 months. Defrost in the microwave or refrigerator.
Top with the shredded cheese and broil for 5 to 6 minutes or until hot and bubbly on the top. Bon appétit!

289. Greek Salad with Yogurt

(Ready in about 15 minutes + chilling time | Servings 4)

Per serving: 318 Calories; 24.3g Fat; 4.1g Carbs; 15.4g Protein; 0.9g Fiber

INGREDIENTS

1 cucumber, sliced
6 radishes, sliced
1 teaspoon basil
1 tablespoon fresh lemon juice

1/2 teaspoon oregano
1/4 cup fresh scallions, thinly sliced
1 cup Greek-style yogurt
2 tablespoons green garlic, minced

Sea salt and ground black pepper, to taste
8 green oak lettuce leaves, torn into pieces

DIRECTIONS

Whisk the yogurt with green garlic, lemon juice, basil, and oregano.
Toss the remaining ingredients in a mixing bowl. Dress the salad and toss to combine well.

STORING

Place the salad in airtight containers and keep in your refrigerator for up to 2 days. Enjoy!

290. Artichoke Salad with Mozzarella Cheese

(Ready in about 25 minutes | Servings 6)

Per serving: 146 Calories; 9.4g Fat; 6.1g Carbs; 5.8g Protein; 6g Fiber

INGREDIENTS

2 tablespoons olive oil
3 artichoke hearts, defrosted
Sea salt and black pepper, to taste
3/4 cup scallions, peeled and finely chopped
12/3 cup arugula

1/3 cup mustard greens
1/3 cup green cabbage
3 tablespoons capers, drained
1 chili pepper, sliced thin
3 teaspoon fresh lemon juice
1 ½ teaspoons deli mustard

2 tablespoons balsamic vinegar
2 tomatoes, sliced
2 ounces Kalamata olives, pitted and sliced
4 ounces Mozzarella cheese, crumbled

DIRECTIONS

Start by preheating your oven to 350 degrees F. Line a baking sheet with parchment paper or a silicone mat.
Brush the artickohe hearts with olive oil. Roast the artichoke hearts in the preheated oven at 360 degrees F for about 20 minutes. Season with salt and pepper to taste.
Meanwhile, toss the vegetables with capers, lemon juice, mustard and balsamic vinegar until well combined.

STORING

Place the cooked artichokes in airtight containers and keep in your refrigerator for up to 4 days.
Place the cooked artichokes on a cookie sheet and freeze. Once they are frozen, put in a plastic bag and place in your freezer.
They will maintain best quality for 10 to 12 months.
Serve the roasted artichokes on the top of your salad and garnish with olives and Mozzarella cheese.

291. Pancetta and Goat Cheese-Stuffed Mushrooms

(Ready in about 25 minutes | Servings 6)

Per serving: 98 Calories; 5.8g Fat; 3.9g Carbs; 8.4g Protein; 0.6g Fiber

INGREDIENTS

12 medium-sized button mushrooms, stems removed
3 slices of pancetta, chopped
2 ounces goat cheese, crumbled
2 tablespoons butter, melted

1 tablespoon oyster sauce
Sea salt and black pepper, to taste
1 teaspoon basil
1 teaspoon fresh rosemary, minced

DIRECTIONS

Brush your mushrooms with melted butter and oyster sauce. Season them with salt and pepper to taste.
Mix the pancetta, basil, rosemary, and goat cheese. Spoon the mixture into the mushroom caps and arrange them on a parchment-lined baking sheet.
Bake in the preheated oven at 360 degrees F for about 20 minutes or until tender.

STORING

Place the stuffed mushrooms in airtight containers; keep in your refrigerator for 3 to 5 days.
Place the stuffed mushrooms on the parchment-lined baking sheet, about 1-inch apart from each other; freeze for about 2 to 3 hours.
Remove the stuffed mushrooms to a freezer bag for long-term storage; they will maintain the best quality for 10 to 12 months. This system enables you to defrost a few mushrooms and keep the rest frozen. Enjoy!

292. The Easiest Roasted Asparagus Ever

(Ready in about 20 minutes | Servings 4)

Per serving: 48 Calories; 1.6g Fat; 4.4g Carbs; 5.5g Protein; 2.5g Fiber

INGREDIENTS

1 pound asparagus spears
4 tablespoons pancetta, chopped
1/4 teaspoon caraway seeds

1/2 teaspoon dried rosemary
Salt and freshly ground black pepper, to your liking
1 teaspoon shallot powder

DIRECTIONS

Toss the asparagus spears with spices.
Bake in the preheated oven at 450 degrees F for about 15 minutes.
Top with the pancetta and continue to bake an additional 5 to 6 minutes.

STORING

Place the roasted asparagus in airtight containers; keep in your refrigerator for 3 to 5 days.
For freezing, place the roasted asparagus in a freezable container; they can be frozen for 10 to 12 months. Enjoy!

293. Roasted Autumn Vegetables

(Ready in about 35 minutes | Servings 6)

Per serving: 137 Calories; 11.1g Fat; 3.1g Carbs; 1.2g Protein; 2.3g Fiber

INGREDIENTS

3 tablespoons olive oil
1 onion, cut into wedges
1 fresh chili pepper, minced
1/2 pound celery, quartered
1/2 pound bell peppers, sliced

1/2 pound turnips, cut into wedges
Sea salt and ground black pepper, to taste
1 teaspoon dried thyme
1 teaspoon dried basil
1 garlic clove, minced

DIRECTIONS

Toss all ingredients in a roasting pan. Roast in the preheated oven at 410 degrees F for 30 minutes.
Taste and adjust the seasoning.

STORING

Place the roasted vegetables in airtight containers or Ziploc bags; keep in your refrigerator for up to 3 to 5 days.
To freeze, arrange the roasted vegetables on a baking sheet in a single layer; freeze for about 2 hours. Transfer the frozen fries to freezer storage bags. Freeze for up to 12 months. Bon appétit!

294. Easy Keto Coleslaw

(Ready in about 10 minutes + chilling time | Servings 4)

Per serving: 242 Calories; 20.5g Fat; 6.2g Carbs; 1g Protein; 3.1g Fiber

INGREDIENTS

3/4 pound cabbage, cored and shredded
1/4 cup fresh cilantro, chopped
1/4 cup fresh chives, chopped
1 teaspoon fennel seeds
Salt and pepper, to taste

1 large-sized celery, shredded
1 teaspoon deli mustard
2 tablespoons sesame seeds, lightly toasted
1 cup mayonnaise

DIRECTIONS

Toss the cabbage, celery, mayonnaise, mustard, cilantro, chives, fennel seeds, salt, and pepper in a bowl.
Sprinkle toasted sesame seeds over your salad.

STORING

Place the salad in airtight containers or Ziploc bags; keep in your refrigerator for up to 3 days.

295. Grilled Zucchini with Mediterranean Sauce

(Ready in about 15 minutes | Servings 4)

Per serving: 132 Calories; 11.1g Fat; 4.1g Carbs; 3.1g Protein; 1.3g Fiber

INGREDIENTS

1 pound zucchini, cut lengthwise into quarters
1/2 teaspoon red pepper flakes, crushed
Salt, to season
1/4 cup extra-virgin olive oil
1 teaspoon garlic, minced

For the Sauce:
1 tablespoon fresh scallions, minced
1 tablespoon fresh basil, chopped
1 teaspoon fresh rosemary, finely chopped
3/4 cup Greek-style yogurt

DIRECTIONS

Begin by preheating your grill to a medium-low heat.
Toss the zucchini slices with the olive oil, garlic, red pepper, and salt. Grill your zucchini on a lightly-oiled grill for about 10 minutes until tender and slightly charred.
Make the sauce by whisking all of the sauce ingredients.

STORING

Place the zucchini in airtight containers or Ziploc bags; keep in your refrigerator for 3 to 5 days.
Place the sauce in airtight containers; keep in your refrigerator for 3 to 5 days.
Place the zucchini in a freezable container; they can be frozen for up to 10 to 12 months.
Bake the thawed zucchini at 200 degrees F until they are completely warm. Serve with the sauce on the side. Enjoy!

296. Keto Noodles with Oyster Mushroom Sauce

(Ready in about 15 minutes | Servings 4)

Per serving: 85 Calories; 3.5g Fat; 6.4g Carbs; 5.8g Protein; 3.3g Fiber

INGREDIENTS

2 zucchinis, cut into thin strips
2 tablespoons olive oil
1 yellow onion, minced

2 garlic cloves, minced
1 pound oyster mushrooms, chopped
1 cup pureed tomatoes

1 cup vegetable broth
1 teaspoon Mediterranean sauce

DIRECTIONS

Parboil the zucchini noodles for one minute or so. Reserve.
Then, heat the oil in a saucepan over a moderately-high heat. Sauté the onion and garlic for 2 to 3 minutes.
Add in the mushrooms and continue to cook for 2 to 3 minutes until they release liquid.
Add in the remaining ingredients and cover the pan; let it simmer for 10 minutes longer until everything is cooked through.
Top your zoodles with the prepared mushroom sauce.

STORING

Place your zoodles in airtight containers or Ziploc bags; keep in your refrigerator for 3 to 5 days.
Place your zoodles in a freezable container; they can be frozen for up to 10 to 12 months. Bake the thawed zucchini at 200 degrees F until they are completely warm. Enjoy!

297. Autumn Eggplant and Squash Stew

(Ready in about 35 minutes | Servings 6)

Per serving: 113 Calories; 7.9g Fat; 3.7g Carbs; 2.8g Protein; 2.2g Fiber

INGREDIENTS

2 tablespoons olive
2 garlic cloves, finely chopped
3 ounces acorn squash, chopped
1 celery, chopped

2 tablespoons fresh parsley, roughly chopped
Sea salt and pepper, to taste
1/2 teaspoon ancho chili powder

2 tomatoes, pureed
2 tablespoons port wine
1 large onion, chopped
3 ounces eggplant, peeled and chopped

DIRECTIONS

In a heavy-bottomed pot, heat olive oil over a moderately-high heat. Sauté the onion and garlic about 5 minutes.
Add in the acorn squash, eggplant, celery and parsley; continue to cook for 5 to 6 minutes.
Add in the other ingredients; turn the heat to a simmer. Continue to cook for about 25 minutes.

STORING

Spoon the stew into airtight containers; keep in your refrigerator for up to 3 to 4 days.
For freezing, place the stew in airtight containers or heavy-duty freezer bags. It will maintain the best quality for about 5 months. Defrost in the refrigerator. Enjoy!

298. Vegetables with Spicy Yogurt Sauce

(Ready in about 45 minutes | Servings 4)

Per serving: 357 Calories; 35.8g Fat; 5.2g Carbs; 3.4g Protein; 2.5g Fiber

INGREDIENTS

1/4 cup olive oil
1/2 teaspoon garlic, sliced
1/2 pound broccoli, cut into sticks
2 celery stalks, cut into sticks

2 bell peppers, deveined and sliced
1 red onion, sliced into wedges
For the Spicy Yogurt Sauce:
1 ½ cups Greek-Style yogurt

Salt and pepper, to taste
2 tablespoons mayonnaise
1 poblano pepper, finely minced
1 tablespoon lemon juice

DIRECTIONS

Toss the vegetables with olive oil and garlic. Arrange your vegetables on a parchment-lined baking sheet.
Roast in the preheated oven at 380 degrees F for about 35 minutes, rotating the pan once or twice.
Thoroughly combine all ingredients for the sauce.

STORING

Place the roasted vegetables in airtight containers or Ziploc bags; keep in your refrigerator for up to 3 to 5 days.
Place the spicy yogurt sauce in airtight containers or Ziploc bags; keep in your refrigerator for up to 3 to 5 days.
To freeze, arrange the roasted vegetables on a baking sheet in a single layer; freeze for about 2 hours. Transfer the frozen fries to freezer storage bags. Freeze for up to 12 months. Bon appétit!

299. Cheesy Italian Pepper Casserole

(Ready in about 1 hour | Servings 4)

Per serving: 408 Calories; 28.9g Fat; 4.6g Carbs; 24.9g Protein; 3.5g Fiber

INGREDIENTS

8 Italian sweet peppers, deveined and
cut into fourths lengthwise
6 whole eggs

1/2 cup Greek-style yogurt
3/4 pound Asiago cheese, shredded
1 leek, thinly sliced

1/2 teaspoon garlic, crushed
Sea salt and ground black pepper, to taste
1 teaspoon oregano

DIRECTIONS

Arrange the peppers in a lightly greased baking dish.
Top with half of the shredded cheese; add a layer of sliced leeks and garlic. Repeat the layers.
After that, beat the eggs with the yogurt, salt, pepper, and oregano. Pour the egg/yogurt mixture over the peppers. Cover with a piece of foil and bake for about 30 minutes.
Remove the foil and bake for a further 10 to 15 minutes.

STORING

Slice the casserole into four pieces. Divide the pieces between airtight containers; it will last for 3 to 4 days in the refrigerator.
For freezing, place each portion in a separate heavy-duty freezer bag. Freeze up to 2 to 3 months. Defrost in the microwave or refrigerator.
Bon appétit!

300. The Best Keto Pizza Ever

(Ready in about 25 minutes | Servings 4)

Per serving: 234 Calories; 16.1g Fat; 6.3g Carbs; 13.6g Protein; 3.6g Fiber

INGREDIENTS

For the Crust:
1/4 cup double cream
1 tablespoon olive oil
1 pound cauliflower florets
1/2 cup Colby cheese

4 medium-sized eggs
Salt and pepper, to taste
For the Topping:
1 tomato, pureed
1/2 cup green mustard

1 tablespoon fresh basil
1/4 cup black olives, pitted and sliced
1 cup mozzarella cheese
1/2 cup romaine lettuce
1 cup lollo rosso

DIRECTIONS

Parboil the cauliflower florets in a large pot of salted water until it is crisp-tender; add in the cheese, eggs, cream, olive oil, salt, and pepper.
Press the crust mixture into the bottom of a lightly oiled baking pan. Bake in the middle of the oven at 385 degrees F. Bake for 13 to 15 minutes or until the crust is firm.

STORING

Place the cauliflower crust in airtight container or heavy-duty freezer bags; keep in the refrigerator for a week.
For freezing, place the cauliflower crust in a heavy-duty freezer bag; freeze up to 3 months. Defrost in your microwave for a few minutes.
Top with the other ingredients, ending with the mozzarella cheese; bake until the cheese is bubbly and hot. Bon appétit!

301. Easy Vegetable Ratatouille

(Ready in about 1 hour | Servings 4)

Per serving: 159 Calories; 10.4g Fat; 5.7g Carbs; 6.4g Protein; 5g Fiber

INGREDIENTS

1 large onion, sliced
1/3 cup Parmesan cheese, shredded
1 celery, peeled and diced
1 poblano pepper, minced
1 eggplant, cut into thick slices

1 cup grape tomatoes, halved
1/2 garlic head, minced
2 tablespoons extra-virgin olive oil
1 tablespoon fresh basil leaves, snipped

DIRECTIONS

Sprinkle the eggplant with 1 teaspoon of salt and let it stand for about 30 minutes; drain and rinse under running water.
Place the eggplant slices in the bottom of a lightly-oiled casserole dish. Add in the remaining vegetable. Add in the olive oil and basil leaves.
Bake in the preheated oven at 350 degrees F for about 30 minute or until thoroughly cooked.

STORING

Place the vegetable ratatouille in airtight containers or Ziploc bags; keep in your refrigerator for up to 3 to 5 days.
To freeze, place the vegetable ratatouille in freezer storage bags. Freeze for up to 12 months. Top with the cheese and place under the pre-heated broiler for 5 to 6 minutes. Bon appétit!

302. Champinones Al Ajillo with Keto Naan

(Ready in about 20 minutes | Servings 6)

Per serving: 281 Calories; 21.4g Fat; 6.1g Carbs; 6.4g Protein; 1.4g Fiber

INGREDIENTS

1 pound button mushrooms, thinly sliced
1 teaspoon Spanish paprika
1/4 teaspoon flaky sea salt
8 tablespoons coconut oil, melted
1 egg plus 1 egg yolk, beaten
1/4 cup coconut flour

1/2 cup almond flour
1/2 teaspoon baking powder
2 tablespoons psyllium powder
1 tablespoon butter
1 teaspoon garlic, minced

DIRECTIONS

Mix the flour with the baking powder, psyllium and salt until well combined.
Add in 6 tablespoons of coconut oil, egg and egg yolk; pour in the water and stir to form a dough; let it stand for about 15 minutes.
Divide the dough into 6 pieces and roll them out to form a disc. Use the remaining 2 tablespoons of coconut oil to bake naan bread.
In a sauté pan, cook the mushrooms and garlic in hot butter until the mushrooms release liquid; season with Spanish paprika. Taste and adjust seasonings.

STORING

Place the mushrooms in airtight containers; keep in your refrigerator for 3 to 5 days.
Place the naan bread in airtight containers; keep in your refrigerator for 3 to 5 days.
Place the mushrooms in a plastic freezer bags; they will maintain the best quality for 10 to 12 months.

303. Spring Mixed Greens Salad

(Ready in about 10 minutes | Servings 4)

Per serving: 190 Calories; 17.6g Fat; 7.6g Carbs; 4.3g Protein; 3.9g Fiber

INGREDIENTS

1 cup romaine lettuce
1 cup lollo rosso
1/3 cup goat cheese, crumbled
2 tablespoons fresh parsley, chopped
2 tablespoons extra-virgin olive oil

1/2 lime, freshly squeezed
2 cups baby spinach
1/2 cup blueberries
1 cup avocado, pitted, peeled and sliced
Sea salt and white pepper, to taste

DIRECTIONS

Toss all ingredients in a mixing bowl. Taste and adjust seasonings.
Place in your refrigerator until ready to use.

STORING

Place the salad in airtight container or heavy-duty freezer bags; keep in the refrigerator for up to 3 to 4 days.

304. Aromatic Chinese Cabbage

(Ready in about 15 minutes | Servings 4)

Per serving: 142 Calories; 11.6g Fat; 5.7g Carbs; 2g Protein; 1.8g Fiber

INGREDIENTS

4 tablespoons sesame oil

1 pound Chinese cabbage, outer leaves discarded, cored and shredded

1 tablespoon rice wine

1 celery rib, thinly sliced

1/4 teaspoon fresh ginger root, grated

1/2 teaspoon sea salt

1/2 cup onion, chopped

1 teaspoon garlic, pressed

1/2 teaspoon Sichuan pepper

1/4 cup vegetable stock

DIRECTIONS

In a wok, heat the sesame oil over a medium-high flame. Stir fry the onion, and garlic for 1 minute or until just tender and fragrant.

Add in the cabbage, celery, and ginger and continue to cook for 7 to 8 minutes more, stirring frequently to ensure even cooking.

Stir in the remaining ingredients and continue to cook for a further 3 minutes.

STORING

Place the Chinese cabbage in airtight containers or Ziploc bags; keep in your refrigerator for up to 3 to 4 days.

For freezing, place the Chinese cabbage in airtight containers or heavy-duty freezer bags. Freeze up to 2 to 3 months. Defrost in the refrigerator. Bon appétit!

VEGAN

305. Italian Stuffed Mushrooms

(Ready in about 35 minutes | Servings 4)

Per serving: 206 Calories; 13.4g Fat; 5.6g Carbs; 12.7g Protein; 4g Fiber

INGREDIENTS

1 pound button mushrooms, stems removed
2 tablespoons coconut oil, melted
1 pound broccoli florets
1 Italian pepper, chopped
1 teaspoon Italian herb mix

Salt and pepper, to taste
1 shallot, finely chopped
2 garlic cloves, minced
1 cup vegan parmesan

DIRECTIONS

Parboil the broccoli in a large pot of salted water until crisp-tender, about 6 minutes. Mash the broccoli florets with a potato masher.
In a saucepan, melt the coconut oil over a moderately-high heat. Once hot, cook the shallot, garlic, and pepper until tender and fragrant. Season with the spices and add in the broccoli.
Fill the mushroom cups with the broccoli mixture and bake in the preheated oven at 365 degrees F for about 10 minutes.
Top with the vegan parmesan and bake for 10 minutes more or until it melts.

STORING

Place the stuffed mushrooms in airtight containers; keep in your refrigerator for 3 to 5 days.
Place the stuffed mushrooms on the parchment-lined baking sheet, about 1-inch apart from each other; freezer for about 2 to 3 hours.
Remove the frozen mushrooms to a plastic freezer bag for long-term storage; they will maintain the best quality for 10 to 12 months. Enjoy!

306. One-Pot Mushroom Stroganoff

(Ready in about 25 minutes | Servings 4)

Per serving: 114 Calories; 7.3g Fat; 5.2g Carbs; 2.1g Protein; 3.1g Fiber

INGREDIENTS

2 tablespoons canola oil
1 parsnip, chopped
1 cup fresh brown mushrooms, sliced
1 cup onions, chopped
2 garlic cloves, pressed
1/2 cup celery rib, chopped
1 teaspoon Hungarian paprika

3 ½ cups roasted vegetable broth
1 cup tomato puree
1 tablespoon flaxseed meal
2 tablespoons sherry wine
1 rosemary sprig, chopped
1/2 teaspoon dried basil
1/2 teaspoon dried oregano

DIRECTIONS

In a heavy-bottomed pot, heat the oil over a moderately-high flame. Cook the onion and garlic for 2 minutes or until tender and aromatic.
Add in the celery, parsnip, and mushrooms, and continue to cook until they've softened; reserve.
Add in the sherry wine to deglaze the bottom of your pot. Add in the seasonings, vegetable broth, and tomato puree.
Continue to simmer, partially covered, for 15 to 18 minutes. Add in the flaxseed meal and stir until the sauce has thickened.

STORING

Spoon the stew into four airtight containers or Ziploc bags; keep in your refrigerator for up to 3 to 4 days.
For freezing, place the stew in airtight containers. Freeze up to 4 to 6 months. Defrost in the refrigerator. Bon appétit!

307. Avocado with Pine Nuts

(Ready in about 10 minutes | Servings 4)

Per serving: 263 Calories; 24.8g Fat; 6.5g Carbs; 3.5g Protein; 6.1g Fiber

INGREDIENTS

2 avocados, pitted and halved
1 tablespoon coconut aminos
1/2 teaspoon garlic, minced
1 teaspoon fresh lime juice

Salt and pepper, to taste
5 ounces pine nuts, ground
1 celery stalk, chopped

DIRECTIONS

Thoroughly combine the avocado pulp with the pine nuts, celery, garlic, fresh lime juice, and coconut aminos. Season with salt and pepper to taste.
Spoon the filling into the avocado halves.

STORING

Place your avocado in airtight containers; keep in your refrigerator for up to 3 days.

308. Zucchini Noodles with Famous Cashew Parmesan

(Ready in about 15 minutes | Servings 4)

Per serving: 145 Calories; 10.6g Fat; 5.9g Carbs; 5.5g Protein; 1.6g Fiber

INGREDIENTS

For Zoodles:
2 tablespoons canola oil
4 zucchinis, peeled and sliced into noodle-shape strands

Salt and pepper, to taste
For Cashew Parmesan:
1/2 cup raw cashews
1/4 teaspoon onion powder

1 garlic clove, minced
2 tablespoons nutritional yeast
Sea salt and pepper, to taste

DIRECTIONS

In a saucepan, heat the canola oil over medium heat; once hot, cook your zoodles for 1 minute or so, stirring frequently to ensure even cooking.
Season with salt and pepper to taste.
In your food processor, process all ingredients for the cashew parmesan. Toss the cashew parmesan with the zoodles and enjoy!

STORING

Place your zoodles in airtight containers or Ziploc bags; keep in your refrigerator for 3 to 5 days.
Place your zoodles in a freezable container; they can be frozen for up to 10 to 12 months. Bake the thawed zucchini at 200 degrees F until they are completely warm. Enjoy!

309. Cream of Broccoli Soup

(Ready in about 15 minutes | Servings 4)

Per serving: 252 Calories; 20.3g Fat; 5.8g Carbs; 8.1g Protein; 4.5g Fiber

INGREDIENTS

1 pound broccoli, cut into small florets
8 ounces baby spinach
4 cups roasted vegetable broth
2 tablespoons olive oil
1 yellow onion, chopped

2 garlic cloves, minced
1/2 cup coconut milk
Salt and pepper, to taste
2 tablespoons parsley, chopped

DIRECTIONS

Heat the oil in a soup pot over a moderately-high flame. Then, sauté the onion and garlic until they're tender and fragrant.
Add in the broccoli, spinach, and broth; bring to a rolling boil. Immediately turn the heat to a simmer.
Pour in the coconut milk, salt, pepper, and parsley; continue to simmer, partially covered, until cooked through.
Puree your soup with an immersion blender.

STORING

Spoon the soup into airtight containers and keep in your refrigerator for up 3 to 4 days.
For freezing, place your soup in airtight containers or heavy-duty freezer bags. Freeze up to 4 to 6 months. Defrost in the microwave or refrigerator. Enjoy!

310. Swiss Chard Chips with Avocado Dip

(Ready in about 20 minutes | Servings 6)

Per serving: 269 Calories; 26.7g Fat; 3.4g Carbs; 2.3g Protein; 4.1g Fiber

INGREDIENTS

1 tablespoon coconut oil
Sea salt and pepper, to taste
2 cups Swiss chard, cleaned

Avocado Dip:
3 ripe avocados, pitted and mashed
2 garlic cloves, finely minced

2 tablespoons extra-virgin olive oil
2 teaspoons lemon juice
Salt and pepper, to taste

DIRECTIONS

Toss the Swiss chard with the coconut oil, salt, and pepper.
Bake the Swiss chard leaves in the preheated oven at 310 degrees F for about 10 minutes until the edges brown but are not burnt.
Thoroughly combine the ingredients for the avocado dip.

STORING

Place the Swiss chard chips in airtight containers; keep at room temperature for a week.
Place the avocado dip in airtight containers or Ziploc bags; keep in your refrigerator for 3 to 5 days. Enjoy!

311. Banana Blueberry Smoothie

(Ready in about 5 minutes | Servings 4)

Per serving: 247 Calories; 21.7g Fat; 4.9g Carbs; 2.6g Protein; 3g Fiber

INGREDIENTS

1/2 cup fresh blueberries
1/2 banana, peeled and sliced
1/2 cup water

1 ½ cups coconut milk
1 tablespoon vegan protein powder, zero carbs

DIRECTIONS

Blend all ingredients until creamy and uniform.

STORING

Spoon the smoothie into airtight containers and keep in your refrigerator for up to 2 days.
Spoon the smoothie into airtight containers. Use vacuum sealing for maximum protection. Store in your freezer for a few weeks.

312. Cajun Artichoke with Tofu

(Ready in about 30 minutes | Servings 4)

Per serving: 138 Calories; 8.9g Fat; 6.8g Carbs; 6.4g Protein; 5g Fiber

INGREDIENTS

1 pound artichokes, trimmed and cut into pieces
2 tablespoons coconut oil, room temperature
1 block tofu, pressed and cubed
1 teaspoon fresh garlic, minced

1 teaspoon Cajun spice mix
1 Spanish pepper, chopped
1/4 cup vegetable broth
Salt and pepper, to taste

DIRECTIONS

Parboil your artichokes in a pot of lightly salted water for 13 to 15 minutes or until they're crisp-tender; drain.
In a large saucepan, melt the coconut oil over medium-high heat; fry the tofu cubes for 5 to 6 minutes or until golden-brown.
Add in the garlic, Cajun spice mix, Spanish pepper, broth, salt, and pepper. Add in the reserved artichokes and continue to cook until for 5 minutes more.

STORING

Place your artichokes in airtight containers and keep in your refrigerator for up to 4 days.
Place your artichokes in airtight containers and keep in your freezer for 10 to 12 months.

313. Mushroom and Cauliflower Medley

(Ready in about 30 minutes | Servings 4)

Per serving: 113 Calories; 6.7g Fat; 6.6g Carbs; 5g Protein; 2.7g Fiber

INGREDIENTS

8 ounces brown mushrooms, halved
1 head cauliflower, cut into florets
1/4 cup olive oil
1/2 teaspoon turmeric powder

1 teaspoon garlic, smashed
1 cup tomato, pureed
Salt and pepper, to taste

DIRECTIONS

Toss all ingredients in a lightly oiled baking pan.
Roast the vegetable in the preheated oven at 380 degrees F for 25 to 30 minutes.

STORING

Spoon your medley into airtight containers and keep in your refrigerator for up 3 to 4 days.
For freezing, place your medley in airtight containers or heavy-duty freezer bags. Freeze up to 4 to 6 months. Defrost in the microwave or refrigerator. Enjoy!

314. Spicy and Peppery Fried Tofu

(Ready in about 20 minutes | Servings 2)

Per serving: 223 Calories; 15.9g Fat; 5.1g Carbs; 15.6g Protein; 3.3g Fiber

INGREDIENTS

2 bell peppers, deveined and sliced
1 chili pepper, deveined and sliced
1 ½ tablespoons almond meal
Salt and pepper, to taste

1 teaspoon ginger-garlic paste
1 teaspoon onion powder
6 ounces extra-firm tofu, pressed and cubed

1/2 teaspoon ground bay leaf
1 tablespoon sesame oil

DIRECTIONS

Toss your tofu, with almond meal, salt, pepper, ginger-garlic paste, onion powder, ground bay leaf.
In a sauté pan, heat the sesame oil over medium-high heat.
Fry the tofu cubes along with the peppers for about 6 minutes.

STORING

Divide the tofu and peppers between two airtight container or Ziploc bags; keep in your refrigerator for up to 3 to 4 days.
To freeze, divide the tofu and pepper into two airtight container or Ziploc bags. Freeze up to 5 months. Defrost in the refrigerator. Enjoy!

315. Colorful Creamy Soup

(Ready in about 25 minutes | Servings 6)

Per serving: 142 Calories; 11.4g Fat; 5.6g Carbs; 2.9g Protein; 1.3g Fiber

INGREDIENTS

2 cups Swiss chard, torn into pieces
Sea salt and pepper, to taste
2 thyme sprigs, chopped
2 teaspoons sesame oil
1 onion, chopped

2 bay leaves
6 cups vegetable broth
1 cup grape tomatoes, chopped
1 cup almond milk, unflavored
1 teaspoon garlic, minced

2 celery stalks, chopped
1 zucchini, chopped
1/2 cup scallions, chopped

DIRECTIONS

In a heavy bottomed pot, heat the sesame oil in over a moderately-high heat. Sauté the onion, garlic, and celery, until they've softened.
Add in the zucchini, Swiss chard, salt, pepper, thyme, bay leaves, broth, and tomatoes; bring to a rapid boil. Turn the heat to a simmer.
Leave the lid slightly ajar and continue to simmer for about 13 minutes. Add in the almond milk and scallions; continue to cook for 4 minutes more or until thoroughly warmed.

STORING

Spoon the soup into airtight containers and keep in your refrigerator for up 3 to 4 days.
For freezing, place your soup in airtight containers or heavy-duty freezer bags. Freeze up to 4 to 6 months. Defrost in the microwave or refrigerator. Enjoy!

316. Tofu Stuffed Zucchini

(Ready in about 50 minutes | Servings 4)

Per serving: 208 Calories; 14.4g Fat; 8.8g Carbs; 6.5g Protein; 4.3g Fiber

INGREDIENTS

4 zucchinis, cut into halves lengthwise and scoop out the pulp
6 ounces firm tofu, drained and crumbled

2 garlic cloves, pressed
1/2 cup onions, chopped
1 tablespoon olive oil
1 cup tomato puree

1 tablespoon nutritional yeast
2 ounces pecans, chopped
1/4 teaspoon curry powder
Sea salt and pepper, to taste

DIRECTIONS

In a saucepan, heat the olive oil over a moderately-high heat; cook the tofu, garlic, and onion for about 5 minutes.
Stir in the tomato puree and scooped zucchini pulp; add all seasonings and continue to cook for a further 5 to 6 minutes.
Spoon the filling into the zucchini "shells" and arrange them in a lightly greased baking dish.
Bake in the preheated oven at 365 degrees F for 25 to 30 minutes. Top with nutritional yeast and pecans nuts; bake for a further 5 minutes.

STORING

Place the stuffed zucchini in airtight containers or Ziploc bags; keep in your refrigerator for 3 to 4 days.
Wrap each zucchini tightly in several layers of plastic wrap and squeeze the air out. Place them in a freezable container; they can be frozen for up to 1 month.
Bake the thawed zucchini at 200 degrees F until they are completely warm. Enjoy!

317. Kadai Broccoli Masala

(Ready in about 15 minutes | Servings 4)

Per serving: 100 Calories; 8.2g Fat; 4.7g Carbs; 3.7g Protein; 4g Fiber

INGREDIENTS

1/4 cup sesame oil
1 pound broccoli florets
1/2 teaspoon Garam Masala

1 tablespoon Kasuri Methi (dried fenugreek leaves)
1 Badi Elaichi (black cardamom)

1 teaspoon garlic, pressed
Salt and pepper, to taste

DIRECTIONS

Parboil the broccoli for 6 to 7 minutes until it is crisp-tender.
Heat the sesame oil in a wok or saucepan until sizzling. Once hot, cook your broccoli for 3 to 4 minutes. Add in the other ingredients and give it a quick stir.
Adjust the spices to suit your taste.

STORING

Divide the broccoli masala into four portions; divide the portions between four airtight containers; keep in your refrigerator for up 3 to 5 days.
For freezing, place the broccoli masala in airtight containers. Freeze up to 10 to 12 months. Defrost in the refrigerator. Bon appétit!

318. Italian-Style Tomato Crisps

(Ready in about 5 hours | Servings 6)

Per serving: 161 Calories; 14g Fat; 6.2g Carbs; 4.6g Protein; 2.6g Fiber

INGREDIENTS

1 tablespoon Italian spice mix
1 ½ pounds Romano tomatoes, sliced
1/4 cup extra-virgin olive oil

For Vegan Parmesan:
1/4 cup sunflower seeds
Salt and pepper, to taste
1/4 teaspoon dried dill weed

1 teaspoon garlic powder
1/4 cup sesame seeds
1 tablespoon nutritional yeast

DIRECTIONS

Process all ingredients for the vegan parmesan in your food processor.
Toss the sliced tomatoes with the extra-virgin olive oil, Italian spice mix, and vegan parmesan.
Arrange the tomato slices on a parchment-lined baking sheet in a single layer. Bake at 220 degrees F about 5 hours.

STORING

Place your vegetables in airtight containers or Ziploc bags, keep at room temperature for up to a week.

319. Lebanese Asparagus with Baba Ghanoush

(Ready in about 45 minutes | Servings 6)

Per serving: 149 Calories; 12.1g Fat; 6.3g Carbs; 3.6g Protein; 4.6g Fiber

INGREDIENTS

1/4 cup sesame oil
1 ½ pounds asparagus spears, med
1/2 teaspoon red pepper flakes
Salt and pepper, to taste

For Baba Ghanoush:
2 tablespoons fresh lime juice
2 teaspoons olive oil
1/2 cup onion, chopped
3/4 pound eggplant
1 teaspoon garlic, minced

1 tablespoon sesame paste
1/2 teaspoon allspice
1/4 teaspoon ground nutmeg
1/4 cup fresh parsley leaves, chopped
Salt and ground black pepper, to taste

DIRECTIONS

Toss the asparagus spears with sesame oil, salt, and pepper. Arrange the asparagus spears on a foil-lined baking pan.
Roast in the preheated oven at 380 degrees F for 8 to 10 minutes.
Meanwhile, make your Baba Ghanoush. Bake eggplants in the preheated oven at 420 degrees F for 25 to 30 minutes; discard the skin and stems.
In a saucepan, heat 2 the olive oil over a moderately-high heat. Cook the onion and garlic until tender and fragrant; heat off.
Add the roasted eggplant, sautéed onion mixture, sesame paste, lime juice, and spices to your blender or food processor. Pulse until creamy and smooth.

STORING

Place the roasted asparagus in airtight containers; keep in your refrigerator for 3 to 5 days.
Place the Baba Ghanoush in airtight containers; keep in your refrigerator for up to 6 days.
For freezing, place the roasted asparagus in a freezable container; they can be frozen for 10 to 12 months.
For freezing, place the Baba Ghanoush in a freezable bag; squeeze as much air as you can from the bag and seal it; it can be frozen for 3 months.

320. Greek-Style Spicy Tofu

(Ready in about 40 minutes | Servings 4)

Per serving: 162 Calories; 10.9g Fat; 5.8g Carbs; 9.5g Protein; 3.3g Fiber

INGREDIENTS

6 ounces tofu, pressed and cut into
1/4-inch thick slices
2 tablespoons balsamic vinegar
2 tablespoons olive oil
1 cup onions, chopped

1/2 teaspoon garlic, minced
1 tablespoon schug sauce
For Vegan Tzatziki:
1 cup coconut yogurt
1/2 cucumber, shredded

1 teaspoon garlic, smashed
2 tablespoons fresh lime juice
Sea salt and pepper, to taste
1 teaspoon dill weed, minced

DIRECTIONS

Place the tofu, garlic, schug sauce, and balsamic vinegar in a ceramic bowl; let your tofu marinate for 30 minutes in your refrigerator.
In a frying pan, heat the olive oil over a moderately-high heat. Cook the tofu with onions for 5 to 6 minutes until it is golden brown.
Then, make the vegan tzatziki by whisking all ingredients in your bowl.

STORING

Place the tofu in airtight containers or Ziploc bags; keep in your refrigerator for up to 3 to 4 days.
Place the vegan tzatziki in airtight containers or Ziploc bags; keep in your refrigerator for up to 3 days.
To freeze, place the tofu in airtight containers or Ziploc bags. Freeze up to 5 months. Defrost in the refrigerator. Enjoy!

321. Walnut-Stuffed Mushrooms

(Ready in about 30 minutes | Servings 4)

Per serving: 139 Calories; 11.2g Fat; 5.4g Carbs; 4.8g Protein; 1.8g Fiber

INGREDIENTS

1 pound button mushrooms, stems removed and chopped
Salt and pepper, to taste
1/4 cup walnuts, chopped
2 tablespoons parsley, chopped

2 tablespoons olive oil
1 cup shallots, chopped
1/2 teaspoon garlic, minced

DIRECTIONS

Preheat your oven to 365 degrees F. Line a baking pan with a parchment paper.
In a saucepan, heat the olive oil over medium-high flame. Now, sauté the shallot and garlic until tender and aromatic.
Add in the mushrooms stems and continue to cook until they've softened. Remove from the heat and season with salt and pepper.
Stir in the chopped walnuts and parsley; stuff the mushroom caps with the prepared filling. Place your mushrooms on the prepared baking pan.
Bake for 20 to 25 minutes until heated through.

STORING

Place the stuffed mushrooms in airtight containers; keep in your refrigerator for 3 to 5 days.
Place the stuffed mushrooms on the parchment-lined baking sheet, about 1-inch apart from each other; freezer for about 2 to 3 hours.

322. Hungarian-Style Oyster Mushroom Stew

(Ready in about 50 minutes | Servings 4)

Per serving: 65 Calories; 2.7g Fat; 6g Carbs; 2.7g Protein; 2.9g Fiber

INGREDIENTS

2 teaspoons canola oil
2 ½ cups oyster mushrooms, chopped
1 tablespoon Hungarian paprika
2 thyme sprigs, chopped
1 bay laurel

Salt and pepper, to taste
1 red onion, chopped
1/2 teaspoon garlic, finely minced
1 cup celery, chopped
2 bell peppers, chopped

1 ½ cups water
2 vegetable bouillon cubes
1 cup tomato puree

DIRECTIONS

Heat canola oil in a soup pot over a moderately-high heat. Sauté the onion and garlic until they've softened.
Stir in the celery, peppers, and mushrooms. Now, continue to cook for about 10 minutes, adding a splash of water to prevent sticking.
Add in the remaining ingredients. Turn the heat to a simmer. Continue to cook, partially covered, for a further 30 minutes.

STORING

Spoon the stew into four airtight containers or Ziploc bags; keep in your refrigerator for up to 3 to 4 days.
For freezing, place the stew in airtight containers. Freeze up to 4 to 6 months. Defrost in the refrigerator. Bon appétit!

323. Zuppa Toscana with Zucchini

(Ready in about 45 minutes | Servings 4)

Per serving: 165 Calories; 13.4g Fat; 6.7g Carbs; 2.2g Protein; 6g Fiber

INGREDIENTS

3 cups zucchini, peeled and chopped
1 tomato, pureed
1 avocado pitted, peeled and mashed
1 cup scallions, chopped
1 celery, sliced

1 parsnip, sliced
3 teaspoons olive oil
Salt and black pepper, to taste
4 cups vegetable broth

DIRECTIONS

In a soup pot, heat the oil over a moderately-high heat. Sauté the scallion, celery, parsnip, and zucchini until they've softened.
Add in the salt, pepper, vegetable broth, and pureed tomato; bring it to a boil. Turn the heat to a simmer.
Continue to simmer for about 25 minutes. Remove from the heat and fold in the mashed avocado.
Puree your soup with an immersion blender.

STORING

Spoon the soup into airtight containers and keep in your refrigerator for up 3 to 4 days.
For freezing, place your soup in airtight containers or heavy-duty freezer bags. Freeze up to 4 to 6 months. Defrost in the microwave or refrigerator. Enjoy!

324. Vegetables with Crunchy Topping

(Ready in about 40 minutes | Servings 4)

Per serving: 242 Calories; 16.3g Fat; 6.7g Carbs; 16.3g Protein; 3.2g Fiber

INGREDIENTS

1/2 pound Brussels sprouts, quartered
2 tablespoons fresh parsley, chopped
1 cup vegetable broth
2 tablespoons sesame oil
1 cup onions, chopped

2 celery stalks, chopped
Sea salt and pepper, to taste
1 teaspoon porcini powder
1 cup vegan parmesan

DIRECTIONS

In a frying pan, heat the sesame oil over a moderately-high heat. Cook the onions, celery, and Brussels sprouts until they have softened.
Spoon the vegetable mixture into a lightly greased baking dish.
Whisk the vegetable broth with the salt, pepper, and porcini powder. Pour the mixture over the vegetables.
Top with the vegan parmesan and parsley; bake in the preheated oven at 365 degrees F for 25 to 30 minutes.

STORING

Slice the casserole into four pieces. Divide the pieces between airtight containers; it will last for 3 to 4 days in the refrigerator.
For freezing, place each portion in a separate heavy-duty freezer bag. Freeze up to 2 to 3 months. Defrost in the microwave or refrigerator.
Bon appétit!

325. Peanut Butter Berry Smoothie

(Ready in about 5 minutes | Servings 1)

Per serving: 114 Calories; 8.2g Fat; 5.9g Carbs; 4.2g Protein; 1.8g Fiber

INGREDIENTS

1 tablespoon peanut butter
1/3 cup mixed berries
3/4 cup coconut milk, unsweetened

1 teaspoon Swerve
1/2 cup lettuce

DIRECTIONS

Blend all ingredients until creamy and smooth.

STORING

Spoon your smoothie into an airtight container and keep in your refrigerator for up to 2 days.
Spoon your smoothie into an airtight container. Store in your freezer for a few weeks.

326. Swiss Chard Dip

(Ready in about 25 minutes | Servings 6)

Per serving: 75 Calories; 3g Fat; 6g Carbs; 2.9g Protein; 0.8g Fiber

INGREDIENTS

2 cups Swiss chard
2 teaspoons sesame oil
Salt and pepper, to taste
1 teaspoon dried Mediterranean spice mix

1 cup tofu, pressed and crumbled
1 teaspoon fresh garlic, smashed
1/2 cup almond milk
2 teaspoons nutritional yeast

DIRECTIONS

Parboil the Swiss chard in a pot of lightly salted water for about 6 minutes. Transfer the mixture to the bowl of a food processor; add in the other ingredients.
Process the ingredients until the mixture is homogeneous.
Bake in the preheated oven at 390 degrees F for about 10 minutes.

STORING

Place your dip in airtight containers or Ziploc bags; keep in your refrigerator for up to 3 to 4 days.
To freeze, place your dip in airtight containers or Ziploc bags. Freeze up to 5 months. Defrost in the refrigerator. Enjoy!

327. Dark Chocolate Smoothie

(Ready in about 10 minutes | Servings 2)

Per serving: 335 Calories; 31.7g Fat; 5.7g Carbs; 7g Protein; 1.9g Fiber

INGREDIENTS

1 tablespoon chia seeds
1 tablespoon unsweetened cocoa powder
2 tablespoons Swerve
8 almonds

1/2 cup coconut milk
1/2 cup water
1 ½ cups baby spinach

DIRECTIONS

Process all ingredients until smooth and creamy.

STORING

Spoon your smoothie into two airtight containers and keep in your refrigerator for up to 2 days.
Spoon your smoothie into two airtight containers and store in your freezer for a few weeks.

328. Cauliflower and Pepper Masala

(Ready in about 30 minutes | Servings 4)

Per serving: 166 Calories; 13.9g Fat; 5.4g Carbs; 3g Protein; 3.1g Fiber

INGREDIENTS

1 pound cauliflower florets
1/4 cup sesame oil
1 cup vegetable broth
2 bell peppers, halved
1 garlic clove, minced
2 sprigs curry leaves

1 teaspoon fennel seeds
1 tablespoon khus khus
1/2 of a star anise
1/2 teaspoon nigella seeds
Salt and pepper, to taste

DIRECTIONS

Parboil the cauliflower in a pot of a lightly-salted water for 5 to 6 minutes until crisp-tender.
Dry roast all the apices on a low flame for about 3 minutes; reserve.
In a wok, or a saucepan, heat the sesame oil until sizzling. Cook the cauliflower, peppers, and garlic for 5 to 6 minutes.
Add in the salt, pepper, and broth and continue to cook for 10 minutes.

STORING

Divide the cauliflower and pepper masala into four portions; divide the portions between four airtight containers; keep in your refrigerator for up 3 to 5 days.
For freezing, place the cauliflower and pepper masala in airtight containers. Freeze up to 10 to 12 months. Defrost in the refrigerator. Bon appétit!

329. Savoy Cabbage with Tempeh

(Ready in about 20 minutes | Servings 4)

Per serving: 179 Calories; 11.7g Fat; 2.1g Carbs; 10.5g Protein; 2.3g Fiber

INGREDIENTS

1/2 pound savoy cabbage, shredded
2 tablespoons sesame oil
6 ounces tempeh, crumbled
1 teaspoon garlic, minced

1/2 cup white onion, chopped
2 tablespoons vegetable broth
2 tablespoons coconut aminos
Sea salt and pepper, to season

DIRECTIONS

In a wok, heat the sesame oil over a moderately-high heat. Sauté the garlic and onion until tender and fragrant.
Now, add in the remaining ingredients and cook for 15 minutes or until thoroughly cooked.

STORING

Place the Savoy cabbage with the tempeh in airtight containers or Ziploc bags; keep in your refrigerator for up to 3 to 4 days.
For freezing, place the Savoy cabbage with the tempeh in airtight containers or heavy-duty freezer bags. Freeze up to 2 to 3 months. Defrost in the refrigerator. Bon appétit!

330. Pine Nut and Cauliflower Soup

(Ready in about 25 minutes | Servings 4)

Per serving: 114 Calories; 6.5g Fat; 6.4g Carbs; 3.8g Protein; 3.5g Fiber

INGREDIENTS

1/4 cup pine nuts, ground
1 pound cauliflower, broken into florets
4 cups vegetable broth
1 tablespoon sesame oil
1 cup onions, chopped

1 celery with leaves, chopped
Salt and pepper, to taste
1 teaspoon garlic, smashed
1 tablespoon fresh coriander, minced

DIRECTIONS

In a heavy-bottomed pot, heat sesame oil over a moderately-high flame. Sauté the onion, celery and garlic until tender and aromatic.
Add in the cauliflower, vegetable broth, salt, pepper, and pine nuts. Bring to a boil.
Immediately reduce the heat to simmer; continue to cook, partially covered, for about 18 minutes.
Afterwards, add in the fresh coriander and puree your soup with an immersion blender.

STORING

Spoon the soup into four airtight containers and keep in your refrigerator for up 3 to 4 days.
For freezing, place the soup in airtight containers or heavy-duty freezer bags. Freeze up to 4 to 6 months. Defrost in the microwave or refrigerator. Enjoy!

331. Easy Vegan Granola

(Ready in about 1 hour | Servings 8)

Per serving: 262 Calories; 24.3g Fat; 5.2g Carbs; 5.1g Protein; 2.2g Fiber

INGREDIENTS

1/2 cup pine nuts, chopped
1/2 cup almonds, slivered
2 tablespoons sunflower seeds
2 tablespoons sesame seeds
1/4 cup flax seeds
2 tablespoons granulated Swerve
2 tablespoons coconut oil, melted

A pinch of Himalayan salt
1 teaspoon grated orange peel
1/8 teaspoon allspice, freshly grated
1 teaspoon ground cinnamon
1/3 cup shredded coconut flakes
1 ½ cups almond milk, unsweetened

DIRECTIONS

Toss all ingredients in a parchment-lined baking pan.
Roast in the preheated oven at 290 degrees F for about 70 minutes; check and stir every 20 minutes.

STORING

Place the granola in airtight containers or Ziploc bags; keep at room temperature for up to a month.

332. Keto "Oats" with Mixed Berries

(Ready in about 5 minutes + chilling time | Servings 4)

Per serving: 176 Calories; 12.7g Fat; 6g Carbs; 9.7g Protein; 3.2g Fiber

INGREDIENTS

1/2 cup hemp hearts
1/4 cup sunflower seeds
8 tablespoons granulated Swerve
1/2 teaspoon ground cinnamon

1/2 cup water
1/2 cup coconut milk, unsweetened
1 cup mixed berries

DIRECTIONS

Thoroughly combine the water, milk, hemp hearts, sunflower seeds, Swerve, and cinnamon in an airtight container.
Cover and let it stand in your refrigerator overnight.

STORING

Place the keto oats in airtight containers or Ziploc bags; keep in your refrigerator for up 2 to 3 days.
Top with fresh strawberries and serve.

333. Hemp and Chia Pudding

(Ready in about 5 minutes + prep time | Servings 3)

Per serving: 153 Calories; 8g Fat; 6.7g Carbs; 6.7g Protein; 2.6g Fiber

INGREDIENTS

2 cups coconut milk, unsweetened
9 blackberries, fresh or frozen
1/4 cup hemp hearts
1/4 cup chia seeds
1/4 teaspoon ground cloves

1/4 teaspoon grated nutmeg
1/4 teaspoon ground cinnamon
1/8 teaspoon coarse sea salt
A few drops of liquid Stevia

DIRECTIONS

Thoroughly combine the coconut milk, hemp hearts, chia seeds, ground cloves, nutmeg, cinnamon, salt, and Stevia in an airtight container.
Cover and let it stand in your refrigerator overnight.

STORING

Place your pudding in airtight containers or Ziploc bags; keep in your refrigerator for up 2 to 3 days.
Top with blackberries and serve.

334. Autumn Squash Smoothie Bowl

(Ready in about 5 minutes | Servings 2)

Per serving: 71 Calories; 2.3g Fat; 4.1g Carbs; 4.3g Protein; 2.4g Fiber

INGREDIENTS

1/2 cup butternut squash, roasted
1/2 teaspoon pumpkin spice mix
2 tablespoons cocoa powder, unsweetened

1 ½ cups almond milk, unsweetened
1/2 cup butterhead lettuce

DIRECTIONS

Blend all ingredients until well combined.

STORING

Spoon your smoothie into two airtight containers and keep in your refrigerator for up to 2 days.
Spoon your smoothie into two airtight containers and store in your freezer for a few weeks.

335. Chinese-Style Tofu in Spicy Sauce

(Ready in about 20 minutes | Servings 4)

Per serving: 336 Calories; 22.2g Fat; 5.8g Carbs; 27.6g Protein; 3.4g Fiber

INGREDIENTS

6 ounces smoked tofu, pressed, drained and cubed
1/2 teaspoon Chinese five-spice powder
2 tablespoons sesame oil
1 cup onions, chopped
2 garlic cloves, minced
1/2 cup vegetable broth

For the Sauce:
1 teaspoon Sriracha sauce
1/2 tablespoon sesame oil
1/2 teaspoon cardamom
1 cup tomatoes, pureed
2 tablespoons Shaoxing rice wine

DIRECTIONS

In a wok, heat 2 tablespoons of sesame oil over medium-high flame.
Cook the tofu cubes until they are slightly browned or about 5 minutes. Add in the onions, garlic, vegetable broth, and Chinese five-spice powder.
Stir fry for 5 to 7 minutes more until almost all liquid has evaporated.
To make the Chinese sauce, heat 1/2 tablespoon of sesame oil over a moderate flame. Add in the pureed tomatoes and cook until thoroughly warmed.
Add in the remaining ingredients and turn the heat to a simmer; continue to simmer for 8 to 10 minutes or until the sauce has reduced by half. Fold in tofu cubes and gently stir to combine.

STORING

Place the Chinese-style tofu in airtight containers or Ziploc bags; keep in your refrigerator for up to 3 to 4 days.
To freeze, place the Chinese-style tofu in airtight containers or Ziploc bags. Freeze up to 5 months. Defrost in the refrigerator. Enjoy!

336. Easy Authentic Guacamole

(Ready in about 10 minutes + chilling time | Servings 8)

Per serving: 112 Calories; 9.9g Fat; 6.5g Carbs; 1.3g Protein; 2.4g Fiber

INGREDIENTS

2 tomatoes, pureed
2 avocados, peeled, pitted, and mashed
1 teaspoon garlic, smashed
1 ancho chili pepper, deveined and minced

Sea salt and pepper, to taste
1 shallot, chopped
2 tablespoons cilantro, chopped
2 tablespoons fresh lemon juice

DIRECTIONS

Thoroughly combine all ingredients
Keep in your refrigerator until ready to serve. Bon appétit!

STORING

Place the tofu and sauce in airtight containers or Ziploc bags; keep in your refrigerator for up to 3 to 4 days.
To freeze, place the tofu and sauce in airtight containers or Ziploc bags. Freeze up to 5 months. Defrost in the refrigerator. Enjoy!

337. Cauliflower Slaw with Almonds

(Ready in about 15 minutes + chilling time | Servings 4)

Per serving: 281 Calories; 26.8g Fat; 5.6g Carbs; 4.2g Protein; 3.4g Fiber

INGREDIENTS

1 pound cauliflower florets
1/2 cup almonds, coarsely chopped
1 tablespoon balsamic vinegar
1 teaspoon deli mustard
Salt and pepper, to taste

1/2 cup black olives, pitted and chopped
3/4 cup yellow onions, chopped
1 roasted pepper, chopped
1/4 cup olive oil

DIRECTIONS

Parboil the cauliflower florets in a lightly-salted water for about 5 minutes until crisp-tender; transfer the cauliflower to a bowl.

STORING

Divide the cauliflower into four portions; divide the portions between four airtight containers; keep in your refrigerator for up 3 to 5 days.
For freezing, place the cauliflower in airtight containers. Freeze up to 10 to 12 months. Defrost in the refrigerator.
Toss the cauliflower with the remaining ingredients. Bon appétit!

338. Chocolate and Berry Shake

(Ready in about 5 minutes | Servings 2)

Per serving: 103 Calories; 5.9g Fat; 6.1g Carbs; 4.1g Protein; 2.4g Fiber

INGREDIENTS

1 cup mixed berries
1 tablespoon cocoa, unsweetened
1 tablespoon peanut butter
1 tablespoon flax seeds, ground

1/4 teaspoon ground cloves
1/2 teaspoon ground cinnamon
2 tablespoons Swerve
1 cup water

DIRECTIONS

Blend all ingredients until smooth, creamy, and uniform.

STORING

Spoon your smoothie into two airtight containers and keep in your refrigerator for up to 2 days.
Spoon your smoothie into two airtight containers and store in your freezer for a few weeks.

339. Spicy Celery and Carrot Salad

(Ready in about 10 minutes | Servings 4)

Per serving: 196 Calories; 17.2g Fat; 6g Carbs; 1.2g Protein; 2.2g Fiber

INGREDIENTS

1/4 pound carrots, coarsely shredded
3/4 pound celery, shredded
1/4 cup fresh parsley, chopped
For the Vinaigrette:
2 garlic cloves, smashed
Sea salt and pepper, to taste

1/3 cup olive oil
1 lemon, freshly squeezed
2 tablespoons balsamic vinegar
1/2 teaspoon ground allspice
1/2 teaspoon Sriracha sauce

DIRECTIONS

Toss the carrots, celery, and parsley in a bowl until everything is well combined.
Mix all ingredients for a vinaigrette and dress your salad.

STORING

Place your salad in airtight containers or Ziploc bags; keep in your refrigerator for up to 3 to 4 days.

340. Traditional Ethiopian-Style Peppers

(Ready in about 40 minutes | Servings 4)

Per serving: 77 Calories; 4.8g Fat; 5.4g Carbs; 1.6g Protein; 3.1g Fiber

INGREDIENTS

4 bell peppers, seeds removed, and halved
1 cup tomato puree
1 ½ tablespoons avocado oil
1 teaspoon ancho chili powder
1 teaspoon Berbere

1 shallot, chopped
1/2 teaspoon garlic, smashed
1/2 pound cauliflower rice
Kosher salt and red pepper, to season

DIRECTIONS

Start by preheating your oven to 365 degrees F.
Roast the peppers for about 15 minutes until the skin is slightly charred.
In a saucepan, heat the avocado oil over medium-high flame. Sauté the shallot and garlic until they are just tender.
Stir in the cauliflower rice, ancho chili powder, and Berbere spice and cook for 5 to 6 minutes.
Spoon the cauliflower mixture into pepper halves. Place the peppers in a lightly greased casserole dish.
Add the tomato, salt and pepper around to the casserole dish and bake for about 15 minutes.

STORING

Place stuffed peppers in airtight containers; keep in your refrigerator for 3 to 4 days.
Wrap each stuffed pepper tightly in several layers of plastic wrap and squeeze the air out. Place them in airtight containers; they can be frozen for up to 1 month.

341. Mushroom and Dijon Mustard-Stuffed Avocado

(Ready in about 10 minutes | Servings 8)

Per serving: 245 Calories; 23.2g Fat; 6.2g Carbs; 2.4g Protein; 4g Fiber

INGREDIENTS

4 avocados, halved
1 tablespoon Dijon mustard
1 shallot, chopped
2 garlic cloves, minced
Salt and pepper, to taste

2 tablespoons sesame oil
2 cups brown mushrooms, chopped
1 cup grape tomatoes, diced
1/2 lemon, freshly squeezed

DIRECTIONS

In a frying pan, heat sesame oil over a moderately-high heat. Sauté the mushrooms, shallot, and garlic until they are tender and fragrant.
Scoop out about 1 tablespoon of the avocado flesh from each half.
Add the avocado flash to the mushroom mixture along with the salt, pepper, Dijon mustard, and tomatoes.
Divide the mushroom mixture among the avocado halves. Drizzle each avocado with lemon juice.

STORING

Place the stuffed avocado in airtight containers; keep in your refrigerator for up to 3 days.

342. Tofu Cubes with Pine Nuts

(Ready in about 13 minutes | Servings 4)

Per serving: 232 Calories; 21.6g Fat; 5.3g Carbs; 8.3g Protein; 2.4g Fiber

INGREDIENTS

1 cup extra firm tofu, pressed and cubed
1/4 cup pine nuts, coarsely chopped
2 teaspoons lightly toasted sesame seeds
3 teaspoons avocado oil
1 ½ tablespoons coconut aminos
3 tablespoons vegetable broth

1/2 teaspoon porcini powder
1/2 teaspoon ground cumin
Salt and pepper, to season
2 garlic cloves, minced
1 teaspoon red pepper flakes

DIRECTIONS

In a wok, heat the avocado oil over a moderately-high heat. Now, fry the tofu cubes for 5 to 6 minutes until golden brown on all sides.
Stir in the pecans, coconut aminos, broth, garlic, red pepper, porcini powder, cumin, salt, and pepper and continue to stir for about 8 minutes.
Top with toasted sesame seeds.

STORING

Place the tofu in airtight containers or Ziploc bags; keep in your refrigerator for up to 3 to 4 days.
To freeze, place the tofu in airtight containers or Ziploc bags. Freeze up to 5 months. Defrost in the refrigerator. Bon appétit!

343. Mediterranean Crunchy Salad with Seeds

(Ready in about 15 minutes | Servings 4)

Per serving: 208 Calories; 15.6g Fat; 6.2g Carbs; 7.6g Protein; 6g Fiber

INGREDIENTS

For Dressing:
2 tablespoons onions, chopped
1/2 teaspoon garlic, chopped
1 cup sunflower seeds, soaked overnight
1/2 cup almond milk
1 lemon, freshly squeezed
1/2 teaspoon Mediterranean herb mix
Salt and pepper, to taste

1/2 teaspoon paprika
For the Salad:
2 tablespoons black olives, pitted
1 cup cherry tomatoes, halved
1 Lebanese cucumbers, sliced
1 head Romaine lettuce, separated into leaves
1 tablespoon cilantro leaves, coarsely chopped

DIRECTIONS

Process all of the dressing ingredients until creamy and smooth.
Toss all of the salad ingredients in a bowl. Dress your salad.

STORING

Place the salad in airtight container or heavy-duty freezer bags; keep in the refrigerator for up to 2 to 3 days.

344. Thai-Style Braised Cabbage

(Ready in about 15 minutes | Servings 6)

Per serving: 186 Calories; 17g Fat; 5.3g Carbs; 2.1g Protein; 2g Fiber

INGREDIENTS

2 pounds Chinese cabbage, cut into wedges
1 Thai bird chili, minced
1 teaspoon sesame seeds
1/4 teaspoon cinnamon
1/2 cup vegetable broth

2 tablespoons fresh chives, chopped
4 tablespoons sesame oil
1/4 teaspoon cardamom
Salt and black pepper, to taste

DIRECTIONS

In a wok or a large saucepan, heat the sesame oil over medium-high heat. Then, fry the cabbage until crisp-tender.
Stir in the remaining ingredients and continue to cook for 10 minutes more or until heated through.

STORING

Place the Thai cabbage in airtight containers or Ziploc bags; keep in your refrigerator for up to 3 to 4 days.
For freezing, place the Thai cabbage in airtight containers or heavy-duty freezer bags. Freeze up to 2 to 3 months. Defrost in the refrigerator.
Bon appétit!

345. Eggplant and Cashew Soup

(Ready in about 1 hour 20 minutes | Servings 4)

Per serving: 159 Calories; 9.4g Fat; 7.1g Carbs; 4.2g Protein; 4g Fiber

INGREDIENTS

1 pound eggplant, sliced
1/3 cup raw cashews, soaked overnight
1 teaspoon garlic, chopped
1/2 teaspoon Mediterranean herb mix
3 cups vegetable broth

1 tablespoon peanut oil
1 cup tomato puree
1 medium onion, chopped
Salt and pepper, to season

DIRECTIONS

Brush the eggplant slices with peanut oil. Roast in the preheated oven at 380 degrees F for about 35 minutes.
Thoroughly combine the eggplant flesh with tomato, onion, garlic, Mediterranean herb mix, and vegetable broth in a heavy-bottomed pot.
Leave the lid slightly ajar and continue to simmer for 35 to 40 minutes or until heated through. Puree the soup in your food processor or blender.
Blend the soaked cashews with 1 cup of water until creamy and smooth. Spoon the cashew cream into the soup and stir until well combined. Season with salt and pepper to taste.

STORING

Spoon the soup into airtight containers; keep in your refrigerator for up to 3 to 4 days.
For freezing, place the soup in airtight containers or heavy-duty freezer bags. It will maintain the best quality for about 5 months. Defrost in the refrigerator. Enjoy!

346. Garlicky Brussels Sprouts

(Ready in about 25 minutes | Servings 4)

Per serving: 118 Calories; 7g Fat; 3.4g Carbs; 2.9g Protein; 4g Fiber

INGREDIENTS

1/2 teaspoon Sichuan peppercorns, crushed
1/2 teaspoon Cassia
1/2 teaspoon jiāng (ginger)
1 pound Brussels sprouts, torn into pieces

2 tablespoons sesame oil
1/2 head garlic, smashed
Salt and ground black pepper, to the taste

DIRECTIONS

Parboil the Brussels sprouts in a pot of a lightly salted water for 15 to 17 minutes over a moderately-high heat. Drain.
In a wok, heat the sesame oil over a moderately-high heat. Then, sauté the garlic for a minute or so.
Add in the reserved Brussels sprouts and spices; continue to cook until everything is cooked through.

STORING

Place the Brussels sprout in airtight containers or Ziploc bags; keep in your refrigerator for 3 to 5 days.
Place the Brussels sprout in freezable containers; they can be frozen for up to 3 months. Defrost in the refrigerator or microwave.

347. Paprika Cauliflower Soup

(Ready in about 20 minutes | Servings 4)

Per serving: 94 Calories; 7.2g Fat; 7g Carbs; 2.7g Protein; 2.8g Fiber

INGREDIENTS

1/2 teaspoon paprika
2 heads of cauliflower, broken into florets

1/4 teaspoon mustard powder
1/2 teaspoon fenugreek
1/4 teaspoon ground cloves

1 ½ tablespoons vegetable broth
2 tablespoons extra-virgin olive oil

DIRECTIONS

Parboil the cauliflower florets for about 12 minutes until crisp-tender.
Add in the remaining ingredients and stir to combine.
Let it simmer, partially covered, for about 10 minutes or until cooked through. Puree the mixture using your immersion blender.

STORING

Spoon the soup into four airtight containers and keep in your refrigerator for up 3 to 4 days.
For freezing, place the soup in airtight containers or heavy-duty freezer bags. Freeze up to 4 to 6 months. Defrost in the microwave or refrigerator. Enjoy!

348. Spanish-Style Roasted Vegetables

(Ready in about 45 minutes | Servings 4)

Per serving: 165 Calories; 14.3g Fat; 5.6g Carbs; 2.1g Protein; 1.9g Fiber

INGREDIENTS

4 tablespoons olive oil
4 tablespoons cream of mushroom soup
1 teaspoon Ñora
1 teaspoon saffron

2 zucchinis, cut into thick slices
1 onion, quartered
4 garlic cloves, halved
3 Spanish peppers, deveined and sliced

1/2 head of cauliflower, broken into large florets
1 teaspoon dried sage, crushed
Salt and pepper, to taste

DIRECTIONS

Toss all ingredients in a parchment-lined roasting pan.
Roast in the preheated oven at 420 degrees F for 35 to 40 minutes.
Toss your vegetables halfway through the cook time. Taste and adjust the seasonings.

STORING

Place the roasted vegetables in airtight containers or Ziploc bags; keep in your refrigerator for up to 3 to 5 days.
To freeze, arrange the roasted vegetables on a baking sheet in a single layer; freeze for about 2 hours. Transfer the frozen vegetables to freezer storage bags. Freeze for up to 12 months.

349. Fennel with Light Mediterranean Sauce

(Ready in about 20 minutes | Servings 4)

Per serving: 135 Calories; 13.6g Fat; 3g Carbs; 0.9g Protein; 1.9g Fiber

INGREDIENTS

1 fennel, thinly sliced
1/4 cup vegetable broth
2 tablespoons olive oil
1/2 teaspoon garlic, minced
Salt and pepper, to taste
1 bay laurel

For the Sauce:
1 cloves garlic, minced
1 cayenne pepper, minced
1 bunch fresh basil, leaves picked
1 teaspoon oregano
1 cup cherry tomatoes

2 tablespoons olive oil
1 teaspoon rosemary
1/2 cup red onion, chopped
Sat and pepper, to taste

DIRECTIONS

Heat 2 tablespoons of olive oil in a frying pan over a moderate flame. Sauté the garlic until aromatic.
Add in the fennel, broth, salt, pepper, and bay laurel. Continue to cook until the fennel is just tender.
Puree the sauce ingredients in your food processor until smooth and creamy. Heat the sauce over-medium low flame.
Add in the fennel mixture and continue to cook for 5 to 6 minutes more or until everything is cooked through.

STORING

Divide the fennel along with sauce into four portions; divide the portions between four airtight containers; keep in your refrigerator for up 3 to 5 days.
For freezing, place the fennel along with sauce in airtight containers. Freeze up to 10 to 12 months. Defrost in the refrigerator. Bon appétit!

350. Rich and Easy Granola

(Ready in about 1 hour | Servings 6)

Per serving: 449 Calories; 44.9g Fat; 6.9g Carbs; 9.3g Protein; 2.3g Fiber

INGREDIENTS

1/3 cup coconut oil, melted
1/2 cup almonds, chopped
1 teaspoon lime zest
1/3 cup water

1 cup pecans, chopped
1/3 cup chia seeds
1/3 cup pumpkin seeds
A few drops of Stevia

1/3 cup flax meal
1/3 cup almond milk
1 teaspoon ground cinnamon
1 teaspoon freshly grated nutmeg

DIRECTIONS

Preheat an oven to 310 degrees F. Coat a cookie sheet with parchment paper.
Toss all ingredients together and spread the mixture out in an even layer onto the prepared cookie sheet.
Bake about for 50 to 55 minutes, stirring every 15 to 20 minutes.

STORING

Place your granola in airtight containers or Ziploc bags; keep at room temperature for up to a month.

351. Vegetable Noodles with Classic Avocado Sauce

(Ready in about 15 minutes | Servings 4)

Per serving: 233 Calories; 20.2g Fat; 6g Carbs; 1.9g Protein; 4g Fiber

INGREDIENTS

3 tablespoons olive oil
1 yellow onion, chopped
1 poblano pepper, deveined and minced

Salt and pepper, to season
1 avocado, peeled and pitted
1 lime, juiced and zested
2 tablespoons parsley, chopped

1/2 pound zucchini, spiralized
1/2 pound bell peppers, spiralized

DIRECTIONS

In a saucepan, heat 1 tablespoon of olive oil over a moderately-high heat. Sauté the zucchini and peppers until crisp-tender or about 5 minutes.
In your blender or food processor, pulse the other ingredients until well combined.
Pour the avocado sauce over the vegetable noodles and toss to combine.

STORING

Place your noodles in airtight containers or Ziploc bags; keep in your refrigerator for 3 to 5 days.
Place your noodles in a freezable container; they can be frozen for up to 10 to 12 months. Bake the thawed noodles at 200 degrees F until they are completely warm. Enjoy!

352. Vegan Skillet with Tofu and Cabbage

(Ready in about 25 minutes | Servings 4)

Per serving: 128 Calories; 8.3g Fat; 6.5g Carbs; 5.1g Protein; 3.2g Fiber

INGREDIENTS

1 pound cabbage, trimmed and quartered
8 ounces tofu, pressed, drained and cubed
1 celery stalk, chopped
1/2 cup onions, chopped
2 tablespoons sesame oil
1 teaspoon red pepper flakes, crushed

Salt and pepper, to taste
1/2 teaspoon curry paste
1/4 teaspoon dried oregano
2 garlic cloves, pressed
2 tablespoons coconut aminos

DIRECTIONS

Heat the sesame oil in a nonstisk skillet over a moderately-high heat. Then, fry the tofu cubes for about 7 minutes or until golden brown on all sides.
Add in the celery and onions, and continue to cook for a further 5 minutes until they are just tender.
Add in the other ingredients and continue to cook, partially covered, for 7 to 8 minutes longer. Fold in the tofu cubes and gently stir to combine.

STORING

Place the tofu and cabbage in airtight containers or Ziploc bags; keep in your refrigerator for up to 3 to 4 days.
To freeze, place the tofu and cabbage in airtight containers or Ziploc bags. Freeze up to 5 months. Defrost in the refrigerator. Bon appétit!

353. Keto Crunch Cereal

(Ready in about 10 minutes | Servings 4)

Per serving: 279 Calories; 23.6g Fat; 5.9g Carbs; 7.2g Protein; 2.2g Fiber

INGREDIENTS

16 almonds, roughly chopped
1/3 cup coconut shreds
2 ½ cups almond milk, full-fat
1/2 cup water
2 tablespoons coconut oil, melted

4 tablespoons Swerve
1/2 cup hemp hearts
A pinch of sea salt
A pinch of grated nutmeg
1/2 teaspoon ground cinnamon

DIRECTIONS

Place all ingreidnets, excepr for the almonds, in a deep saucepan over medium-low heat.
Let it simmer, partially covered, for 5 to 6 minutes or until slightly thickened.
Top each serving with slivered almonds.

STORING

Place the keto crunch cereal in airtight containers or Ziploc bags; keep in your refrigerator for up to 3 days.

354. Pancetta and Chives Deviled Eggs

(Ready in about 20 minutes | Servings 10)

Per serving: 128 Calories; 9.7g Fat; 3.3g Carbs; 6.8g Protein; 0.1g Fiber

INGREDIENTS

10 eggs
1/4 cup pancetta, chopped
1 tablespoon deli mustard
1/4 teaspoon Sriracha sauce

1/2 cup mayonnaise
1 tablespoon fresh basil, finely chopped
2 teaspoons champagne vinegar

DIRECTIONS

Place the eggs in a saucepan and cover them with water by 1 inch. Cover and bring the water to a boil over high heat. Boil for 6 to 7 minutes over medium-high heat.
Peel the eggs and slice them in half lengthwise; mix the yolks with the remaining ingredients.
Divide the mixture between the egg whites and arrange the deviled eggs on a nice serving platter.

STORING

Place the deviled eggs in an airtight container or Ziploc bag; transfer to your refrigerator; they should be consumed within 2 days.
For freezing, spoon out the yolk mixture from the deviled eggs. Add the egg yolk mixture to an airtight container or Ziploc bag.
Place the container in the freezer for up to 3 months. To defrost, let them sit overnight in the refrigerator until they are fully thawed out.
Enjoy!

355. Easy Antipasto Skewers

(Ready in about 10 minutes | Servings 6)

Per serving: 249 Calories; 19.3g Fat; 6g Carbs; 9.7g Protein; 1.4g Fiber

INGREDIENTS

1 cup bacon, diced
4 ounces feta cheese, cubed
1/2 cup olives, pitted
6 ounces pickled cornichons, no sugar added

2 bell peppers, sliced
1/3 cup balsamic vinegar
1/3 cup olive oil
1/2 teaspoon cumin seeds

DIRECTIONS

Toss all ingredients in a mixing bowl.
Thread the pickled cornichons, bell peppers, feta cheese, bacon, and olives onto long wooden skewers, alternating the ingredients.

STORING

Place the antipasto skewers in airtight containers or Ziploc bags; transfer to your refrigerator; they should be consumed within 3 days.

356. Cheese Cucumber Rounds

(Ready in about 10 minutes | Servings 10)

Per serving: 63 Calories; 4.3g Fat; 2.7g Carbs; 4g Protein; 0.1g Fiber

INGREDIENTS

2 cucumbers, cut into thick slices
2 tablespoons ham, chopped
1/4 cup chives, chopped

1 teaspoon ancho chili powder
1 cup goat cheese

DIRECTIONS

Mix the cheese, ham, chives, and ancho chili powder until well combined.
Divide the mixture between cucumber slices.

STORING

Place the cucumber bites in airtight containers or Ziploc bags; transfer to your refrigerator; they should be consumed within 3 days.

357. Bell Pepper Bites

(Ready in about 20 minutes | Servings 4)

Per serving: 252 Calories; 13.7g Fat; 5.6g Carbs; 26g Protein; 1.4g Fiber

INGREDIENTS

4 bell peppers, deveined and quartered
2 tablespoons ghee, softened
2 ounces chorizo, chopped
1 yellow onion, minced
2 garlic cloves, minced

1 tablespoon fresh cilantro, finely chopped
Salt and pepper, to taste
1/2 pound ground turkey
6 ounces cream cheese, softened

DIRECTIONS

In a frying pan, melt the ghee over a moderately high flame. Once hot, sauté the onion until tender and translucent.
Add in the ground turkey and continue to cook for a further 5 minutes or until no longer pink. Remove from the heat.
Add in the cheese, garlic, cilantro, salt, and pepper. Divide the meat/cheese mixture between your peppers. Top with the chorizo and arrange your peppers on a parchment-lined baking sheet.
Bake in the preheated oven at 370 degrees F for about 15 minutes or until the peppers are tender.

STORING

Place the stuffed peppers in airtight containers; keep in your refrigerator for 3 to 4 days.
Wrap each stuffed pepper tightly in several layers of plastic wrap and squeeze the air out. Place them in airtight containers; they can be frozen for up to 1 month.
Bake the thawed stuffed peppers at 200 degrees F until they are completely warm.

358. Sour Cream and Bacon Dip

(Ready in about 5 minutes | Servings 6)

Per serving: 147 Calories; 10.6g Fat; 2.7g Carbs; 10.2g Protein; 0.4g Fiber

INGREDIENTS

5 ounces sour cream
1/2 cup Canadian bacon, crumbled
2 tablespoons fresh parsley, chopped

1 cup mozzarella cheese, shredded
5 ounces cream cheese, at room temperature

DIRECTIONS

Mix all ingredients until well combined.

STORING

Place your dip in an airtight container and keep in your refrigerator for 3 to 4 days. Enjoy!

359. Genoa Salami and Egg Balls

(Ready in about 5 minutes + chilling time | Servings 6)

Per serving: 327 Calories; 25.7g Fat; 6.4g Carbs; 17g Protein; 0.4g Fiber

INGREDIENTS

1/2 cup Ricotta cheese, softened
1/3 cup mayonnaise
6 hard-boiled eggs, peeled and chopped
1/2 teaspoon Italian seasoning mix

Sea salt and pepper, to taste
1/2 teaspoon paprika
6 slices genoa salami, chopped

DIRECTIONS

Thoroughly combine all ingredients until well combined.
Roll the mixture into balls.

STORING

Place the salami and egg bites in an airtight container and keep in your refrigerator for 3 to 4 days. Bon appétit!

360. Easy Bacon Chips

(Ready in about 15 minutes | Servings 6)

Per serving: 409 Calories; 31.6g Fat; 1.1g Carbs; 28g Protein; 0.4g Fiber

INGREDIENTS

1 pound bacon, cut into 1-inch squares
1 teaspoon Sriracha sauce
1 teaspoon lime juice

1 teaspoon lime zest
1 tablespoon smoked paprika

DIRECTIONS

Toss all ingredients in a mixing dish.
Bake in the preheated oven at 365 degrees F approximately 15 minutes.

STORING

Divide the bacon chips between airtight containers or Ziploc bags; keep in your refrigerator for up to 4 days.
To freeze, divide the bacon chips between airtight containers. Freeze up to 2 months. Defrost and reheat in your oven until it is crisp. Enjoy!

361. Swiss Cheese and Salami Cups

(Ready in about 20 minutes | Servings 6)

Per serving: 162 Calories; 13.1g Fat; 2.5g Carbs; 8.7g Protein; 1.7g Fiber

INGREDIENTS

12 winter salami slices
1/2 cup spicy tomato sauce
1 teaspoon Italian spice mix

1 cup Swiss cheese, shredded
1/2 cup black olives, pitted and chopped

DIRECTIONS

Spritz 12-cup muffin tin with a nonstick cooking spray. Place a salami slice in each muffin cup.
Add in the cheese, tomato sauce, Italian spice mix, and olives.
Bake in the preheated oven at 365 degrees F approximately 16 minutes.

STORING

Place the cheese and salami cups in the airtight containers or Ziploc bags; keep in the refrigerator for a week.
For freezing, divide the cheese and salami cups among three Ziploc bags and freeze up to 3 months. Defrost in your microwave for a couple of minutes. Enjoy!

362. Cheesy Carrot Sticks

(Ready in about 35 minutes | Servings 6)

Per serving: 216 Calories; 18.7g Fat; 5.4g Carbs; 3.5g Protein; 3.6g Fiber

INGREDIENTS

1 ½ pounds carrot, cuti into sticks
1/4 teaspoon mustard seeds
1 tablespoon Swerve
1 teaspoon basil

1/2 cup Colby cheese, grated
1 stick butter, melted
Salt and pepper, to taste

DIRECTIONS

Preheat your oven to 390 degrees F.
Toss the carrot sticks with the melted butter, salt, pepper, mustard seeds, Swerve, and basil.
Roast the carrot sticks in the preheated oven for 25 to 30 minutes, stirring every 10 minutes.

STORING

Place the carrot sticks in airtight containers or Ziploc bags; keep in your refrigerator for up to 3 to 5 days.
To freeze, arrange the carrot sticks on a baking sheet in a single layer; freeze for about 2 hours. Transfer to freezer storage bags. Freeze for up to 3 months.
Top with the shredded cheese and broil an additional 5 minutes or until the cheese is slightly browned. Bon appétit!

363. Keto Paprika Crackers

(Ready in about 30 minutes | Servings 12)

Per serving: 119 Calories; 8g Fat; 4.7g Carbs; 2.6g Protein; 1.1g Fiber

INGREDIENTS

1/2 cup sesame seeds
1/4 tablespoons sunflower seeds
2 tablespoons flax seeds
1 tablespoon pine nuts, ground

1/3 cup pumpkin seeds, ground
1/4 cup psyllium husks
Coarse sea salt, to taste
1 teaspoon paprika

DIRECTIONS

Mix all the above ingredients in a bowl. Add in the warm water to form a smooth dough ball.
Then, roll the dough out as thin as possible. Use a pizza cutter to cut dough into 1-inch squares.
Bake in the preheated oven at 365 degrees F for about 12 minutes or until golden and crispy. Turn your crackers over and bake for further 8 to 10 minutes.

STORING

Place the keto crackers in airtight containers or Ziploc bags; keep in your refrigerator for up to 10 days.

364. Spicy Double Cheese Chips

(Ready in about 20 minutes | Servings 6)

Per serving: 225 Calories; 19.3g Fat; 0.6g Carbs; 12.1g Protein; 0.2g Fiber

INGREDIENTS

4 slices prosciutto, crumbled
1 poblano pepper, finely chopped
1 cup Parmesan cheese, finely shredded
1 cup Cheddar cheese, shredded

1/2 teaspoon cayenne pepper
1/2 teaspoon allspice
Salt and pepper, to taste

DIRECTIONS

Start by preheating your oven to 390 degrees F. Coat a baking sheet with a sheet of parchment paper.
Mix all ingredients until well combined.
Add the mixture in small heaps on the prepared baking sheet; be sure to leave enough room in between your crisps.
Bake in the preheated oven approximately 10 minutes. Let them cool on a cooling rack.

STORING

Divide the crisps between airtight containers or Ziploc bags; keep in your refrigerator for up to 4 days.
To freeze, divide the crisps between airtight containers. Freeze up to 2 months. Defrost and reheat in your oven until it is crisp. Enjoy!

365. Italian Fried Cheese Sticks

(Ready in about 15 minutes | Servings 5)

Per serving: 338 Calories; 26.5g Fat; 3.4g Carbs; 21g Protein; 2.3g Fiber

INGREDIENTS

1 teaspoon Italian spice mix
1/4 cup almond meal
1/4 cup flaxseed meal
1/3 cup Romano cheese, grated

2 tablespoons buttermilk
2 eggs
10 pieces mozzarella cheese sticks
Vegetable oil for frying

DIRECTIONS

Mix the Italian spice mix, almond meal, flaxseed meal, and Romano cheese in a shallow bowl.
In another dish, whisk buttermilk with eggs.
Dip each cheese stick into the egg mixture; then, dredge them into the almond meal mixture, then quickly again in the egg mixture and again in the almond meal mixture.
Fill a frying pan with about 2 inches of oil. Heat the oil over high heat.
Deep fry the cheese sticks for 2 minutes per side until the crust is golden brown. Place the fried cheese sticks on paper towels to drain excess oil.

STORING

Divide the cheese sticks between airtight containers or Ziploc bags; keep in your refrigerator for up to 4 days.
To freeze, divide the cheese sticks between airtight containers. Freeze up to 2 months. Defrost and reheat in your oven until it is crisp. Enjoy!

366. Cherry Tomatoes with Creamy Chive Sauce

(Ready in about 25 minutes | Servings 6)

Per serving: 230 Calories; 21g Fat; 6g Carbs; 5.1g Protein; 2.5g Fiber

INGREDIENTS

1 Adobo spice mix
1/4 cup extra-virgin olive oil
1 ½ pounds cherry tomatoes
For the Sauce:

1/2 cup aïoli
1/2 cup fresh chives, chopped
1 cup cream cheese

DIRECTIONS

Toss your tomatoes with the Adobo spice mix and olive oil.
Roast in the preheated oven at 420 degrees F for about 20 minutes.
In the meantime, make the sauce by whisking all the sauce ingredients.

STORING

Place the roasted tomatoes in airtight containers or Ziploc bags; keep in your refrigerator for 3 to 4 days.
Place the sauce in airtight containers or Ziploc bags; keep in your refrigerator for 3 to 4 days.
Place the roasted tomatoes in freezable containers; they can be frozen for up to 1 month. Enjoy!

367. Saucy Cocktail Weenies

(Ready in about 2 hours 30 minutes | Servings 6)

Per serving: 271 Calories; 22.2g Fat; 4.5g Carbs; 12.3g Protein; 3.2g Fiber

INGREDIENTS

1 ½ pounds mini cocktail sausages
1 bottle barbecue sauce, no sugar added
1 tablespoon Erythritol
1 teaspoon granulated garlic

3 tablespoons deli mustard
1 teaspoon shallot powder
1 teaspoon porcini powder

DIRECTIONS

Sear the sausage in a preheated nonstick skillet for 3 to 4 minutes.
Place all ingredients in your slow cooker.
Cook on the Lowest setting for 2 hours. Serve with cocktail sticks or toothpicks.

STORING

Place the cocktail Weenies in airtight containers or Ziploc bags; keep in your refrigerator for 3 to 4 days.
Place the cocktail Weenies in freezable containers; they can be frozen for up to 1 month. Enjoy!

368. Chives Cheese Bites

(Ready in about 10 minutes + chilling time | Servings 6)

Per serving: 108 Calories; 9g Fat; 2.2g Carbs; 4.8g Protein; 0.2g Fiber

INGREDIENTS

1/2 cup fresh chives, finely chopped
1/4 teaspoon champagne vinegar
Salt and pepper, to taste

1 cup Cottage cheese
3 tablespoons butter

DIRECTIONS

Thoroughly combine the cheese, butter, and vinegar. Season with salt and pepper to taste.
Place the cheese mixture in the refrigerator to chill for 2 to 3 hours.
Roll the mixture into bite-sized balls and roll them in the chopped chives.

STORING

Place the cheese bites in airtight containers or Ziploc bags; keep in your refrigerator for 10 days.
To freeze, arrange the cheese bites on a baking tray in a single layer; freeze for about 2 hours. Transfer cheese bites to an airtight container. Freeze for up to 2 months. Serve well chilled!

369. Hungarian Paprika Bacon Crisps

(Ready in about 20 minutes | Servings 4)

Per serving: 118 Calories; 10g Fat; 1.9g Carbs; 5g Protein; 0.4g Fiber

INGREDIENTS

1 tablespoon Hungarian paprika
12 bacon strips, cut into small squares

2 tablespoons Erythritol

DIRECTIONS

Start by preheating your oven to 365 degrees F
Toss the bacon strips with Erythritol and Hungarian paprika.
Place the bacon squares on a parchment lined baking sheet and bake for 13 to 15 minutes.

STORING

Divide the bacon crisps between airtight containers or Ziploc bags; keep in your refrigerator for up to 4 days.
To freeze, divide the bacon crisps between airtight containers. Freeze up to 2 months. Defrost and reheat in your oven until it is crisp. Enjoy!

370. Garlic Romano Chicken Wings

(Ready in about 1 hour 10 minutes | Servings 6)

Per serving: 312 Calories; 23g Fat; 0.9g Carbs; 24.6g Protein; 0.3g Fiber

INGREDIENTS

2 pounds chicken wings, bone-in
1 teaspoon hot sauce
1 cup Romano cheese, grated
Salt and black pepper, to taste

2 cloves garlic, smashed
1 stick butter
1 tablespoon champagne vinegar
1/2 cup Italian parsley, chopped

DIRECTIONS

Line a large rimmed baking sheet with a metal rack.
Preheat an oven to 420 degrees F. Set a metal rack on top of a baking sheet.
Toss the wings with salt and black pepper. Bake in the preheated oven at 410 degrees F until golden and crispy, for 45 to 50 minutes.
Place the garlic, butter, vinegar and hot sauce in a saucepan; cook over low heat until the sauce has thickened slightly.
Remove from the heat and fold in the cheese; toss the wings with the cheese mixture until well coated. Bake an additional 8 minutes and top with parsley.

STORING

Place the chicken wings in airtight containers or Ziploc bags; keep in your refrigerator for up 3 to 4 days.
For freezing, place the chicken wings in airtight containers or heavy-duty freezer bags. Freeze up to 3 months. Once thawed in the refrigerator, heat in the preheated oven at 375 degrees F for 20 to 25 minutes or until heated through. Enjoy!

371. Bacon and Broccoli Mini Frittatas

(Ready in about 30 minutes | Servings 6)

Per serving: 375 Calories; 27.6g Fat; 6g Carbs; 24.8g Protein; 1.6g Fiber

INGREDIENTS

6 eggs, whisked
5 ounces cooked bacon, chopped
1 ½ cups cheddar cheese, freshly grated
1 head broccoli, grated
1 cup onions, chopped
Sea salt and pepper, to taste
1/2 teaspoon Adobo seasoning mix

For the Dipping Sauce:
1 Spanish pepper, chopped
2 vine-ripened tomatoes, chopped
1/2 teaspoon garlic, chopped
1/2 shallot, minced
2 tablespoons sesame oil
1 teaspoon basil

DIRECTIONS

In a mixing bowl, combine the eggs, bacon, cheese, broccoli, onions, salt, pepper, and Adobo seasoning mix.
Preheat your oven to 385 degrees F.
Spoon the mixture into lightly buttered muffin cups and bake for 20 to 30 minutes, or until golden brown.
In the meantime, place all the sauce ingredients in a saucepan over medium-low heat. Let it simmer until reduced by half.

STORING

Place the mini frittatas in an airtight container and keep in your refrigerator for 3 to 4 days.
Place the tomato sauce in an airtight container and keep in your refrigerator for up to 3 days.
To freeze, place the mini frittatas in separate Ziploc bags and freeze up to 3 months. To defrost, place in your microwave for a few minutes.
To freeze, place the tomato sauce in separate Ziploc bags and freeze up to 3 months.

372. Cheese and Ground Meat Sauce

(Ready in about 15 minutes | Servings 10)

Per serving: 195 Calories; 12g Fat; 1.5g Carbs; 19.5g Protein; 0g Fiber

INGREDIENTS

8 ounces cream cheese, at room temperature
6 ounces Cheddar cheese, grated
1/2 pound ground pork
1/2 pound ground turkey
1 teaspoon shallot powder
1/2 teaspoon mustard powder
1/2 teaspoon porcini powder
1 tablespoon olive oil
1/2 teaspoon granulated garlic
1/2 teaspoon cayenne pepper
Salt and black pepper, to taste

DIRECTIONS

Heat the oil in a saucepan over a moderately-high flame. Cook the ground meat for about 5 minutes until no longer pink.
Add in the remaining ingredients and continue to simmer over low heat for about 4 minutes.

STORING

Place your sauce in airtight containers; keep in your refrigerator for 3 to 5 days.
For freezing, place your sauce in a freezable container; it can be frozen for 4 to 5 months. Enjoy!

373. Rich and Easy Ground Meat Pie

(Ready in about 25 minutes | Servings 6)

Per serving: 231 Calories; 16.4g Fat; 3.5g Carbs; 17.3g Protein; 0.7g Fiber

INGREDIENTS

1 ½ cups ground turkey
1 shallot, chopped
1 teaspoon garlic, crushed
1 cup sharp Cheddar cheese, shredded
1 cup Monterey-Jack cheese, shredded
1 cup Colby cheese, shredded
Salt and black pepper, to your liking
1/2 teaspoon mustard powder
2 tomatoes, crushed

DIRECTIONS

Preheat your oven to 395 degrees F. Coat a baking sheet with a piece of parchment paper.
Spread the shredded cheese on the bottom of your baking sheet. Bake for 11 to 13 minutes or until golden-browned on top.
Meanwhile, preheat a lightly oiled skillet over a moderately-high heat and cook the shallot until just tender and translucent.
Add in the garlic and continue to sauté until aromatic. Stir in the ground turkey and spices and continue to cook, breaking it up in the pan to cook through.
Top the cheese "crust" with the meat mixture; return it to the oven and bake an additional 7 minutes. Top with the tomatoes.

STORING

Cut your pie into six pieces. Place each of them in an airtight container; place in the refrigerator for up 3 to 4 days.
To freeze, place the pieces in separate Ziploc bags and freeze up to 3 months. To defrost, place in your microwave for a few minutes.

374. Sesame Shrimp Bites

(Ready in about 15 minutes | Servings 6)

Per serving: 107 Calories; 4.9g Fat; 1g Carbs; 15.3g Protein; 0.8g Fiber

INGREDIENTS

1 pound shrimp, deveined and shelled
2 tablespoons sesame seeds
1/4 cup fish stock

2 garlic cloves, pressed
2 tablespoons sesame oil
1/2 cup onions, chopped

1 teaspoon chili powder
2 tablespoons dry white wine
Salt and ground black pepper, to taste

DIRECTIONS

Heat the oil in a saucepan over a moderately-high heat. Cook the shrimp, garlic and onions for about 3 minutes.
Add in the remaining ingredients and cook for 10 minutes more until cooked through.

STORING

Place the shrimp in airtight containers or Ziploc bags; keep in your refrigerator for up 3 to 4 days.
For freezing, arrange cooked shrimp in a single layer on a baking tray; place in your freezer for about 15 minutes, or until it begins to harden.
Transfer the frozen shrimp to heavy-duty freezer bags. Freeze up to 3 months. Defrost in your refrigerator. Enjoy!

375. Easy Turkey Bites with Spicy Sauce

(Ready in about 30 minutes | Servings 8)

Per serving: 153 Calories; 6.7g Fat; 4.6g Carbs; 21.8g Protein; 0.7g Fiber

INGREDIENTS

1/3 cup flax meal
3/4 cup almond flour
2 eggs, whisked
1 ¼ pounds turkey tenderloin, cut into
20 pieces

Salt and black pepper, to season
For the Sauce:
1/2 tablespoon Sriracha sauce
1/2 teaspoon cayenne pepper
1 teaspoon deli mustard

1 teaspoon garlic powder
1/3 cup tomato paste
1/3 teaspoon cumin

DIRECTIONS

Start by preheating your oven to 365 degrees F. Brush the bottom of a baking pan with cooking spray.
Toss the turkey pieces with salt and pepper. Mix the flax meal with the almond meal.
Dip the turkey pieces in the whisked egg, then, coat them with the meal mixture. Bake for 25 to 28 minutes.
Whisk all the sauce ingredients and reserve.

STORING

Wrap the turkey pieces in foil before packing them into an airtight container; keep in your refrigerator for up to 3 to 4 days.
For freezing, place them in airtight containers or heavy-duty freezer bags. Freeze up to 2 to 3 months. Defrost in the refrigerator.
Place the sauce in airtight containers or Ziploc bags; keep in your refrigerator for up 3 to 4 days.
To freeze, place the sauce in separate Ziploc bags and freeze up to 3 months. To defrost, place in your microwave for a few minutes. Bon appétit!

376. Spicy Parm Meatballs

(Ready in about 15 minutes | Servings 10)

Per serving: 158 Calories; 7.9g Fat; 0.4g Carbs; 20.4g Protein; 0.1g Fiber

INGREDIENTS

1 egg, beaten
1/3 cup double cream
3/4 pound ground turkey
1/2 pound ground pork

2 garlic cloves, finely minced
1 teaspoon shallot powder
1/2 teaspoon mustard seeds
1 teaspoon hot sauce

1/4 cup pork rinds, crushed
1/3 cup Parmesan cheese, grated
Sea salt and black pepper, to taste
1 teaspoon fresh basil, minced

DIRECTIONS

In a mixing bowl, combine all ingredients until everything is well incorporated. Roll the mixture into small balls and arrange them on a parchment-lined baking sheet.
Bake in the preheated oven at 390 degrees F for 8 to 10 minutes. Then, flip them over and cook another 8 minutes until they are browned and slightly crisp on top.

STORING

Place the meatballs in airtight containers or Ziploc bags; keep in your refrigerator for up to 3 to 4 days.
Freeze the meatballs in airtight containers or heavy-duty freezer bags. Freeze up to 3 to 4 months. To defrost, slowly reheat in a saucepan.
Bon appétit!

377. Classic Cheese and Artichoke Dip

(Ready in about 5 minutes | Servings 8)

Per serving: 157 Calories; 11g Fat; 5.9g Carbs; 6.5g Protein; 2.7g Fiber

INGREDIENTS

12 ounces canned artichoke hearts, drained
1/2 pound cream cheese
1/2 cup Cheddar cheese, shredded

1/2 cup mayonnaise
1 teaspoon garlic, minced
4 tablespoons chives
2 tablespoons spring onions

Salt and black pepper, to taste
1 teaspoon cayenne pepper

DIRECTIONS

In a deep saucepan, combine artichoke hearts and cream cheese over the lowest heat. Let the cheese melt for a couple of minutes.
Remove from the heat and add in the remaining ingredients.
Taste and adjust the seasonings.

STORING

Place the cheese and artichoke dip in an airtight container and keep in your refrigerator for 3 to 4 days. Enjoy!

378. Sardine Stuffed-Eggs

(Ready in about 20 minutes | Servings 6)

Per serving: 216 Calories; 17.3g Fat; 1.8g Carbs; 12.2g Protein; 0.2g Fiber

INGREDIENTS

1 can sardines, drained
1/2 teaspoon smoked paprika
1 teaspoon fresh or dried basil

1 tablespoon fresh chives, chopped
1 poblano pepper, minced
12 eggs

1/3 cup aioli
Salt and pepper, to taste

DIRECTIONS

Place the eggs in a saucepan and cover them with water by 1 inch. Cover and bring the water to a boil over high heat. Boil for 6 to 7 minutes over medium-high heat.
Peel the eggs and slice them in half lengthwise; mix the yolks with the remaining ingredients.
Divide the mixture among the egg whites.

STORING

Place the deviled eggs in an airtight container or Ziploc bag; transfer to your refrigerator; they should be consumed within 2 days.
For freezing, spoon out the yolk mixture from the deviled eggs. Add the egg yolk mixture to an airtight container or Ziploc bag.
Place the container in the freezer for up to 3 months. To defrost, let them sit overnight in the refrigerator until they are fully thawed out. Enjoy!

379. Chicken Wings with Cheese Dip

(Ready in about 1 hour 15 minutes | Servings 10)

Per serving: 227 Calories; 10.2g Fat; 0.4g Carbs; 31.5g Protein; 0.2g Fiber

INGREDIENTS

3 pounds chicken wings
Salt and red pepper, to taste
1 teaspoon mustard seeds
1 teaspoon olive oil
For Feta Cheese Dip:

2 tablespoons sour cream
1/4 cup fresh parsley leaves, finely chopped
2 cloves garlic, smashed
1 teaspoon porcini powder

1/2 teaspoon ground cumin
1 cup feta cheese, shredded
1/3 cup mayonnaise

DIRECTIONS

Toss the chicken wings with the olive oil, salt, red pepper, and mustard seeds.
Roast in the preheated oven at 380 degrees F approximately 35 minutes.
Turn the oven up to 410 degrees F and bake for a further 35 minutes on the higher shelf until crispy.
In the meantime, mix all ingredients for the cheese sauce.

STORING

Place the chicken wings in airtight containers or Ziploc bags; keep in your refrigerator for up 3 to 4 days.
For freezing, place the chicken wings in airtight containers or heavy-duty freezer bags. Freeze up to 3 months. Once thawed in the refrigerator, heat in the preheated oven at 375 degrees F for 20 to 25 minutes or until heated through.
Place the feta cheese dip in a glass jar with an airtight lid; keep in your refrigerator for 3 to 4 days. Enjoy!

380. Celery Fries with Pecans

(Ready in about 35 minutes | Servings 6)

Per serving: 96 Calories; 8.5g Fat; 4.1g Carbs; 1.5g Protein; 2.6g Fiber

INGREDIENTS

1 ½ pounds celery root, cut into sticks
2 tablespoons sesame oil
1/4 cup pecans, coarsely ground

1 tablespoon Adobo seasoning mix
Salt and pepper, to taste
1/2 teaspoon smoked paprika

DIRECTIONS

Start by preheating your oven to 395 degrees F. Coat a baking sheet with a Silpat mat.
Toss the celery root with the sesame oil, salt, pepper, paprika, and Adobo seasoning mix.
Place the celery stick on the prepared baking sheet and bake in the preheated oven for 30 to 35 minutes, turning them over once or twice.
Sprinkle with pecans.

STORING

Place the celery fries in airtight containers or Ziploc bags; keep in your refrigerator for up to 3 to 4 days.
To freeze, place the celery fries in airtight containers or Ziploc bags. Freeze up to 5 months. Defrost in the refrigerator. Bon appétit!

381. Chicharrones with Cream Cheese Dip

(Ready in about 3 hours 10 minutes | Servings 10)

Per serving: 420 Calories; 43g Fat; 3.1g Carbs; 5g Protein; 0.8g Fiber

INGREDIENTS

1 tablespoon olive oil
1 ½ pounds pork skin, trimmed of excess fat
Sea salt and pepper, to taste
12 ounces cream cheese
1/2 cup mayonnaise

2 cups mustard greens, torn into pieces and steamed
1 tablespoon chili paste (sambal)
1 teaspoon onion powder
1 teaspoon granulated garlic
1/4 teaspoon mustard powder

DIRECTIONS

Toss the pork skin with salt until well coated. Place them on a wire rack over a baking sheet.
Bake in the preheated oven at 350 degrees F for about 3 hours, until skin is completely dried out.
Heat the olive oil in a nonstick skillet and can cook your chicharrónes in batches until they puff up, about 5 minutes. Place on a paper towel-lined plate.
Meanwhile, parboil the mustard greens for about 7 minutes. Add in the remaining ingredients and mix to combine well.

STORING

Place the chicharrones in airtight containers or Ziploc bags; keep in your refrigerator for up to a week. Reheat them in the microwave.
Place the cream cheese dip in airtight containers or Ziploc bags; keep in your refrigerator for up to 4 days.
To freeze, place the chicharrones in in airtight containers or Ziploc bags. Freeze up to 3 months. Defrost in the refrigerator. Bon appétit!

382. Cheesy Cauliflower Florets

(Ready in about 40 minutes | Servings 6)

Per serving: 167 Calories; 13.4g Fat; 2.4g Carbs; 7.5g Protein; 2.4g Fiber

INGREDIENTS

1 ½ pounds cauliflower florets
1 cup Parmigiano-Reggiano cheese, grated
1 teaspoon hot sauce

Sea salt and pepper, to your liking
1 teaspoon lemongrass, grated
1/4 cup butter, melted

DIRECTIONS

Toss the cauliflower with melted butter, salt, pepper, lemongrass, and hot sauce.
Place the cauliflower florets on a parchment-lined baking pan and roast them in the preheated oven at 420 degrees F.
Roast the cauliflower florets for about 35 minutes. Toss with Parmigiano-Reggiano and roast an additional 5 to 7 minutes or until the top is crispy.

STORING

Place the cauliflower florets in airtight containers or Ziploc bags; keep in your refrigerator for up to a week.
To freeze, arrange the cauliflower florets on a baking sheet in a single layer; freeze for about 2 hours. Transfer the frozen vegetables to freezer storage bags. Freeze for up to 3 months.

383. Roasted Zucchini Bites

(Ready in about 40 minutes | Servings 4)

Per serving: 91 Calories; 6.1g Fat; 6g Carbs; 4.2g Protein; 0.4g Fiber

INGREDIENTS

2 tablespoons olive oil
2 egg whites
Salt and pepper, to taste

1/2 teaspoon basil
1/2 teaspoon oregano
4 zucchinis, cut into thick slices

DIRECTIONS

Toss the zucchini with the remaining ingredients.
Roast in the preheated oven at 410 degrees F for about 30 minutes until the slices are crispy and golden.

STORING

Place the zucchini in airtight containers or Ziploc bags; keep in your refrigerator for 3 to 5 days.
Place the zucchini in a freezable container; they can be frozen for up to 10 to 12 months. Bake the thawed zucchini at 200 degrees F until they are completely warm. Enjoy!

384. Nacho Cheese Chips

(Ready in about 15 minutes | Servings 6)

Per serving: 268 Calories; 20.4g Fat; 3.4g Carbs; 18.1g Protein; 0g Fiber

INGREDIENTS

3 cups Mexican blend cheese, shredded
1 tablespoon Taco seasoning mix

DIRECTIONS

Toss the shredded cheese with Taco seasoning mix.
Drop tablespoons of this mixture into small piles. Roast in the preheated oven at 410 degrees F for about 12 minutes.

STORING

Divide the crisps between airtight containers or Ziploc bags; keep in your refrigerator for up to 4 days.
To freeze, divide the crisps between airtight containers. Freeze up to 2 months. Defrost and reheat in your oven until it is crisp. Enjoy!

385. Seafood Stuffed Mushrooms

(Ready in about 25 minutes | Servings 4)

Per serving: 221 Calories; 13.5g Fat; 6g Carbs; 19.8g Protein; 1.9g Fiber

INGREDIENTS

1 teaspoon Old Bay seasoning blend
1 cup Neufchâtel cheese
1/4 cup mayonnaise
1 pound button mushrooms, stems removed
Salt and pepper, to taste

1/2 teaspoon mustard seeds
1/2 pound mixed seafood
1 teaspoon garlic, pressed
1 tablespoon scallions, minced

DIRECTIONS

Start by preheating your oven to 395 degrees F. Brush a baking pan with a nonstick cooking spray.
Sprinkle the mushrooms with salt, pepper, mustard seeds, and Old Bay seasoning blend.
Mix the remaining ingredients to prepare the filling. Divide the filling mixture between mushroom caps.
Bake in the preheated oven for about 18 minutes or until cooked through.

STORING

Place the stuffed mushrooms in airtight containers; keep in your refrigerator for 3 to 5 days.
Place the stuffed mushrooms on the parchment-lined baking sheet, about 1-inch apart from each other; freezer for about 2 to 3 hours.
Remove the frozen mushrooms to a plastic freezer bag for long-term storage; they will maintain the best quality for 10 to 12 months.

386. Glazed Oyster Mushrooms

(Ready in about 10 minutes | Servings 4)

Per serving: 75 Calories; 5.2g Fat; 3.3g Carbs; 2.9g Protein; 1.1g Fiber

INGREDIENTS

1 pound oyster mushrooms, sliced
3 tablespoons butter
1 teaspoon garlic, minced

1 tablespoon coconut aminos
1 tablespoons Swerve
Salt and white pepper, to taste

DIRECTIONS

Melt the butter in a saucepan over a moderately-high heat. Now, sauté the garlic for a minute or so.
Stir in the mushrooms and continue to cook them for 3 to 4 minutes, until they release the liquid.
Add in the other ingredients and continue to cook until the mushrooms are caramelized.

STORING

Place your mushrooms in airtight containers; keep in your refrigerator for 3 to 5 days.
To freeze, divide your mushrooms between airtight containers. Freeze up to 10 months. Defrost and reheat in a saucepan.

387. Chicken Drumettes with Tomatillo Dip

(Ready in about 50 minutes | Servings 4)

Per serving: 161 Calories; 3.5g Fat; 8.4g Carbs; 20.6g Protein; 2g Fiber

INGREDIENTS

12 chicken drumettes
1 teaspoon coarse sea salt
1/2 teaspoon ground black pepper, or more to taste
For the Tomatillo Dip:
1 teaspoon chili pepper, deveined and finely minced

2 tablespoons coriander, finely chopped
2 tablespoons red wine vinegar
4 medium tomatillos, crushed
1 onion, finely chopped
1 cup peppers, chopped

DIRECTIONS

Toss the chicken drumettes with salt and black pepper. Bake them in the preheated oven at 390 degrees F for about 40 minutes or until they are golden and crispy.
In a mixing bowl, thoroughly combine all ingredients for the dip.

STORING

Place the chicken drumettes in airtight containers or Ziploc bags; keep in your refrigerator for up 3 to 4 days.
For freezing, place the chicken drumettes in airtight containers or heavy-duty freezer bags. Freeze up to 3 months. Once thawed in the refrigerator, heat in the preheated oven at 375 degrees F for 20 to 25 minutes or until heated through.
Place the tomatillo dip in a glass jar with an airtight lid; keep in your refrigerator for 3 to 4 days. Enjoy!

388. Chunky Ground Meat Dip

(Ready in about 10 minutes | Servings 24)

Per serving: 153 Calories; 11.2g Fat; 2.2g Carbs; 10.8g Protein; 0.4g Fiber

INGREDIENTS

3 cups cream cheese
1 cup feta cheese
1/2 cup tomato paste
1 pound ground beef

1/2 pound ground turkey
1 teaspoon garlic, minced
1 cup black olives, pitted and chopped
1 teaspoon Greek seasoning mix

DIRECTIONS

Preheat a lightly oiled nonstick pan over a moderately-high heat. Cook ground meat for 5 to 6 minutes until no longer pink, breaking apart with a fork.
Thoroughly combine the cheese, tomato paste, garlic, and spices. Place 1/2 of meat mixture in a bowl.
Top with 1/2 of the cheese mixture; repeat the layers and top with olives.

STORING

Place the ground meat mixture in airtight containers; keep in your refrigerator for 3 to 4 days.
Freeze the ground meat mixture in airtight containers or heavy-duty freezer bags. Freeze up to 2 to 3 months.
Defrost them in the refrigerator and reheat in your microwave.

389. Celery Bites with Crab and Cheese

(Ready in about 10 minutes | Servings 16)

Per serving: 29 Calories; 1.9g Fat; 0.7g Carbs; 2.5g Protein; 1.9g Fiber

INGREDIENTS

8 celery sticks, cut into halves
6 ounces crab meat

1 teaspoon Mediterranean spice mix
2 tablespoons apple cider vinegar

1 cup cream cheese
Salt and pepper, to taste

DIRECTIONS

In a mixing bowl, combine the crab meat, apple cider vinegar, cream cheese, salt, pepper, and Mediterranean spice mix.
Divide the crab mixture between celery sticks.

STORING

Place the celery bites in airtight containers or Ziploc bags; keep in your refrigerator for up to 3 to 5 days.
To freeze, place the celery bites on a baking sheet in a single layer; freeze for about 2 hours. Transfer the frozen celery bites to freezer storage bags. Freeze for up to 12 months. Bon appétit!

390. Cauliflower Bites with Greek Dip

(Ready in about 30 minutes | Servings 6)

Per serving: 182 Calories; 13.1g Fat; 5.9g Carbs; 11.5g Protein; 1.7g Fiber

INGREDIENTS

1 ½ cups cheddar cheese, grated
1 pound cauliflower florets
1 shallot, finely chopped
1/2 teaspoon garlic, minced

Salt and pepper, to taste
3 eggs, whisked
For Greek Dip:
1/2 cup feta cheese

1 teaspoon lime juice
1/2 teaspoon garlic, minced
2 tablespoons mayonnaise
1/2 cup Greek yogurt

DIRECTIONS

Parboil the cauliflower in a pot of a lightly-salted water until crisp-tender, for 5 to 6 minutes.
Then, place the cauliflower florets, cheese, eggs, shallot, garlic, salt, and pepper in your food processor. Pulse until well blended.
Roll the cauliflower mixture into bite-sized balls and arrange them in a parchment-lined baking pan.
Bake in the preheated oven at 395 degrees F for about 20 minutes. Meanwhile, make the sauce by whisking the remaining ingredients.

STORING

Transfer the balls to the airtight containers and place in your refrigerator for up to 3 to 4 days.
For freezing, place the balls in freezer safe containers and freeze up to 1 month. Defrost in the microwave for a few minutes.
Place the sauce in a glass jar with an airtight lid; keep in your refrigerator for up to 3 days.

391. Homemade Tortilla Chips

(Ready in about 20 minutes | Servings 10)

Per serving: 109 Calories; 8.4g Fat; 5.3g Carbs; 2.2g Protein; 3.1g Fiber

INGREDIENTS

For the chips:
1 tablespoon coconut oil
1/4 teaspoon baking powder
1/4 cup psyllium husk powder
2 tablespoons canola oil
3/4 cup almond meal

2 tablespoons flax seed meal
For the Guacamole:
1 serrano jalapeno pepper, stems and
seeds removed, minced
1/2 cup green onions, chopped
1 cup tomatoes, chopped

2 ripe avocados, seeded and peeled
Juice of 1 fresh lemon
Salt and pepper, to taste
2 tablespoons fresh cilantro, chopped
2 garlic cloves, finely minced

DIRECTIONS

Mix all ingredients for the tortilla chips. Pour in hot water to form a dough.
Place the dough in between two large pieces of parchment pepper; roll it out as thin as possible. Cut the dough into triangles.
Bake your tortilla chips in the preheated oven at 360 degrees F for about 12 minutes until the chips are crisp, but not too browned.
Make your guacamole by mixing the remaining ingredients in your blender or food processor.

STORING

Place the tortilla chips in airtight containers or Ziploc bags; keep at room temperature for 1 to 2 weeks.
Place your guacamole in airtight containers. Add a squirt of extra lime juice. Cover your guacamole with plastic wrap before you put the lid on; place in your refrigerator for up to 3 to 5 days.
For freezing, place your guacamole in freezer safe containers and freeze up to 4 weeks.

392. Winter Cheese and Kulen Roll-Ups

(Ready in about 10 minutes | Servings 5)

Per serving: 381 Calories; 31.2g Fat; 4.8g Carbs; 17.6g Protein; 0.4g Fiber

INGREDIENTS

10 slices Kulen salami
10 slices Cheddar cheese
4 ounces mayonnaise

10 slices bacon
10 olives, pitted

DIRECTIONS

Spread a thin layer of mayo onto each slice of Cheddar cheese. Add a slice of bacon on top of the mayo.
Top with a slice of salami. Roll them up, garnish with olives and secure with toothpicks.

STORING

Place the roll-ups in airtight containers; keep in your refrigerator for up to 5 days.
For freezing, place roll-ups in airtight containers. Freeze up to 3 months. Defrost in the refrigerator. Enjoy!

393. Provençal-Style Mini Muffins

(Ready in about 20 minutes | Servings 6)

Per serving: 269 Calories; 20.7g Fat; 5g Carbs; 15.5g Protein; 2.4g Fiber

INGREDIENTS

2 eggs
1/2 cup Greek-style yogurt
10 slices hunter salami, chopped
1/3 cup almond meal
1/3 cup flaxseed meal
1/3cup coconut flour

2 tablespoons granulated Swerve
1/2 teaspoon baking powder
2 teaspoons psyllium
Salt and pepper, to taste
1 teaspoon herbes de Provence

DIRECTIONS

Preheat your oven to 365 degrees F. Brush a muffin tin with a nonstick spray.
Thoroughly combine the almond meal, flaxseed meal, coconut flour, Swerve, baking powder, psyllium, salt, pepper, and herbes de Provence.
Fold in the eggs, Greek-style yogurt, and chopped hunter salami. Spoon the mixture into the prepared muffin tin.
Bake in the preheated oven for 13 to 15 minutes until golden brown. Place on a wire rack to cool slightly before unmolding.

STORING

Place the muffins in airtight containers and refrigerate for a week.
To freeze, place the muffins on a baking tray and freeze for 2 hours. Now, place them in airtight containers. They can be frozen for 2 to 3 months. Bon appétit!

394. Ciauscolo and Cheese Fat Bombs

(Ready in about 10 minutes | Servings 5)

Per serving: 341 Calories; 30.6g Fat; 3.4g Carbs; 12.8g Protein; 1g Fiber

INGREDIENTS

5 ounces mozzarella cheese
5 ounces Ciauscolo salami, chopped
1 teaspoon Roman mustard
1/2 teaspoon smoked paprika

4 large egg yolks, hard-boiled
2 tablespoons sesame seeds, lightly toasted
2 tablespoons extra-virgin olive oil

DIRECTIONS

Thoroughly combine all ingredients, except for the sesame seeds, in a mixing dish.
Now, roll your mixture into 10 small balls. Roll each ball over the toasted sesame seeds until well coated on all sides.

STORING

Place the fat bombs in airtight containers or Ziploc bags; keep in your refrigerator for 10 days.
To freeze, arrange the fat bombs on a baking tray in a single layer; freeze for about 2 hours. Transfer the fat bombs to an airtight container. Freeze for up to 2 months. Serve well chilled!

395. Classic Cajun Shrimp Skewers

(Ready in about 15 minutes | Servings 4)

Per serving: 218 Calories; 11g Fat; 5.1g Carbs; 23.5g Protein; 1.4g Fiber

INGREDIENTS

3 tablespoons olive oil
1 pound large shrimp, peeled and deveined
2 tablespoons fresh scallions, chopped

1 teaspoon garlic, minced
1 tablespoon Cajun seasoning mix
1 tablespoon fresh lemon juice
1 tablespoon white vinegar

2 tablespoons minced coriander
2 Italian peppers, diced
1 cup cherry tomatoes

DIRECTIONS

In a saucepan, heat olive oil over a moderately-high flame.
Cook the shrimp and scallions for about 4 minutes. Stir in the garlic and Cajun seasoning mix and continue to sauté for a minute or so, until aromatic.
Heat off; toss your shrimp with lemon juice, vinegar and coriander. Tread the prawns onto bamboo skewers, alternating them with Italian peppers and cherry tomatoes.

STORING

Place shrimp skewers in airtight containers or Ziploc bags; keep in your refrigerator for up 3 to 4 days.
Place shrimp skewers in heavy-duty freezer bags. Freeze up to 3 months. Defrost in your refrigerator. Enjoy!

396. The Ultimate Ranch Cheese Ball

(Ready in about 10 minutes | Servings 6)

Per serving: 182 Calories; 15.5g Fat; 3g Carbs; 7.6g Protein; 1.1g Fiber

INGREDIENTS

6 slices of ham, chopped
1/4 cup mayonnaise
6 black olives, pitted and sliced

1 teaspoon poppy seeds
1 tablespoon ketchup
6 ounces cream cheese

1 ounce package Ranch seasoning
Salt and pepper, to taste

DIRECTIONS

Thoroughly combine the cream cheese, Ranch seasoning, mayonnaise, ketchup, chopped ham, salt, pepper, and poppy seeds.
Shape the mixture into a ball. Garnish with black olives.

STORING

Place your cheese ball in an airtight container or Ziploc bags; keep in your refrigerator for up to 3 to 4 days.
For freezing, place your cheese ball in an airtight container. Freeze up to 1 month. Defrost in the refrigerator. Enjoy!

397. Pork Rinds with Mexican Sauce

(Ready in about 2 hours 30 minutes | Servings 6)

Per serving: 199 Calories; 16.1g Fat; 6.5g Carbs; 7.5g Protein; 3.8g Fiber

INGREDIENTS

1 whole pork skin from a pork belly
Salt, to taste
For Mexican Sauce:
1 Anaheim pepper, deveined and minced
2 tablespoons fresh-squeezed lemon juice
1 cup tomatillo, chopped

2 tablespoons cilantro, chopped
1 teaspoon garlic, smashed
2 avocados, seeded, peeled and chopped
1/4 teaspoon ground mustard seeds
1/2 cup scallions, finely chopped

DIRECTIONS

Toss the pork skin with salt until well coated.
Bake in the preheated oven at 350 degrees F for 2 hours 30 minutes, until skin is completely dried out.
Meanwhile, make the Mexican sauce by whisking all of the ingredients in the order listed above.

STORING

Place the pork rinds in airtight containers or Ziploc bags; keep in your refrigerator for up to a week. Reheat them in the microwave.
To freeze, place the pork rinds in airtight containers or Ziploc bags. Freeze up to 3 months. Defrost in the refrigerator. Bon appétit!
Place the Mexican sauce in airtight containers. Add a squirt of extra lime juice. Cover Mexican sauce with plastic wrap before you put the lid on; place in your refrigerator for up to 3 to 5 days.
For freezing, place the Mexican sauce in freezer safe containers and freeze up to 4 weeks.

398. Mascarpone Fat Bombs

(Ready in about 10 minutes + chilling time | Servings 6)

Per serving: 214 Calories; 20.4g Fat; 1.2g Carbs; 5.6g Protein; 0.3g Fiber

INGREDIENTS

1 cup Mascarpone cheese
Salt and pepper, to season
1/2 cup fresh parsley, finely chopped

3 ounces bacon, chopped
1/4 teaspoon champagne vinegar

DIRECTIONS

In a mixing bowl, thoroughly combine the cheese, bacon, vinegar, salt, and pepper. Cover the bowl and place in your refrigerator for 2 to 3 hours to help firm it up.
Roll the mixture into balls.
Roll the fat bombs over chopped parsley until well coated.

STORING

Place the fat bombs in airtight containers or Ziploc bags; keep in your refrigerator for 10 days.
To freeze, arrange the fat bombs on a baking tray in a single layer; freeze for about 2 hours. Transfer fat bombs to an airtight container. Freeze for up to 2 months. Serve well chilled!

399. Rich and Easy Cocktail Meatballs

(Ready in about 40 minutes | Servings 5)

Per serving: 244 Calories; 13.3g Fat; 3.7g Carbs; 28.1g Protein; 1.1g Fiber

INGREDIENTS

1/3 pound ground chicken
2/3 pound ground pork
1/2 cup ground pine nuts
2 ounces Pecorino cheese, grated
1/2 cup green onions, chopped
2 tablespoons green garlic, minced

1 tablespoon deli mustard
2 tablespoons buttermilk
2 eggs, whisked
1 poblano pepper, deveined and minced
Salt and black pepper, to taste

DIRECTIONS

In a mixing bowl, combine all of the above ingredients, except for the ground nuts. Shape the mixture into small balls.
Roll these balls over the ground nuts until they're coated on all sides.
Preheat a lightly greased skillet over a moderately-high heat. Fry your meatballs in batches until the juice is clear.

STORING

Place the meatballs in airtight containers or Ziploc bags; keep in your refrigerator for up to 3 to 4 days.
Freeze the meatballs in airtight containers or heavy-duty freezer bags. Freeze up to 3 to 4 months. To defrost, slowly reheat in a saucepan. Bon appétit!

400. Mediterranean Broccoli Dip

(Ready in about 10 minutes | Servings 8)

Per serving: 134 Calories; 10.2g Fat; 6.5g Carbs; 5.1g Protein; 1.6g Fiber

INGREDIENTS

1/3 cup mayonnaise
1 pound broccoli florets
Salt and pepper, to taste

1/2 cup Greek-style yogurt
1/2 cup blue cheese
1 teaspoon Mediterranean seasoning mix

DIRECTIONS

Parboil broccoli florets for about 7 minutes or until crisp-tender. Place the broccoli florets in a bowl of your food processor.
Add in the yogurt, cheese, and spices and blend briefly to combine.
Fold in the well-chilled mayonnaise and continue to blend until everything is well incorporated.

STORING

Place the Mediterranean broccoli dip in airtight containers or Ziploc bags; keep in your refrigerator for up to 5 days.

401. Mozzarella-Stuffed Meatballs

(Ready in about 25 minutes | Servings 10)

Per serving: 214 Calories; 12.6g Fat; 1.6g Carbs; 21.9g Protein; 0.4g Fiber

INGREDIENTS

1/3 cup Pecorino-Romano cheese, grated
2 eggs
1 cup Mozzarella cheese, cubed
Sea salt and pepper, to taste
1 teaspoon paprika

1 teaspoon fish sauce
1/2 cup shallots, finely chopped
1/2 pound ground chuck
1 pound ground pork
1 teaspoon garlic, smashed

DIRECTIONS

In a mixing dish, combine all ingredients, except for the Mozzarella cheese.
Roll this mixture into golf ball sized meatballs using your hands. Press a Mozzarella cheese cube into the middle of each meatball, fully enclosing it.
Bake in the preheated oven at 395 degrees F for 18 to 22 minutes until they are fully cooked.

STORING

Place the meatballs in airtight containers or Ziploc bags; keep in your refrigerator for up to 3 to 4 days.
Freeze the meatballs in airtight containers or heavy-duty freezer bags. Freeze up to 3 to 4 months. To defrost, slowly reheat in a saucepan.
Bon appétit!

402. Pepperoni and Ricotta Balls

(Ready in about 15 minutes + chilling time | Servings 5)

Per serving: 323 Calories; 28.4g Fat; 2.6g Carbs; 13.1g Protein; 0.3g Fiber

INGREDIENTS

5 ounces pepperoni, chopped
1 teaspoon brown mustard
2 teaspoons tomato paste
10 ounces Ricotta cheese, room temperature

1/4 cup mayonnaise
1 teaspoon tequila
1 teaspoon lime juice, freshly squeezed
8 black olives, pitted and chopped

DIRECTIONS

Mix all ingredients in a bowl until well combined. Place in your refrigerator for 2 hours.
Roll the mixture into balls.

STORING

Place the pepperoni and ricotta balls in airtight containers or Ziploc bags; keep in your refrigerator for 10 days.
To freeze, arrange the pepperoni and ricotta balls on a baking tray in a single layer; freeze for about 2 hours. Transfer them to an airtight container. Freeze for up to 2 months.
Serve well chilled!

DESSERTS

403. Chia Pudding with Coconut and Lemon

(Ready in about 1 hour | Servings 4)

Per serving: 270 Calories; 24.7g Fat; 6.5g Carbs; 4.6g Protein; 4g Fiber

INGREDIENTS

1/3 cup chia seeds
1/2 cup Greek-style yogurt
1/3 teaspoon vanilla extract
1/2 teaspoon ground cloves

1/4 teaspoon ground cinnamon
1/2 cup coconut milk
1 cup coconut cream
2 tablespoons Erythritol

DIRECTIONS

Place all ingredients in a glass jar and let it sit in your refrigerator for 1 hour.

STORING

Place the chia pudding in airtight containers or Ziploc bags; keep in your refrigerator for 3 days.

404. Mini Brownies with Almonds

(Ready in about 25 minutes | Servings 12)

Per serving: 251 Calories; 21.5g Fat; 4.6g Carbs; 6.4g Protein; 0.8g Fiber

INGREDIENTS

4 ounces cocoa powder
1/2 cup almonds, ground
5 eggs
1/2 teaspoon ground cinnamon
6 ounces sour cream

2 tablespoons Swerve
2/3 cup coconut oil, melted
1 teaspoon rum extract
3/4 teaspoon baking powder

DIRECTIONS

Begin by preheating your oven to 365 degrees F. Brush a muffin tin with a nonstick spray.
Mix all ingredients in a bowl and scrape the batter into the muffin cups.
Bake for about 20 minutes; let it cool slightly before unmolding and storing.

STORING

Divide your mini brownies between four airtight containers; keep in the refrigerator for 3 to 4 days.
For freezing, divide your mini brownies among four Ziploc bags and freeze up to 4 to 5 months. Defrost in your microwave for a couple of minutes. Enjoy!

405. Peanut Butter Fudge Cake

(Ready in about 3 hours | Servings 8)

Per serving: 180 Calories; 18.3g Fat; 4.5g Carbs; 1g Protein; 1.1g Fiber

INGREDIENTS

3/4 cup peanut butter, sugar-free, preferably homemade
3 tablespoons cocoa nibs, unsweetened and melted
1/4 teaspoon baking powder
3 tablespoons coconut oil, at room temperature
1 teaspoon vanilla extract

1 stick butter
1/3 cup almond milk
1/3 cup Swerve
A pinch of salt
A pinch of grated nutmeg

DIRECTIONS

Melt the butter in your microwave. Stir in the milk, 1/4 cup of Swerve, salt, nutmeg, and baking powder.
Spoon the batter into a parchment-lined baking dish. Refrigerate for about 3 hours or until set.
Meanwhile, make the sauce by whisking the remaining ingredients until everything is well incorporated.
Spoon the sauce over your fudge cake.

STORING

Cover your fudge with foil or plastic wrap to prevent drying out. It will last for about 1 to 2 days at room temperature.
Cover with aluminum foil or plastic wrap and refrigerate for a week.
To freeze, wrap your fudge tightly with foil or place in a heavy-duty freezer bag. Freeze for up to 4 to 6 months. Enjoy!

406. Rum Chocolate Pralines

(Ready in about 10 minutes + chilling time | Servings 8)

Per serving: 70 Calories; 3.4g Fat; 5.1g Carbs; 2.4g Protein; 1.6g Fiber

INGREDIENTS

1 cup bakers' chocolate, sugar-free
2 tablespoons dark rum
1/8 teaspoon ground cloves
1/8 teaspoon cinnamon powder
1/2 teaspoon almond extract

1/2 teaspoon rum extract
3 tablespoons cocoa powder
1/4 cup almond butter
1 cup almond milk

DIRECTIONS

Microwave the chocolate, cocoa and almond butter until they have completely melted.
Add in the other ingredients and mix to combine well. Pour the mixture into silicone molds and place in your refrigerator until set.

STORING

Place the chocolate pralines in airtight containers or Ziploc bags; keep in your refrigerator for 3 weeks to 1 month.
To freeze, arrange the chocolate pralines on a baking tray in a single layer; freeze for about 2 hours. Transfer the frozen chocolate pralines to an airtight container. Freeze for up to a month. Bon appétit!

407. Mom's Coconut Tarts

(Ready in about 40 minutes + chilling time | Servings 4)

Per serving: 304 Calories; 27.7g Fat; 6.6g Carbs; 11.6g Protein; 1.5g Fiber

INGREDIENTS

1 cup coconut cream, unsweetened
A pinch of nutmeg
1/4 teaspoon ground cinnamon
1/2 cup granulated Erythritol

1 teaspoon pure almond extract
4 eggs
1/2 cup almond butter
A pinch of salt

DIRECTIONS

Melt the coconut cream in a sauté pan over medium-low heat. Remove form heat.
Mix the remaining ingredients until well combined. Now, gradually pour the egg mixture into the warm coconut cream, whisking to combine well.
Spoon the mixture into small tart cases. Bake in the preheated oven at 350 degrees F for about 30 minutes until they are golden and firm.

STORING

Place the coconut tarts in airtight containers or Ziploc bags; keep at room temperature up to 3 days.
Place the coconut tarts in airtight containers or Ziploc bags; keep in your refrigerator for 3 weeks.
To freeze, arrange the coconut tarts on a baking tray in a single layer; freeze for about 2 hours. Transfer the frozen coconut tarts to an airtight container. Freeze for up to 2 months. Bon appétit!

408. Vanilla Berry Meringues

(Ready in about 2 hours | Servings 10)

Per serving: 51 Calories; 0g Fat; 4g Carbs; 12g Protein; 0.1g Fiber

INGREDIENTS

1 teaspoon vanilla extract
3 tablespoons freeze-dried mixed berries, crushed
3 large egg whites, at room temperature

1/3 cup Erythritol
1 teaspoon lemon rind

DIRECTIONS

In a mixing bowl, beat the egg whites until foamy. Add in vanilla extract, lemon rind, and Erythritol; continue to mix, using an electric mixer until stiff and glossy.
Add the crushed berries and mix again until well combined. Use two teaspoons to spoon meringue onto parchment-lined cookie sheets.
Bake at 220 degrees F for about 1 hour 45 minutes.

STORING

Place the meringues in airtight containers or Ziploc bags; keep in a cool, dry place for 2 weeks.
To freeze, place meringues in airtight containers. Freeze for up to 3 months. Bon appétit!

409. Bourbon Vanilla Cheesecake

(Ready in about 30 minutes + chilling time | Servings 10)

Per serving: 211 Calories; 19g Fat; 4.4g Carbs; 7g Protein; 0.5g Fiber

INGREDIENTS

For the Crust:
2 tablespoons walnuts, chopped
4 tablespoons peanut butter, room temperature
1 cup coconut flour
For the Filling:
1/2 teaspoon vanilla essence

2 tablespoons bourbon
1 teaspoon fresh ginger, grated
10 ounces cream cheese, room temperature
2 eggs
1/2 teaspoon Monk fruit sweetener

DIRECTIONS

Mix all of the crust ingredients. Press the crust into a parchment-lined springform pan and bake at 330 degrees F for about 10 minutes.
Place the springform pan in a deep baking tray filled with 2 inches of warm water to help create steam during baking.
Make the cheesecake filling by mixing all the ingredients using an electric mixer. Spread the filling onto the crusts and bake an additional 20 minutes.

STORING

Cut your cheesecake into squares and place them in airtight containers and refrigerate for a week.
To freeze, place the cheesecake squares on a baking tray and freeze for 2 hours. Now, place them in airtight containers. They can be frozen for 2 to 3 months. Bon appétit!

410. Mother's Day Pecan Truffles

(Ready in about 25 minutes + chilling time | Servings 6)

Per serving: 113 Calories; 8.5g Fat; 5.9g Carbs; 1.7g Protein; 3.3g Fiber

INGREDIENTS

1/2 cup toasted pecans, finely chopped
1/2 cup double cream
1 teaspoon vanilla paste
3 bars chocolate, sugar-free

1/4 teaspoon ground cardamom
1/4 teaspoon ground cinnamon
1/4 teaspoon coarse salt

DIRECTIONS

In a medium stainless steel bowl set over a pot of gently simmering water, melt the chocolate and cream.
Add in the vanilla, cardamom, cinnamon, and salt and place in your refrigerator for 7 to 8 hours or until firm.
Shape the mixture into balls and roll the balls into the chopped pecans.

STORING

Place the pecan truffles in airtight containers or Ziploc bags; keep in your refrigerator for 3 weeks to 1 month.
To freeze, arrange the pecan truffles on a baking tray in a single layer; freeze for about 2 hours. Transfer the frozen pecan truffles to an airtight container. Freeze for up to a month. Bon appétit!

411. Easy Lemon Panna Cotta

(Ready in about 10 minutes + chilling time | Servings 10)

Per serving: 221 Calories; 21.5g Fat; 3.8g Carbs; 4.3g Protein; 0g Fiber

INGREDIENTS

1 teaspoon lemon juice
1 teaspoon lemon rind, grated
1 teaspoon vanilla extract
1 ½ teaspoons gelatins powder, unsweetened

1/2 cup almond milk
1 cup double cream
1/4 cup erythritol

DIRECTIONS

Place the gelatin and milk in a saucepan and let it sit for 2 minutes. Add in the other ingredients and stir to combine.
Let it simmer for 3 to 4 minutes until the gelatin has dissolved completely. Pour the mixture into 4 ramekins and transfer to your refrigerator; cover and let it sit overnight or at least 6 hours.

STORING

Cover your panna cotta with plastic wrap to prevent it from drying out; keep in your refrigerator for up to 5 days. Enjoy!

412. Blueberry and Coconut Protein Shake

(Ready in about 10 minutes | Servings 4)

Per serving: 274 Calories; 26.8g Fat; 7.5g Carbs; 3.9g Protein; 1.3g Fiber

INGREDIENTS

1/2 cup blueberries, frozen
1/2 teaspoon vanilla essence
1/2 teapsoon Monk fruit powder
2 tablespoons collagen protein

2 tablespoons coconut cream
1/4 cup coconut shreds
1 cup coconut milk

DIRECTIONS

Pulse the frozen blueberries in your blender.
Add in the other ingredients and mix until creamy, smooth and uniform.

STORING

Spoon the protein shake into airtight containers and keep in your refrigerator for up to 2 days.
Spoon the protein shake into airtight containers. Use vacuum sealing for maximum protection. Store in your freezer for a few weeks.

413. Frozen Walnut Dessert

(Ready in about 10 minutes + chilling time | Servings 6)

Per serving: 84 Calories; 8.9g Fat; 1.5g Carbs; 0.8g Protein; 0.7g Fiber

INGREDIENTS

1/2 stick butter, melted
1/2 teaspoon almond extract
A few drops Monk fruit powder

2 tablespoons cocoa powder
2 tablespoons walnuts, chopped

DIRECTIONS

Melt the butter in your microwave; add in the almond extract, Monk fruit powder, and cocoa powder.
Spoon the mixture into a parchment-lined baking tray. Scatter the chopped walnuts on top and place in your freezer until set.

STORING

Place your dessert in airtight containers. Keep in your refrigerator for up to 8 days.
Freeze up to 3 to 4 months. Defrost in the refrigerator. Bon appétit!

414. Classic Chocolate Bars

(Ready in about 25 minutes + chilling time | Servings 10)

Per serving: 119 Calories; 11.7g Fat; 5.2g Carbs; 1.1g Protein; 5g Fiber

INGREDIENTS

1/2 stick butter, cold
1 ½ cups whipped cream
A pinch of coarse salt
8 ounces chocolate chunks, sugar-free
1/4 teaspoon cinnamon
1/2 teaspoon rum extract

1 teaspoon vanilla extract
1/4 cup coconut flour
1/4 cup flaxseed meal
1 cup almond meal
2 packets stevia

DIRECTIONS

Start by preheating your oven to 340 degrees F. Coat a baking dish with a piece of parchment paper.
Add the coconut flour, flaxseed meal, almond meal, stevia, cinnamon, rum extract, vanilla, and salt to your blender. Blend until everything is well incorporated.
Cut in the cold butter and continue to blend until well combined.
Spoon the batter into the bottom of the prepared baking pan. Bake for 12 to 15 minutes and place on a wire rack to cool slightly.
Bring the whipped cream to a simmer; add in the chocolate chunks and whisk to combine. Spread the chocolate filling over the crust and place in your refrigerator until set. Cut into bars.

STORING

Wrap the chocolate bars tightly with heavy-duty aluminum foil or plastic wrap. Then, keep in your refrigerator for up to 7 days.
These chocolate bars can be frozen in an airtight container. Put a piece of baking parchment between each bar to prevent them from sticking together. Freeze up to 4 months. Defrost in the refrigerator. Bon appétit!

415. Coconut and Berry Ice Cream

(Ready in about 10 minutes + chilling time | Servings 4)

Per serving: 305 Calories; 18.3g Fat; 4.5g Carbs; 1g Protein; 2.7g Fiber

INGREDIENTS

1 ¼ cups coconut milk
1/2 teaspoon xanthan gum
1/3 cup double cream

A few drops Monk fruit
1/2 cup coconut flakes

DIRECTIONS

In a mixing bowl, combine coconut milk, double cream, Monk fruit, and coconut flakes.
Add in the xanthan gum, whisking constantly, until the mixture has thickened.
Then, prepare your ice cream in the ice cream maker according to manufacturer's instructions.

STORING

Spoon your ice cream in an airtight container. Store your ice cream in the very back of the freezer. Freeze up to 2 to 4 months. Bon appétit!

416. The Best Chocolate Cake Ever

(Ready in about 50 minutes + chilling time | Servings 10)

Per serving: 313 Calories; 30.7g Fat; 7.5g Carbs; 7.3g Protein; 1.9g Fiber

INGREDIENTS

5 eggs
1/2 teaspoon ground cinnamon
A pinch of coarse salt
1/2 cup water
3/4 cup erythritol

14 ounces chocolate, unsweetened
2 sticks butter, cold

For Peanut-Choc Ganache:
9 ounces chocolate, unsweetened
1/4 cup smooth peanut butter
A pinch of coarse salt
3/4 cups whipped cream

DIRECTIONS

In a medium-sized pan, bring the water to a boil; add in the erythritol and let it simmer until it has dissolved.
Melt the chocolate and butter; beat the mixture with an electric mixer.
Add the chocolate mixture to the hot water mixture. Fold in the eggs, one at a time, beating continuously.
Add in the cinnamon and salt, and stir well to combine. Spoon the mixture into a parchment-lined baking pan and wrap with foil.
Lower the baking pan into a larger pan that is filled with hot water about 1 inch deep. Bake in the preheated oven at 365 degrees F for about 45 minutes.
Meanwhile, place the whipped cream in a pan over a moderately-high heat and bring to a boil. Pour the hot cream over the chocolate and whisk to combine.
Add in the peanut butter and salt; continue to mix until creamy and smooth. Glaze your cake and place in the refrigerator until set.

STORING

Cover your cake loosely with aluminum foil or plastic wrap and refrigerate for a week.
To freeze, place your cake on a baking pan and freeze for 2 hours; then, place in a heavy-duty freezer bag. It will maintain the best quality for about 4 to 6 months. Enjoy!

417. Mixed Berry Scones

(Ready in about 25 minutes | Servings 10)

Per serving: 245 Calories; 21.6g Fat; 7.4g Carbs; 3.8g Protein; 0.6g Fiber

INGREDIENTS

1 cup mixed berries
1 ½ sticks butter
1 cup double cream
1 cup Swerve

A pinch of salt
A pinch of grated nutmeg
1 cup almond meal
1 cup coconut flour

1 teaspoon baking powder
2 eggs
1 teaspoon vanilla paste

DIRECTIONS

Thoroughly combine the almond meal, coconut flour, baking powder, salt, nutmeg, and berries.
In another bowl, whisk the eggs with the butter and double cream. Stir in Swerve and vanilla paste; stir until everything is well combined.
Add the egg mixture to the almond flour mixture; stir until a soft dough forms.
Shape the dough into 16 triangles and place them on a foil-lined baking sheet. Bake in the preheated oven at 360 degrees F for about 20 minutes.

STORING

Place your scones in airtight containers and refrigerate for a week.
Freeze the scones on a baking tray until they are solid; place them in airtight containers and freeze for up to 3 months.

418. Creamsicle Pudding with Coconut

(Ready in about 1 hour 5 minutes | Servings 4)

Per serving: 226 Calories; 17.9g Fat; 7g Carbs; 5.9g Protein; 4.6g Fiber

INGREDIENTS

1 cup unsweetened coconut milk
1 cup water
1/4 cup coconut flakes
2 tablespoons Swerve

1/2 teaspoon ground star anise
1 cup double cream
1 teaspoon coconut extract
1 cup chia seeds

DIRECTIONS

Mix the ingredients until everything is well incorporated. Place in your refrigerator for about 1 hour.

STORING

Divide the pudding among four airtight containers; refrigerate for 3 days.
To freeze, pour the mixture into ice-pop molds. Cover and insert sticks. Freeze until firm, at least 4 hours. Dip molds briefly in hot water to release pops. Freeze up to 1 month. Enjoy!

419. Greek Frappé Coffee

(Ready in about 2 hours | Servings 2)

Per serving: 222 Calories; 15.8g Fat; 7.1g Carbs; 5.9g Protein; 0.3g Fiber

INGREDIENTS

1 tablespoon cacao butter
1 cup almond milk
1/2 cup prepared instant espresso, cooled

1/2 teaspoon Monk fruit powder
2 tablespoons coconut whipped cream

DIRECTIONS

In your blender, mix the cacao butter, almond milk, instant espresso, and Monk fruit powder until well combined.

STORING

Spoon your Frappé into two airtight containers and keep in your refrigerator for up to 2 days.
Spoon your Frappé into two airtight containers and store in your freezer for a few weeks.
Serve topped with coconut whipped cream. Enjoy!

420. Old-Fashioned Walnut Cheesecake

(Ready in about 1 hour | Servings 14)

Per serving: 393 Calories; 38g Fat; 4.1g Carbs; 9.8g Protein; 1.1g Fiber

INGREDIENTS

The Crust:
1/3 cup Swerve
1/4 teaspoon ground cinnamon
8 ounces walnuts, chopped
A pinch of salt
1 stick butter, melted
1/4 teaspoon ground cloves

For the Filling:
1 cup Swerve
1 teaspoon pure vanilla extract
4 eggs
14 ounces Greek-style yogurt
22 ounces Neufchâtel cheese, at room temperature

DIRECTIONS

Mix all ingredients for the crust; press the mixture into a baking pan and set it aside
Whip the Neufchâtel cheese using your electric mixer on low speed.
Add in 1 cup of Swerve and vanilla. Fold in the eggs, one at a time, mixing constantly on low speed. Add in Greek-style yogurt and gently stir to combine.
Bake in the preheated oven at 290 degrees F for 50 to 55 minutes.

STORING

Place your cheesecake in airtight containers and refrigerate for a week.
To freeze, place your cheesecake on a baking tray and freeze for 2 hours. Now, place them in airtight containers. They can be frozen for 2 to 3 months. Bon appétit!

421. Father's Day Ice Cream

(Ready in about 15 minutes + chilling time | Servings 8)

Per serving: 89 Calories; 9.3g Fat; 1.5g Carbs; 0.8g Protein; 0g Fiber

INGREDIENTS

3/4 cup double cream
1/2 cup coconut milk
1 tablespoon rum flavoring
24 packets of stevia

A pinch of grated nutmeg
A pinch of salt
1/4 cup Greek-style yogurt

DIRECTIONS

Melt the double cream and coconut milk in a saucepan over a medium-low heat. Stir until there are no lumps.
Allow it to cool and add in the other ingredients.
Beat the ingredients using an electric mixer until creamy and uniform.

STORING

Spoon your ice cream in an airtight container.
Store your ice cream in the very back of the freezer for up to 2 to 4 months. Bon appétit!

422. Chocolate Nut Clusters

(Ready in about 15 minutes + chilling time | Servings 8)

Per serving: 166 Calories; 17.2g Fat; 2.2g Carbs; 1.2g Protein; 1.1g Fiber

INGREDIENTS

1/2 cup walnuts, chopped
1/2 cup coconut oil, at room temperature
1/4 cup cocoa powder, unsweetened

1/4 cup Erythritol
A pinch of coarse salt

DIRECTIONS

Melt the coconut oil in your microwave; add in cocoa powder and Erythritol. Remove from the heat and stir well.
Add in the ground walnuts and coarse salt and stir until everything is well combined.
Drop by teaspoonfuls onto foil-lined baking sheets. Chill in your refrigerator until firm.

STORING

Place the chocolate nut clusters in airtight containers or Ziploc bags; keep in your refrigerator for 3 weeks to 1 month.
To freeze, arrange the chocolate nut clusters on a baking tray in a single layer; freeze for about 2 hours. Transfer the frozen truffles to an airtight container. Freeze for up to a month. Bon appétit!

423. Classic Chocolate Fudge

(Ready in about 15 minutes + chilling time | Servings 8)

Per serving: 220 Calories; 20g Fat; 7g Carbs; 1.7g Protein; 2.1g Fiber

INGREDIENTS

3/4 cup chocolate chunks, unsweetened
2 tablespoons coconut oil
4-5 drops Monk fruit sweetener

1/2 cup double cream
1/2 cup butter, at room temperature
1 cup full-fat milk

DIRECTIONS

Microwave the chocolate and milk until they've completely melted; spoon into a foil-lined pie pan and freeze until firm.
Then, melt the butter, coconut oil, Monk fruit sweetener, and double cream; mix with a wire whisk to combine well.
Spoon the cream mixture over the chocolate layer and freeze until solid.

STORING

Cover your fudge with foil or plastic wrap to prevent drying out; keep in your refrigerator for a week.
To freeze, wrap your fudge tightly with foil or place in a heavy-duty freezer bag. Freeze for up to 4 to 6 months. Enjoy!

424. Hazelnut Cake Squares

(Ready in about 30 minutes | Servings 8)

Per serving: 241 Calories; 23.6g Fat; 3.7g Carbs; 5.2g Protein; 1g Fiber

INGREDIENTS

2 cups almond meal
3 eggs
1 teaspoon almond extract
3/4 cup heavy cream
A pinch of sea salt
1/2 cup coconut oil, at room temperature

1/2 cup hazelnuts, chopped
3/4 teaspoon baking powder
1 cup Erythritol
1/2 teaspoon ground cinnamon
1/4 teaspoon ground cardamom

DIRECTIONS

Start by preheating your oven to 365 degrees F. Coat the bottom of your baking pan with parchment paper.
Thoroughly combine the almond meal, baking powder, Erythritol, cinnamon, cardamom, and salt.
After that, stir in the coconut oil, eggs, almond extract, and heavy cream; whisk until everything is well incorporated.
Stir in the chopped hazelnuts. Scrape the batter into the prepared baking pan.
Bake in the preheated oven for about 25 minutes.

STORING

Cover the hazelnut squares with foil or plastic wrap to prevent drying out. It will last for about 1 day at room temperature.
Cover with aluminum foil or plastic wrap and refrigerate for two weeks.
To freeze, wrap the hazelnut squares tightly with foil or place in a heavy-duty freezer bag. Freeze for up to 3 to 4 months. Enjoy!

425. Butterscotch Pudding Popsicles

(Ready in about 1 hour | Servings 6)

Per serving: 248 Calories; 20.8g Fat; 7g Carbs; 4.6g Protein; 4.1g Fiber

INGREDIENTS

1 teaspoon orange juice
1 cup buttermilk
1 cup coconut milk
1 tablespoon butterscotch extract

1 cup Swerve
1/8 teaspoon xanthan gum
3 avocados, pitted, peeled and mashed

DIRECTIONS

Place all ingredients in your blender. Process until well combined.

STORING

Spoon the pudding into plastic cups and insert wooden pop sticks into the center of each cup. Freeze up to 1 month. Enjoy!

426. Chocolate Jaffa Custard

(Ready in about 15 minutes | Servings 4)

Per serving: 154 Calories; 13g Fat; 6.3g Carbs; 5.3g Protein; 1.7g Fiber

INGREDIENTS

3 ounces cream cheese, at room temperature
2 egg yolks
1/4 teaspoon ground cardamom
1/4 teaspoon grated nutmeg

1/4 cup Swerve
1/4 cup cocoa powder, unsweetened
3/4 cup double cream
1 tablespoon orange juice, freshly squeezed

DIRECTIONS

Whip the egg yolks using an electric mixer until pale and frothy.
Warm the cream and gradually fold in the hot cream into the beaten eggs.
Let it simmer for about 4 minutes, stirring continuously, until the mixture has reduced and thickened slightly.
In another mixing bowl, beat the remaining ingredients until everything is creamy and uniform. Fold the avocado mixture into the egg/cream mixture; gently stir until well combined.

STORING

Spoon your custard into four airtight containers; keep in your refrigerator for 5 to 6 days.
To freeze, place your custard in four airtight containers; freeze up to 1 month.
Defrost in the refrigerator. Enjoy!

427. American-Style Mini Cheesecakes

(Ready in about 25 minutes | Servings 12)

Per serving: 134 Calories; 12.5g Fat; 3.3g Carbs; 4.6g Protein; 0.4g Fiber

INGREDIENTS

6 ounces Neufchatel cheese, at room temperature
7 tablespoons coconut oil, melted
5 eggs
1/4 teaspoon ground cinnamon
1/4 cup Swerve

2 ounces cocoa powder, unsweetened
1 teaspoon vanilla paste
1 teaspoon rum extract
1/3 teaspoon baking powder

DIRECTIONS

Beat the ingredients using your electric mixer on high speed. Line a mini muffin pan with 12 liners.
Spoon the mixture into prepared muffins cups.
Bake in the preheated oven at 350 degrees F for about 20 minutes.

STORING

Place the mini cheesecakes in airtight containers and refrigerate for a week.
To freeze, place the mini cheesecakes on a baking tray and freeze for 2 hours. Now, place them in airtight containers. They can be frozen for 2 to 3 months. Bon appétit!

428. Perfect Lemon Curd

(Ready in about 10 minutes + chilling time | Servings 6)

Per serving: 180 Calories; 17.6g Fat; 5.2g Carbs; 2.8g Protein; 0.1g Fiber

INGREDIENTS

4 ounces fresh lemon juice
1 ½ cups Erythritol
A pinch of salt

A pinch of nutmeg
2 eggs + 1 egg yolk, well whisked
1/2 cup butter, at room temperature

DIRECTIONS

In a sauté pan, beat the eggs over a low heat.
Add in the remaining ingredients and cook for about 5 minutes, whisking constantly.
Turn the heat to the lowest setting and continue to stir with a wire whisk for 1 to 2 minutes longer.
Cover with a plastic wrap.

STORING

Spoon the lemon curd into four airtight containers; keep in your refrigerator for 5 to 6 days.
To freeze, place the lemon curd in four airtight containers; freeze up to 1 month.
Defrost in the refrigerator. Enjoy!

429. Peanut Butter Cupcakes

(Ready in about 10 minutes + chilling time | Servings 10)

Per serving: 266 Calories; 28.1g Fat; 2.6g Carbs; 3.3g Protein; 0.5g Fiber

INGREDIENTS

1 stick butter
4 tablespoons heavy cream

1 tablespoon Erythritol
1 cup peanut butter

DIRECTIONS

Place a bowl over a saucepan of simmering water. Add in all of the above ingredients and stir continuously until well melted and blended.
Spoon the batter into muffin cups lined with cupcake wrappers.
Allow them to harden for about 1 hour in your freezer.

STORING

Cover the peanut butter cupcakes with foil or plastic wrap to prevent drying out. It will last for about 1 to 2 days at room temperature.
Cover with aluminum foil or plastic wrap and refrigerate for a week.
To freeze, wrap the peanut butter cupcakes tightly with foil or place in a heavy-duty freezer bag. Freeze for up to 4 to 6 months. Enjoy!

430. Autumn Pear Crumble

(Ready in about 30 minutes | Servings 8)

Per serving: 152 Calories; 11.8g Fat; 6.2g Carbs; 2.5g Protein; 1.7g Fiber

INGREDIENTS

2 ½ cups pears, cored and sliced
1/2 cup coconut flour
3/4 cup granulated Swerve

2 eggs, whisked
1/2 tablespoon fresh lime juice
1/3 teaspoon xanthan gum

3/4 cup almond meal
5 tablespoons butter

DIRECTIONS

Preheat your oven to 365 degrees F. Brush the sides and bottom of a baking dish with a nonstick spray.
Arrange your pears on the bottom of the baking dish. Drizzle the lime juice and xanthan gum over them.
In a mixing dish, thoroughly combine the almond meal, coconut flour, and Swerve. Fold in the eggs, one at a time, mixing constantly until your mixture resembles coarse meal.
Spread this mixture over the pear layer.
Cut in the cold butter and bake in the preheated oven for 20 to 23 minutes or until golden brown on the top.

STORING

Place the pear crumble in four airtight containers; keep in your refrigerator for 4 to 5 days.
To freeze, place the pear crumble in four airtight containers or Ziploc bags; it can be frozen for 3 months. Defrost in your microwave for a few minutes. Bon appétit!

431. Old-Fashioned Walnut Candy

(Ready in about 1 hour | Servings 10)

Per serving: 162 Calories; 14.6g Fat; 5.9g Carbs; 2.3g Protein; 1.7g Fiber

INGREDIENTS

4 tablespoons walnuts, coarsely chopped
1 tablespoon rum
1/2 teaspoon pure vanilla extract
1/2 cup lightly toasted walnuts, chopped

1/2 cup chocolate, sugar-free
1/2 coconut oil, room temperature
4 ounces coconut cream
1/4 cup confectioners' Swerve

DIRECTIONS

Melt the coconut oil in a double boiler and fold in the coconut cream and confectioners' Swerve; stir to combine well. Remove from the heat and add in the rum, vanilla extract and chopped walnuts.
Let it cool to room temperature. Roll into 20 balls and chill for about 50 minutes.
Then, melt the chocolate and dip each ball into the chocolate glaze.
Roll your candies in the chopped walnuts until well coated.

STORING

Place the walnut candy in airtight containers or Ziploc bags; keep in your refrigerator for 3 weeks to 1 month.
To freeze, arrange the walnut candy on a baking tray in a single layer; freeze for about 2 hours. Transfer the frozen walnut candy to an airtight container. Freeze for up to a month. Bon appétit!

432. Espresso Pudding Shots

(Ready in about 10 minutes + chilling time | Servings 6)

Per serving: 218 Calories; 24.7g Fat; 1.1g Carbs; 0.4g Protein; 0.7g Fiber

INGREDIENTS

2 teaspoons butter, softened
A pinch of grated nutmeg
1 teaspoon pure vanilla extract

4 ounces coconut oil
3 tablespoons powdered Erythritol
4 ounces coconut milk creamer

1 teaspoon espresso powder

DIRECTIONS

Melt the butter and coconut oil in a double boiler over medium-low heat.
Add in the remaining ingredients and stir to combine.
Pour into silicone molds.

STORING

Store the pudding shots in your refrigerator for 5 to 6 days.
Freeze up to 1 month. Enjoy!

433. Cashew and Pecan Fat Bombs

(Ready in about 40 minutes | Servings 12)

Per serving: 114 Calories; 10.6g Fat; 3.4g Carbs; 3.1g Protein; 1g Fiber

INGREDIENTS

2/3 cup pecans, chopped
10 drops Monk fruit powder
1 teaspoon vanilla essence
1/4 cup almond flour

2 tablespoons cocoa powder, unsweetened
1/2 cup cashew butter
1/2 cup coconut oil

DIRECTIONS

Mix all ingredients in a bowl until well combined.
Drop by teaspoonfuls onto foil-lined baking sheets. Chill in your refrigerator until firm.

STORING

Place the fat bombs in airtight containers or Ziploc bags; keep in your refrigerator for 3 weeks to 1 month.
To freeze, arrange the fat bombs on a baking tray in a single layer; freeze for about 2 hours. Transfer the frozen fat bombs to an airtight container. Freeze for up to a month. Bon appétit!

434. Creamy Gelatin Dessert

(Ready in about 45 minutes | Servings 10)

Per serving: 56 Calories; 5.5g Fat; 0.4g Carbs; 1.5g Protein; 0g Fiber

INGREDIENTS

2 envelopes lemon gelatin
5 tablespoons powdered Erythritol
1 ¼ cups double cream

1/2 teaspoon ginger, minced
1 teaspoon vanilla extract
3/4 cup boiling water

DIRECTIONS

Combine the gelatin, Erythritol, ginger, and vanilla in a heatproof dish. Pour in the boiling water.
Stir until the gelatin has dissolved completely.
Stir in the double cream; continue to stir with a wire whisk. Pour the mixture into molds and transfer to your refrigerator for 30 to 35 minutes or until they are solid.

STORING

Place your dessert in airtight containers or Ziploc bags; keep in your refrigerator for 7 to 10 days.

435. Chocolate Sheet Pan Cookie Cake

(Ready in about 30 minutes | Servings 10)

Per serving: 157 Calories; 14.8g Fat; 3.5g Carbs; 4.5g Protein; 2.2g Fiber

INGREDIENTS

1/2 cup coconut oil
2 eggs
5 drops liquid Monk fruit
1/4 teaspoon ground cinnamon
1/2 cup walnuts, chopped
1/3 cup baker's chocolate chunks, unsweetened

3/4 cup coconut flour
1 cup almond meal
1/2 teaspoon baking powder
1/4 teaspoon ground cardamom
1/2 teaspoon almond extract

DIRECTIONS

Start by preheating your oven to 360 degrees F. Line a baking sheet with a parchment paper.
Melt the coconut oil in a double over low heat.
Thoroughly combine the almond extract, eggs, and Monk fruit. Add in the melted coconut oil along with the remaining ingredients. Stir to combine well.
Scrape the mixture into the prepared baking sheet. Bake in the preheated oven for 25 to 30 minutes.

STORING

Cover your cake with foil or plastic wrap to prevent drying out; keep in your refrigerator for a week.
To freeze, wrap your cake tightly with foil or place in a heavy-duty freezer bag. Freeze for up to 4 to 6 months. Enjoy!

436. Easy Coconut Mousse

(Ready in about 15 minutes+ chilling time | Servings 6)

Per serving: 303 Calories; 30g Fat; 3.1g Carbs; 3.5g Protein; 2.7g Fiber

INGREDIENTS

1/2 cup coconut milk
A pinch of grated nutmeg
1 cup double cream

1/2 cup panela cheese
2 tablespoons powdered Erythritol
1/2 cup coconut creamer

1 ½ cups avocado, pitted, peeled and mashed

DIRECTIONS

Warm the coconut milk and creamer over low heat. Remove from the heat.
Stir in the avocado and nutmeg; continue to stir until everything is well incorporated.
Add in the remaining ingredients. Beat using an electric mixer on medium-high speed. Place in your refrigerator until firm.

STORING

Spoon your mousse into six airtight containers; keep in your refrigerator for 5 to 6 days.
To freeze, place your mousse in six airtight containers. Freeze up to 1 month. Defrost in the refrigerator. Enjoy!

437. Almond Fluff Fudge

(Ready in about 2 hours | Servings 8)

Per serving: 167 Calories; 17.1g Fat; 6.8g Carbs; 2.4g Protein; 0.9g Fiber

INGREDIENTS

2 ounces almonds, chopped
1/2 teaspoon vanilla extract
1/4 teaspoon orange zest

1 cup Swerve
1 cup coconut milk, unsweetened
1/2 cup butter, at room temperature

DIRECTIONS

Combine the Swerve and coconut milk in a double boiler over low heat.
Add in the butter and vanilla extract and beat the mixture using an electric mixer at low speed.
Fold in the chopped almond and orange zest. Scrape the batter into a lightly greased baking dish and freeze until firm about 1 hour 50 minutes.

STORING

Cover your fudge with foil or plastic wrap to prevent drying out; keep in your refrigerator for a week.
To freeze, wrap your fudge tightly with foil or place in a heavy-duty freezer bag. Freeze for up to 4 to 6 months. Enjoy!

438. Cheesecake Squares with Berry Topping

(Ready in about 30 minutes | Servings 6)

Per serving: 333 Calories; 28.4g Fat; 6.3g Carbs; 11.7g Protein; 0.1g Fiber

INGREDIENTS

For the Cheesecake Squares:
1 cup soft cheese
1 teaspoon vanilla essence
3 tablespoons Swerve
1/2 cup butter, melted
4 eggs

For the Berry Topping:
1/2 teaspoon lime juice
1 ½ tablespoons coconut milk
3/4 cup, frozen mixed berries
2 tablespoons Swerve

DIRECTIONS

Start by preheating your oven to 340 degrees F. Line a baking pan with a Silpat mat.
In a mixing bowl, combine all ingredients for the cheesecake squares using an electric mixer. Press the crust into the baking pan.
Bake in the preheated oven for about 23 minutes.
Warm all of the topping ingredients in a saucepan over a moderate flame. Reduce the heat to a simmer and continue to cook until the sauce has reduced by half.
Spoon the berry topping over the chilled cheesecake.

STORING

Cut your cheesecake into squares and place them in airtight containers and refrigerate for a week.
To freeze, place the cheesecake squares on a baking tray and freeze for 2 hours. Now, place them in airtight containers. They can be frozen for 2 to 3 months. Bon appétit!

439. Easy Cappuccino Creamsicles

(Ready in about 10 minutes + chilling time | Servings 8)

Per serving: 117 Calories; 11.2g Fat; 5g Carbs; 1.3g Protein; 3g Fiber

INGREDIENTS

1 ½ cups avocado, pitted, peeled and mashed
2 tablespoons cocoa powder
3 tablespoons Swerve

1/2 teaspoon cappuccino flavor extract
1 cup brewed coffee
1 cup double cream

DIRECTIONS

Using a stand mixer with a whisk attachment, whip the double cream until soft peaks form.
Process all ingredients in your blender or food processor until everything is creamy and smooth.
Pour the mixture into popsicle molds and freeze overnight.

STORING

Store the cappuccino creamsicles in your freezer up to 1 month. Enjoy!

440. Classic Coconut Truffles

(Ready in about 15 minutes + chilling time | Servings 16)

Per serving: 90 Calories; 6.3g Fat; 4.9g Carbs; 3.7g Protein; 0.5g Fiber

INGREDIENTS

4 tablespoons coconut flakes
1/4 cup unsweetened cocoa powder
1/4 cup coconut oil
1 cup whipped cream

1 ½ cups bakers' chocolate, unsweetened
3 tablespoons Swerve
1 teaspoon vanilla extract
1 tablespoon rum

DIRECTIONS

Melt the chocolate in your microwave. Add in the coconut flakes, coconut oil, cream, Swerve, vanilla extract, and rum.
Place in your refrigerator until the batter is well-chilled. Roll the mixture into balls and cover with cocoa powder on all sides.

STORING

Place the coconut truffles in airtight containers or Ziploc bags; keep in your refrigerator for 3 weeks to 1 month.
To freeze, arrange the coconut truffles on a baking tray in a single layer; freeze for about 2 hours. Transfer the frozen coconut truffles to an airtight container. Freeze for up to a month. Bon appétit!

441. Greek-Style Coconut Cheesecake

(Ready in about 30 minutes | Servings 12)

Per serving: 246 Calories; 22.2g Fat; 5.7g Carbs; 8.1g Protein; 1.9g Fiber

INGREDIENTS

5 ounces Greek-style yogurt
1 ounce coconut flakes
10 ounces almond meal
1/4 teaspoon grated nutmeg
1 teaspoon lemon zest

5 ounces soft cheese
1 teaspoon baking powder
4 eggs, lightly beaten
4 ounces Swerve
1/4 coconut oil

DIRECTIONS

Brush two spring form pans with a nonstick spray.
Mix the almond meal, coconut flakes, nutmeg, and baking powder. Add in the eggs, one at a time, whisking constantly; add in 2 ounces of Swerve.
Spoon the mixture into spring form pans and bake at 360 degrees F for 23 minutes.
In another bowl, combine the coconut oil, lemon zest, yogurt, soft cheese, and the remaining 2 ounces of Swerve. Mix to combine and spoon the filling over the first crust. Spread half of the filling over it.
Top with another crust and spread the rest of the filling over the top.

STORING

Place your cheesecake in airtight containers and refrigerate for a week.
To freeze, place your cheesecake on a baking tray and freeze for 2 hours. Now, place them in airtight containers. They can be frozen for 2 to 3 months. Bon appétit!

442. Butterscotch Cheesecake Cupcakes

(Ready in about 30 minutes + chilling time | Servings 8)

Per serving: 165 Calories; 15.6g Fat; 5.4g Carbs; 5.2g Protein; 1.7g Fiber

INGREDIENTS

2 eggs
1 tablespoon whiskey
2 packets stevia
3 tablespoons butter, melted
10 ounces soft cheese, at room temperature
1/2 teaspoon ground cinnamon

For the Frosting:
1 teaspoon butterscotch extract
1/2 stick butter, at room temperature
1/2 cup powdered erythritol
1 ½ tablespoons coconut milk, unsweetened

DIRECTIONS

Start by preheating your oven to 365 degrees F.
Mix 3 tablespoons of butter, soft cheese, whiskey, eggs, stevia, and cinnamon until well combined.
Scrape the batter into the muffin pan and bake approximately 15 minutes; place the muffin pan in the freezer for 2 hours.
In a mixing bowl, beat 1/2 stick of butter with powdered erythritol and butterscotch extract.
Gradually pour in the milk and mix again. Afterwards, frost the chilled cupcakes.

STORING

Place your cupcakes in airtight containers and refrigerate for a week.
To freeze, place your cupcakes on a baking tray and freeze for 2 hours. Now, place them in airtight containers. They can be frozen for 2 to 3 months. Bon appétit!

443. The Best Keto Birthday Cake

(Ready in about 40 minutes + chilling time | Servings 10)

Per serving: 241 Calories; 22.6g Fat; 4.2g Carbs; 6.6g Protein; 0.7g Fiber

INGREDIENTS

For the Cake Base:
2/3 cup coconut flour
2 ½ tablespoons butter
4 eggs
1 cup full-fat milk
1 teaspoon vanilla extract

1 ½ cups almond meal
1/2 teaspoon baking powder
A pinch of coarse salt
1 cup erythritol

For the Frosting:
1/3 cup erythritol
3 ounces coconut oil, at room temperature
A few drops coconut flavor
10 ounces soft cheese

DIRECTIONS

Mix all ingredients for the cake base until well combined.
Press the crust into a parchment-lined springform pan. Bake at 365 degrees F for 30 minutes or until a toothpick comes out clean; allow it to cool to room temperature.
Meanwhile, beat the cheese using your electric mixer until creamy. Stir in the remaining ingredients and continue to mix until well combined. Frost your cake and serve well-chilled.

STORING

Place your cheesecake in airtight containers and refrigerate for a week.
To freeze, place your cheesecake on a baking tray and freeze for 2 hours. Now, place them in airtight containers. They can be frozen for 2 to 3 months. Bon appétit!

444. Tangerine Chocolate Pudding

(Ready in about 15 minutes + chilling time | Servings 6)

Per serving: 158 Calories; 15.7g Fat; 7.2g Carbs; 2.2g Protein; 1.6g Fiber

INGREDIENTS

3 1/3 tablespoons Dutch-processed brown cocoa powder
2 cups whipped cream

Fresh juice and zest of 1/2 tangerine
1/4 teaspoon ground cloves
1/2 teaspoon crystallized ginger

6 ounces chocolate, unsweetened
3 tablespoons powdered erythritol

DIRECTIONS

Using a stand mixer with a whisk attachment, whip the cream until soft peaks form.
Add in the powdered erythritol and cocoa powder and beat again. Add in the remaining ingredients and beat until everything is well incorporated.

STORING

Spoon your pudding into six airtight containers; keep in your refrigerator for 5 to 6 days.
To freeze, place your pudding in six airtight containers; freeze up to 1 month.

445. Peanut Butter Mousse

(Ready in about 15 minutes | Servings 4)

Per serving: 288 Calories; 27.3g Fat; 6.9g Carbs; 6.2g Protein; 5.2g Fiber

INGREDIENTS

1/2 cup peanut butter
1 ½ cups avocado, peeled, pitted, and diced
1 teaspoon vanilla extract
1 tablespoon lemon juice

1/2 cup coconut cream
1 teaspoon monk fruit powder
1/2 cup coconut milk

DIRECTIONS

Place all ingredients in your blender or food processor. Process until well combined.

STORING

Spoon your mousse into four airtight containers; keep in your refrigerator for 5 to 6 days.

446. Decadent Macchiato Penuche

(Ready in about 10 minutes + chilling time | Servings 8)

Per serving: 145 Calories; 12.8g Fat; 6.2g Carbs; 0.9g Protein; 1.2g Fiber

INGREDIENTS

1 teaspoon warm coffee
1 teaspoon caramel flavor
6 tablespoons butter

1 tablespoon peanut butter
3 ounces dark chocolate, unsweetened
1 teaspoon liquid Monk fruit

DIRECTIONS

Microwave the butter and chocolate until they are completely melted.
Fold in the remaining ingredients. Spoon the batter into a foil-lined baking pan, smoothing out the top.
Place in your refrigerator for 30 minutes before cutting.

STORING

Cover your penuche with foil or plastic wrap to prevent drying out; keep in your refrigerator for a week.
To freeze, wrap your penuche tightly with foil or place in a heavy-duty freezer bag. Freeze for up to 4 to 6 months. Enjoy!

447. White Chocolate Fudge Squares

(Ready in about 15 minutes + chilling time | Servings 12)

Per serving: 202 Calories; 21.3g Fat; 2.3g Carbs; 2.4g Protein; 2.2g Fiber

INGREDIENTS

3 ounces white chocolate, unsweetened
3/4 cup coconut oil
1/3 cup almond milk

2 tablespoons Swerve
1/8 teaspoon coarse sea salt
1 ¼ cups almond butter

DIRECTIONS

Microwave the coconut oil, almond butter, and white chocolate until they are melted. Add in the remaining ingredients and process in your blender.
Scrape the mixture into a parchment-lined baking tray. Cut into squares and serve.

STORING

Cover your fudge squares with foil or plastic wrap to prevent drying out; keep in your refrigerator for a week.
To freeze, wrap your fudge squares tightly with foil or place in a heavy-duty freezer bag. Freeze for up to 4 to 6 months. Enjoy!

448. Coconut and Peanut Bark

(Ready in about 10 minutes + chilling time | Servings 12)

Per serving: 316 Calories; 31.6g Fat; 4.6g Carbs; 6.6g Protein; 2.6g Fiber

INGREDIENTS

3/4 cup coconut oil
1/2 teaspoon pure almond extract
1/2 cup coconut, shredded

3/4 cup peanut butter
1 cup powdered Erythritol

DIRECTIONS

Melt all ingredients in a double boiler over medium-low heat.
Scrape the batter into a parchment-lined baking pan. Place in your freezer for about 1 hour; break your bark into pieces.

STORING

Place your bark in airtight containers or Ziploc bags; keep in your refrigerator for 1 month.
Place your bark in freezable containers; it will maintain the best quality for 4 months. Defrost in the refrigerator. Bon appétit!

449. Homemade Mint Chocolate

(Ready in about 35 minutes | Servings 8)

Per serving: 140 Calories; 14g Fat; 5.9g Carbs; 2g Protein; 2.4g Fiber

INGREDIENTS

4 ounces cacao butter
1 teaspoon vanilla paste
1/4 teaspoon grated nutmeg
1/2 cup hazelnuts, chopped

1 tablespoon coconut oil
8 tablespoons cocoa powder
1/4 cup Erythritol
1 teaspoon peppermint oil

DIRECTIONS

Microwave the cacao butter and coconut oil for about 1 minute.
Now, stir in the cocoa powder, Erythritol, peppermint oil, vanilla, and nutmeg.
Spoon the mixture into an ice cube tray. Fold in the chopped hazelnuts and place in your freezer for about 30 minutes until set.

STORING

Wrap the chocolate tightly with heavy-duty aluminum foil or plastic wrap. Then, keep in your refrigerator for up to 7 days.
It can be frozen in an airtight container. Freeze up to 4 months. Bon appétit!

450. Orange Crème Brûlée

(Ready in about 45 minutes + chilling time | Servings 5)

Per serving: 205 Calories; 16.4g Fat; 6.5g Carbs; 7.4g Protein; 0g Fiber

INGREDIENTS

3/4 cup Erythritol
6 eggs
1 ½ cups double cream
1 teaspoon orange rind, grated

1 teaspoon orange juice
1/2 teaspoon star anise, ground
3/4 cup water

DIRECTIONS

In a saute pan, melt Erythritol until it has caramelized. Spoon the caramelized Erythritol into 5 ramekins.
Bring the cream along with water to a boil.
Whisk the eggs until pale and frothy; add in the remaining ingredients and stir to combine well. Add the mixture to the warm cream mixture and stir to combine well.
Spoon the egg/cream mixture over the caramelized Erythritol. Lower the ramekins into a large cake pan. Pour hot water into the pan to come halfway up the sides of your ramekins.
Bake at 325 degrees F for about 45 minutes. Refrigerate for at least 2 hours.

STORING

Spoon the Crème Brûlée into airtight containers; keep in your refrigerator for 5 to 6 days.
To freeze, place the Crème Brûlée in airtight containers; freeze up to 1 month.
Defrost in the refrigerator. Enjoy!

451. Brazilian Berry Brigadeiro

(Ready in about 15 minutes + chilling time | Servings 10)

Per serving: 334 Calories; 37g Fat; 5.3g Carbs; 1.6g Protein; 0.6g Fiber

INGREDIENTS

4 ounces bakers' chocolate chunks, unsweetened
1/2 teaspoon vanilla extract
1/2 teaspoon coconut extract
1/4 cup butter

1/2 cup peanut butter
3/4 cup coconut oil
1 cup freeze-dried mixed berries, crushed

DIRECTIONS

Melt the butter, peanut butter, and coconut oil in a double boiler over medium-low heat. Fold in the chocolate chunks, mixed berries, vanilla extract, and coconut extract.

Shape the batter into small balls and let them harden in your refrigerator.

STORING

Place the Brazilian Brigadeiro in airtight containers or Ziploc bags; keep in your refrigerator for 3 weeks to 1 month.

To freeze, arrange the Brazilian Brigadeiro on a baking tray in a single layer; freeze for about 2 hours. Transfer the frozen Brazilian Brigadeiro to an airtight container. Freeze for up to a month. Bon appétit!

KETO FAVORITES

452. Rich Chia Pudding

(Ready in about 35 minutes | Servings 4)

Per serving: 93 Calories; 5.1g Fat; 7.2g Carbs; 4.4g Protein; 0.7g Fiber

INGREDIENTS

3/4 cup coconut milk, preferably homemade
1/4 cup water
3 tablespoons orange flower water
2 tablespoons chocolate chunks, unsweetened

2 tablespoons peanut butter
1/2 cup chia seeds
1 teaspoon liquid Monk fruit

DIRECTIONS

Thoroughly combine the coconut milk, water, peanut butter, chia seeds, Monk fruit, and orange flower water.
Let the mixture stand for 30 minutes in your refrigerator. Scatter the chopped chocolate over the top of each serving.

STORING

Place the chia pudding in four airtight containers; place in the refrigerator for up to 3 to 4 days.
To freeze, place in separate containers and freeze up to 2 months. Thaw in the refrigerator before ready to serve.

453. Mediterranean Mezze Platter

(Ready in about 20 minutes | Servings 4)

Per serving: 542 Calories; 46.4g Fat; 6.2g Carbs; 23.7g Protein; 4g Fiber

INGREDIENTS

12 ounces Halloumi cheese, cut into 1/4-1/3-inch slices
3 teaspoons olive oil
1 teaspoon Greek seasoning blend
1 tablespoon olive oil
6 eggs

Sea salt and ground black pepper, to taste
1 ½ cups avocado, pitted and sliced
1 cup grape tomatoes, halved
4 tablespoons Kalamata olives

DIRECTIONS

Preheat a grill pan over medium-high heat, about 395 degrees F.
Grill your halloumi for about 3 minutes or until golden brown grill marks appear.
Heat the oil in a nonstick skillet over moderately-high plate; scramble the eggs with a wide spatula.

STORING

Divide the scrambled eggs between four airtight containers or Ziploc bags. Refrigerate for up to 3 days.
Divide the grilled cheese between four airtight containers or Ziploc bags. Refrigerate for up to 3 days.
For freezing, place the scrambled eggs in four Ziploc bags and freeze up to 6 months. Defrost in your refrigerator or microwave.
Season with sea salt, black pepper, and Greek seasoning blend. Garnish with the avocado, tomatoes, and olives.

454. Bacon and Mascarpone Fat Bombs

(Ready in about 15 minutes | Servings 4)

Per serving: 88 Calories; 6.5g Fat; 0.7g Carbs; 6.5g Protein; 0.3g Fiber

INGREDIENTS

4 bacon slices, chopped
1 teaspoon paprika
1 teaspoon onion powder
1/2 teaspoon garlic powder

1/2 cup mascarpone cheese
1/2 teaspoon smoke flavor
1/4 teaspoon apple cider vinegar

DIRECTIONS

Thoroughly combine all ingredients until well combined.
Roll the mixture into bite-sized balls.

STORING

Place the fat bombs in airtight containers or Ziploc bags; keep in your refrigerator for 10 days.
To freeze, arrange the fat bombs on a baking tray in a single layer; freeze for about 2 hours. Transfer the frozen bombs to an airtight container. Freeze for up to 2 months. Serve well chilled!

455. Spanish Tortilla Pizza

(Ready in about 15 minutes | Servings 2)

Per serving: 397 Calories; 31g Fat; 6.1g Carbs; 22g Protein; 1.4g Fiber

INGREDIENTS

For the Crust:
4 eggs, beaten
1/2 teaspoon coriander, minced
Salt and pepper, to taste
1 tablespoon extra-virgin olive oil
1/4 cup cream cheese

2 tablespoons flax seed meal
1 teaspoon chili pepper, deveined and minced
For the Toppings:
2 ounces Manchego cheese, shredded
2 tablespoons tomato paste

DIRECTIONS

In a mixing bowl, combine ingredients for the crust. Divide the batter into two pieces.
Cook in a frying pan for about 5 minutes; flip your tortilla and cook on the other side until crisp and golden-brown on their edges.
Repeat with another tortilla. Spread the tomato paste and cheese over the top of each of the prepared tortillas.
Place under the preheated broiler for about 5 minutes until the cheese is hot and bubbly.

STORING

Place the tortilla pizza in airtight containers; place in the refrigerator for up to 3 to 4 days.
To freeze, place in separate Ziploc bags and freeze up to 3 months. Defrost in your microwave for a few minutes.

456. Prosciutto and Cheddar Muffins

(Ready in about 30 minutes | Servings 9)

Per serving: 294 Calories; 21.4g Fat; 3.5g Carbs; 21g Protein; 0.2g Fiber

INGREDIENTS

9 slices prosciutto, chopped
1/2 cup cheddar cheese, shredded
1/4 teaspoon garlic powder
1/2 teaspoon cayenne pepper

Sea salt and pepper, to taste
9 eggs
1/2 cup green onions, chopped

DIRECTIONS

Thoroughly combine all ingredients in a mixing bowl. Spoon the batter into a lightly oiled muffin pan.
Bake in the preheated oven at 395 degrees F for about 25 minutes.

STORING

Place your muffins in the airtight containers or Ziploc bags; keep in the refrigerator for a week.
For freezing, divide your muffins among Ziploc bags and freeze up to 3 months. Defrost in your microwave for a couple of minutes. Bon appétit!

457. Anchovy and Cheese Mousse

(Ready in about 20 minutes + chilling time | Servings 5)

Per serving: 100 Calories; 5.8g Fat; 4.1g Carbs; 8g Protein; 0.5g Fiber

INGREDIENTS

3 ounces anchovies, chopped
2 ounces soft cheese
1 ½ teaspoons gelatin, powdered
1 garlic clove, minced
1 teaspoon poblano pepper, deveined and minced

Sea salt and pepper, to taste
3 tablespoons water
3 tablespoons mayonnaise
1/4 cup scallions, chopped

DIRECTIONS

Dissolve the gelatin in water for about 10 minutes.
Warm the soft cheese over low heat heat; fold in the gelatin and whisk until it is well incorporated.
Let it cool to room temperature. Add in the other ingredients and mix to combine.
Spoon the mixture into ramekins and place in your refrigerator until set.

STORING

Cover your mousse with plastic wrap and refrigerate for up to 5 days. Enjoy!

458. Avocado Stuffed with Tomato and Cheese

(Ready in about 25 minutes | Servings 4)

Per serving: 264 Calories; 24.4g Fat; 6g Carbs; 3.7g Protein; 5g Fiber

INGREDIENTS

2 avocados, halved and pitted
1/2 cup tomatoes, chopped
3 ounces mascarpone cheese

1 teaspoon olive oil
8 black olives, pitted and sliced

DIRECTIONS

Mix the olive oil, tomatoes, cheese and black olives in a bowl. Spoon the mixture into the avocado halves. Bake in the preheated oven at 365 degrees F for about 20 minutes or until everything is cooked through.

STORING

Place the stuffed avocado in airtight containers; keep in your refrigerator for 3 to 4 days. Bon appétit!

459. Rich Keto Grits with Hemp

(Ready in about 20 minutes | Servings 4)

Per serving: 405 Calories; 37g Fat; 6.6g Carbs; 14.8g Protein; 2.3g Fiber

INGREDIENTS

1/4 cup hemp hearts
2 tablespoons butter, softened
1 teaspoon coconut extract
1/4 teaspoon coarse salt
8 walnuts, chopped

4 eggs, lightly whisked
1/4 cup flax seed, freshly ground
2 teaspoons liquid Monk fruit
1/4 teaspoon pinch psyllium husk powder

DIRECTIONS

Mel the butter in a sauté pan over medium-low heat. Add in the remaining ingredients and continue to cook until the mixture starts to boil. Remove from heat and stir in the chopped walnuts; stir to combine.

STORING

Divide your grits into four portions; store each portion in an airtight container. Keep in the refrigerator for up to 5 days.
To freeze, place each portion in an airtight container; freeze for up to 3 months. Reheat the keto grits in a microwave, stirring and adding some extra liquid if necessary. Bon appétit!

460. Mom's Homemade Bread

(Ready in about 40 minutes | Servings 6)

Per serving: 109 Calories; 10.2g Fat; 1g Carbs; 3.9g Protein; 0.8g Fiber

INGREDIENTS

5 eggs whites
1/2 teaspoon sea salt
1 tablespoon poppy seeds
1 tablespoon flax seeds
1 tablespoon sesame seeds
1/2 teaspoon cream of tartar

1/4 cup butter, softened
1 teaspoon baking powder
1 teaspoon baking soda
1 3/4 cups almond flour
1/4 cup psyllium husk flour

DIRECTIONS

Start by preheating your oven to 365 degrees F.
Beat the eggs with the cream of tartar using your electric mixer until stiff peaks form.
Add in the flour, butter, baking powder, baking soda, and salt; blend until everything is well combined.
Add the egg mixture to the flour mixture; add in seeds and stir again. Spoon the batter into a lightly buttered loaf pan.
Bake in the preheated oven for about 30 minutes.

STORING

Store the keto bread in an airtight container in the refrigerator for up to 7 days.
For freezing, wrap the loaf with clear plastic bread bags. Freeze up to 1 month. To thaw the frozen bread, let it come to room temperature.
Just before serving, place it in an oven heated to 400 degrees F for about 4 minutes.

461. Pecan Cream Pie

(Ready in about 30 minutes + chilling time | Servings 6)

Per serving: 305 Calories; 30.6g Fat; 4.7g Carbs; 4.6g Protein; 0.5g Fiber

INGREDIENTS

For the Crust:
3/4 cup almond meal
1/3 cup coconut flour
1/4 cup coconut oil
1/3 cup Swerve

For the Custard:
3 egg yolks
1/3 cup almond meal
1 ¼ cups whipping cream
1/3 cup Swerve
3/4 cup water
1/2 teaspoon ground cinnamon
1 teaspoon vanilla essence

For the Topping:
1 cup whipping cream
2 tablespoons pecans, chopped

DIRECTIONS

Microwave the coconut oil; add in 1/3 cup of Swerve and whisk until it has dissolved completely.
Stir in the almond meal and coconut flour and mix again. Press the crust mixture into the bottom of a parchment-lined baking pan. Place in your refrigerator to harden.
Melt the whipping cream and egg yolks until everything is well incorporated.
Whisk in the remaining ingredients for custard. Spread the custard mixture over the crust and place in your refrigerator for at least 1 hour.
Beat 1 cup of whipping cream using an electric mixer until peaks are completely stiff. Top your pie with the cream and garnish with chopped pecans.

STORING

Cut your pie into slices and divide them between airtight containers; they can be stored in the refrigerator up to 3 days.
Place the pie slices in heavy-duty freezer bags. Store in your freezer up to 1 month. Bon appétit!

462. Nutty Breakfast Porridge

(Ready in about 25 minutes | Servings 2)

Per serving: 430 Calories; 41.1g Fat; 5.8g Carbs; 11.4g Protein; 0.1g Fiber

INGREDIENTS

3 eggs
3 tablespoons erythritol

1/2 cup sour cream
1 ½ tablespoons butter

1/2 teaspoon star anise
1/4 cup almonds

DIRECTIONS

Whisk the eggs, erythritol, and sour cream until well combined.
Melt the butter and add in the egg mixture along with star anise; continue to cook on medium-low heat until thoroughly warmed.
Top with slivered almonds.

STORING

Divide your porridge between two airtight containers. Keep in the refrigerator for up to 5 days.
To freeze, place the porridge in airtight containers; freeze for up to 3 months. Reheat the porridge in a microwave, stirring and adding some extra liquid if necessary. Bon appétit!

463. Cheesy Mashed Cauliflower

(Ready in about 15 minutes | Servings 4)

Per serving: 230 Calories; 17.7g Fat; 7.2g Carbs; 11.9g Protein; 3.5g Fiber

INGREDIENTS

1 ½ pounds cauliflower florets
1/2 teaspoon dried oregano
2 cups goat cheese, crumbled

Salt and pepper, to taste
2 tablespoons butter, softened
1 thyme sprig, chopped

1 teaspoon dried basil
1 teaspoon garlic, minced

DIRECTIONS

Steam the cauliflower florets for about 10 minutes or until they are crisp-tender.
Puree the cauliflower in your blender or food processor, adding the cooking liquid periodically.
Add in the remaining ingredients and pulse until everything is well combined.

STORING

Place the mashed cauliflower place it in airtight containers or Ziploc bags; keep in your refrigerator for up to 3 to 4 days.

464. Keto Pancakes with Blueberry Topping

(Ready in about 20 minutes | Servings 4)

Per serving: 237 Calories; 16.3g Fat; 5.5g Carbs; 14.5g Protein; 0.9g Fiber

INGREDIENTS

For the Batter:
6 ounces soft cheese
1 teaspoon baking powder
5 eggs
For the Topping:

1 cup fresh blueberries
2 tablespoons Swerve
2 tablespoons canola oil
1/2 cup sour cream

DIRECTIONS

In a mixing bowl, whisk all the batter ingredients.
Brush your pan with a small amount of the oil.
Once hot, spoon the batter onto the pan and form into circles. Cover and cook until bubbles start to form. Flip and cook on the other side until browned. Repeat with the rest of the batter.

STORING

Place your pancakes in airtight containers or Ziploc bags; keep in your refrigerator for up 3 to 4 days.
To freeze, place a sheet of wax paper between each pancake and stack together. Wrap the tightly in aluminum foil. Freeze up to 1 to 2 months.
Divide the fresh berries among the prepared pancakes; sprinkle with Swerve, and top with a dollop of sour cream.

465. Italian Savory Panna Cotta

(Ready in about 15 minutes + chilling time | Servings 6)

Per serving: 489 Calories; 47.4g Fat; 6.9g Carbs; 12.7g Protein; 1.6g Fiber

INGREDIENTS

2 ounces button mushrooms, chopped
8 ounces goat cheese
1 cup Greek-style yogurt
1 tablespoon canola oil

1 teaspoon Italian herb mix
1/4 cup almonds, slivered
2 teaspoons powdered gelatin
1 1/3 cups double cream

DIRECTIONS

Heat the oil in a saucepan over medium-high heat; once hot, sauté the mushrooms for 4 to 5 minutes until they release the liquid.
Add in the gelatin and cream and continue to cook for 3 to 4 minutes more. Remove from the heat.
Add in the remaining ingredients and transfer to your refrigerator until set.

STORING

Cover your panna cotta with plastic wrap and refrigerate for up to 5 days. Enjoy!

466. Decadent Omelet with Blueberries

(Ready in about 10 minutes | Servings 1)

Per serving: 488 Calories; 42g Fat; 8g Carbs; 15.3g Protein; 0.3g Fiber

INGREDIENTS

2 eggs, whisked
2 tablespoons double cream
1/2 teaspoon ground cardamom

1 tablespoon coconut oil
2 tablespoons soft cheese
6 fresh blueberries, sliced

DIRECTIONS

Beat the eggs with the cream and cardamom until well combined.
In a saucepan, melt the coconut oil over a medium-high flame. Now, cook the egg mixture for 3 to 4 minutes.

STORING

Place your omelet in an airtight container or Ziploc bag; place in the refrigerator for up to 3 to 4 days.
To freeze, place your omelet in a Ziploc bag and freeze up to 3 months. Defrost in your microwave for a few minutes.
Serve with soft cheese and blueberries. Bon appétit!

467. French-Style Bacon Fat Bombs

(Ready in about 15 minutes + chilling time | Servings 5)

Per serving: 206 Calories; 16.5g Fat; 0.6g Carbs; 13.4g Protein; 0.1g Fiber

INGREDIENTS

1/2 teaspoon red pepper flakes, crushed
6 ounces Camembert
3 ounces bacon
1 chili pepper, seeded and minced

DIRECTIONS

Cook the bacon over a moderately high flame until it is browned on all sides; chop the bacon and set aside.
Mix the remaining ingredients until well blended. Place the mixture in your refrigerator for 1 hour.
Roll the mixture into bite-sized balls; roll the balls over chopped bacon.

STORING

Place the fat bombs in airtight containers or Ziploc bags; keep in your refrigerator for 10 days.
To freeze, arrange the fat bombs on a baking tray in a single layer; freeze for about 2 hours. Transfer the frozen bombs to an airtight container. Freeze for up to 2 months. Serve well chilled!

468. Authentic Greek Aioli

(Ready in about 10 minutes | Servings 8)

Per serving: 116 Calories; 13.2g Fat; 0.2g Carbs; 0.4g Protein; 0.1g Fiber

INGREDIENTS

1 tablespoon white vinegar
1 teaspoon dried dill weed
Salt and pepper, to taste

1/2 cup olive oil
1 egg yolk, at room temperature
1/2 teaspoon garlic, crushed

DIRECTIONS

In your blender, process the vinegar, egg yolk, garlic, salt, and pepper; pulse until smooth and uniform. Turn to low setting.
Gradually drizzle in the olive oil and continue to mix until well blended.
Add in the dried dill and place in your refrigerator.

STORING

Place your aioli in a glass jar, cover, and keep in your refrigerator for up to week.

469. Festive Triple Cheese Fondue

(Ready in about 15 minutes | Servings 10)

Per serving: 148 Calories; 10.2g Fat; 1.5g Carbs; 9.3g Protein; 0.2g Fiber

INGREDIENTS

1 tomato, pureed
1 tablespoon xanthan gum
1/2 teaspoon garlic, minced
1 teaspoon onion powder
3/4 cup dry white wine

1/2 tablespoon lime juice
Cayenne pepper, to taste
1/3 pound soft cheese, chopped
1/3 pound goat cheese, shredded
1/2 cup Parmesan, freshly grated

DIRECTIONS

Melt the cheese in a double boiler; add in the remaining ingredients and stir to combine.
Then, place the cheese mixture under the preheated broiler for about 7 minutes, until the cheese is hot and bubbly.

STORING

Place your dip in an airtight container and keep in your refrigerator for 3 to 4 days. Enjoy!

470. Pizza Dipping Sauce

(Ready in about 20 minutes | Servings 10)

Per serving: 160 Calories; 12.7g Fat; 2.4g Carbs; 8.9g Protein; 0.8g Fiber

INGREDIENTS

8 ounces pepperoni, chopped
1 cup marinara sauce
1 teaspoon dried basil
Salt and black pepper, to taste
1/2 cup black olives, to garnish

1/2 teaspoon cayenne pepper
1/2 teaspoon dried oregano
8 ounces cream cheese, room temperature
2 ounces Parmesan cheese, shredded

DIRECTIONS

Begin by preheating your oven to 365 degrees F.
Mix the cheese, marinara sauce, and spices in a bowl. Place the mixture in a lightly oiled baking dish.
Top with the pepperoni and olives and bake for 15 to 18 minutes or until hot and bubbly on top.

STORING

Place your dip in an airtight container and keep in your refrigerator for 3 to 4 days. Enjoy!

471. Autumn Nut and Seed Granola

(Ready in about 35 minutes | Servings 8)

Per serving: 281 Calories; 26.6g Fat; 7.7g Carbs; 5.4g Protein; 3.3g Fiber

INGREDIENTS

2 tablespoons hemp hearts
1/4 cup sunflower seeds
1 teaspoon pumpkin pie spice mix
3/4 cup almonds, chopped
1/2 cup cashews, chopped

1 tablepsoon Monk fruit powder
1 cup coconut flakes
3 tablespoons coconut oil
1/4 cup pepitas seeds
1/4 cup flaxseeds

DIRECTIONS

Toss all ingredients in a rimmed baking pan.
Bake in the preheated oven 290 degrees F, tossing once or twice.

STORING

Place your granola in airtight containers or Ziploc bags; keep at room temperature for up to a month.

472. Chicken Skin Chips

(Ready in about 15 minutes | Servings 4)

Per serving: 119 Calories; 10.5g Fat; 1.1g Carbs; 5.1g Protein; 0.3g Fiber

INGREDIENTS

Skin from 4 chicken wings
1/4 cup soft cheese
2 tablespoons Greek-style yogurt
1 tablespoon butter

1/2 teaspoon mustard seeds
2 tablespoons scallions, chopped
Salt and pepper, to season

DIRECTIONS

Bake the chicken skins in the preheated oven at 365 degrees F for about 10 minutes; cut the skin into small pieces.
Meanwhile, mix the remaining ingredients to make the sauce.

STORING

Divide the chicken skin between four airtight containers; keep in your refrigerator for up 3 to 4 days.
For freezing, place the chicken skin in airtight containers or heavy-duty freezer bags. Freeze up to 3 months. Defrost in the refrigerator.
Place the sauce in an airtight container and keep in your refrigerator for 3 to 4 days. Enjoy!

473. Cheese Chicken Tenders

(Ready in about 20 minutes | Servings 4)

Per serving: 416 Calories; 26g Fat; 3.2g Carbs; 40.7g Protein; 0.3g Fiber

INGREDIENTS

1 pound chicken tenders
1 tablespoon butter
1/3 cup chicken stock
2 tablespoon tomato paste

1 cup Cheddar cheese, shredded
1 teaspoon garlic, minced
1/2 cup double cheese

DIRECTIONS

In a frying pan, melt the butter over a moderately-high flame; cook the chicken for 5 to 6 minutes until no longer pink.
Add in the garlic and continue to sauté for 1 minuet or so; reserve.
Cook the cream, stock, and tomato paste until it has reduced by half.
Remove from the heat. Add in the reserved chicken and garlic; scatter the cheese over the top. Cover and let it sit for about 10 minutes.

STORING

Place the chicken tenders in airtight containers or Ziploc bags; keep in your refrigerator for up 1 to 2 days.
For freezing, place the chicken tenders in airtight containers or heavy-duty freezer bags. Freeze up to 2 to 3 months. Defrost in the refrigerator or microwave. Bon appétit!

474. Omelet with Spring Onions

(Ready in about 15 minutes | Servings 2)

Per serving: 319 Calories; 25g Fat; 7.4g Carbs; 14.9g Protein; 2.7g Fiber

INGREDIENTS

4 eggs, beaten
2 teaspoons olive oil
2 tomatoes, chopped
1 chili pepper, minced

Salt and black pepper, to taste
2 spring onions, chopped
1 teaspoon spring garlic, minced
8 ounces Greek-style yogurt

DIRECTIONS

In a frying pan, heat the olive oil over a moderate flame. Once hot, cook the spring onion and garlic until they've softened or about 2 minutes.
Beat the eggs with the Greek-style yogurt. Pour the egg mixture into the pan; cook until the eggs are puffy and golden-brown.
Place the tomatoes and pepper on one side of the omelet. Sprinkle with salt and pepper and fold the omelet in half.

STORING

Slice the omelet into two pieces. Place each of them in an airtight container or Ziploc bag; place in the refrigerator for up to 3 to 4 days.
To freeze, place in separate Ziploc bags and freeze up to 3 months. Defrost in your microwave for a few minutes.

475. Spicy Chorizo with Vegetables

(Ready in about 25 minutes | Servings 4)

Per serving: 227 Calories; 18g Fat; 7g Carbs; 7.1g Protein; 0.7g Fiber

INGREDIENTS

2 chorizo sausages, sliced
1 tablespoon olive oil
1 teaspoon Taco seasoning mix
1 poblano pepper, minced

2 Spanish peppers, sliced
2 cloves garlic, minced
2 zucchinis, sliced
1 celery, sliced

DIRECTIONS

In a large skillet, heat the olive oil over a moderately-high heat. Sear the sausage for 7 to 8 minutes.
Add in the other ingredients and continue to cook, partially covered, for about 15 minutes.

STORING

Place the sausage and vegetables in four Ziploc bags; keep in the refrigerator for a week.
For freezing, divide the sausage and vegetables among Ziploc bags and freeze up to 3 to 4 months. Thaw them in the refrigerator. You can reheat the sausage and vegetables in the pan. Enjoy!

476. Comte Cheese Custard with Chanterelles

(Ready in about 45 minutes | Servings 6)

Per serving: 263 Calories; 22.4g Fat; 6.1g Carbs; 10g Protein; 0.2g Fiber

INGREDIENTS

1 tablespoon ghee, room temperature
4 ounces Chanterelle mushrooms, chopped
1/2 teaspoon fresh garlic, minced
1 ½ cups double cream

4 ounces Comté cheese, crumbled
3 eggs, whisked
Salt and pepper, to taste

DIRECTIONS

Melt the cream and add in the cheese; stir until melted. Add in the whisked eggs, salt, and pepper; continue to stir for about 2 minutes or until well combined.
Spoon the mixture into 6 ramekins; place the ramekins into a large pan with hot water (depth of about 1-inch).
Bake in the preheated oven at 310 degrees F for about 35 minutes or until set.
Sauté the mushrooms in hot ghee until they release liquid; add in the garlic and continue to sauté a minute more or until aromatic. Top each custard with sautéed chanterelles.

STORING

Keep your custard in the refrigerator for 5 to 6 days.
To freeze, wrap your custard with foil and freeze up to 1 month. Defrost in the refrigerator. Enjoy!

477. Great-Grandma's Cheesy Meatballs

(Ready in about 35 minutes | Servings 5)

Per serving: 342 Calories; 23.7g Fat; 4.3g Carbs; 31.7g Protein; 0.6g Fiber

INGREDIENTS

1 pound ground beef
1 egg, beaten
Salt and pepper, to taste

2 tablespoons olive oil
1 cup Swiss cheese, shredded
1 celery, grated

1 teaspoon garlic, minced
1 yellow onion, chopped
1 teaspoon Fajita seasoning mix

DIRECTIONS

Mix all ingredients, except for cheese, until everything is well incorporated.
Roll the mixture into small meatballs and bake at 365 degrees F for about 30 minutes.

STORING

Place the meatballs in airtight containers or Ziploc bags; keep in your refrigerator for up to 3 to 4 days.
Freeze the meatballs in airtight containers or heavy-duty freezer bags. Freeze up to 3 to 4 months.
Scatter the cheese over the balls and place under the preheated broil for about 6 minutes. Bon appétit!

478. Cheese Bites with Celery Chips

(Ready in about 25 minutes | Servings 8)

Per serving: 177 Calories; 12.9g Fat; 6.8g Carbs; 8.8g Protein; 1.3g Fiber

INGREDIENTS

1 cup Swiss cheese, shredded
1 teaspoon Italian herb mix
2 tablespoons chili pepper, minced
Salt and pepper, to taste

1 cup Parmesan cheese, freshly grated
1/2 cup Greek-style yogurt
2 tablespoons tomato paste

For Celery Chips:
2 tablespoons avocado oil
1 pound celery, cut into sticks
Salt and pepper, to taste

DIRECTIONS

Mix the Swiss cheese, Parmesan cheese, Greek-style yogurt, tomato paste, Italian herb mix, chili pepper, salt, and pepper in a bowl.
Roll the mixture into balls and place in your refrigerator.
Toss the celery with avocado oil, salt, and pepper. Roast in the preheated oven at 420 degrees F for about 20 minutes.

STORING

Divide the cheese bites between airtight containers or Ziploc bags; keep in your refrigerator for up to 3 to 4 days.
For freezing, place the cheese bites in airtight containers. Freeze up to 1 month. Defrost in the refrigerator.
Place the celery chips in an airtight container and keep at room temperature up to 10 days.

479. Classic Egg, Chèvre and Salami Breakfast

(Ready in about 5 minutes | Servings 3)

Per serving: 303 Calories; 22.4g Fat; 3.6g Carbs; 21.6g Protein; 0.4g Fiber

INGREDIENTS

3 teaspoons olive oil
3 slices salami, chopped
Salt and pepper, to taste
1 teaspoon deli mustard

6 eggs
1/2 cup Chèvre cheese, shredded
1/2 cup soft cheese
Salt and pepper, to taste

DIRECTIONS

Brush three mason jars with olive oil.
Crack two eggs into each jar. Add the other ingredients to your jars and cover them.
Shake until everything is well combined. Uncover and microwave for 2 minutes on high.

STORING

Keep your jars in the refrigerator for 3 to 4 days.

480. Italian Bacon and Gorgonzola Waffles

(Ready in about 20 minutes | Servings 3)

Per serving: 453 Calories; 37g Fat; 4.5g Carbs; 25.6g Protein; 1.8g Fiber

INGREDIENTS

6 large-sized eggs, separated
3 tablespoons tomato paste
3 ounces bacon, chopped
3 ounces Gorgonzola cheese, shredded

1 teaspoon baking powder
4 tablespoons butter
1 teaspoon Italian seasoning mix
Salt and pepper, to taste

DIRECTIONS

Combine the egg yolks, baking powder, butter, salt, pepper, and Italian seasoning mix.
Beat the egg whites with an electric mixer until pale and frothy. Fold in the egg whites into the egg yolk mixture.
Heat you waffle iron. Cook 1/4 cup of the batter until golden. Repeat with the remaining ingredients; you will have six waffles.
Spread your toppings onto three waffle; top with remaining waffles and cook until the cheese is melted.

STORING

Place the waffles in the airtight containers or Ziploc bags; keep in the refrigerator for a week.
For freezing, divide the waffles among three Ziploc bags and freeze up to 3 months. Defrost in your microwave for a couple of minutes. Enjoy!

481. Mexican-Style Avocado Fat Bombs

(Ready in about 20 minutes + chilling time | Servings 8)

Per serving: 145 Calories; 12.6g Fat; 3.7g Carbs; 5.5g Protein; 1.7g Fiber

INGREDIENTS

2 ounces bacon bits

1/2 teaspoon chili powder

1/4 teaspoon mustard powder

6 ounces avocado flash

6 ounces Cotija cheese

1 tablespoon cayenne pepper

DIRECTIONS

Thoroughly combine all ingredients until everything is well incorporated.
Roll the mixture into eight balls. Place in the refrigerator for about 1 hour.

STORING

Place the fat bombs in airtight containers or Ziploc bags; keep in your refrigerator for 5 days.
To freeze, arrange the fat bombs on a baking tray in a single layer; freeze for about 2 hours. Transfer the frozen bombs to an airtight container. Freeze for up to 2 months. Bon appétit!

482. Greek-Style Loaded Cheeseburgers

(Ready in about 20 minutes | Servings 6)

Per serving: 252 Calories; 15.5g Fat; 1.2g Carbs; 26g Protein; 0.3g Fiber

INGREDIENTS

3 ounces Cheddar cheese, grated
1/2 pound ground beef
1/2 pound ground lamb

1/2 cup onions, chopped
1 teaspoon garlic, chopped
2 ounces soft cheese

2 tablespoons olive oil
Se salt and black pepper, to taste
1/2 teaspoon red pepper flakes

DIRECTIONS

Thoroughly combine the ground meat, onions, garlic, salt, black pepper, and red pepper.
Roll the mixture into six balls; flatten them using your hands to make 6 burgers.
In a separate bowl, combine soft cheese with Cheddar cheese. Place the cheese into the center of each ball, and enclose inside the meat mixture.
Heat the olive oil in a frying pan over a moderately-high flame. Cook your burgers approximately 5 minutes per side.

STORING

Place your burgers in airtight containers or Ziploc bags; keep in your refrigerator for up to 3 to 4 days.
Freeze your burgers in airtight containers or heavy-duty freezer bags. Freeze up to 3 to 4 months. To defrost, slowly reheat in a saucepan. Bon appétit!

483. Gorgonzola and Pancetta Cups

(Ready in about 20 minutes | Servings 6)

Per serving: 268 Calories; 18.3g Fat; 0.7g Carbs; 26.2g Protein; 0.3g Fiber

INGREDIENTS

2 ounces Gorgonzola cheese, diced
12 small thin slices of pancetta
1/4 cup scallions, chopped

2 ounces soft cheese
6 eggs, whisked
Salt and pepper, to season

DIRECTIONS

Line 6 ramekins with 2 slices of pancetta each. Mix the remaining ingredients until everything is well incorporated.
Divide the egg mixture between ramekins. Cover with a double layer of foil.
Bake in the preheated oven at 395 degrees F for 15 to 18 minutes or until the top is golden brown.

STORING

Place the pancetta cups in the airtight containers or Ziploc bags; keep in the refrigerator for a week.
For freezing, divide the pancetta cups among Ziploc bags and freeze up to 3 months. Defrost in your microwave for a couple of minutes. Enjoy!

484. Easy Peppery Ribs

(Ready in about 15 minutes | Servings 4)

Per serving: 490 Calories; 44g Fat; 5.5g Carbs; 16.9g Protein; 0.6g Fiber

INGREDIENTS

2 Italian peppers, deveined and thinly sliced
2 tablespoons scallions, chopped
1 pound ribs, cut into small chunks

Salt and black pepper, to taste
1 tablespoon lard, at room temperature
1 teaspoon garlic, minced

DIRECTIONS

Melt the lard in a saucepan over medium-high heat. Cook the ribs for about 5 minutes or until the meat reaches an internal temperature of 160 degrees F.
Add in the other ingredients and cook for 2 minutes more.
Place under the preheated broiler until it is crispy in top.

STORING

Divide the peppery ribs into four portions. Place each portion of ribs in an airtight container; keep in your refrigerator for 3 to 5 days.
For freezing, place the ribs in airtight containers or heavy-duty freezer bags. Freeze up to 4 to 6 months. Defrost in the refrigerator. Reheat in your oven at 250 degrees F until heated through. Bon appétit!

485. Old Bay Crabmeat Frittata

(Ready in about 25 minutes | Servings 3)

Per serving: 265 Calories; 15.8g Fat; 7.1g Carbs; 22.9g Protein; 0.6g Fiber

INGREDIENTS

4 ounces crabmeat, flaked
1 tablespoon butter, melted
1 teaspoon Old Bay seasoning mix
6 eggs, slightly beaten

1/2 cup sour cream
1 yellow onion, chopped
1 teaspoon garlic, minced

DIRECTIONS

Begin by preheating your oven to 360 degrees F.
Heat the oil in an oven-proof skillet over moderately-high heat.
Sauté the onions until they are tender and translucent; add the crabmeat and garlic and continue to cook for 2 minutes or until fragrant.
Mix the eggs and sour cream until well combined; pour the egg mixture into the skillet.
Bake for 18 to 20 minutes or until the eggs are puffed and opaque.

STORING

Cut the frittata into three wedges. Place each of them in an airtight container; place in the refrigerator for up 3 to 4 days.
To freeze, place in separate Ziploc bags and freeze up to 3 months. To defrost, place in your microwave for a few minutes.

486. Smoked Fish Pâté

(Ready in about 10 minutes + chilling time | Servings 12)

Per serving: 64 Calories; 2.9g Fat; 1.3g Carbs; 7.9g Protein; 0.2g Fiber

INGREDIENTS

3/4 cup soft cheese
2 ounces coriander, finely chopped
Salt and pepper, to taste
1/2 teaspoon cayenne pepper

2 tablespoons butter
1/2 teaspoon deli mustard
12 ounces smoked salmon, skinned, deboned, and flaked

DIRECTIONS

Pulse all of the above ingredients in your food processor and place in your refrigerator.

STORING

Place the fish pâté in an airtight container; keep in the refrigerator for a week.
You can freeze them in silicone molds. Once frozen, unmold and put some wax paper between each little pâté to prevent them from sticking to each other.
Now, place them in a freezer-safe container for up to 3 months. Thaw in your refrigerator.

487. Easy Mexican Quesadilla

(Ready in about 15 minutes | Servings 4)

Per serving: 323 Calories; 24g Fat; 7.4g Carbs; 18.8g Protein; 2.3g Fiber

INGREDIENTS

1 pound cauliflower florets
1/2 cup Muenster cheese, shredded
1/2 pound bacon, cut into strips
1 cup whipping cream

1 tablespoon butter
2 garlic cloves, minced
2 tablespoons white vinegar

DIRECTIONS

In a preheated sauté pan, cook the bacon for 2 to 3 minutes and reserve.
Melt the butter in the same pan. Sauté the cauliflower florets in the pan drippings until they are crisp-tender.
Pour the whipping cream into the pan. Add in the garlic and vinegar and continue to cook for 3 minutes longer, stirring frequently.
Add in the reserved bacon along with cheese; continue to cook for 2 to 3 minutes, or until the cheese has melted.

STORING

Place your Quesadilla in airtight containers or Ziploc bags; keep in your refrigerator for up to a week.
To freeze, place your Quesadilla in storage bags. Freeze for up to 3 months.

488. Mini Meatloaves with Cheese and Pancetta

(Ready in about 30 minutes | Servings 6)

Per serving: 276 Calories; 18.3g Fat; 1.2g Carbs; 29.2g Protein; 0.1g Fiber

INGREDIENTS

2 ounces pancetta, chopped
4 ounces Teleme cheese, cubed
1/2 pound ground beef
1/2 ground pork
1 egg, beaten

1 teaspoon Dijon mustard
2 tablespoons scallions, chopped
2 garlic cloves, smashed
Sea salt and pepper, to taste
1 teaspoon Italian herb mix

DIRECTIONS

Begin by preheating your oven to 360 degrees F.
In a mixing bowl, thoroughly combine the scallions, garlic, ground meat, pancetta, egg and mustard.
Season with salt, black pepper, and Italian herb mix.
Mix until well combined. Spoon the mixture into muffin cups. Insert one cube of cheese into each cup; seal the top to cover the cheese.
Bake in the preheated oven for 18 to 20 minutes or until the internal temperature reaches 165 degrees F.

STORING

Wrap the mini meatloaves tightly with heavy-duty aluminum foil or plastic wrap. Then, keep in your refrigerator for up to 3 to 4 days.
For freezing, wrap the mini meatloaves tightly to prevent freezer burn. Freeze up to 3 to 4 months. Defrost in the refrigerator. Bon appétit!

489. Caramel Cheese Balls

(Ready in about 5 minutes | Servings 4)

Per serving: 180 Calories; 17.3g Fat; 3.4g Carbs; 5.3g Protein; 1.1g Fiber

INGREDIENTS

3 ounces walnuts, chopped
1/2 teaspoon caramel flavoring

3 ounces soft cheese
1/4 teaspoon ground cinnamon

DIRECTIONS

Pulse all ingredients in your blender until well combined.
Roll the mixture into 8 balls.

STORING

Divide the cheese balls between airtight containers or Ziploc bags; keep in your refrigerator for up to 3 to 4 days.
For freezing, place the cheese balls in airtight containers. Freeze up to 1 month. Defrost in the refrigerator.

490. Fluffy Almond Bars

(Ready in about 20 minutes | Servings 4)

Per serving: 278 Calories; 30.1g Fat; 2.2g Carbs; 2.2g Protein; 0.1g Fiber

INGREDIENTS

1 cup whipped cream
2 tablespoons almond butter
1/2 cup almonds, chopped

1/4 teaspoon nutmeg
1/4 teaspoon cinnamon
2 tablespoons butter

DIRECTIONS

Beat the cream with nutmeg and cardamom, and spread the mixture on the bottom of a foil-lined baking pan.
Then, mix the regular butter and almond butter. Spread this mixture over the creamed mixture.
Scatter the chopped almonds over the top. Cut into bars.

STORING

Cover the almond bars with foil or plastic wrap to prevent drying out. It will last for about 1 day at room temperature.
Cover with aluminum foil or plastic wrap and refrigerate for two weeks.
To freeze, wrap them tightly with foil or place in a heavy-duty freezer bag. Freeze for up to 3 to 4 months. Enjoy!

491. Pillowy-Soft Chocolate Donuts

(Ready in about 25 minutes | Servings 6)

Per serving: 218 Calories; 20g Fat; 6g Carbs; 4.8g Protein; 0.3g Fiber

INGREDIENTS

1/4 cup coconut oil, room temperature
1/2 cup soft cheese
1/2 teaspoon cinnamon, ground
1/4 teaspoon grated nutmeg
1/3 cup coconut flour

1/3cup almond flour
1/4 cup Swerve
1 ½ teaspoons baking powder
A pinch of coarse sea salt
1 egg

1 teaspoon vanilla extract
For the Frosting:
1 cup whipping cream
1 cup bakers' chocolate chunks, unsweetened

DIRECTIONS

Thoroughly combine the coconut flour, almond flour, Swerve, baking powder, cinnamon, nutmeg, and salt.
In a separate bowl, thoroughly combine the coconut oil with cheese, egg, and vanilla. Beat until everything is well mixed. Add the cheese mixture to the dry flour mixture.
Scrape the batter evenly into a lightly buttered donut pan. Bake in the preheated oven at 365 degrees F approximately 20 minutes.
Meanwhile, warm the cream in a saucepan; then, fold in the chocolate chunks and whisk to combine well. Frost the prepared donuts.

STORING

Place the donuts in three airtight containers or Ziploc bags; keep in the refrigerator for a week.
For freezing, wrap the glazed donuts in foil before packing them into an airtight container. Place the container in the freezer for up to 3 to 4 months.
Thaw the donuts in the refrigerator. You can reheat them in an oven.

492. Egg, Olive and Pancetta Balls

(Ready in about 35 minutes | Servings 6)

Per serving: 174 Calories; 15.2g Fat; 4.3g Carbs; 5.9g Protein; 0.6g Fiber

INGREDIENTS

3 eggs
3 tablespoons aioli
Salt and pepper, to taste
3 slices pancetta, chopped

1/4 cup butter, softened
8 Kalamata olives, pitted and coarsely chopped
2 tablespoons sesame seeds, toasted

DIRECTIONS

Thoroughly combine the eggs, butter, Kalamata olives, aioli, salt and pepper.
Fold in the chopped pancetta. Roll the mixture into balls.
Place the sesame seeds in a shallow dish; roll your balls over the seeds to coat on all sides.

STORING

Place the pancetta balls in airtight containers or Ziploc bags; keep in your refrigerator for 10 days.
To freeze, arrange the pancetta balls on a baking tray in a single layer; freeze for about 2 hours. Transfer the frozen bombs to an airtight container. Freeze for up to 2 months. Bon appétit!

493. Keto Flat Bread with Kulen

(Ready in about 30 minutes | Servings 6)

Per serving: 464 Calories; 33.6g Fat; 5.1g Carbs; 31.1g Protein; 1.2g Fiber

INGREDIENTS

10 ounces soft cheese, melted
3 tablespoons butter
1/2 cup tomato paste

12 large slices of kulen
4 large eggs, beaten
1/2 cup pork rinds, crushed

2 teaspoons baking powder
1/4 teaspoon sea salt
2 ½ cups Romano cheese, shredded

DIRECTIONS

Thoroughly combine the cheese, eggs, butter, pork rinds, baking powder, and salt.
Preheat a frying pan over a moderately-high flame.
Cook your flatbread for about 5 minutes.

STORING

Place your flatbread in airtight containers or Ziploc bags; keep in your refrigerator for up 3 to 4 days.
To freeze, place a sheet of wax paper between each flatbread and stack together. Wrap the tightly in aluminum foil. Freeze up to 1 to 2 months.
Spread the tomato paste over flatbread and top with kulen. Bon appétit!

494. Bacon and Turkey Roulade

(Ready in about 50 minutes | Servings 6)

Per serving: 275 Calories; 9.5g Fat; 1.3g Carbs; 44.5g Protein; 0.5g Fiber

INGREDIENTS

6 slices bacon
6 (4-ounce) turkey fillets
2 tablespoons fresh cilantro, roughly chopped
2 garlic cloves, chopped

Salt and pepper, to taste
1/2 teaspoon chili pepper, chopped
1 tablespoon olive oil
3 tablespoons Dijon mustard

DIRECTIONS

Rub the olive oil and Dijon mustard all over the turkey fillets.
Place the fresh cilantro, garlic, chili pepper, salt, and pepper on each turkey fillet. Roll the fillets in the bacon and secure with a toothpick.
Bake in the preheated oven at 395 degrees F for about 40 minutes.

STORING

Place the turkey roulade in airtight containers or Ziploc bags; keep in your refrigerator for up to 3 to 4 days.
For freezing, place the turkey roulade in airtight containers or heavy-duty freezer bags. Freeze up to 2 to 3 months. Once thawed in the refrigerator, reheat them in a saucepan. Bon appétit!

495. Basic Crustless Pizza

(Ready in about 15 minutes | Servings 4)

Per serving: 266 Calories; 23.6g Fat; 6.6g Carbs; 9g Protein; 1g Fiber

INGREDIENTS

2 bell peppers, chopped
1 cup tomatoes, chopped
1 teaspoon garlic, minced
Salt and pepper, to season

2 tablespoons butter, melted
1/2 cup Colby cheese, shredded
1 3/4 cups soft cheese
2 tablespoons sour cream

DIRECTIONS

In a large pan, melt the butter over medium heat.
Spread the cheese on the bottom and cook for 4 to 5 minutes until it is crispy on top.
Add the sour cream, garlic, bell peppers and tomatoes. Season with salt and pepper, and continue to cook for 2 to 3 minutes more.

496. French-Style Cheese Sauce

(Ready in about 15 minutes | Servings 6)

Per serving: 110 Calories; 10.5g Fat; 0.7g Carbs; 3.4g Protein; 0.2g Fiber

INGREDIENTS

1/3 cup double cream
1/2 teaspoon dried dill
1/2 teaspoon garlic powder
1 teaspoon onion powder
1/3 teaspoon cayenne pepper

1 ½ tablespoons butter
3 tablespoons coconut milk
1/2 cup Roquefort cheese
1/3 cup Brie, grated

DIRECTIONS

Melt the double cream and butter in a sauté pan over a moderate heat. Once hot, add in the cheese along with the other ingredients.
Cook for 4 to 5 minutes, stirring continuously.

STORING

Place your dip in an airtight container and keep in your refrigerator for 3 to 4 days. Enjoy!

497. Autumn Pumpkin Pudding

(Ready in about 15 minutes + chilling time | Servings 6)

Per serving: 368 Calories; 33.7g Fat; 5.6g Carbs; 13.8g Protein; 1.7g Fiber

INGREDIENTS

1 cup double cream
1/2 teaspoon ground ginger
1/4 teaspoon ground cloves
1/2 teaspoon ground cinnamon

1/8 teaspoon grated nutmeg
1/8 teaspoon kosher salt
1 cup cream cheese
3 eggs

1 ¼ cups pumpkin puree
1/2 cup Swerve

DIRECTIONS

Melt the cream, cheese, and Swerve in a sauté pan, whisking frequently.
Whisk the eggs in a mixing bowl.
Add in the eggs, whisking constantly and continue to cook for about 3 minutes, or until the mixture has reduced slightly.
Remove from the heat and fold in the pumpkin puree and spices. Spoon the mixture into serving bowls and place in your refrigerator.

STORING

Spoon your pudding into six airtight containers; keep in your refrigerator for 5 to 6 days.
To freeze, place your pudding in six airtight containers. Freeze up to 1 month. Defrost in the refrigerator. Enjoy!

498. Butter Rum Pancakes

(Ready in about 25 minutes | Servings 6)

Per serving: 243 Calories; 19.6g Fat; 5.5g Carbs; 11g Protein; 0.1g Fiber

INGREDIENTS

6 ounces soft cheese
1/4 cup almond meal
1 ½ teaspoons baking powder
1/2 teaspoon ground cinnamon
6 eggs
4 tablespoons Erythritol

For the Syrup:
1 tablespoon ghee
3/4 cup Erythritol
1 tablespoon rum extract
3/4 cup water

DIRECTIONS

Thoroughly combine the soft cheese, eggs, Erythritol, almond meal, baking powder, and cinnamon.
Brush a frying pan with nonstick cooking oil and cook your pancakes over a moderate flame until the edges begin to brown.
Flip and cook your pancake on the other side for about 3 minutes more.
Whisk the water, ghee, Erythritol, and rum extract in a saucepan over medium heat; let it simmer for 5 to 6 minutes or until thickened and reduced.

STORING

Place your pancakes in airtight containers or Ziploc bags; keep in your refrigerator for up 3 to 4 days.
Place the syrup in a glass jar and keep in your refrigerator for up 3 to 4 days.
To freeze, place a sheet of wax paper between each pancake and stack together. Wrap the tightly in aluminum foil. Freeze up to 1 to 2 months. Bon appétit!

499. Iced Bulletproof Coffee

(Ready in about 10 minutes | Servings 4)

Per serving: 161 Calories; 13.7g Fat; 4.4g Carbs; 0.7g Protein; 0.4g Fiber

INGREDIENTS

4 cups coffee, chilled
4 teaspoons MCT oil
1/4 cup almond milk

1 teaspoon vanilla liquid stevia
1/4 teaspoon ground cinnamon
4 tablespoons coconut whipped cream

DIRECTIONS

Blend the coffee with the remaining ingredients, except for the heavy cream.
Spoon your coffee along with ice cubes into four chilled glasses.

STORING

Spoon your coffee into four airtight containers and keep in your refrigerator for up to 2 days.
Spoon your coffee into airtight containers and store in your freezer for a few weeks.
Serve topped with coconut whipped cream. Enjoy!

500. Puffy Pancetta and Cheese Muffins

(Ready in about 25 minutes | Servings 5)

Per serving: 240 Calories; 15.3g Fat; 7g Carbs; 16.1g Protein; 0.2g Fiber

INGREDIENTS

4 slices pancetta
1/2 cup almond flour
1 teaspoon baking powder

1 cup goat cheese, diced
Sea salt and black pepper, to taste
4 eggs, beaten

DIRECTIONS

Preheat a nonstick skillet over a moderately-high heat. Cook the pancetta for about 4 minutes until it is browned; place the pancetta on paper towels.

Chop the pancetta and add in the remaining ingredients; stir to combine. Now, spoon the batter into paper-lined muffin cups (3/4 full). Bake in the preheated oven at 395 degrees F for 15 to 17 minutes.

STORING

Place your muffins in airtight containers and refrigerate for a week.

To freeze, place your muffins on a baking tray and freeze for 2 hours. Now, place them in airtight containers. They can be frozen for 2 to 3 months. Bon appétit!

MORE KETO RECIPES

501. Peanut Butter Fudge

(Ready in about 3 hours | Servings 8)

Per serving: 180 Calories; 18.3g Fat; 4.5g Carbs; 1g Protein; 1.1g Fiber

INGREDIENTS

3/4 cup peanut butter
1/4 cup Swerve
1/8 teaspoon salt
3 tablespoons coconut butter, melted

1 teaspoon vanilla
3 tablespoons cocoa powder, unsweetened
1/2 cup ghee

1/3 cup almond milk
1 tablespoon liquid Stevia

DIRECTIONS

Melt the peanut butter and ghee in your microwave.
Add in the almond milk, 1/4 cup Swerve, and salt; stir to combine well and scrape the base into a foil-lined baking pan.
Refrigerate for about 3 hours or until set.
Now, make the sauce by whisking the other ingredients until well combined. Spread the sauce over your fudge. Cut into squares.

STORING

Cover your fudge with foil or plastic wrap to prevent drying out; keep in your refrigerator for a week.
To freeze, wrap your fudge tightly with foil or place in a heavy-duty freezer bag. Freeze for up to 4 to 6 months. Enjoy!

502. Rich New Orleans Jambalaya

(Ready in about 35 minutes | Servings 6)

Per serving: 427 Calories; 26.2g Fat; 7.6g Carbs; 35.2g Protein; 4.1g Fiber

INGREDIENTS

1 parsnip, chopped
1 teaspoon cayenne pepper
1 tablespoon Creole spice mix
4 cups roasted vegetable broth
1/4 cup flaxseed meal

1 (14-ounce) can diced tomatoes
1 pound pork butt, cubed
8 ounces andouille sausage, sliced
1 onion, chopped
1 ½ tablespoons lard

1 teaspoon gumbo file
1 cup boiling water
1 green bell peppers, deveined and thinly sliced
Sea salt and black pepper, to taste

DIRECTIONS

In a soup pot, melt the lard over a moderately-high heat. Sear the pork and sausage until just browned on all sides and set aside.
Stir in the onion and continue to cook until tender and translucent. Add in the remaining ingredients, except for the flaxseed meal, and bring it to a boil.
Turn to a simmer and continue to cook for a further 20 minutes.
Afterwards, add in the flax seed meal and let it simmer for 4 to 5 minutes or until the liquid has thickened.

STORING

Spoon your Jambalaya into airtight containers; keep in your refrigerator for up to 3 to 4 days.
For freezing, place your Jambalaya in airtight containers or heavy-duty freezer bags. It will maintain the best quality for about 5 months. Defrost in the refrigerator. Enjoy!

503. Perfect Family Steak

(Ready in about 20 minutes + marinating time | Servings 6)

Per serving: 350 Calories; 17.3g Fat; 2.1g Carbs; 42.7g Protein; 0.4g Fiber

INGREDIENTS

1 ½ tablespoons canola oil
2 tablespoons coconut aminos
2 garlic cloves, minced

1/2 cup white onions, chopped
1 tablespoon white vinegar
1/4 cup dry red wine

2 pounds skirt steak
1/2 teaspoon ground bay leaf
Salt and pepper, to taste

DIRECTIONS

Combine the oil, coconut aminos, garlic, onions, vinegar, and red wine in a ceramic dish. Add in the steak, ground bay leaf, salt, and pepper. Let it marinate overnight.
Sear the steak in a nonstick skillet over a moderately-high flame. Sear the steak for 8 to 11 minutes per side.

STORING

Cut the steak into six pieces; divide the pieces between six airtight containers; keep in your refrigerator for up to 3 to 4 days.
For freezing, place the steaks in airtight containers or heavy-duty freezer bags. Freeze up to 2 to 3 months. Defrost in the refrigerator. Bon appétit!

504. Mexican Sausage and Vegetable Bake

(Ready in about 30 minutes | Servings 4)

Per serving: 424 Calories; 32.4g Fat; 6.8g Carbs; 23.7g Protein; 2.9g Fiber

INGREDIENTS

1 tablespoon lard, softened
1 onion, sliced
1 cup broccoli florets
1 parsnip, sliced

1 bell pepper, sliced
1 chili pepper, finely chopped
1 teaspoon garlic, finely chopped
Salt and pepper, to season

1 ¼ cups vegetable broth
4 Mexican sausages, sliced
1 celery stalk, chopped

DIRECTIONS

Melt the lard in a frying pan over a moderately-high heat. Cook the sausage until no longer pink and reserve.
In the pan drippings, cook the onion, broccoli, parsnip, celery, peppers, and garlic until they've softened.
Season with salt and pepper to taste and spoon the mixture into a lightly buttered baking dish. Nestle the sausages within the sautéed vegetables.
Pour in the vegetable broth and bake in the preheated oven at 360 degrees F for 15 minutes.

STORING

Slice the casserole into four pieces. Divide the pieces between airtight containers; it will last for 3 to 4 days in the refrigerator.
For freezing, place each portion in a separate heavy-duty freezer bag. Freeze up to 2 to 3 months. Defrost in the microwave or refrigerator.
Bon appétit!

505. Beef Salad Bowl

(Ready in about 15 minutes | Servings 4)

Per serving: 404 Calories; 32.9g Fat; 8g Carbs; 12.8g Protein; 6g Fiber

INGREDIENTS

1/2 pound flank steak, cut into strips
1 cucumber, sliced
1 celery, sliced
1 tablespoon fresh basil, snipped
1 poblano chili, minced

Sea salt and ground black pepper, to taste
2 tablespoons olive oil
1 teaspoon coconut aminos
2 tablespoons lime juice, freshly squeezed

1 tablespoon fresh lime juice
1/4 cup sesame seeds, lightly toasted
1 shallot, peeled and sliced
1/2 teaspoon ginger-garlic paste
2 avocados, pitted, peeled and sliced

DIRECTIONS

In a large frying pan, heat the oil over medium-low flame. Sauté the shallot until tender or about 3 minutes.
Add in the steak and cook for 5 to 6 minutes per side. Season the steak with salt and pepper.

STORING

Divide the steaks between four airtight containers or Ziploc bags; keep in your refrigerator for up to 3 to 4 days.
For freezing, place the steaks in airtight containers or heavy-duty freezer bags. Freeze up to 3 months. Defrost in the refrigerator. Bon appétit
Toss the remaining igredients in a bowl and top your salad with steak. Enjoy!

506. Middle Eastern Brussels Sprouts

(Ready in about 20 minutes +marinating time | Servings 4)

Per serving: 321 Calories; 14g Fat; 7.3g Carbs; 36.7g Protein; 2g Fiber

INGREDIENTS

1 pound tenderloin, cut into small pieces
1 teaspoon garlic, finely chopped
1 cup Brussels sprouts, halved

1 Italian pepper, chopped
1 chili pepper, deseeded and chopped
1 tablespoon coconut aminos
2 tablespoons olive oil

1 onion, chopped
1 tablespoon lime juice
Sea salt and black pepper, to taste
1 teaspoon Za'atar

DIRECTIONS

Place the tenderloin, coconut aminos, lime juice, salt, salt, black pepper and Za'atar seasoning in a ceramic bowl. Let it marinate in your refrigerator a couple of hours.
Heat the oil in a frying pan over a medium-high heat. Sear the steaks for about 5 minutes on each side.
Add in the onions, garlic, Brussels sprouts, and peppers; turn the heat to a simmer. Continue to cook for about 15 minutes until thoroughly cooked.

STORING

Place the steak and vegetables in airtight containers; keep in your refrigerator for up to 3 to 4 days.
For freezing, place the steak and vegetables in airtight containers or heavy-duty freezer bags. Freeze up to 2 to 3 months. Defrost in the refrigerator. Bon appétit!

507. Thai-Style Sausage and Vegetable Bowl

(Ready in about 40 minutes | Servings 4)

Per serving: 250 Calories; 17.5g Fat; 5.4g Carbs; 6.8g Protein; 2.1g Fiber

INGREDIENTS

4 beef sausages, sliced
1 cup tomato Nam Prik, no sugar added
2 tablespoons sesame oil
1 medium onion, chopped
1 tablespoon lemongrass, sliced

Salt and pepper, to taste
1 Bird's eye chili, deveined and chopped
1 parsnip, chopped
1 ½ cups chicken broth
1/4 cup Marsala wine

1 teaspoon fresh turmeric
2 rosemary sprigs
1 teaspoon garlic, minced
1 green bell pepper, deveined and chopped

DIRECTIONS

Ina wok, heat the sesame oil over a moderately-high heat. Sear the sausage for about 3 minutes or until no longer pink.
Add in the onion, garlic, peppers, parsnip, lemongrass, salt, and pepper. Cook an additional 6 to 7 minutes.
Add in the remaining ingredients and bring it to a rapid boil. Reduce the heat to a simmer. Continue to simmer for 20 to 25 minutes.

STORING

Place the sausage and vegetables in airtight containers; keep in your refrigerator for up to 3 to 4 days.
For freezing, place the sausage and vegetables in airtight containers or heavy-duty freezer bags. Freeze up to 2 to 3 months. Defrost in the refrigerator. Bon appétit!

508. Chinese-Style Fish Chowder

(Ready in about 30 minutes | Servings 6)

Per serving: 165 Calories; 5.5g Fat; 4g Carbs; 25.4g Protein; 0.6g Fiber

INGREDIENTS

2 tablespoons sesame oil
1 celery rib, diced
1 bell pepper, deveined and sliced
1 chili pepper, deveined and sliced
1/2 cup Thai shallots, sliced

1 ¼ pounds cod fish fillets, cut into small chunks
3/4 cup full-fat milk
1 tablespoon galangal, chopped
1/2 teaspoon cayenne pepper

1 garlic clove, smashed
1 tablespoon oyster sauce
2 ½ cups fish stock
1 teaspoon Five-spice powder

DIRECTIONS

In a heavy-bottomed pot, heat the oil over a moderately-high flame. Sauté the shallots until they are just tender and fragrant.
Add in the remaining ingredients, except fish and milk. Continue to cook, covered, for about 15 minutes.
Add in the fish and continue to cook, partially covered, an additional 13 minutes or until the fish is opaque. Add in the milk, stir, and remove from heat.

STORING

Spoon the chowder into six airtight containers or Ziploc bags; keep in your refrigerator for up to 3 to 4 days.
For freezing, place the chowder in airtight containers. It will maintain the best quality for about 4 months. Defrost in the refrigerator. Bon appétit!

509. Coconut Ice Cream

(Ready in about 10 minutes + chilling time | Servings 4)

Per serving: 260 Calories; 24.3g Fat; 6.5g Carbs; 2.5g Protein; 2.7g Fiber

INGREDIENTS

1 ¼ cups coconut milk
17 drops liquid Monk fruit
1/2 cup coconut flakes

1/2 teaspoon xanthan gum
1/3 cup double cream

DIRECTIONS

Thoroughly combine all ingredients, except for the xanthan gum, using your electric mixer.
Add in the xanthan gum, mixing constantly, until the mixture has thickened.
Prepare your ice cream in a machine following the manufacturer's instructions.

STORING

Spoon your ice cream in an airtight container. Store your ice cream in the very back of the freezer. Freeze up to 2 to 4 months. Bon appétit!

510. Almond and Blueberry Shake

(Ready in about 2 hours | Servings 2)

Per serving: 371 Calories; 37.8g Fat; 7.1g Carbs; 3.4g Protein; 0.3g Fiber

INGREDIENTS

16 blueberries, frozen
2 teaspoons instant coffee
1/4 cup cold water
1 cup coconut milk

2 tablespoons whipped cream
4 drops liquid Monk fruit
1 tablespoon cacao butter

DIRECTIONS

Combine the instant coffee, Monk fruit, cacao butter and cold water. Shake for about 30 seconds.
Divide the frozen blueberries between two glasses. Pour the coffee mixture over them. Add in the coconut milk.

STORING

Spoon your coffee into airtight containers and keep in your refrigerator for up to 2 days.
Spoon your coffee into airtight containers and store in your freezer for a few weeks.
Serve topped with coconut whipped cream.

511. Mustard Bacon Chips

(Ready in about 15 minutes | Servings 6)

Per serving: 409 Calories; 31.6g Fat; 1.1g Carbs; 28g Protein; 0g Fiber

INGREDIENTS

1 tablespoon deli mustard
1 pound bacon, cut into small squares

1 tablespoon cayenne pepper

DIRECTIONS

Toss all ingredients in a rimmed baking pan.
Bake in the preheated oven at 365 degrees F for about 15 minutes.

STORING

Place the bacon chips in an airtight container or wrap tightly with heavy-duty aluminum foil; transfer to your refrigerator; they should be consumed within 3 to 4 days.
To freeze, place in an airtight container and freeze up to 2 to 3 months. It has been thawed in the refrigerator and can be kept for an additional 3 to 4 days in the refrigerator before serving. Enjoy!

512. Creole Seafood Bowl

(Ready in about 10 minutes | Servings 4)

Per serving: 260 Calories; 13.6g Fat; 5.9g Carbs; 28.1g Protein; 4g Fiber

INGREDIENTS

1 bell pepper, sliced
1/2 pound shrimp, deveined
1/2 pound sea scallops, halved horizontally
2 cloves garlic, minced
Sea salt and black pepper, to taste
1 teaspoon Creole spice mix

1/2 cup black olives, pitted
1 head of Romaine lettuce, torn into bite-sized pieces
1/2 tablespoon Dijon mustard
1/4 cup olive oil
2 tablespoons lime juice
1 cup cherry tomatoes, halved

DIRECTIONS

Parboil the seafood in a pot of a lightly salted water for about 2 minutes; rinse and place in a bowl.

STORING

Place the prepared seafood in airtight containers or Ziploc bags; keep in your refrigerator for up 3 to 4 days.
For freezing, arrange the prepared seafood in a single layer on a baking tray; place in the freezer for about 15 minutes, or until it begins to harden.
Transfer frozen seafood to heavy-duty freezer bags. Freeze up to 3 months. Defrost in your refrigerator.

513. Flank Steak with Eggs

(Ready in about 30 minutes | Servings 6)

Per serving: 429 Calories; 27.8g Fat; 3.2g Carbs; 39.1g Protein; 0.6g Fiber

INGREDIENTS

2 tablespoons lard, melted
1 ½ pounds flank steak, cut into strips
Salt and black pepper, to taste

1/2 teaspoon cayenne pepper
1/2 cup onions, finely chopped
2 garlic cloves, minced

2 Spanish peppers, chopped
6 eggs

DIRECTIONS

In a nonstick skillet, melt the lard over a moderately-high heat. Sear the steak for 10 minutes, stirring frequently to ensure even cooking. Season with salt, black pepper, and cayenne pepper and set aside.

In the same skillet, sauté the onion, garlic, and peppers for about 4 minutes or until they are tender and fragrant. Add the meat back to the skillet.

Create six indentions in the sautéed mixture. Crack an egg into each indention. Cover and continue to cook for about 5 minutes or until the eggs are set.

STORING

Divide your dish between airtight containers. Refrigerate for up to 3 days.

For freezing, place each serving into individual plastic wrap and squeeze as much air as possible. Place them inside an airtight container and freeze up to 6 months.

Thaw your dish before reheating in the microwave. Enjoy!

514. Fluffy Tuna Pâté

(Ready in about 10 minutes | Servings 6)

Per serving: 384 Calories; 20.4g Fat; 2.5g Carbs; 45.9g Protein; 0.8g Fiber

INGREDIENTS

6 ounces tuna in oil, drained
1 teaspoon stone-ground mustard
1 tablespoon fresh coriander, chopped

A bunch of fresh scallions
1/2 cup soft cheese
1/2 teaspoon curry paste

2 ounces walnuts, ground

DIRECTIONS

Process all ingredinets in your blender or food processor until smooth and creamy.

STORING

Place the tuna pâté in an airtight container; keep in the refrigerator for a week.

You can freeze them in silicone molds. Once frozen, unmold and put some wax paper between each little pâté to prevent them from sticking to each other.

Now, place them in a freezer-safe container for up to 3 months. Thaw in your refrigerator.

515. Blade Roast with Cheese

(Ready in about 8 hours | Servings 6)

Per serving: 397 Calories; 31.4g Fat; 3.9g Carbs; 23.5g Protein; 0.5g Fiber

INGREDIENTS

1 ½ pounds boneless blade roast
2 tablespoons olive oil
1/4 cup red wine

1 cup chicken stock
1 teaspoon garlic, minced
1 teaspoon coriander seeds

1/2 teaspoon mustard seeds
6 ounces goat cheese, crumbled
1 onion, chopped

DIRECTIONS

In a frying pan, heat the oil over medium-high heat. Cook the onion until tender and translucent.

Add in the garlic and continue to sauté for a further 30 seconds; transfer the sautéed mixture to your slow cooker.

Sear the beef until golden-brown and transfer to the slow cooker. Add in the remaining ingredients, except for cheese.

Cover and cook on Low heat setting for about 7 hours or until the meat has softened.

STORING

Cut the beef into thin pieces using a knife, slicing against the grain; divide the pieces between six airtight containers; keep in your refrigerator for up to 3 to 4 days.

For freezing, place the beef in airtight containers or heavy-duty freezer bags. Freeze up to 2 to 3 months. Defrost in the refrigerator. Serve topped with goat cheese.

516. Soft Cheese and Parsley Balls

(Ready in about 10 minutes + chilling time | Servings 6)

Per serving: 108 Calories; 9g Fat; 2.2g Carbs; 4.8g Protein; 0.3g Fiber

INGREDIENTS

1/4 teaspoon white vinegar
Salt and pepper, to taste
1/2 cup fresh parsley, minced

1 cup soft cheese
3 tablespoons butter

DIRECTIONS

Mix all ingredients, except for the parsley, in your blender or food processor.
Place the mixture in the refrigerator until firm.
Shape the mixture into bite-sized balls and roll them in the parsley until coated on all sides.

STORING

Divide the soft cheese balls between airtight containers or Ziploc bags; keep in your refrigerator for up to 3 to 4 days.
For freezing, place the soft cheese balls in airtight containers. Freeze up to 1 month. Defrost in the refrigerator. Enjoy!

517. Rum Spiked Chocolates

(Ready in about 25 minutes + chilling time | Servings 10)

Per serving: 119 Calories; 11.7g Fat; 5.2g Carbs; 1.1g Protein; 4g Fiber

INGREDIENTS

1 cup coconut flour
1/2 stick cold butter
1 ½ cups whipped cream
8 ounces chocolate chips, unsweetened
1/2 cup almond meal

1/4 teaspoon cinnamon
1 teaspoon pure vanilla extract
1 tablespoon rum
A pinch of grated nutmeg
2 packets stevia

DIRECTIONS

Begin by preheating your oven to 340 degrees F.
Mix the coconut flour, almond meal, nutmeg, stevia, cinnamon, vanilla, and rum in your blender or food processor.
Cut in the cold butter and mix again.
Press the mixture into molds. Bake for about 10 minutes and place on a wire rack.
Heat the double cream over medium-low flame; once it is warmed, fold in the chocolate and stir to combine well. Spread the filling over the base and place in your refrigerator.

STORING

Place the chocolates in airtight containers or Ziploc bags; keep in your refrigerator for 3 weeks to 1 month.
To freeze, arrange the chocolates on a baking tray in a single layer; freeze for about 2 hours. Transfer the frozen chocolates to an airtight container. Freeze for up to a month. Bon appétit!

518. Skinny Garlic Portobellos

(Ready in about 10 minutes | Servings 4)

Per serving: 75 Calories; 5.2g Fat; 3.3g Carbs; 2.9g Protein; 1.1g Fiber

INGREDIENTS

1 pound Portobello mushrooms, sliced
2 cloves garlic, minced
1 tablespoon white wine

Salt and black pepper, to taste
2 tablespoons butter

DIRECTIONS

In a wok or large saucepan, melt the butter over a moderately-high flame. Sauté the garlic for a minute or so until aromatic.
Add in the mushrooms and continue to sauté them for 3 to 4 minutes until they are caramelized.
Add in the wine, salt, and pepper and continue to cook for 3 to 4 minutes more until heated through.

STORING

Place the mushrooms in airtight containers; keep in your refrigerator for 3 to 5 days.
Place your mushrooms in a plastic freezer bag; they will maintain the best quality for 10 to 12 months.

519. Hot and Spicy Mexican Wings

(Ready in about 50 minutes | Servings 6)

Per serving: 236 Calories; 13.5g Fat; 6g Carbs; 19.4g Protein; 1.7g Fiber

INGREDIENTS

12 chicken wings
Salt and red pepper, to taste
For the Dip:
1 cup tomatillos, peeled
2 tablespoons lime juice, freshly squeezed

1 Habanero pepper, minced
2 tablespoons coriander, minced
4 ripe tomatoes
1 shallot, finely chopped

DIRECTIONS

Toss the chicken wings with salt and red pepper; brush them with a nonstick spray.
Bake in the preheated oven at 396 degrees F for 45 to 50 minutes or until they're crispy.
In your blender, process the remaining ingredients to make the sauce.

STORING

Place the chicken wings in airtight containers or Ziploc bags; keep in your refrigerator for up 3 to 4 days.
For freezing, place the chicken wings in airtight containers or heavy-duty freezer bags. Freeze up to 3 months. Once thawed in the refrigerator, heat in the preheated oven at 375 degrees F for 20 to 25 minutes or until heated through.
Place the tomato dip in a glass jar with an airtight lid; keep in your refrigerator for 3 to 4 days. Enjoy!

520. Coconut Blueberry Crisp

(Ready in about 30 minutes | Servings 8)

Per serving: 152 Calories; 11.8g Fat; 6.2g Carbs; 2.5g Protein; 1.5g Fiber

INGREDIENTS

2 ½ cups blueberries, cored and sliced
1/2 cup coconut flour
3/4 cup Swerve
2 eggs, whisked

5 tablespoons butter, melted
1/2 tablespoon lime juice
1/3 teaspoon xanthan gum
3/4 cup almond meal

DIRECTIONS

Preheat your oven to 365 degrees F. Lightly oil a baking pan with a cooking spray.
Arrange the blueberries on the bottom of the baking pan. Drizzle with lime juice and xanthan gum.
Mix the almond meal, coconut flour, xylitol and eggs until the mixture resembles coarse meal. Spread the mixture over the blueberries.
Drizzle melted butter over the topping. Bake for 25 to 30 minutes.

STORING

Place the blueberry crisp in airtight containers; keep in your refrigerator for 4 to 5 days.
To freeze, place the blueberry crisp in airtight containers or Ziploc bags; it can be frozen for 3 months. Defrost in your microwave for a few minutes. Bon appétit!

521. Coconut Cream Mocha Espresso

(Ready in about 10 minutes + chilling time | Servings 6)

Per serving: 218 Calories; 24.7g Fat; 1.1g Carbs; 0.4g Protein; 0g Fiber

INGREDIENTS

1 teaspoon instant espresso powder
1/2 teaspoon pure coconut extract
1/2 teaspoon pure vanilla extract
3 tablespoons erythritol

A pinch of salt
4 ounces coconut oil
5 ounces coconut cream

DIRECTIONS

Melt the coconut oil in a double boiler; add in the remaining ingredients. Remove from heat and stir to combine well.
Pour into a silicone mold and place in your freezer.

522. Buttery Greens with Cheddar Cheese

(Ready in about 25 minutes | Servings 5)

Per serving: 160 Calories; 10g Fat; 7.1g Carbs; 11g Protein; 6g Fiber

INGREDIENTS

1 tablespoon olive oil
1 teaspoon garlic, minced
1 red onion, finely chopped
2 pounds mustard greens, trimmed and torn into pieces
1/4 cup vegetable broth

1 tablespoon white vinegar
1 teaspoon red pepper flakes
Sea salt and ground black pepper, to taste
1 cup Cheddar cheese, shredded

DIRECTIONS

In a saucepan, heat the oil over a moderately-high flame. Sauté the garlic and onions for 2 to 3 minutes or until fragrant.
Stir in the mustard greens and vegetable broth; continue to cook until the leaves have wilted and all liquid has evaporated, about 15 minutes.
Now, add in the vinegar, red pepper, salt and black pepper. Remove from heat.

STORING

Place the mustard greens in airtight containers; keep in your refrigerator for 3 to 5 days.
For freezing, place the mustard greens in a freezable container; they can be frozen for 4 to 5 months.
Top with the Cheddar cheese and reheat until melted. Enjoy!

523. Chicken Salad with Avocado

(Ready in about 20 minutes | Servings 4)

Per serving: 408 Calories; 34.2g Fat; 4.8g Carbs; 22.7g Protein; 3.1g Fiber

INGREDIENTS

2 chicken breasts
Sea salt and red pepper, to taste
1/2 teaspoon deli mustard

1/3 cup extra-virgin olive oil
1 tablespoon soy sauce
1/2 teaspoon Italian seasoning mix

1 tablespoon lemon juice
1 avocado, pitted and sliced
2 egg yolks

DIRECTIONS

Toss the chicken breasts with salt, red pepper and Italian seasoning mix. Cook the chicken on the preheated grill for 4 minutes per side.
Cut the chicken into the strips.

STORING

Place the chicken in airtight containers or Ziploc bags; keep in your refrigerator for 3 to 4 days.
For freezing, place the chicken in airtight containers or heavy-duty freezer bags. It will maintain the best quality for about 4 months. Defrost in the refrigerator.
Place the avocado slices in 4 serving plates. Make the dressing by whisking the remaining ingredients.
Dress your salad and serve!

524. Sausage with Spicy Tomato Sauce

(Ready in about 15 minutes | Servings 4)

Per serving: 156 Calories; 4.2g Fat; 5.1g Carbs; 16.2g Protein; 0.9g Fiber

INGREDIENTS

4 turkey sausages, sliced
1 cup cherry tomatoes, chopped
2 cloves garlic, smashed

2 teaspoons olive oil, at room temperature
1 cup Italian peppers, chopped
1 shallot, diced

2 tablespoons fresh parsley, minced
3 teaspoons lemon juice
1/4 cup white wine

DIRECTIONS

In a nonstick skillet, heat the olive oil over moderately-high heat.
Then, sear the sausage until well browned on all sides; pour in the wine and continue to cook for about 4 minutes. Set aside.
Make the salsa by blending the remaining ingredients.

STORING

Place the sausage in airtight containers or Ziploc bags; keep in your refrigerator for up 3 to 4 days.
For freezing, place the sausage in airtight containers or heavy-duty freezer bags. Freeze up to 3 months. Once thawed in the refrigerator, heat in the preheated oven at 375 degrees F for 20 to 25 minutes or until heated through.
Place the tomato dip in a glass jar with an airtight lid; keep in your refrigerator for 3 to 4 days. Enjoy!

525. Chicken with Mustard Sauce

(Ready in about 25 minutes | Servings 4)

Per serving: 311 Calories; 16.9g Fat; 2.1g Carbs; 33.6g Protein; 0.9g Fiber

INGREDIENTS

1 pound chicken breasts
Salt and red pepper, to season
1 tablespoon olive oil

1/2 cup onions, chopped
2 garlic cloves, minced
1/2 cup low-sodium chicken broth

1/2 cup whipped cream
2 tablespoons deli mustard
1/2 cup fresh chives, chopped

DIRECTIONS

Rub the chicken with salt and pepper.
Heat the oil in a frying pan over a moderately-high heat. Sear the chicken for about 8 minutes and set aside.
Then, sauté the onion and garlic for about 3 minutes until aromatic.
Pour in the broth and cook until the liquid has reduced by half. Stir in the whipped cream and mustard.
Add the sauce and chives to the reserved chicken.

STORING

Place the chicken in airtight containers or Ziploc bags; keep in your refrigerator for up 3 to 4 days.
For freezing, place the chicken in airtight containers or heavy-duty freezer bags. Freeze up to 3 months.
Once thawed in the refrigerator, heat in the preheated oven at 375 degrees F for 20 to 25 minutes or until heated through. Bon appétit!

526. Chicken Sausage with Cabbage

(Ready in about 50 minutes | Servings 4)

Per serving: 189 Calories; 12g Fat; 6.6g Carbs; 9.4g Protein; 3.1g Fiber

INGREDIENTS

4 chicken sausages, sliced
1 pound cabbage
1 tablespoon lard, at room temperature

Salt and pepper, to season
1 cup vegetable broth
1/2 cup whipped cream

6 ounces Cotija cheese, grated
1 onion, chopped

DIRECTIONS

Begin by preheating your oven to 365 degrees F. Melt the lard in a saucepan; once hot, cook the sausage until no longer pink and reserve.
Then, in the pan drippings, sauté the onion and cabbage until they've softened. Add in the salt, pepper, and vegetable broth and continue to cook for about 3 minutes or until cooked through.
Place the sautéed cabbage in a lightly buttered casserole dish. Top with the reserved sausage.
Cover with foil and bake in the preheated oven for 40 to 45 minutes.

STORING

Slice the casserole into four pieces. Divide the pieces between airtight containers; it will last for 3 to 4 days in the refrigerator.
For freezing, place each portion in a separate heavy-duty freezer bag. Freeze up to 2 to 3 months. Defrost in the microwave or refrigerator.
In a bowl, mix the whipped cream with the Cotija cheese. Pour this mixture over the sausage and bake an additional 5 minutes or until hot and bubbly. Enjoy!

527. Turkey and Vegetable Kebabs

(Ready in about 30 minutes | Servings 6)

Per serving: 293 Calories; 13.8g Fat; 5.7g Carbs; 34.5g Protein; 1g Fiber

INGREDIENTS

1 cup red onion, cut into wedges
1 ½ cups grape tomatoes, sliced
1 tablespoon fresh cilantro, chopped

1 ½ pounds turkey breast, cubed
1 tablespoon Italian seasoning mix
1 cup bell peppers, sliced

1 cup zucchini, cut into thick slices
2 tablespoons olive oil

DIRECTIONS

Toss the turkey breast with olive oil and Italian seasoning mix. Thread the turkey onto skewers, alternating them with the vegetables.
Continue until all the ingredients are used up.
Grill the kebabs for about 10 minutes, turning them occasionally to ensure even cooking. Toss the kebabs with the cilantro.

STORING

Wrap your kebabs in foil before packing them into airtight containers; keep in your refrigerator for up to 3 to 4 days.
For freezing, place your kebabs in airtight containers or heavy-duty freezer bags. Freeze up to 2 to 3 months. Defrost in the refrigerator.
Bon appétit!

528. Cheese and Broccoli Bake

(Ready in about 25 minutes | Servings 3)

Per serving: 195 Calories; 12.7g Fat; 6.7g Carbs; 11.6g Protein; 7.1g Fiber

INGREDIENTS

3 tablespoons olive oil
1/2 teaspoon mustard powder
Sea salt and black pepper, to season
2 ounces Colby cheese, shredded

1 onion, minced
2 cloves garlic, finely chopped
1/2 cup whipped cream
1/2 teaspoon curry paste

1/2 pound broccoli florets
3 eggs, well-beaten

DIRECTIONS

Start by preheating your oven to 320 degrees F.
Melt the olive oil in a sauté pan over a moderately-high heat. Once hot, sauté the onion and garlic until they are tender and fragrant.
Add in the broccoli florets and continue to cook until they've softened. Spoon the mixture into a lightly buttered baking dish.
In another bowl, whisk the eggs, cream, curry paste, mustard powder, salt, and black pepper.
Pour the cream/egg mixture over the broccoli mixture. Bake for 20 to minutes or until thoroughly cooked.

STORING

Slice the casserole into three pieces. Divide the pieces between airtight containers; it will last for 3 to 4 days in the refrigerator.
For freezing, place each portion in a separate heavy-duty freezer bag. Freeze up to 2 to 3 months. Defrost in the microwave or refrigerator.
Top with the cheese and place under the preheated broiler for about 5 minutes or until hot and bubbly. Enjoy!

529. Bok Choy with Celery and Bacon

(Ready in about 20 minutes | Servings 6)

Per serving: 259 Calories; 18.1g Fat; 6.6g Carbs; 15.5g Protein; 1g Fiber

INGREDIENTS

1 tablespoon butter, at room temperature
1/2 pound bacon, chopped
1 cup chicken bone broth
1/2 teaspoon red pepper flakes

1 celery stalk, finely chopped
1 garlic clove, minced
1 pound Bok choy, shredded

DIRECTIONS

Melt the butter in a wok over a moderately-high heat. Now, cook Bok choy, celery, and garlic until they've softened.
Add in the remaining ingredients and turn the heat to a simmer. Let it simmer, covered, for 10 to 12 minutes longer.

STORING

Place the Bok choy with bacon in airtight containers or Ziploc bags; keep in your refrigerator for up to 3 to 4 days.
For freezing, place the Bok choy with bacon in airtight containers or heavy-duty freezer bags. Freeze up to 2 to 3 months. Defrost in the refrigerator. Bon appétit!

530. Vegetable and Mushroom Medley

(Ready in about 30 minutes | Servings 4)

Per serving: 133 Calories; 3.7g Fat; 6.7g Carbs; 14g Protein; 1g Fiber

INGREDIENTS

1/2 pound button mushrooms, chopped
1 cup onion, chopped
Salt and pepper, to taste
1/2 teaspoon ground allspice

1 teaspoon ground bay leaves
1/3 cup fresh parsley, chopped
1 teaspoon jalapeno pepper, finely minced
2 garlic cloves, minced

2 celery stalks, chopped
1 tablespoon lard, melted
3 cups vegetable broth
1 cup tomato puree

DIRECTIONS

In a heavy-bottomed pot, melt the lard over medium-high heat. Cook the onion, jalapeno pepper, garlic, celery, and mushrooms for 7 to 8 minutes.
Add in the vegetable broth, tomato puree, and spices, and bring to a boil. Turn the heat to a simmer; cover and let it cook for about 20 minutes.

STORING

Spoon the medley into four airtight containers or Ziploc bags; keep in your refrigerator for up to 3 to 4 days.
For freezing, place the medley in airtight containers. Freeze up to 4 to 6 months. Defrost in the refrigerator. Bon appétit!

531. Baked Breaded Chicken

(Ready in about 30 minutes + marinating time | Servings 6)

Per serving: 420 Calories; 28.2g Fat; 5g Carbs; 35.3g Protein; 0.8g Fiber

INGREDIENTS

1/2 stick butter, melted
2 cloves garlic, minced
2 eggs
1/4 cup flax seeds, ground
Salt and black pepper, to taste

2 tablespoons coconut aminos
3 teaspoons red wine vinegar
1 pound chicken, cut into strips
1/2 teaspoon Sriracha sauce
2 tablespoons marinara sauce

DIRECTIONS

Start by preheating your oven to 400 degrees F. Brush the bottom and sides of a casserole dish with a cooking spray.
Toss the chicken with the butter, salt, pepper, coconut aminos, vinegar, Sriracha sauce, marinara sauce and garlic. Let it marinate in your refrigerator at least 1 hour.
In a mixing bowl, whisk the eggs with the ground flax seeds. Dip each chicken strip in the egg mixture. Transfer the chicken strips to the casserole dish.
Bake for about 25 minutes, turning once or twice. Place under the preheated broiler until the top is crispy.

STORING

Place the breaded chicken in airtight containers or Ziploc bags; keep in your refrigerator for up 1 to 2 days.
For freezing, place the breaded chicken in airtight containers or heavy-duty freezer bags. Freeze up to 2 to 3 months. Defrost in the refrigerator or microwave. Enjoy!

532. Chinese-Style Pork Shoulder

(Ready in about 1 hour 15 minutes | Servings 8)

Per serving: 369 Calories; 20.2g Fat; 2.9g Carbs; 41.3g Protein; 1.2g Fiber

INGREDIENTS

2 pounds pork shoulder, cut into strips
Salt and Sichuan pepper, to taste
1/2 teaspoon celery seeds
1 cup coconut milk, unsweetened
1 ½ cups chicken broth
1 tablespoon sesame oil
1/2 teaspoon mustard powder

1/2 cup onion, chopped
1 bell pepper, deveined and chopped
1 chili pepper, deveined and chopped
1 teaspoon garlic, minced
1/2 tablespoon turmeric powder
1 cup tomato puree

DIRECTIONS

Heat the sesame oil in a wok over a moderately-high heat. Toss the pork with salt, pepper and mustard powder.
Sear the pork for 8 to 10 minutes, stirring continuously to ensure even cooking.
Now, sauté the onion, garlic, and turmeric powder in the pan drippings. Place the mixture into the slow cooker.
Add in the remaining ingredients and continue to cook, covered, for 1 hour 30 minutes on Low setting.

STORING

Place the pork in airtight containers or Ziploc bags; keep in your refrigerator for 3 to 4 days.
For freezing, wrap the pork tightly with heavy-duty aluminum foil or freezer wrap. It will maintain the best quality for 2 to 3 months. Defrost in the refrigerator. Enjoy!

533. Cheesy Meatloaf in a Mug

(Ready in about 10 minutes | Servings 2)

Per serving: 327 Calories; 16.6g Fat; 5.8g Carbs; 40g Protein; 1.8g Fiber

INGREDIENTS

1/2 pound ground pork
1/2 cup marinara sauce
Salt and pepper, to season
2 garlic cloves, minced

1/2 cup Swiss cheese, shredded
1/2 teaspoon mustard powder
1/2 teaspoon red pepper flakes
1 teaspoon shallot powder

DIRECTIONS

In a mixing bowl, combine all ingredients until everything is well combined.
Spoon the mixture into two microwave-safe mugs.
Microwave at 70 percent power for about 6 minutes until no longer pink in the center.

534. Ground Pork Soup with Avocado

(Ready in about 20 minutes | Servings 6)

Per serving: 423 Calories; 31.8g Fat; 6.5g Carbs; 25.9g Protein; 3.5g Fiber

INGREDIENTS

1 ¼ pounds pork butt, cut into chunks
2 tablespoons olive oil
1 medium-sized leek, chopped
1 teaspoon garlic, minced
1 celery stalk, chopped

1/4 cup fresh cilantro, roughly chopped
1 avocado, pitted and sliced
3 cups vegetable broth
Salt and pepper, to taste
1 cup tomato puree

DIRECTIONS

In a stock pot, heat the olive oil over a moderately-high flame. Sauté the leek, garlic, and celery for about 3 minutes or until the vegetable are tender and fragrant.
Add in the pork and continue to cook for 4 to 5 minutes more, stirring frequently to ensure even cooking. Add in the remaining ingredients. Leave the lid slightly ajar. Turn the heat to a simmer for 10 to 12 minutes.

STORING

Spoon the soup into airtight containers or Ziploc bags; keep in your refrigerator for up to 3 to 4 days.
For freezing, place the soup in airtight containers. Freeze up to 4 to 6 months. Defrost in the refrigerator. Serve topped with fresh cilantro and sliced avocado. Bon appétit!

535. Herring Salad Boats

(Ready in about 10 minutes | Servings 4)

Per serving: 120 Calories; 5.4g Fat; 5.8g Carbs; 12.3g Protein; 1.4g Fiber

INGREDIENTS

7 ounces canned herring, chopped
Salt and black pepper, to taste
1 tablespoon fresh cilantro, chopped
4 red pickled peppers, slice into halves

1 teaspoon Dijon mustard
2 tablespoons lemon juice
1 celery, chopped
1/2 cup onions, chopped

DIRECTIONS

Thoroughly combine the herring, Dijon mustard, celery, onions, lemon juice, salt, black pepper, and fresh cilantro.
Mix until everything is well combined.
Spoon the herring mixture into the pickle boats.

STORING

Place the peppers in airtight containers; keep in your refrigerator for 3 to 4 days.
Wrap each pepper tightly in several layers of plastic wrap and squeeze the air out. Place them in airtight containers; they can be frozen for up to 1 month.
Bake the peppers at 200 degrees F until they are completely warm.

536. Hot and Spicy Egg Salad

(Ready in about 15 minutes | Servings 8)

Per serving: 174 Calories; 13g Fat; 2.7g Carbs; 7.4g Protein; 0.6g Fiber

INGREDIENTS

10 eggs
1 teaspoon lemon juice
Salt and pepper, to season
1 head butterhead lettuce, torn into pieces
1 tablespoon Dijon mustard

1/2 cup onions
1/2 stalk of celery, minced
3/4 cup mayonnaise
1 teaspoon hot sauce

DIRECTIONS

Place the eggs in a saucepan and cover them with water by 1 inch. Cover and bring the water to a boil over high heat. Boil for 6 to 7 minutes over medium-high heat.
Peel the eggs and chop them coarsely. Add in the remaining ingredients and toss to combine well.

STORING

Place the egg salad in an airtight container or Ziploc bag; transfer to your refrigerator; it should be consumed within two days. Bon appétit!

537. Authentic Hungarian Goulash (Pörkölt)

(Ready in about 1 hour 25 minutes | Servings 4)

Per serving: 357 Calories; 15.8g Fat; 7g Carbs; 40.2g Protein; 2.5g Fiber

INGREDIENTS

2 tablespoons lard, at room temperature
1 bay leaf
1 celery stalk, chopped
2 bell pepper, chopped
1 tablespoon flaxseed meal
1 ¼ pounds stewing beef, cut into 1/2-inch pieces

Sea salt and pepper, to taste
1 tablespoon Hungarian paprika
1/2 teaspoon caraway seeds, coarsely crushed
4 cups beef broth
1 cup onion, chopped

DIRECTIONS

In a heavy-bottomed pot, sear the meat until no longer pink, for about 4 minutes; reserve. Season with salt, pepper, Hungarian paprika, and caraway seeds.
Pour in a splash of broth to scrape up any browned bits from the bottom of the pot.
Add in the remaining beef broth, bay leaf, onion, celery and bell pepper and continue to cook, covered, for 1 hour 10 minutes over a moderate heat.
Add in the flaxseed meal to thicken the cooking liquid; whisk for 2 to 3 minutes.

STORING

Spoon the goulash into four airtight containers or Ziploc bags; keep in your refrigerator for up to 3 to 4 days.
For freezing, place the goulash in airtight containers. Freeze up to 4 to 6 months. Defrost in the refrigerator. Bon appétit!

538. Classic Tilapia Fish Cakes

(Ready in about 30 minutes | Servings 6)

Per serving: 234 Calories; 10.6g Fat; 2.5g Carbs; 31.2g Protein; 1.2g Fiber

INGREDIENTS

2 tablespoons olive oil
1 ½ pounds tilapia, boned and flaked
1/2 cup soft cheese, at room temperature

2 teaspoons deli mustard
Salt and pepper, to season
2 eggs, whisked

1/3 cup almond meal
2 tablespoons flaxseed meal
2 tablespoons fresh chives, chopped

DIRECTIONS

Begin by preheating your oven to 395 degrees F. Line a baking pan with parchment paper.
In a mixing bowl, combine all ingredients until everything is well incorporated.
Form the mixture into 12 patties using your hands. Arrange them on the baking pan and bake for about 15 minutes; turn them over and cook for another 10 minutes.

STORING

Place the fish cakes in airtight containers; it will last for 3 to 4 days in the refrigerator.
For freezing, place the fish cakes in airtight containers or heavy-duty freezer bags. Freeze up to 2 to 3 months. Defrost in the refrigerator and reheat in your oven. Bon appétit!

539. The Best Vegetarian Tacos Ever

(Ready in about 10 minutes | Servings 6)

Per serving: 346 Calories; 25.7g Fat; 6.9g Carbs; 20.5g Protein; 1.4g Fiber

INGREDIENTS

1 pound Mexican cheese blend, grated
1 teaspoon taco seasoning mix

1 ½ cups salsa
1 cup sour cream

2 cups lettuce, torn into pieces

DIRECTIONS

Thoroughly combine the cheese and taco seasoning mix. Scatter the cheese all over the preheated pan, covering the bottom.
Cook for about 3 minutes, flip them over, and continue to cook for 2 to 3 minutes more until the bubbles start to form.
Top with the salsa, sour cream and lettuce; roll them up and serve immediately. Bon appétit!

STORING

Divide the tacos between airtight containers or Ziploc bags; keep in your refrigerator for up to 4 days.
To freeze, divide the tacos between airtight containers. Freeze up to 2 months. Defrost and reheat in your oven until it is crisp. Enjoy!

540. Authentic Greek Salad

(Ready in about 15 minutes + chilling time | Servings 4)

Per serving: 318 Calories; 24.3g Fat; 4.1g Carbs; 15.4g Protein; 1.1g Fiber

INGREDIENTS

2 cucumbers, sliced
1 teaspoon Greek seasoning mix
12 cherry tomatoes, halved
Sea salt and black pepper, to taste
4 large lettuce leaves

1 teaspoon garlic, minced
1 tablespoon lemon juice
1 onion, thinly sliced
1 cup Greek-style yogurt

DIRECTIONS

Thoroughly combine the Greek-style yogurt, garlic, lemon juice, and Greek seasoning mix.
Toss the onions, cucumbers, and tomatoes in a bowl; dress the salad and season with salt and pepper to taste.
Mound your salad onto each lettuce leaf.

STORING

Place the Greek salad in airtight containers or Ziploc bags; keep in your refrigerator for up to 3 to 4 days.

541. Orange and Chocolate Creamsicle Pudding

(Ready in about 15 minutes | Servings 4)

Per serving: 154 Calories; 13g Fat; 6.3g Carbs; 5.3g Protein; 1.8g Fiber

INGREDIENTS

1/4 cup Swerve
1/4 cup cocoa powder, unsweetened
3/4 cup double cream
3 ounces soft cheese, at room temperature

1 tablespoon orange juice, freshly squeezed
2 egg yolks
1/2 teaspoon ground cinnamon

DIRECTIONS

Beat the egg yolks using your electric mixer until frothy.
Warm the cream in a saucepan over a moderate heat. Stir in the hot cream into the egg yolks.
Turn the heat to a simmer and continue to cook for 5 to 6 minutes, stirring constantly, until your mixture has thickened.
Beat in the remaining ingredients using your electric mixer until creamy and uniform.

STORING

Divide your pudding among four airtight containers; refrigerate for 3 days.
To freeze, pour the mixture into ice-pop molds. Cover and insert sticks. Freeze until firm, at least 4 hours. Dip the molds briefly in hot water to release pops. Freeze up to 1 month. Enjoy!

542. Chocolate Truffles with Coconut and Rum

(Ready in about 15 minutes + chilling time | Servings 16)

Per serving: 90 Calories; 6.3g Fat; 4.9g Carbs; 3.7g Protein; 0.5g Fiber

INGREDIENTS

4 tablespoons coconut, shredded
1/4 cup cocoa powder unsweetened
1/4 teaspoon grated nutmeg
1 teaspoon vanilla
1 tablespoon rum

1/4 cup coconut oil
1 cup whipped cream
1 ½ cups dark chocolate, sugar-free, broken into chunks
3 tablespoons granulated Swerve
1/2 teaspoon almond extract

DIRECTIONS

In a mixing bowl, combine the chocolate, coconut, coconut oil, whipped cream, Swerve, almond extract, nutmeg, and vanilla.
Microwave the mixture for 1 minute on medium-high and then, let it cool down for a few minutes. Add in the rum and stir again.
Place in your refrigerator for 2 to 3 hours until firm. Roll the mixture into balls; roll each ball in the cocoa powder.

STORING

Place your truffles in airtight containers or Ziploc bags; keep in your refrigerator for 3 weeks to 1 month.
To freeze, arrange the coconut truffles on a baking tray in a single layer; freeze for about 2 hours. Transfer the frozen coconut truffles to an airtight container. Freeze for up to a month. Bon appétit!

543. Chorizo and Cheese Bites

(Ready in about 15 minutes + chilling time | Servings 5)

Per serving: 327 Calories; 25.7g Fat; 6.4g Carbs; 17g Protein; 0.3g Fiber

INGREDIENTS

10 ounces Chorizo sausage, chopped
1/2 teaspoon Dijon mustard
2 teaspoons tomato paste, no sugar added
8 black olives, pitted and chopped

2 tablespoons butter
2 tablespoons mayonnaise
10 ounces soft cheese, softened

DIRECTIONS

Sear the sausage in the preheated skillet until no longer pink. Add in the remaining ingredients and place it in the refrigerator. Roll the batter into bite-sized balls and serve.

STORING

Divide the chorizo balls between airtight containers or Ziploc bags; keep in your refrigerator for up to 3 to 4 days. For freezing, place the chorizo balls in airtight containers. Freeze up to 1 month. Defrost in the refrigerator. Enjoy!

544. Spicy Eggplant Casserole

(Ready in about 1 hour | Servings 4)

Per serving: 159 Calories; 10.4g Fat; 7.7g Carbs; 6.4g Protein; 3g Fiber

INGREDIENTS

3/4 pound eggplant, cut into slices
1 chili pepper, minced
1 teaspoon Italian seasoning mix
2 tablespoons olive oil
1 celery stalk, peeled and sliced

1/3 cup Romano cheese, shredded
1 cup tomatoes, sliced
4 garlic cloves, crushed
1 onion, sliced

DIRECTIONS

Place the eggplant with 1 teaspoon of coarse salt in a bowl; let it stand for about 30 minutes; drain and rinse the eggplant.
Preheat your oven to 340 degrees F. Brush the bottom and sides of a casserole dish with a cooking spray.
Place the vegetables along with the spices and olive oil in the prepared casserole dish. Roast the vegetables for 18 to 20 minutes.
Place the cheese on the top and continue to bake for a further 10 minutes.

STORING

Slice the casserole into four pieces. Divide the pieces between four airtight containers; it will last for 3 to 4 days in the refrigerator.
For freezing, place each portion in a separate heavy-duty freezer bag. Freeze up to 2 to 3 months. Defrost in the microwave or refrigerator. Bon appétit!

545. Salmon Steaks with Cauliflower

(Ready in about 25 minutes | Servings 4)

Per serving: 508 Calories; 22.9g Fat; 4.7g Carbs; 68.6g Protein; 2.6g Fiber

INGREDIENTS

4 salmon steaks
Salt and red pepper flakes, to season
1 cup Cheddar cheese, shredded

1 pound cauliflower florets
2 tablespoons butter, melted
1 teaspoon Creole seasoning mix

DIRECTIONS

Preheat your oven to 395 degrees F. Brush the sides and bottom of a baking dish with 1 tablespoon of butter.
Parboil the cauliflower in a pot of a lightly-salted water until crisp-tender.
Transfer the cauliflower florets to the buttered baking dish. Season with salt and red pepper and bake for 15 to 17 minutes.
Meanwhile, heat the remaining tablespoon of butter over a moderately-high heat. Cook the salmon until golden and crisp on all sides. Season with Creole seasoning mix.

STORING

Divide the salmon and cauliflower into four airtight containers; it will last for 3 to 4 days in the refrigerator.
For freezing, place each portion in a separate heavy-duty freezer bag. Freeze up to 2 to 3 months. Defrost in the microwave or refrigerator.
Place the shredded cheese on top and place under the preheated broiler for 5 to 6 minutes. Bon appétit!

546. Oven-Baked Sea Bass

(Ready in about 30 minutes | Servings 4)

Per serving: 195 Calories; 8.2g Fat; 0.5g Carbs; 28.7g Protein; 0.8g Fiber

INGREDIENTS

4 sea bass fillets
2 tablespoons butter, at room temperature
2 garlic cloves, minced

1 tablespoon lime juice
1 teaspoon lime zest
1/2 tablespoon deli mustard
1 teaspoon onion powder

Salt and pepper, to season
1 teaspoon paprika
1/4 cup fresh parsley, chopped

DIRECTIONS

Begin by preheating your oven to 410 degrees F. Then, grease a baking dish with a cooking spray.
In a mixing bowl, combine the butter, mustard, garlic, lime juice and zest, and spices. Rub the mixture on all sides of fish fillets.
Bake for about 20 minutes or until opaque.

STORING

Place the sea bass fillets in airtight containers; it will last for 3 to 4 days in the refrigerator.
For freezing, place the sea bass fillets in airtight containers or heavy-duty freezer bags. Freeze up to 2 to 3 months. Defrost in the refrigerator. Bon appétit!

547. Chicken and Mozzarella Stuffed Tomatoes

(Ready in about 25 minutes | Servings 4)

Per serving: 413 Calories; 28.2g Fat; 7.8g Carbs; 35.2g Protein; 3.2g Fiber

INGREDIENTS

4 medium-sized tomatoes
1/2 teaspoon garlic, minced
1 tablespoon fresh cilantro, chopped

2 cups mozzarella cheese, freshly grated
1/2 cup marinara sauce
1 tablespoon avocado oil

1/2 cup onion, chopped
Salt and black pepper, to taste
1/2 pound ground chicken

DIRECTIONS

Slice the tomatoes in half horizontally and scoop out pulp and seeds using a spoon.
Heat the oil in a frying pan over a moderately-high heat. Once hot, sear the ground chicken for about 4 minutes and reserve.
In the same frying pan, cook the onion and garlic until they've softened or about 5 minutes. Add in the reserved meat, tomato pulp, cilantro, salt, and black pepper.
Place the tomatoes in a baking dish. Spoon the stuffing into your tomatoes and pour the marinara sauce around them.
Now, bake in the middle of the preheated oven at 365 degrees F for about 20 minutes.

STORING

Place the stuffed tomatoes in airtight containers or Ziploc bags; keep in your refrigerator for 3 to 4 days.
Wrap each stuffed tomato tightly in several layers of plastic wrap and squeeze the air out. Place them in a freezable container; they can be frozen for up to 1 month.
Top each tomato with cheese. Bake the thawed stuffed tomatoes in your oven at 200 degrees F until they are completely warm. Bon appétit!

548. Crispy Chicken Drumettes

(Ready in about 30 minutes | Servings 4)

Per serving: 165 Calories; 9.8g Fat; 7.7g Carbs; 12.4g Protein; 3g Fiber

INGREDIENTS

4 chicken drumettes
2 tablespoons butter, room temperature
2 tomatoes, pureed

1 tablespoon coconut aminos
1 teaspoon Mediterranean herb mix
1 parsnip, sliced
1 teaspoon garlic, minced

1 teaspoon paprika
Salt and black pepper, to taste
1/2 cup onions, chopped
1 cup chicken broth

DIRECTIONS

In a frying pan, melt the butter over medium-high heat. Season the chicken drumettes with the salt and black pepper.
Sear the chicken drumettes until they are no longer pink; reserve. Cook the vegetables until they've softened for about 5 minutes.
Turn the heat to a simmer and add in the remaining ingredients along with the reserved chicken drumettes. Leave the lid slightly ajar and let it simmer, partially covered, for about 20 minutes.

STORING

Place the chicken drumettes in airtight containers or Ziploc bags; keep in your refrigerator for up 3 to 4 days.
For freezing, place the chicken drumettes in airtight containers or heavy-duty freezer bags. Freeze up to 3 months.
Once thawed in the refrigerator, heat in the preheated oven at 375 degrees F for 20 to 25 minutes or until heated through. Enjoy!

549. Herby Turkey Wings

(Ready in about 1 hour + marinating time | Servings 2)

Per serving: 488 Calories; 24.5g Fat; 2.1g Carbs; 33.6g Protein; 1g Fiber

INGREDIENTS

2 turkey wings
2 tablespoons red wine vinegar

1 tablespoon Taco seasoning mix
Salt and red pepper, to taste

2 tablespoons olive oil

DIRECTIONS

In a mixing bowl, combine the red wine vinegar, Taco seasoning mix, olive oil and turkey wings. Let the turkey wings marinate at least 2 hours in the refrigerator.
Grill the turkey wings on a lightly greased grill pan until a meat thermometer has reached the temperature of 180 degrees F. Sprinkle with salt and red pepper on all sides.

STORING

Wrap the turkey wings in foil before packing them into an airtight container; keep in your refrigerator for up to 3 to 4 days.
For freezing, place them in airtight containers or heavy-duty freezer bags. Freeze up to 2 to 3 months. Defrost in the refrigerator. Bon appétit!

550. Spare Ribs with Kale

(Ready in about 25 minutes + marinating time | Servings 6)

Per serving: 234 Calories; 11g Fat; 2g Carbs; 29.8g Protein; 1g Fiber

INGREDIENTS

1 ½ pounds spare ribs
1 medium leek, sliced
1 celery stalk, sliced
1 bell pepper, chopped

2 cups kale
2 tablespoons coconut aminos
Salt and pepper, to season
2 teaspoons olive oil

2 tablespoons red wine vinegar
1/4 cup red wine
2 garlic cloves, minced

DIRECTIONS

Season the pork ribs with salt and pepper. In a bowl, make the marinade by whisking the coconut aminos, vinegar, red wine, and garlic. Allow the spare ribs to marinate for at least 3 hours in your refrigerator.
Heat 1 teaspoon of the oil in a frying pan over a moderately-high heat; cook the leeks, celery and bell pepper for 4 to 5 minutes until they are crisp tender.
Heat the remaining teaspoon of the olive oil and sear the pork, adding the marinade as needed; cook for about 12 minutes.
Add in the kale and continue to simmer until the leaves are wilted, about 5 minutes.

STORING

Divide the ribs into six portions. Place each portion of ribs along with the cooking juices in an airtight container; store in your refrigerator for 3 to 5 days.
For freezing, place the ribs in airtight containers or heavy-duty freezer bags. Freeze up to 4 to 6 months. Defrost in the refrigerator. Reheat in your oven at 250 degrees F until heated through. Bon appétit!

551. Hamburger and Cabbage Chowder

(Ready in about 35 minutes | Servings 4)

Per serving: 307 Calories; 23.6g Fat; 6.4g Carbs; 14.8g Protein; 2.7g Fiber

INGREDIENTS

3/4 pound ground beef
2 tablespoons oil
1 teaspoon garlic, chopped
1 parsnip, diced

1 cup green cabbage, shredded
1 celery stalk, diced
1 cup tomato, puree
4 cups vegetable broth

1 bay leaf
Salt and black pepper, to taste
1 cup full-fat sour cream
1/2 cup onions, chopped

DIRECTIONS

In a stockpot, heat the olive oil over medium-high heat. Cook the ground beef for about 5 minutes and reserve.
Now, cook the onions, garlic, parsnip, cabbage, and celery in the pan drippings, stirring constantly, until they've softened.
Stir in the remaining ingredients along with the reserved ground beef and bring to a boil. Immediately, turn the heat to a simmer and continue to cook for another 25 minutes.

STORING

Spoon the chowder into four airtight containers or Ziploc bags; keep in your refrigerator for up to 3 to 4 days.
For freezing, place the chowder in airtight containers. It will maintain the best quality for about 4 to 6 months. Defrost in the refrigerator. Serve dolloped with sour cream. Bon appétit!

552. Country Boil Soup

(Ready in about 30 minutes | Servings 4)

Per serving: 170 Calories; 5.8g Fat; 6.2g Carbs; 20g Protein; 2.8g Fiber

INGREDIENTS

1 ¼ pounds tilapia, chopped
1/4 cup Marsala wine
1/2 cup coconut milk
3 teaspoons olive oil

1 cup onion, chopped
1 celery stalk, chopped
1 teaspoon Creole seasonings mix
3 ½ cups fish stock

1 parsnip, chopped
2 bell pepper, chopped
Sea salt and black pepper, to taste

DIRECTIONS

Heat the oil in a heavy-bottomed pan over medium-high flame. Once hot, sauté all vegetables until they are just tender or about 5 minutes. Add in the seasonings.
Add in the tilapia along with fish stock; partially cover and continue to cook for about 13 minutes or until cooked through.
Pour in the wine and coconut milk and bring to a rapid boil. Let it simmer for about 13 minutes.

STORING

Spoon the soup into four airtight containers or Ziploc bags; keep in your refrigerator for up to 3 to 4 days.
For freezing, place the soup in airtight containers. It will maintain the best quality for about 4 months. Defrost in the refrigerator. Bon appétit!

553. Tuna and Chèvre Stuffed Tomatoes

(Ready in about 30 minutes | Servings 6)

Per serving: 303 Calories; 22.9g Fat; 5.8g Carbs; 17g Protein; 2.1g Fiber

INGREDIENTS

10 ounces tuna, flaked
1 ½ cups Chèvre cheese, crumbled
6 tomatoes
2 tablespoons parsley, chopped
1 teaspoon garlic, smashed

1/2 cup mayonnaise
1 teaspoon deli mustard
1 onion, finely chopped
Sea salt and black pepper, to season

DIRECTIONS

Begin by preheating your oven to 395 degrees F. Slice your tomatoes in half horizontally and scoop out the pulp, set them aside.
Thoroughly combine the tuna, onion, garlic, parsley, mayonnaise, deli mustard, salt, and black pepper.
Divide the filling between tomatoes and bake for about 23 minutes until they are thoroughly cooked.

STORING

Place the stuffed tomatoes in airtight containers or Ziploc bags; keep in your refrigerator for 3 to 4 days.
Wrap each stuffed tomato tightly in several layers of plastic wrap and squeeze the air out. Place them in a freezable container; they can be frozen for up to 1 month.
Top each tomato with cheese. Bake the thawed stuffed tomatoes in your oven at 200 degrees F until they are completely warm. Bon appétit!

554. Frozen Cocoa Dessert

(Ready in about 10 minutes + chilling time | Servings 6)

Per serving: 84 Calories; 8.9g Fat; 1.5g Carbs; 0.8g Protein; 1g Fiber

INGREDIENTS

2 tablespoons cocoa powder
2 tablespoons coconut flakes
1/4 cup coconut oil, melted

1 teaspoon vanilla extract
10 drops liquid Monk fruit

DIRECTIONS

Melt the coconut oil, vanilla, and liquid Monk fruit in a pan over a moderately-high heat.
Add in the cocoa powder and stir to combine.
Spoon the mixture into a silicone candy mold tray. Top with coconut flakes and place in your freezer until set.

STORING

Place in a heavy-duty freezer bag. Freeze up to 3 to 4 months. Bon appétit!

555. Deviled Eggs with Smoked Herring

(Ready in about 20 minutes | Servings 6)

Per serving: 203 Calories; 13.3g Fat; 3.8g Carbs; 17.2g Protein; 0.3g Fiber

INGREDIENTS

1 (6.7-ounce) can smoked herring, drained
1 teaspoon paprika

12 eggs
1/4 cup tarragon
2 pickled jalapenos, minced

Salt and pepper, to taste
1/3 cup aioli
1 tablespoon small capers, drained

DIRECTIONS

Place the eggs in a saucepan and cover them with water by 1 inch. Cover and bring the water to a boil over high heat. Boil for 6 to 7 minutes over medium-high heat.
Peel the eggs and slice them in half lengthwise; mix the yolks with the aioli, herring, paprika, capers, tarragon, jalapenos, salt, and pepper. Divide the mixture between the egg whites and arrange the deviled eggs on a nice serving platter.

STORING

Place the deviled eggs in an airtight container or Ziploc bag; transfer to your refrigerator; they should be consumed within 2 days.
For freezing, spoon out the yolk mixture from the deviled eggs. Add the egg yolk mixture to an airtight container or Ziploc bag.
Place the container in the freezer for up to 3 months. To defrost, let them sit overnight in the refrigerator until they are fully thawed out. Enjoy!

556. Avocado and Salmon Bites

(Ready in about 5 minutes | Servings 4)

Per serving: 316 Calories; 24.4g Fat; 5.9g Carbs; 17.4g Protein; 6g Fiber

INGREDIENTS

1 avocado, pitted and peeled
1/2 cup scallions, chopped
1/2 teaspoon dried oregano

8 ounces canned salmon, drained
1 ounce pumpkin seeds, chopped
1 ounce sunflower seeds

1 ounce hemp seeds
Salt and pepper, to taste
1/2 teaspoon cayenne pepper

DIRECTIONS

Combine all ingredients until well mixed.
Roll the mixture into eight balls and place in your refrigerator until set.

STORING

Place the salmon bites in airtight containers; keep in your refrigerator for 5 to 6 days.
To freeze, place the salmon bites in four airtight containers for up to 1 month. Defrost in the refrigerator. Enjoy!

557. Nonna's Traditional Beef Casserole

(Ready in about 25 minutes | Servings 4)

Per serving: 509 Calories; 29.6g Fat; 6.1g Carbs; 45.2g Protein; 2g Fiber

INGREDIENTS

1 pound ground chuck
1 ¼ cups marinara sauce
Sea salt and ground black pepper, to taste

1 tablespoon tallow, melted
1 teaspoon Italian seasoning mix
1 cup Swiss cheese
3/4 cup Greek-style yogurt

2 garlic cloves, minced
1/2 cup onion, finely chopped

DIRECTIONS

Begin by preheating your oven to 395 degrees F.
In a frying pan, melt the tallow over a moderately-high flame. Once hot, cook the ground chuck, breaking apart with a spatula. Then, sauté the onion and garlic until just tender and fragrant.
Add in the marinara sauce, salt, pepper, Italian seasoning mix,
Spoon the sautéed mixture into a casserole dish. Bake in the preheated oven for about 20 minutes.

STORING

Slice your casserole into four pieces; divide between airtight containers or Ziploc bags; keep in your refrigerator for up to 3 days.
For freezing, place your casserole in airtight containers or heavy-duty freezer bags. Freeze up to 3 months. Defrost in the refrigerator.
Mix the swiss cheese and yogurt in a bowl. Spoon the mixture over your casserole and place under the preheated broiler for about 5 minutes until hot and bubbly.

558. Stuffed Peppers with Salmon and Cheese

(Ready in about 25 minutes | Servings 4)

Per serving: 273 Calories; 13.9g Fat; 5.1g Carbs; 28.9g Protein; 1.7g Fiber

INGREDIENTS

4 bell peppers
Salt and red pepper flakes, to taste
1 teaspoon Mediterranean spice mix

1/3 cup mayonnaise
1/3 cup black olives, pitted and chopped
1 cup soft cheese

10 ounces canned salmon, drained
1 red onion, finely chopped
1/2 teaspoon garlic, minced

DIRECTIONS

Broil the bell peppers for 5 to 6 minutes, turning them halfway through the cook time.
Cut the peppers into halves and remove the seeds and skin.
In a mixing bowl, combine the salmon, onion, garlic, mayonnaise, olives, salt, red pepper, Mediterranean spice mix, and soft cheese.
Divide the mixture between the peppers and bake them in the preheated oven at 390 degrees F for 10 to 12 minutes or until cooked through.

STORING

Place the stuffed peppers in airtight containers; keep in your refrigerator for 3 to 4 days.
Wrap each stuffed pepper tightly in several layers of plastic wrap and squeeze the air out. Place them in airtight containers; they can be frozen for up to 1 month.
Reheat the thawed stuffed peppers at 200 degrees F until they are completely warm.

559. Cheesy Roasted Asparagus

(Ready in about 15 minutes | Servings 6)

Per serving: 128 Calories; 9.4g Fat; 2.9g Carbs; 6.4g Protein; 2.6g Fiber

INGREDIENTS

1/2 cup shallots, chopped
1 cup goat cheese, crumbled
1/2 cup fresh cilantro, roughly chopped

1 teaspoon fresh garlic, minced
1 ½ pounds asparagus spears
2 tablespoons olive oil

Salt and red pepper, to season

DIRECTIONS

Begin by preheating your oven to 410 degrees F. Brush the bottom of a rimmed pan with nonstick spray.
Brush the asparagus with the olive oil. Toss the asparagus spears with the shallots, garlic, salt, and red pepper.
Place the asparagus on the rimmed pan in a single layer. Roast for about 15 minutes.

STORING

Place the roasted asparagus in airtight containers; keep in your refrigerator for 3 to 5 days.
For freezing, place the roasted asparagus in a freezable container; they can be frozen for 10 to 12 months.
Scatter the crumbled cheese and cilantro over the asparagus spears. Enjoy!

560. Boston Butt with Goat Cheese Sauce

(Ready in about 30 minutes | Servings 6)

Per serving: 495 Calories; 36.9g Fat; 3.6g Carbs; 33.4g Protein; 0.3g Fiber

INGREDIENTS

1 ½ pounds boneless Boston butt, and
cut into 6 pieces
1 teaspoon fresh garlic, minced
1/3 cup port wine
1 tablespoon olive oil

1/2 cup scallions, chopped
1 tablespoon coconut aminos
6 ounces Chevre goat cheese
1/3 cup whipped cream
1/3 cup roasted vegetable broth

1/2 teaspoon hot chili flakes
Salt and black pepper, to taste
1 teaspoon Mediterranean spice mix

DIRECTIONS

Rub each piece of the pork with salt, black pepper, and Mediterranean spice mix.
Heat the oil in a saucepan over moderately-high heat. Sear the pork for about 20 minutes (an internal temperature of 145 degrees F); reserve.
In the same saucepan, sauté the scallions and garlic until they are soft and aromatic. Add in the port wine and broth and stir to deglaze the pan.
Turn the heat to a simmer and stir in the remaining ingredients; let it simmer until the liquid has thickened and reduced by evaporation.
Add the pork back to the saucepan.

STORING

Place the pork pieces in six airtight containers or Ziploc bags; keep in your refrigerator for 3 to 4 days.
For freezing, wrap tightly with heavy-duty aluminum foil or freezer wrap. It will maintain the best quality for 2 to 3 months. Defrost in the refrigerator. Enjoy!

561. Balsamic Glazed Meatloaf with Cheese

(Ready in about 1 hour 10 minutes | Servings 8)

Per serving: 318 Calories; 14.7g Fat; 6.2g Carbs; 39.3g Protein; 1.3g Fiber

INGREDIENTS

2 eggs, beaten
1 tablespoon deli mustard
1/2 cup tomato paste, no sugar added
1 tablespoon Swerve
1/2 cup green onions, chopped

1/2 cup salsa, no sugar added
8 ounces Swiss cheese, shredded
1 teaspoon cayenne pepper
Salt and black pepper, to season
1 tablespoon balsamic vinegar

1/2 teaspoon garlic, minced
1 pound ground pork
1 pound ground beef

DIRECTIONS

Begin by preheating your oven to 365 degrees F.
Thoroughly combine the ground meat, eggs, green onions, salsa, Swiss cheese, garlic, cayenne pepper, salt, and black pepper.
Press the mixture into a lightly oiled loaf pan.
Whisk the balsamic vinegar, deli mustard, tomato paste, and Swerve until well combined; pour the mixture over the top of your meatloaf.
Bake for about 1 hour, rotating the pan once to ensure even cooking. Lastly, place under the preheated broiler for about 5 minutes or until the top has caramelized.

STORING

Wrap your meatloaf tightly with heavy-duty aluminum foil or plastic wrap. Then, keep in your refrigerator for up to 3 to 4 days.
For freezing, wrap your meatloaf tightly to prevent freezer burn. Freeze up to 3 to 4 months. Defrost in the refrigerator. Bon appétit!

562. Mini Meatloaves with Parsnip

(Ready in about 35 minutes | Servings 6)

Per serving: 321 Calories; 16.3g Fat; 8.8g Carbs; 32.8g Protein; 2.1g Fiber

INGREDIENTS

1 egg, beaten
1 cup Colby cheese, shredded
1 cup tomato puree
1 ounce envelope onion soup mix

1 tablespoon coconut aminos
1 tablespoon deli mustard
1 teaspoon garlic, smashed
1 pound pork, ground

1/2 pound chuck, ground
1 cup parsnip, shredded
Sea salt and black pepper, to season
1 teaspoon Mediterranean herb mix

DIRECTIONS

Begin by preheating your oven to 360 degrees F.
Thoroughly combine all ingredients for the mini meatloaves.
Scrape the mixture into a lightly buttered muffin tin. Bake in the preheated oven for 30 to 35 minutes.

STORING

Wrap the meatloaf muffins tightly with heavy-duty aluminum foil or plastic wrap. Then, keep in your refrigerator for up to 3 to 4 days.
For freezing, wrap the meatloaf muffins tightly to prevent freezer burn. Freeze up to 3 to 4 months. Defrost in the refrigerator. Bon appétit!

563. Spicy Beef with Leeks

(Ready in about 20 minutes + marinating time | Servings 4)

Per serving: 292 Calories; 14.3g Fat; 3.9g Carbs; 36.9g Protein; 0.8g Fiber

INGREDIENTS

1 ½ pounds bottom eye roast, cubed
1/4 teaspoon fennel seeds
1 tablespoon fresh cilantro, chopped
2 tablespoons coconut aminos

1 teaspoon hot sauce
2 teaspoons garlic, minced
1/2 cup leeks, chopped
1/2 tablespoon butter

Salt and pepper, to taste
1 teaspoon deli mustard
1 teaspoon Taco seasoning blend

DIRECTIONS

Whisk the coconut aminos, hot sauce and garlic in a mixing dish. Add in the salt, pepper, mustard, Taco seasoning blend, and leeks.
Add the bottom eye roast and let it marinate for 1 hour in your refrigerator.
Melt the butter in a saucepan over a moderately-high heat. Cook the marinated bottom eye roast for about 16 minutes, stirring periodically to ensure even cooking.
Season with fennel seeds and cilantro.

STORING

Cut the bottom eye roast into thin pieces using a knife, slicing against the grain; divide the pieces between four airtight containers; keep in your refrigerator for up to 3 to 4 days.
For freezing, place the bottom eye roast in airtight containers or heavy-duty freezer bags. Freeze up to 2 to 3 months. Defrost in the refrigerator. Bon appétit!

564. Saucy Porterhouse Steaks

(Ready in about 2 hours 15 minutes | Servings 4)

Per serving: 238 Calories; 9.2g Fat; 6.3g Carbs; 27.4g Protein; 1.4g Fiber

INGREDIENTS

1 tablespoon olive oil
1/3 cup red wine
2 tablespoons coconut aminos
1 ½ cups vegetable broth
1 red onion, sliced

1 parsnip, chopped
1 teaspoon garlic, minced
1 teaspoon lemon zest
1/2 teaspoon cayenne pepper
1 pound Porterhouse steaks, thinly sliced

DIRECTIONS

In a frying pan, heat the olive oil in over a moderate heat. Sear the Porterhouse steaks for about 12 minutes and reserve.
In the same skillet, cook the onion, parsnip and garlic for about 3 minutes, stirring frequently to ensure even cooking.
Add in the remaining ingredients and bring to a boil. Turn the heat to a simmer and continue to cook for about 2 hours.

STORING

Divide the Porterhouse steaks between airtight containers; keep in your refrigerator for up to 3 to 4 days.
For freezing, place the Porterhouse steaks in airtight containers or heavy-duty freezer bags. Freeze up to 2 to 3 months. Defrost in the refrigerator. Bon appétit!

565. Mixed Greens with Ricotta Cheese

(Ready in about 10 minutes | Servings 4)

Per serving: 208 Calories; 13.5g Fat; 6g Carbs; 14.5g Protein; 4.4g Fiber

INGREDIENTS

2 pounds mixed greens, torn into pieces
1/4 cup butter
Sea salt and pepper, to taste

1/2 teaspoon curry powder
1 cup Ricotta cheese
1 teaspoon garlic, minced

DIRECTIONS

Melt the butter in a large saucepan over a moderately-high heat. Once hot, cook the garlic until just tender and aromatic.
Add in the mixed greens, salt, pepper, and curry powder; cook for a further 3 minutes, stirring frequently.
Turn the heat on high and continue to cook for about 2 minutes more.

STORING

Place the mixed greens in airtight containers; keep in your refrigerator for 3 to 5 days.
For freezing, place the mixed greens in freezable containers; they can be frozen for 4 to 5 months. Top with cheese and reheat in the saucepan until cheese melts completely. Enjoy!

566. Vegetable and Cheese Fritters

(Ready in about 15 minutes | Servings 6)

Per serving: 153 Calories; 11.8g Fat; 6.6g Carbs; 6.4g Protein; 0.3g Fiber

INGREDIENTS

1 garlic clove, crushed
1 cup Colby cheese, grated
2 tablespoons butter, melted
1 egg yolk
Salt and pepper, to taste

1 large parsnip, shredded
1 large celery stalk, shredded
2 cups zucchini, shredded
2 tablespoons cilantro, chopped
1 cup shallots, chopped

DIRECTIONS

Place the shredded vegetables in a colander to drain away the excess liquid. Mix in the other ingredients until everything is well combined.
Divide the mixture into 12 patties. Place them in a parchment-lined baking pan.
Bake in the preheated oven at 365 degrees F for about 10 minutes.

STORING

Divide your fritters between airtight containers or heavy-duty freezer bags; keep in the refrigerator for a week.
For freezing, divide the fritters among three heavy-duty freezer bags; freeze up to 3 months. Defrost in your microwave for a few minutes. Bon appétit!

567. Grandma's Beef Stew

(Ready in about 40 minutes | Servings 6)

Per serving: 259 Calories; 10.1g Fat; 4.1g Carbs; 35.7g Protein; 0.6g Fiber

INGREDIENTS

1 tablespoon lard, at room temperature
1 tablespoon Steak dry rub
4 cups beef bone broth

1 egg, lightly whisked
1 cup onion, thinly sliced
1 teaspoon garlic, minced

1 cup brown mushrooms, thinly sliced
Salt and pepper, to taste
1 ½ pounds chuck, cubed

DIRECTIONS

Melt the lard in a heavy-bottomed pot over a moderately-high flame.
Brown the beef for about 8 minutes or until no longer pink.
In the same pot, cook the onion and garlic until they are just tender and aromatic. Stir in the mushrooms and cook until they release the liquid.
Add in the other ingredients, and continue to cook, covered, approximately 35 minutes. Fold in the whisked egg and stir for 1 minute or until completely dissolved.

STORING

Spoon the stew into airtight containers or Ziploc bags; keep in your refrigerator for up to 3 to 4 days.
For freezing, place the stew in airtight containers. Freeze up to 4 to 6 months. Defrost in the refrigerator and reheat on the stove pot. Serve with fresh cilantro. Bon appétit!

568. Muffins with Ground Meat and Herbs

(Ready in about 25 minutes | Servings 6)

Per serving: 600 Calories; 42.3g Fat; 6.5g Carbs; 27.9g Protein; 4.1g Fiber

INGREDIENTS

3 eggs, lightly beaten
2 tablespoons whipped cream
1 teaspoon dried marjoram
1/2 pound ground beef

1 pound ground pork
1 tablespoon olive oil
1 stick butter
1 cup almond meal

1/4 cups flaxseed meal
1 teaspoon baking powder
Salt and pepper, to season

DIRECTIONS

In a saucepan, heat the olive oil over a moderate flame. Sear the ground meat for about 5 minutes the juices run clear.
Add in the remaining ingredients and mix to combine well.
Spoon the mixture into lightly greased muffin cups. Bake in the preheated oven at 365 degrees F for about 17 minutes.

STORING

Wrap your muffins tightly with heavy-duty aluminum foil or plastic wrap. Then, keep in your refrigerator for up to 3 to 4 days.
For freezing, wrap your muffins tightly to prevent freezer burn. Freeze up to 3 to 4 months. Defrost in the refrigerator. Bon appétit!

569. Decadent Pork and Vegetable Soup

(Ready in about 20 minutes | Servings 6)

Per serving: 423 Calories; 31.8g Fat; 6g Carbs; 25.9g Protein; 2.6g Fiber

INGREDIENTS

1 ¼ pounds pork butt, cut into bite-sized pieces
2 tablespoons olive oil
1 avocado, pitted, peeled and sliced
1 onion, peeled and chopped
1 teaspoon garlic, peeled and minced
1 teaspoon chili pepper, seeded and minced

1 celery stalk, chopped
3 cups roasted vegetable broth
Sea salt and black pepper, to taste
1 cup tomato puree
1/4 cup fresh cilantro, roughly chopped

DIRECTIONS

In a heavy-bottomed pot, heat the oil until sizzling. Once hot, sauté the onion, garlic, pepper and celery for about 3 minutes or until the vegetables have softened.
Stir in the pork and continue to cook for 4 minutes longer or until no longer pink. Add in the remaining ingredients.
Turn the heat to a simmer, partially cover, and continue to cook for about 15 minutes.

STORING

Spoon the soup into airtight containers or Ziploc bags; keep in your refrigerator for up to 3 to 4 days.
For freezing, place the soup in airtight containers. Freeze up to 4 to 6 months. Defrost in the refrigerator.
Serve topped with fresh avocado. Bon appétit!

570. Steaks in Port Wine Sauce

(Ready in about 30 minutes | Servings 4)

Per serving: 451 Calories; 34.4g Fat; 3.6g Carbs; 29.7g Protein; 1.2g Fiber

INGREDIENTS

1 ½ pound rib-eye steaks
1/2 cup port wine
2 Italian peppers, deveined and chopped

2 thyme sprigs
2 tablespoons butter, room temperature
1 cup onions, chopped

1 tablespoon Dijon mustard
Salt and pepper, to taste
1 teaspoon garlic, smashed

DIRECTIONS

Rub the steaks with the mustard, salt, pepper, and thyme.
Melt the butter in a nonstick skillet over a moderately heat. Sear your steaks for 8 to 10 minutes per side.
In the same skillet, cook the onions, garlic, and Italian pepper for 3 to 4 minutes. Pour in the wine and scrape up any browned bits from the bottom of the skillet.
Continue to simmer until the liquid has reduced and thickened.

STORING

Divide your steaks between airtight containers; keep in your refrigerator for up to 3 to 4 days.
For freezing, place your steaks in airtight containers or heavy-duty freezer bags. Freeze up to 2 to 3 months. Defrost in the refrigerator. Bon appétit!

571. Burger Soup with Cheddar Cheese

(Ready in about 20 minutes | Servings 4)

Per serving: 326 Calories; 20.5g Fat; 4.5g Carbs; 26.8g Protein; 0.8g Fiber

INGREDIENTS

1/2 pound ground beef
2 tablespoons olive oil
½ cup whipped cream

1 tablespoon fresh basil, chopped
1 cup Cheddar cheese, shredded
1 cup onion, chopped

1/2 cup celery with leaves, chopped
4 cups vegetable broth

DIRECTIONS

In a soup pot, heat olive oil over moderate heat. Now, cook the ground beef until it is no longer pink; reserve.
In the same pot, cook the onion until tender and translucent. Add a splash of vegetable broth to scrape up any browned bits from the bottom of the skillet.
Add in the celery and vegetable broth and bring to a boil. Leave the lid slightly ajar and continue to cook for 8 to 10 minutes, partially covered.
Slowly add in the cream, whisking constantly until well combined. Continue to simmer an additional 5 to 6 minutes.

STORING

Spoon the soup into four airtight containers or Ziploc bags; keep in your refrigerator for up to 3 to 4 days.
For freezing, place the soup in airtight containers. It will maintain the best quality for about 4 to 6 months. Defrost in the refrigerator.
Add in the cheese and reheat in your pot for 5 to 6 minutes until cheese has melted completely. Serve with fresh basil leaves. Bon appétit!

572. Bavarian-Style Sauerkraut with Ground Meat

(Ready in about 20 minutes | Servings 4)

Per serving: 330 Calories; 12.2g Fat; 4.7g Carbs; 44.4g Protein; 4.7g Fiber

INGREDIENTS

18 ounces sauerkraut, rinsed and well drained
1/2 pound ground pork
3/4 pounds ground turkey

1 tablespoon lard, room temperature
1 teaspoon garlic, minced
1 teaspoon fennel seeds
1 teaspoon ancho chile powder

2 bay laurels
Salt and black pepper, to season
1 cup onions, chopped

DIRECTIONS

Melt the lard in a Dutch oven over a moderate flame; once hot, sauté the onions and garlic until they have just browned.
Stir in the ground meat and continue to sauté for about 5 minutes until no longer pink.
Add in the other ingredients and reduce the heat to a simmer. Continue to cook for 5 to 6 minutes or until everything is cooked through.

STORING

Divide the sauerkraut between airtight containers or Ziploc bags; keep in your refrigerator for up to 3 to 5 days.
For freezing, place the sauerkraut in airtight containers or heavy-duty freezer bags. Freeze up to 5 months. Defrost in the refrigerator and reheat on the stove pot. Bon appétit!

573. Steak with Mustard Sauce

(Ready in about 20 minutes | Servings 4)

Per serving: 321 Calories; 13.7g Fat; 1g Carbs; 45g Protein; 0.4g Fiber

INGREDIENTS

4 1 ½-inch thick steaks
1 ½ tablespoons coriander, chopped
Salt and pepper, to taste

1/3 cup sour cream
1 tablespoon Dijon mustard
2 sprigs thyme, chopped

1 tablespoon olive oil

DIRECTIONS

In a bowl, combine the sour cream, Dijon mustard, and coriander; reserve in your refrigerator.
Sprinkle the steaks with salt, pepper, and thyme.
Heat the olive oil in a pan over moderately-high heat; once hot, cook the steak for 4 to 5 minutes per side.

STORING

Divide the steaks between four airtight containers or Ziploc bags; keep in your refrigerator for up to 3 to 4 days.
Spoon the sauce into a glass jar and keep in your refrigerator for up to 3 to 4 days.
For freezing, place the steaks in airtight containers or heavy-duty freezer bags. Freeze up to 3 months. Defrost in the refrigerator. Bon appétit!

574. Veggie-Loaded Mini Meatloaves

(Ready in about 35 minutes | Servings 6)

Per serving: 220 Calories; 6.3g Fat; 5.4g Carbs; 33.8g Protein; 2.2g Fiber

INGREDIENTS

1 pound pork, ground
1 cup tomato puree
1 ounce envelope onion soup mix
1/2 pound chuck, ground

Salt and pepper, to taste
1 tablespoon stone-ground mustard
1 cup soft cheese, shredded
1 teaspoon garlic, smashed

1 egg, beaten
1 cup parsnip, shredded
1 tablespoon soy sauce

DIRECTIONS

In a mixing bowl, thoroughly combine all ingredients until well combined.
Press the mixture into lightly greased muffin cups. Bake in the preheated oven at 356 degrees F for about 35 minutes.

STORING

Wrap the meatloaf muffins tightly with heavy-duty aluminum foil or plastic wrap. Then, keep in your refrigerator for up to 3 to 4 days.
For freezing, wrap the meatloaf muffins tightly to prevent freezer burn. Freeze up to 3 to 4 months. Defrost in the refrigerator. Bon appétit!

575. Cheese-Stuffed Meatballs

(Ready in about 25 minutes | Servings 5)

Per serving: 302 Calories; 17.3g Fat; 1.9g Carbs; 33.4g Protein; 0.5g Fiber

INGREDIENTS

10 (1-inch) cubes of cheddar cheese
1 tablespoon fresh parsley, roughly chopped
1 small onion, minced
1/2 pound ground beef
1 teaspoon garlic, minced

1/2 pound ground pork
1/3 cup double cream
2 eggs, whisked
Salt and pepper, to taste
1 teaspoon dried marjoram

DIRECTIONS

In a mixing bowl, combine the ground meat, double cream, eggs, parsley, onion, garlic, salt, pepper, and marjoram; mix until everything is well combined.
Now, roll the mixture into 10 balls using your hands. Place a piece of cheese in the center of each ball.
Press the ground meat around the piece of cheese, sealing it tightly around cheese.
Bake in the preheated oven at 395 degrees F for about 20 minutes.

STORING

Place your meatballs in airtight containers or Ziploc bags; keep in your refrigerator for up to 3 to 4 days.
Freeze the meatballs in airtight containers or heavy-duty freezer bags. Freeze up to 3 to 4 months. To defrost, slowly reheat in a saucepan. Bon appétit!

576. Spring Salad with Macadamia Nuts

(Ready in about 5 minutes | Servings 4)

Per serving: 184 Calories; 16.8g Fat; 5g Carbs; 2.1g Protein; 2g Fiber

INGREDIENTS

3 tablespoons olive oil
1 teaspoon chili sauce, sugar-free
Salt and pepper, to taste
1 cup grape tomatoes

1 white onion, sliced
1 ounce macadamia nuts, chopped
1 parsnip, grated
2 tablespoons sesame seeds, toasted

1 cup butterhead lettuce, torn into
small pieces
1 tablespoon lemon juice
1 cucumber, thinly sliced

DIRECTIONS

Combine all ingredients, except for the sesame seeds, in a bowl. Toss until everything is well combined.
Top with the sesame seeds.

STORING

Place your salad in airtight containers or Ziploc bags; keep in your refrigerator for up to 3 to 4 days.

577. Chicken Drumsticks with Mediterranean Sauce

(Ready in about 35 minutes | Servings 4)

Per serving: 562 Calories; 43.8g Fat; 2.1g Carbs; 40.8g Protein; 0.6g Fiber

INGREDIENTS

4 chicken drumsticks
1 ½ tablespoons butter, room temperature
1 cup feta cheese, cubed
1 hard-boiled egg yolk, mashed
2 garlic cloves, minced
1 tablespoon lime juice

1/2 cup olive oil
Sea salt and pepper, to taste
2 tablespoons fresh cilantro, roughly chopped
6 black olives, pitted and halved
Sea salt and ground black pepper, to taste

DIRECTIONS

Begin by preheating your oven to 390 degrees F.
In a frying pan, melt the butter over medium-high heat.
Sprinkle the chicken drumsticks with salt and pepper; now, sear the chicken for about 4 minutes or until no longer pink.
Arrange the chicken on a foil-lined baking sheet and place the fresh cilantro and black olives on top.
Meanwhile, make the sauce by blending the remaining ingredients, except for feta cheese. Spread the sauce over the chicken and bake for 20 to 25 minutes.

STORING

Place the chicken drumsticks in airtight containers or Ziploc bags; keep in your refrigerator for up 3 to 4 days.
For freezing, place the chicken drumsticks in airtight containers or heavy-duty freezer bags. Freeze up to 3 months.
Once thawed in the refrigerator, top with the cheese and place under the preheated broiler for about 6 minutes or until hot and bubbly.

578. Old-Fashioned Pork Meatloaf

(Ready in about 45 minutes | Servings 6)

Per serving: 251 Calories; 7.9g Fat; 6.5g Carbs; 34.6g Protein; 4g Fiber

INGREDIENTS

For the Meatloaf:
1 pound ground pork
1 egg, whisked
Sea salt and black pepper, to taste
1 teaspoon chili powder

1/2 pound ground beef
1 large onion, chopped
2 cloves garlic, finely minced
1/4 cup pork rinds, crushed
1/3 cup flaxseed meal

For the Sauce:
1 cup marinara sauce
1 tablespoon balsamic vinegar
1 teaspoon dried coriander
1 ½ tablespoons erythritol

DIRECTIONS

Mix all ingredients for the meatloaf until well combined. Press the mixture into a lightly greased baking pan.
In another bowl, mix all the sauce ingredients until well combined. Spoon the sauce over the meatloaf.
Bake in the preheated oven at 365 degrees F for 40 to 45 minutes or until a meat thermometer registers 165 degrees F.

STORING

Wrap your meatloaf tightly with heavy-duty aluminum foil or plastic wrap. Then, keep in your refrigerator for up to 3 to 4 days.
For freezing, wrap your meatloaf tightly to prevent freezer burn. Freeze up to 3 to 4 months. Defrost in the refrigerator. Bon appétit!

579. The Best Greek Souvlaki Ever

(Ready in about 20 minutes + marinating time | Servings 6)

Per serving: 147 Calories; 4.8g Fat; 5.8g Carbs; 17.3g Protein; 0.6g Fiber

INGREDIENTS

2 pounds pork shoulder, cut into
1-inch cubes
3 cloves garlic, smashed
Salt and black pepper, to taste
1/2 teaspoon dried basil
1/2 teaspoon dried oregano

1/3 cup apple cider vinegar
2 tablespoons parsley, chopped
For Tzatziki Sauce:
1 cup Greek yogurt
1 tablespoon dill weed, finely minced
2 cloves garlic, smashed

2 tablespoons extra-virgin olive oil
1 Lebanese cucumber, shredded and
drained
Sea salt, to taste

DIRECTIONS

Place the pork shoulder along with vinegar, parsley, garlic, salt, pepper, basil, and oregano in a ceramic dish; let it marinate for 2 to 3 hours in your refrigerator.

Thread the pork cubes onto bamboo skewers. Cook the skewers on the preheated grill for about 10 minutes.

Thoroughly combine all ingredients for the Greek tzatziki sauce.

STORING

Divide the pork skewers between six portions; place each portion in a separate airtight container or Ziploc bag; keep in your refrigerator for 3 to 4 days.

Freeze the pork skewers in airtight containers or heavy-duty freezer bags. Freeze up to 4 months. Defrost in the refrigerator. Bon appétit!

580. Pancetta-Wrapped Meatballs

(Ready in about 30 minutes | Servings 6)

Per serving: 399 Calories; 27g Fat; 1.8g Carbs; 37.7g Protein; 1.9g Fiber

INGREDIENTS

1/2 pound ground beef
1/2 pound ground pork
1/2 cup pork rinds, crushed
Salt and pepper, to taste
1 teaspoon paprika
1/2 pound pancetta slices

1 egg, whisked
1 ½ tablespoons olive oil
1/4 cup fresh scallions, finely chopped
2 cloves garlic, minced
For the Parsley Sauce:
1 cup fresh parsley

1 tablespoon pumpkin seeds, chopped
1/2 tablespoon olive oil
Salt and pepper, to taste
1 tablespoon pine nuts, toasted and
chopped

DIRECTIONS

In a mixing bowl, thoroughly combine the ground meat, egg, olive oil, pork rinds, scallions, garlic, salt, pepper, and paprika. Roll the mixture into small meatballs.

Wrap each ball with a slice of pancetta and secure with a toothpick.

Place the meatballs on a baking pan; bake in the preheated oven at 385 degrees F for about 30 minutes.

Meanwhile, make the sauce by mixing all ingredients in your food processor.

STORING

Place your meatballs in airtight containers or Ziploc bags; keep in your refrigerator for up to 3 to 4 days.

Place the sauce in an airtight container and keep in your refrigerator for up 3 to 4 days.

Freeze the meatballs in airtight containers or heavy-duty freezer bags. Freeze up to 3 to 4 months. To defrost, slowly reheat in a saucepan. Bon appétit!

581. Stuffed Avocado with Beef and Cheese

(Ready in about 20 minutes | Servings 6)

Per serving: 407 Calories; 28.8g Fat; 6.4g Carbs; 23.4g Protein; 5g Fiber

INGREDIENTS

3 ripe avocados, pitted and halved
1/2 cup onions, sliced
1/3 cup roasted vegetable broth
3 tablespoons olives, pitted and sliced

1/2 cup aioli
Salt and pepper, to taste
1 cup cherry tomatoes, chopped
1 tablespoon olive oil

3/4 pound beef, ground
3/4 cup Swiss cheese, shredded

DIRECTIONS

Scoop out the middle of each avocado; mash the avocado flash.

In a Dutch oven, heat the olive oil until sizzling. Once hot, sear the ground beef for about 3 minutes, breaking apart with a fork.

Then, stir in the onion and continue to cook for about 2 minutes or until just aromatic.

Add in broth to deglaze the pan; add in salt, pepper, tomatoes, and avocado flash. Spoon this filling into avocado halves.

Bake in the preheated oven at 340 degrees F for about 8 minutes. Top with the cheese, olives and aioli and bake an additional 5 minutes.

STORING

Place the stuffed avocado in airtight containers; keep in your refrigerator for 3 to 4 days. Bon appétit!

582. Sauerkraut with Ground Beef and Pepper

(Ready in about 20 minutes | Servings 4)

Per serving: 330 Calories; 12.2g Fat; 6.7g Carbs; 44.4g Protein; 4.1g Fiber

INGREDIENTS

18 ounces sauerkraut, rinsed and well drained
1 ¼ pounds ground beef
1 tablespoon lard, melted
1 teaspoon paprika
1 teaspoon fennel seeds

1 bell pepper, sliced
1 bay leaf
Sea salt and black peppercorns, to taste
1 large-sized leek, chopped
1 teaspoon garlic, minced

DIRECTIONS

In a Dutch oven, melt the lard over medium-high heat. Once hot, cook the leeks until tender and fragrant.
Add in the ground beef and continue to cook for 3 to 4 minutes or until no longer pink.
Stir in the remaining ingredients and continue to cook for 6 to 7 minutes or until everything is cooked through.

STORING

Divide the sauerkraut between airtight containers or Ziploc bags; keep in your refrigerator for up to 3 to 5 days.
For freezing, place the sauerkraut in airtight containers or heavy-duty freezer bags. Freeze up to 5 months. Defrost in the refrigerator and reheat on the stove pot. Bon appétit!

583. Grilled Cheese and Salmon Salad

(Ready in about 15 minutes | Servings 4)

Per serving: 199 Calories; 10.6g Fat; 3.1g Carbs; 14.2g Protein; 1.4g Fiber

INGREDIENTS

8 ounces halloumi cheese
1 cup cherry tomatoes, halved
1 onion, thinly sliced
1 tablespoon lemon juice
Sea salt and pepper, to taste
1 Lebanese cucumber, sliced

1/2 head lettuce
1/2 cup Italian peppers, thinly sliced
2 tablespoons hem hearts
1 ½ tablespoons extra-virgin olive oil
6 ounces canned salmon, drained

DIRECTIONS

Cook the halloumi cheese in a grill pan over a moderate heat for about 3 minute; cut into cubes.
In a bowl, toss the remaining ingredients until well combined. Place the grilled cheese on top.

STORING

Place the salad in airtight containers; keep in your refrigerator for 3 to 4 days. Bon appétit!

584. Waffles with Prosciutto and Cheese

(Ready in about 20 minutes | Servings 2)

Per serving: 470 Calories; 40.3g Fat; 2.9g Carbs; 24.4g Protein; 0.5g Fiber

INGREDIENTS

4 eggs
1/2 cup gorgonzola cheese, crumbled
4 slices prosciutto, chopped

2 tablespoons ghee, room temperature
Salt and pepper, to taste
1/2 teaspoon red pepper flakes

DIRECTIONS

Start by preheating your waffle iron to the desired temperature.
Thoroughly combine all ingredients in a mixing bowl. Spray your waffle iron with a nonstick cooking spray.
Ladle the batter into the preheated waffle iron; cook your waffles until golden and crisp.

STORING

Place the waffles in separate airtight containers; keep in the refrigerator for a week.
For freezing, divide the waffles among two airtight containers or heavy-duty freezer bags and freeze up to 3 months. Defrost in your microwave for a couple of minutes. Enjoy!

585. Boston Butt with Gorgonzola Sauce

(Ready in about 30 minutes | Servings 6)

Per serving: 495 Calories; 36.9g Fat; 3.6g Carbs; 33.4g Protein; 0.4g Fiber

INGREDIENTS

1 ½ pounds Boston butt, boneless and cut into 6 pieces
1 tablespoon coconut aminos
6 ounces Gorgonzola cheese
1/3 cup whipped cream

Salt and pepper, to taste
1 teaspoon garlic, chopped
1/3 cup port wine
1/3 cup vegetable broth
1 teaspoon cayenne pepper

1 teaspoon Mediterranean spice mix
1 tablespoon olive oil
1/2 cup leek, chopped

DIRECTIONS

Rub the Boston butt with salt, pepper, and Mediterranean spice mix.

Heat the olive oil in a saucepan over a moderately-high heat. Sear the Boston butt on all sides for about 15 minutes and reserve.

In the pan drippings, sauté the leeks and garlic until they are just tender and fragrant. Pour in the wine to deglaze the pan. Now, add in broth, cayenne pepper, and coconut aminos.

Continue to simmer, partially covered, until the sauce has thickened slightly. Add in the cheese and whipped cream and continue to simmer for a couple of minutes until the cheese melts.

STORING

Place the pork pieces into six airtight containers or Ziploc bags; keep in your refrigerator for 3 to 4 days.

For freezing, wrap tightly with heavy-duty aluminum foil or freezer wrap. It will maintain the best quality for 2 to 3 months. Defrost in the refrigerator. Enjoy!

586. Frankfurter Sausage and Mozzarella Balls

(Ready in about 15 minutes + chilling time | Servings 6)

Per serving: 353 Calories; 30.7g Fat; 3g Carbs; 16.1g Protein; 2.5g Fiber

INGREDIENTS

1 tablespoon lard
1/2 shallot, minced
4 ounces Mozzarella cheese
1/2 pound Frankfurter sausage, sliced

Sea salt and black pepper, to taste
4 ounces soft cheese
4 ounces fontina cheese, crumbled
2 tablespoons flaxseed meal

1 cup tomato puree
2 garlic cloves, minced

DIRECTIONS

In a frying pan, melt the lard over a moderately-high heat. Sear the sausage for about 5 minutes, crumbling with a fork or spatula.

Add in the tomato puree, garlic, and shallot and continue to sauté for 5 to 6 minutes more. Add in the remaining ingredients; stir until everything is well combined.

Place the mixture in your refrigerator and roll it into bite-sized balls.

STORING

Divide the sausage and mozzarella balls between airtight containers or Ziploc bags; keep in your refrigerator for up to 3 to 4 days.

For freezing, place the sausage and mozzarella balls in airtight containers. Freeze up to 1 month. Defrost in the refrigerator. Enjoy!

587. Green Beans with Pasta Elias

(Ready in about 15 minutes | Servings 4)

Per serving: 183 Calories; 16.1g Fat; 8.4g Carbs; 3.2g Protein; 3.4g Fiber

INGREDIENTS

1 tablespoon olive oil
1 cup celery, shredded
1/2 teaspoon garlic, minced
1/2 teaspoon cayenne pepper

1 pound green beans
Salt and black pepper, to taste
For Pasta Elias:
1 ½ tablespoons Italian parsley leaves

2 anchovy fillets
1 tablespoon lime juice
3 tablespoons extra-virgin olive oil
1/2 cup Greek olives, pitted

DIRECTIONS

Steam green beans for about 4 minutes or until just tender.

Heat the olive oil in a sauté pan over a moderately-high heat. Add in the celery and garlic and continue to sauté for 3 to 4 minutes, stirring occasionally to ensure even cooking.

Season with cayenne pepper, salt, and black pepper.

In your blender or food processor, pulse all ingredients for the Pasta Elias.

STORING

Place the green beans in airtight containers and keep in your refrigerator for 3 to 4 days.

Place the Pasta Elias in airtight containers and keep in your refrigerator for up to a week.

Spread the chilled green beans in a single layer on a baking sheet. Freeze for about 2 hours. Place the frozen green beans in freezer bags and keep for about 3 months. Reheat in a saucepan and enjoy!

588. Provençal Vegetables with Cheese

(Ready in about 15 minutes | Servings 4)

Per serving: 318 Calories; 24.3g Fat; 5.1g Carbs; 15.4g Protein; 2.9g Fiber

INGREDIENTS

2 tablespoons olive oil
1 teaspoon Herbes de Provence
1/2 pound white mushrooms, chopped
1 cup cauliflower, cut into small florets

1 zucchini, chopped
1/2 cup tomato puree
1/4 cup Provençal wine
8 ounces goat cheese, cubed

1 teaspoon garlic, pressed
1 onion, chopped

DIRECTIONS

In a Dutch oven, heat the olive oil over a moderately-high heat. Sauté the garlic until just tender but not browned for about one minute.
Add in the onion, mushrooms, cauliflower, and zucchini; cook for a further 5 minutes, stirring occasionally to ensure even cooking.
Add in the seasonings, tomato puree, and Provençal wine; partially cover and continue to cook for 4 to 5 minutes.

STORING

Spoon the Provençal vegetables into airtight containers and keep in your refrigerator for up 3 to 4 days.
For freezing, place the Provençal vegetables in airtight containers or heavy-duty freezer bags. Freeze up to 4 to 6 months. Defrost in the microwave or refrigerator.
Serve topped with Halloumi cheese and enjoy!

589. Avocado Boats with Swiss Cheese

(Ready in about 20 minutes | Servings 4)

Per serving: 342 Calories; 30.4g Fat; 6.5g Carbs; 11.1g Protein; 4.9g Fiber

INGREDIENTS

2 avocados, halved and pitted
1 teaspoon garlic, smashed
Salt and red pepper, to taste

4 ounces Swiss cheese, grated
2 eggs, beaten
1 tablespoon fresh coriander, minced

DIRECTIONS

Begin by preheating your oven to 365 degrees F. Place the avocado halves in a baking dish.
In a mixing bowl, thoroughly combine the cheese, eggs, garlic, salt, pepper, and coriander. Spoon the mixture into the avocado halves.
Bake for about 16 minutes or until everything is cooked thorough.

STORING

Place the stuffed avocado in airtight containers; keep in your refrigerator for 3 to 4 days. Bon appétit!

590. Greek Egg Salad with Anchovies

(Ready in about 20 minutes | Servings 8)

Per serving: 285 Calories; 22.5g Fat; 1.8g Carbs; 19.5g Protein; 0.3g Fiber

INGREDIENTS

For the Salad:
1/2 cup Gruyère cheese, crumbled
1 (14-ounce) can anchovy fillets, deboned, drained and flaked
1/3 cup sour cream
1 teaspoon deli mustard
8 eggs
1 cup butterhead lettuce, torn into pieces

1/2 cup onions, chopped
For Aioli:
1 egg
1 teaspoon garlic, minced
1 tablespoon lime juice
1/2 cup extra-virgin olive oil
Salt and pepper, to taste

DIRECTIONS

Place the eggs in a saucepan and cover them with water by 1 inch. Cover and bring the water to a boil over high heat. Boil for 6 to 7 minutes over medium-high heat.
Peel the eggs and coarsely chop them. Add in the remaining ingredients for the salad and toss to combine well.
To make the aioli, beat the egg, garlic, and lime juice with an immersion blender. Add the extra-virgin oil, salt and pepper, and blend until everything is well mixed.
Add the prepared aioli to the salad and gently stir to combine well.

STORING

Place the egg salad in an airtight container or Ziploc bag; transfer to your refrigerator; it should be consumed within two days. Bon appétit!

591. Tilapia with Tomatillo Chutney

(Ready in about 30 minutes | Servings 4)

Per serving: 291 Calories; 9.5g Fat; 5.6g Carbs; 42.5g Protein; 4.3g Fiber

INGREDIENTS

1 ½ pounds tilapia fillets
1 cup Spanish peppers, thinly sliced
1/2 cup shallots, thinly sliced
Salt and black pepper, to taste
2 tablespoons olive oil

1 pound cauliflower florets
1 teaspoon red pepper flakes
For Tomato Chutney:
2 tomatillos, crushed
1 tablespoon mustard seeds

1 teaspoon butter, melted
1 chilli pepper, deseeded and minced
Sea salt and black pepper, to taste
1 teaspoon garlic, chopped

DIRECTIONS

In a saucepan, heat 1 tablespoon of olive oil over moderately-high flame.

Now, cook the cauliflower florets, peppers, and shallots until they've softened; season with salt, black pepper, and red pepper and reserve.

Heat another tablespoon of the olive oil. Cook the fish fillets for 5 to 6 minutes per side or until thoroughly cooked and opaque. Add the sautéed cauliflower mixture.

Then, melt the butter in a frying pan over a moderately-high heat. Now, sauté the garlic until just tender and fragrant.

Add in the tomatillos, mustard seeds, chili pepper, salt, and black pepper and continue to cook, stirring periodically, for 9 to 10 minutes.

STORING

Place the tilapia fillets with sautéed cauliflower mixture in airtight containers and keep in your refrigerator for up to 3 to 4 days.

Place the tomatillo chutney in airtight containers or Ziploc bags; keep in your refrigerator for up 3 to 4 days.

For freezing, place the tilapia fillets with sautéed cauliflower mixture in airtight containers or wrap tightly with freezer wrap. Freeze up to 2 to 3 months.

Defrost in the refrigerator and serve with tomatillo chutney. Enjoy!

592. Stuffed Mushrooms with Bacon

(Ready in about 25 minutes | Servings 6)

Per serving: 98 Calories; 5.8g Fat; 3.9g Carbs; 8.4g Protein; 0.5g Fiber

INGREDIENTS

3 teaspoons olive oil
1 tablespoon coconut aminos
Salt and black pepper, to taste

6 large-sized button mushrooms,
stems removed
2 tablespoons fresh parsley, minced

1 teaspoon fresh basil, minced
2 ounces cheddar cheese, grated
3 slices of bacon, finely chopped

DIRECTIONS

Toss the mushroom caps with the olive oil, coconut amions, salt, and black pepper.

In a mixing bowl, thoroughly combine the bacon, parsley, basil, and cheese. Divide the filling between mushroom caps.

Place the stuffed mushrooms on a parchment-lined baking pan. Bake in the preheated oven at 360 degrees F for 18 to 20 minutes or until just tender and fragrant.

STORING

Place the mushrooms in airtight containers; keep in your refrigerator for 3 to 5 days.

Place your mushrooms in a plastic freezer bag; they will maintain the best quality for 10 to 12 months.

593. Roasted Vegetable with Spicy Dip

(Ready in about 45 minutes | Servings 4)

Per serving: 357 Calories; 35.8g Fat; 5.2g Carbs; 3.4g Protein; 1.1g Fiber

INGREDIENTS

2 celery stalks, cut into sticks
2 bell peppers, sliced
1 onion, sliced
1/4 cup olive oil
2 garlic cloves, minced

1 tablespoon fresh cilantro, minced
1/2 teaspoon cayenne pepper
For the Spicy Sour Cream Dip:
1 ½ cups cream cheese
2 tablespoons aioli

3/4 teaspoon deli mustard
1 chili pepper, finely minced
1 tablespoon lemon juice
Salt and pepper, to taste
2 tablespoons basil, chopped

DIRECTIONS

Begin by preheating your oven to 395 degrees F. Line a baking pan with a piece of parchment paper.

Toss your vegetables with the olive oil, garlic, cilantro, and cayenne pepper.

Arrange the vegetables on the baking pan and roast for 35 to 40 minutes, tossing them halfway through.

Thoroughly combine all ingredients for the dip.

STORING

Place the roasted vegetables in airtight containers or Ziploc bags; keep in your refrigerator for up to 3 to 5 days.

To freeze, arrange the roasted vegetables on a baking sheet in a single layer; freeze for about 2 hours. Transfer the frozen vegetables to freezer storage bags. Freeze for up to 12 months.

Place the sauce in a glass jar with an airtight lid; keep in your refrigerator for up 3 to 4 days.

594. Coleslaw with a Twist

(Ready in about 10 minutes + chilling time | Servings 4)

Per serving: 242 Calories; 20.5g Fat; 6.2g Carbs; 1g Protein; 2.5g Fiber

INGREDIENTS

3/4 pound green cabbage, cored and shredded
1/2 cup fresh cilantro leaves, coarsely chopped
1 large-sized celery stalk, grated
1/2 teaspoon cumin seeds
Salt and pepper, to taste

2 tablespoons pumpkin seeds
1/2 red onion, sliced
1 cup mayonnaise
1 teaspoon Dijon mustard

DIRECTIONS

Add the green cabbage, celery, and onion to a bowl. Add in mayonnaise, Dijon mustard, cilantro, cumin seeds, salt, and pepper. Gently stir to combine and place in your refrigerator. Serve sprinkled with pumpkin seeds.

STORING

Place the salad in airtight containers or Ziploc bags; keep in your refrigerator for up to 3 days.

595. Autumn Cabbage and Cream Soup

(Ready in about 25 minutes | Servings 4)

Per serving: 185 Calories; 16.6g Fat; 2.4g Carbs; 2.9g Protein; 1.2g Fiber

INGREDIENTS

1 cup cabbage, shredded
1 teaspoon garlic, minced
1 celery with leaves, chopped
1 bell pepper, chopped
4 cups broth

1 bay leaf
1 cup sour cream
1 ½ tablespoons olive oil
1 medium-sized leek, chopped

DIRECTIONS

Heat the oil in a heavy-bottomed pot over a moderate flame. Sauté the leek until tender and aromatic. Add in the remaining vegetables and continue to cook for about 6 minutes, stirring occasionally to ensure even cooking.
Add in the broth and bay leaf, leave the lid slightly ajar, and cover partially. Continue to cook for 12 to 15 minutes.
Puree the mixture with an immersion blender.

STORING

Spoon the soup into four airtight containers or Ziploc bags; keep in your refrigerator for up to 3 to 4 days.
For freezing, place the soup in airtight containers. It will maintain the best quality for about 4 to 6 months. Defrost in the refrigerator. Reheat in a soup pot and serve dolloped with chilled sour cream. Enjoy!

596. Chanterelle Mushrooms with Salami

(Ready in about 25 minutes | Servings 6)

Per serving: 98 Calories; 5.8g Fat; 3.9g Carbs; 8.4g Protein; 0.7g Fiber

INGREDIENTS

6 Chanterelle mushrooms, stems removed
3 slices of salami, chopped
2 tablespoons fresh parsley, minced
1 teaspoon fresh basil, minced

2 ounces Swiss cheese, shredded
3 teaspoons olive oil
1 tablespoon soy sauce
Salt and pepper, to taste

DIRECTIONS

Toss the Chanterelle mushrooms with olive oil, soy sauce, salt, and pepper.
Thoroughly combine the salami, parsley, basil, and Swiss cheese; mix well and stuff the mushroom caps.
Bake in the preheated oven at 360 degrees F for about 20 minutes.

STORING

Place the mushrooms in airtight containers; keep in your refrigerator for 3 to 5 days.
Place the mushrooms in a plastic freezer bag; they will maintain the best quality for 10 to 12 months.

597. Oven-Roasted Asparagus with Pancetta

(Ready in about 20 minutes | Servings 4)

Per serving: 48 Calories; 1.6g Fat; 4.4g Carbs; 5.5g Protein; 2.7g Fiber

INGREDIENTS

1 pound asparagus spears
4 tablespoons pancetta, finely chopped
1 teaspoon shallot powder

1/4 teaspoon porcini powder
1/2 teaspoon dried dill weed
Salt and black pepper, to season

DIRECTIONS

Toss your asparagus with the salt, pepper, shallot powder, porcini powder, and dill. Place them on a parchment-lined baking sheet.
Bake in the preheated oven at 440 degrees F for about 20 minutes; toss them halfway through the cook time.
Top with the chopped pancetta.

STORING

Place the roasted asparagus in airtight containers; keep in your refrigerator for 3 to 5 days.
For freezing, place the roasted asparagus in a freezable container; they can be frozen for 10 to 12 months. Enjoy!

598. Grandma's Cauliflower Cakes

(Ready in about 35 minutes | Servings 6)

Per serving: 199 Calories; 13.8g Fat; 6.8g Carbs; 13g Protein; 2.1g Fiber

INGREDIENTS

1 ½ tablespoons sesame oil
1 onion, chopped
1/2 teaspoon dried basil
Salt and pepper, to taste
1/2 teaspoon garlic, minced

1 pound cauliflower, grated
2 eggs, beaten
5 tablespoons almond meal
½ cup cheddar cheese, shredded
1 cup Romano cheese

DIRECTIONS

In a frying pan, heat the sesame oil over a moderate flame. Then, sauté the onions and garlic until they've softened.
Add in the grated cauliflower along with the remaining ingredients. Shape the mixture into patties and arrange them on a parchment-lined baking sheet.
Bake in the preheated oven at 395 degrees F for 20 to 22 minutes. Turn them over and cook on the other side for 8 to 10 minutes more.

STORING

Place the cauliflower cakes in airtight containers or Ziploc bags; keep in your refrigerator for up to a week.
To freeze, arrange the cauliflower cakes on a baking sheet in a single layer; freeze for about 2 hours. Transfer the frozen vegetables to freezer storage bags. Freeze for up to 3 months.

599. Spicy Mushrooms Omelet with Salsa

(Ready in about 15 minutes | Servings 4)

Per serving: 290 Calories; 21.7g Fat; 6.5g Carbs; 10.6g Protein; 5g Fiber

INGREDIENTS

4 eggs
1 pound brown mushroom, chopped
1 cup tomatoes, crushed
2 tablespoons butter, melted
Sea salt and ground black pepper, to taste

1/4 cup salsa
1 medium-sized avocado, pitted and mashed
1 large onion, finely chopped
1/2 teaspoon garlic, smashed

DIRECTIONS

In a frying pan, melt the butter over a moderately-high flame. Sauté the onion and garlic until they've softened.
Add in the brown mushrooms, tomatoes, salt, and pepper; continue to cook for 2 minutes more.
Stir in the eggs and scramble them; top with the salsa sauce.

STORING

Slice the omelet into four pieces. Place each of them in an airtight container or Ziploc bag; place in the refrigerator for up to 3 to 4 days.
To freeze, place in separate Ziploc bags and freeze up to 3 months. Defrost in your microwave for a few minutes.
Serve warm with avocado slices.

600. Refreshing Gorgonzola and Cucumber Bites

(Ready in about 25 minutes | Servings 2)

Per serving: 133 Calories; 9.9g Fat; 6.8g Carbs; 6g Protein; 2.6g Fiber

INGREDIENTS

1 cucumber, grated
2 tablespoons almonds, chopped
1 oz Gorgonzola cheese

1 oz soft cheese, room temperature
1 tablespoon fresh cilantro, chopped

DIRECTIONS

Throw the cucumbers into a colander and sprinkle with sea salt. Let it stand for about 30 minutes and then, press your cucumber to drain away the excess liquid.

Add in the cheese and cilantro; stir to combine well. Place the chopped almonds in a shallow dish.

Form the mixture into 4 balls and roll them over the chopped almonds.

STORING

Divide the keto balls between airtight containers or Ziploc bags; keep in your refrigerator for up to 3 to 4 days.

For freezing, place the keto balls in airtight containers. Freeze up to 1 month. Defrost in the refrigerator.

Made in the USA
Middletown, DE
01 January 2023

20904215R00121